SO IT STARTED THERE

T0322642

SO IT STARTED THERE

FROM PUNK TO PULP

Nick Banks

OMNIBUS PRESS

Copyright © 2023 Omnibus Press
(A division of the Wise Music Group
14–15 Berners Street, London, W1T 3LJ)

Covers designed by Paul Tippett
Cover images by Donald Milne
Special edition cover images Donald Milne
Picture research by the author

ISBN: 978-1-9158-4110-0
Special edition ISBN: 978-1-9158-4117-9

Nick Banks hereby asserts his right to be identified
as the author of this work in accordance with Sections 77 to 78
of the Copyright, Designs and Patents Act 1988.

All rights reserved. No part of this book may be reproduced in any
form or by any electronic or mechanical means, including information
storage or retrieval systems, without permission in writing from the
publisher, except by a reviewer who may quote brief passages.

Every effort has been made to trace the copyright holders of the
photographs in this book but one or two were unreachable. We would
be grateful if the photographers concerned would contact us.

A catalogue record for this book is available from the British Library.

Typeset in Bembo by Palimpsest Book Production Ltd, Falkirk, Stirlingshire.

Printed in Poland by Hussar Books

www.omnibuspress.com

This book goes out to Sarah, Jackson and Jeannie.

Contents

Foreword by Richard Hawley

Nick and I met decades ago – I can't recall exactly when or where – but it was around about when I was 16 years old, and Nick would've been around 17 at the time. It could've been in the Limit Club, The Hallamshire, Washington pubs or even at a Pulp gig. The gig is a good bet, as we were both huge fans of the band years before Nick joined the group. Nick used to come and watch my gigs when I was in Treebound Story, so we became good friends. We still are and always will be. He's one of the calmest, grounded, most joyful and intelligent men I've ever known. He's also funny as fuck. In fact, one of the most constant things in our friendship has been hysterical laughter. He's a very confident guy, but also humble in a way. A perfect example of this humble nature is that it took him many years to tell me that the 1966 World Cup-winning football legend, goal-keeper Gordon Banks, was his uncle. A lot of folks would've mentioned that and exploited it, but not Nick. He kept it quiet.

Nick told me recently that he was going to live to be a hundred years old. At the time I thought, 'Hmm, wishful thinking r kid', remembering the hundreds of times we've met up over the last forty years and managed to get absolutely battered in one form or another. Pubs, clubs and gigs, either watching bands, being in bands together or out with friends and family, the end result is always the same . . . carnage and tremendous fun. The idea of either of us living for half a century (which came to pass some time ago now), let alone a whole century, is a little unrealistic.

I was going to talk about what a brilliantly gifted drummer Nick is, but that would be equally far-fetched. He is by his own admission an average musician, his timing a little questionable . . . I believe I may have coined the phrase 'In and out of time like Dr Who'. However, given the right band he is irreplaceable. I know this because we tried it once when Jarvis, Mackey, Candida, myself and various other Sheffield musicians, DJs and friends played together live for the Big Melt at the Crucible theatre. It was all going well until we tried to play a couple of Pulp songs with a different drummer. It just didn't work at all – it felt and sounded wrong. The songs were perfectly in time and all the beats and notes were correct, but something vital was missing. The energy just wasn't in the room. So we had to get Nick down to play with us to make it work. It did, the gig was ace. Nick's musical style is 100 per cent pure punk in its outlook and execution – you can't fake that, it's for real.

Nick has lived a remarkable life, been showered with awards, sold multi-platinum amounts of records and played at some of the most iconic concerts and events in British music history. He's achieved great things that when we met would've seemed unimaginable and totally unrealistic. Which brings me back to him living to be a hundred years old . . . now I've read this book, I think it just might happen. So enjoy part one of Nick Banks's life, up to now.

Richard Hawley
June 2023

1

Where To Start?

(Countdown)

We're sat in a fluorescently lit Portakabin. It is obscenely bright. We are about to embark on perhaps our greatest triumph or the most fantastic failure, one that will make us the subject of mass ridicule for the rest of our lives. No pressure then.

My ears are under constant assault from the throb of bass that ought to be much further away. It's not. It doesn't stop. The thump of the bass drum is the only punctuation in this low-end rumble. That too doesn't stop. It might be more bearable if I could determine a tune, any tune, but the bass is the only frequency to carry away from the stage and back to us.

I look around the space at the others – y'know: Jarvis, Candida, Steve, Russell and Mark. Everyone has a grey pallor, the colour washed out of concerned faces. No one is speaking much. I'm sat at one of those cloth-seat folding director's chairs. It's vibrating. Though not with the rumble of the not-so-distant stage, but rather the trembling of my own limbs. I realise I have the wooden arms in a fierce grip, seemingly in an attempt to stop the vibrations, or simply to prevent the chair from taking off across the room. It doesn't work. I get up and pace about, the same as everyone else. It's hard to keep still in these circumstances. Actually, it's more of a jostle than a pace, as Portakabins aren't so large and this one is full of people.

My mouth is dry, really dry. It's been that way for hours but no matter how tempting the 'rider' is, I dare not hit the cans. Must stay sober, for my greatest fear at this moment would be cocking up the next couple of hours by hitting the drink too early. Perversely, I can't stop going to the backstage portaloo toilets, provided for the artists' convenience. Believe me, these are a vast improvement on the loos the audience has to deal with, but don't start harbouring any thoughts of 'hygiene', 'comfort', 'odour free', 'heated seats', or even 'bog roll' – they're still a pretty grim affair. At least (for now) the loo seats are still affixed to the pans. A bog trip gives brief respite from the churning in the stomach and the restless limbs. Deep breaths (but only once having exited the lavs).

Various folk pop in to wish us luck and to attempt some chat to relieve the tension. It doesn't.

I step out into the cool evening air. It's a pleasantly dry and warm festival this year and the usual Somme-like quagmire is gratefully absent. Thankfully the wellies have taken a back seat for a change. It's amazing how much of a better festival experience everyone has – entertainer and punter alike – when the sun shines. Even so, late June evenings in Somerset can rapidly cool once the sun reaches the horizon. Having said that, this particular day – 24 June – is close to the summer solstice and the sky won't darken 'til almost 10 p.m., so it's still relatively light around 8.

Even more people are hanging around outside the Portakabin: friends, relatives, members of other bands who have already done their 'bit'. I go to the 'kabin next door. It's where we have our clothes rail and custom-built illuminated mirror (all bands have this kind of thing, don't they?) – perfect for sticking on a bit of slap, adjusting the false eyelashes or deciding which pair of 'out there' sunglasses to wear (in the dark, natch). Anyway, I'm not much of a make-up wearer; I'm the drummer stuck way out at the back (where I like it) and probably the band member least favoured by the camera shot director. Others are more amenable to a lick of eyeliner or so, but I'm more fearful of getting a mid-song eye attack due to a stray spot of glitter or something. Best not risk it. Besides, there's nothing for me in here. I'm already in my stage wear – no fancy designer gear, just a long-sleeve white T-shirt (then it's not a T-shirt, is it?), my fave brown cords and Puma Gazelle trainers.

I return to the other Portakabin and continue to alternatively pace around and attempt to sit. Relaxation is almost impossible. A printed set-list appears eventually. I study each song title and try to imagine playing each one, concentrating on how each song starts and finishes. Tonight we are debuting three songs from our new album, which is still only half recorded. Playing new songs on stage is difficult at the best of times – so many chances to make a mistake, as they will have been played in rehearsal only and can feel ready to unveil to the world. But once they're played *4 real* anything can happen. Cues may not have been fully bedded in yet and the sound you're used to hearing in a rehearsal studio will be totally different on stage (especially at a festival, where no sound checks can take place). All these unknowns can easily throw a song into uncharted territory. Chuck in being watched by 80,000+ people wanting the time of their lives, and countless millions more viewers on TV, and it doesn't make for a comfortable feeling pre-gig. Still the nerves build.

Our amiable tour manager, Richard Priest, eventually ushers the assorted hangers-on/guests/other halves/VIPs out of the main dressing room and then it's just the six of us. Our onstage time is just a few minutes away and something happens that has never happened before: a pep talk. We don't exactly get in a Madonna-style huddle, arms linked, hands clasped in prayer to the gods of live performance – no, none of that. Jarvis merely tells us, 'This is it' (no shit, Sherlock!) and that we should just try to enjoy this moment. Never mind that it's only the most important gig we've ever played — or, as it turns out, will ever play; just enjoy the experience that is about to take place. We all look at each other with a kind of morbid trepidation. Everyone has been suffering the same pre-gig nerves as me. Then Priesty opens the 'kabin door and in his half-serious, half-laughing Coventry accent, says, 'Come on then . . .'

We may have walked to the stage (about 30 metres away) or we may have been transported in golf buggies. Either way, it's a few paces up the ramp to the side of the world-famous Pyramid Stage (though this year it's not pyramid shaped, more on that later). We can see the great multitudes assembled before the stage. Deep breaths.

The roadies give the all-clear that everything's plugged in, tightened, tuned up, turned on. Out we stride.

A hypnotic, robotic voice intones *COMMON PEOPLE, COMMON PEOPLE, COMMON PEOPLE, COMMON PEOPLE . . .*

'Hello,' Jarvis deadpans, and I count us in — '1.2.3.4!'

And we're off.

The question now is: how did I get here?

2

How Did We Get Here?

(Sunrise)

The obvious answer is that I joined a local Sheffield band called Pulp. But is it as easy as trotting that out?

At the risk of getting too 'heavy' too early, we all go through life overlooking the small events that can fundamentally change how our lives turn out – be it for better, or for worse. For example, if I'd stepped off the kerb 10 seconds earlier I would not have seen the bus that could've knocked seven bells out of me that day. Or maybe if I hadn't stayed for that extra pint in the Dog and Duck I wouldn't have bumped into that gorgeous girl and fallen head over heels in love. I could have easily failed to notice a small, scrappy, dog-eared bit of paper stuck to a notice board in The Leadmill nightclub. But I didn't miss it and my life was changed for evermore. (By the way, only one of these events actually happened.) The fickle fortunes of fate, yeah?

But, hold on; I had to get myself into the position that I felt able to call the number on the advert and be confident that I would get the job – no point in doing it if I didn't feel up to it. So, let's go a little further back to see how I got to know that I could take on the role of 'drummer in Pulp'.

Of course, playing in Sheffield bands gave me the desire and a feel for what it 'might' take. Not that we knew at this point what that meant, but by being part of the Sheffield scene I was certainly in the right place at the right time.

But how did I come to be part of that scene, especially when I grew up in the salubrious town of Rotherham, South Yorkshire, seven miles distant from the bright (or not so bright) lights of Sheffield? Seven miles may seem a mere hop, skip and a jump to most, but the gulf cannot be confined to measurements. More significant is the veritable chasm that existed between the two cities in culture and mindset.

In Rotherham, I was the beneficiary of a fairly bog-standard sixties and seventies childhood and adolescence, which prepared me for striding out into the world – well, seven miles up the road to be fair – at age 18. We could go even further, to the moment that led to my coming into this world in the summer of 1965. Two people met and eventually I popped out. It's impossible not to ponder on the profound effect those two had on how I turned out.

We could delve back further through time, examining those fateful moments upon which entire lives turn – remember, that we are all the products of an unbroken line, perhaps of fate, going back to the dawn of time, offspring of offspring that eventually produced all of us, including me (phew – got a bit heavy there, sorry!).

Anyway let's not go back too far, as we'll be here forever. Instead, let's stop this journey into the mists of time on the doorstep of Grandad Ford.

3

Thanks, Young Horace

(Tunnel)

South Yorkshire, along with the North East, Nottinghamshire, South Wales and various other pockets around the UK, was built on coal mining and steel. It requires a hell of a lot of coal, of course, to melt iron ore into steel. So it would be logical to put them together.

In the first quarter of the 20th century the UK had around a million coal miners, my grandad being one of them. James William Ford, born in the year 1900, went down the local pit, New Stubbin Colliery, located in Rawmarsh just to the north of Rotherham, after an initial spell working in a greengrocer's shop, where he met my Grandma Elsie. Grandad thus missed going to France and serving in the trenches of the First World War. There you go – another fateful intervention that swerved a potential non-appearance of yours truly many, many years later. Dodged a bullet there.

Not that digging coal underground was any easier than fighting. The war effort ran on the energy produced by coal: train transport, battleships, heating, energy for the manufacturing of guns, shells, bullets, tanks, tin helmets – the lot. Coal by-products also permeated society, from soap to the gas that lit the nations' households. So, digging coal was strategically vital to Britain's war success and miners were fighting their own underground war to bring up the coal for the nation.

Working underground was always an extremely dangerous occupation and there's numerous ways to die or at least succumb to serious injury. You could get mangled in dangerous machinery. The roof might collapse. You could hit underground water and drown in a flood. The air could turn poisonous, or the ventilation could run out or fail and suffocate you. The coal face could burst under the enormous pressure. Ignition of the gas given off by the coal could cause an explosion – even the coal dust itself could explode, obviously with catastrophic consequences for all concerned. Not nice.

If you survived this underground warzone, then your old age could be scarred by pneumoconiosis; a lung disease that would develop years later from breathing in the filthy black coal-dust-laden air, day after day, year after year. One way or another, the pit will get you.

Grandad will have set off for his shift as usual with his 'snap tin' (lunch box) slung over his shoulders, probably dreading the long descent into the bowels of the earth to dig. Every day was the same: change at the pithead into your pit clothes, pick up your miner's safety lamp and helmet, grab your pick, check in with the safety officer and descend into the pit via the lift-shaft cage, crammed in with around 20 other miners and colleagues – among them, Grandad's younger cousin Horace. Once at the bottom of the shaft, you and your fellow miners would then have to walk a while – maybe even a mile or more – to your place of work, which for Grandad was at the coalface where the actual coal was dug out of the seam.

Grandad was a hewer, which meant he had the job of cutting the coal from the coalface with a pick and shovelling it into squat wheeled trucks to be sent to the surface. This was hot, dangerous stuff; men would often work shirtless or even naked, rarely with enough room to stand up, usually on their knees or even lying down to get at the coal. Miners worked eight-hour shifts, six days' a week. They got Sundays off. And all this for about £2 10s a week (the average wage for British workers back then being about £3 per week).

But today, 29 January 1929, all that was to change.

The coal seam at the face is under tremendous pressure from all the earth above it pushing down. Add to this the fact that as the coal is cut out, there are times when the roof above you is unsupported. A dangerous situation that the miners were used to, but on this day the seam, and the roof along with it, collapsed, burying Grandad and a few of his immediate fellow miners in rock, coal and earth. After the noise of the fall subsided, silence.

Other miners nearby will have rushed over to see who could be saved, perhaps with trepidation, as the roof could go again at any moment. They would've had to work quickly to get props in place before helping any survivors.

One of the rescuers that day was Horace, who worked feverishly to uncover the buried miners. They will have worked in almost pitch darkness, the only light from their handheld safety lamps, pulling at the rock and earth with their bare hands (attacking the fall with picks and shovels could injure buried workers).

Eventually, Grandad was pulled out from the collapse. He was the only survivor from those buried. However, he was gravely injured. His back was broken in three places and his right leg was crushed. It could not be saved and was immediately amputated to prevent catastrophic blood loss and certain death.

He spent many years in and out of hospital and never worked again. He was forever in constant pain from his injuries and wore a large, heavy leather back brace along with a prosthetic leg for the rest of his life. He was a jovial man, though, who had a bit of a daredevil streak. He would love taking me and my brother for rides in his little light blue Invacar (abbreviated from 'invalid carriage') when we were small. Totally illegal, of course, as it had only one seat. If he spotted the police we'd have to duck our heads down so we wouldn't be seen. Great fun, but unsafe? Definitely.

One time, when Grandad had a sore throat, he thought that

drinking perfume would cure it, since perfume was 'nice'. But my favourite memory of Grandad Ford was our Butlin's holiday together.

Butlin's holiday camps are self-contained seaside resorts designed to cater for mass tourism at a keen price. The first camps were built in the thirties, and quickly became very popular among working-class families, with their mix of knobbly knees entertainment and bracing sea air.

Grandma and Grandad Ford were on their annual holiday at Butlin's, Skegness, on the English North Sea coast. Unfortunately, Grandma took badly (became ill, in Sheffield dialect) and needed to be brought home. However, Grandad refused to miss his Butlin's holiday, so there was a spare place going in their chalet for the few days they had left of the week. I volunteered to take the space, and was duly dropped off and Grandma taken away. I was thus given the run of Butlin's, just me and Grandad. I was probably about nine or ten and spent most of my time in the huge (or so it seemed) hall that had a huge Scalextric slot car racing game set up in it. Put your two pence in the slot and you had control of a race car for five minutes or so as it zoomed around the track. Bliss.

Grandad had no problems taking me on the rollercoaster – my first ever. He chucked his crutches – which he needed to walk with – at the attendant to look after, hopped into the little car and off we went, careering around the structure, Grandad completely unfazed.

That Butlin's holiday holds many fond memories. I even had my first 'girlfriend' there. Totally innocent, of course. We rode the futuristic monorail together that transported holidaymakers around the site. Sadly her name is lost in time now; like tears in rain.

Anyway, Grandad Ford's disability clearly didn't stop him living life. He and Grandma Elsie had five kids, one of them being my mum, Brenda. If I had a magic photo as in *Back to the Future*, my outline would now be a little bit more visible.

My mum had a happy childhood, albeit one of great poverty – or so it would seem by today's standards. The Second World War made a huge impression even though she was only young, gas drills at school and planes – both friend and foe – overhead being particularly vivid to her. However, these times did afford the kids of the day a lot of freedom to be out and about having adventures. Along with siblings Audrey, Barbara, Brenda (my mum), Margaret and Roy, they were a tight-knit family. As was the norm in the post-war years, mum left school at 15 and went straight into work at a bakery in Mexborough, South Yorkshire.

Outside of work, the family would spend time visiting relatives in Sheringham, north Norfolk, bit of a break by the sea (in the forties, the eldest sister, Audrey, had married a rugged sailor from Sheringham). They would go on the train, and it was while returning from one of these trips that everything would change again.

In mid-1954, Brenda and Margaret were travelling back to Rotherham on a train that was due to change at Norwich, again at Melton and a final time at Doncaster. At Norwich, they noticed a couple of handsome chaps boarding. The same lads changed, as they did, at Melton and again at Doncaster, destined for Rotherham and on to Sheffield. At some point on the journey the four youngsters struck up a conversation and by the time they parted, arrangements to meet again had been made. One of the lads was a dark-haired bricklayer called David Banks. By the end of the year, David and Brenda were engaged and the pair were married three years later in 1957. My magic picture is suddenly getting more in focus.

David Banks was one of four brothers – the others being John, Michael and Gordon – who grew up in Sheffield again, like Brenda, seemingly in great poverty. They went to school in clogs and often ragged clothing. This may have been more through neglect than lack of money. David's mum, Nellie, didn't take to mothering so it seems, and by all accounts was a fierce character. (My abiding memory of her is that she always made her own bread with a Player's Navy Cut cigarette permanently on the go. The fag never seemed to see an ashtray, as the bread was always flecked with ash that fell off the ciggie as it sat clamped between her tacit jaws. Never did us no harm.)

David had a couple of close shaves as a boy, one of which occurred when he was knocked down a deep hole by a motorcycle, leading to numerous broken bones and a fractured skull. He was only six.

Elsewhere, family life was probably a bit chaotic and as war broke out, all the kids that lived by the steelworks in Sheffield were to be evacuated out to the countryside and safety. But David missed the evacuation bus. No one thought the brothers should be evacuated at a later date – miss the bus, stay in the danger zone. It seemed like nobody cared. All Sheffield steelworks were, of course, a primary target for enemy bombers, and David was right in the firing line. Luck would have it that Hitler's bombs didn't hit The Banks family. (My outline in the photo just got a bit firmer.)

David left school at 15 without much in the way of qualifications and started out as an apprentice bricklayer before going on to do his National Service in the British Army, travelling with the York and Lancaster Regiment to Egypt and the Sudan, then a protectorate of the United Kingdom, as a driver. Some lads in his unit were transported to the conflict in Korea, but thankfully not David. Another bullet dodged.

After a holiday at Great Yarmouth with his mate Gordon Haig, they were waiting on the platform at Norwich Station for their connection when they noticed two young ladies that looked like they were going their way . . .

4

Arrival

(David's Last Summer)

Nicholas David Banks arrived at five minutes to midnight on 28 July 1965. Edward Heath had become leader of the Conservative Party the day before and The Beatles' second film, *Help!*, was to debut in London the next day. So it looks like my arrival was the only noteworthy event on 28 July that year.

However, 1965 was a historic year overall. A year that saw wartime leader Winston Churchill shuffle off this mortal coil, Sir Stanley Matthews play his final First Division game for Stoke City FC and 'great train robber' Ronnie Biggs escape from Wandsworth nick. Elsewhere, Ian Brady and Myra Hindley were charged with the Moors Murders, capital punishment was abolished in the UK and theatre critic Kenneth Tynan said 'fuck' for the first time on British TV. In happier news, The Rolling Stones released '(I Can't Get No) Satisfaction' their first US number one single, the first episode of sci-fi puppet series *Thunderbirds* aired on UK TV and Asda opened its first supermarket in Castleford, West Yorkshire.

So, all in all, my arrival is well up there with the best 1965 had to offer.

I soon settled into getting a few years under my belt in the council house I was born in: 315 Brinsworth Rd, Brinsworth, Rotherham.

Brinsworth lies just over the demarcation line between Sheffield and Rotherham. The M1 motorway that runs from London to Leeds passed within about 50 yards of us, which was handy for breathing in all those vehicle fumes and lead pollution from the cars and lorries that thundered by all day every day. Lovely. It was, and still is, an everyday neighbourhood of stout-hearted working-class folk. Sadly I have virtually no memories of living there, except for a vague notion of going round to next door to play with the lad who lived there.

Mum, Dad, elder brother Richard and I moved out when I was four or so (in 1969) to a more salubrious address in the posh end of Rotherham (though this is a relative term, of course – can anywhere in Rotherham be really termed 'posh'? Maybe nouveau riche?). Dad's business was obviously doing well. He was a bookie with his brothers Jack and Michael (bookie = turf accountant in posh parlance, or betting shops to you and me). The three of them would take bets mainly on horse racing and greyhound racing, but sometimes other sports too. I always thought that I had been fed and clothed on the backs of the financial hopes and dreams of countless working men of Sheffield and Rotherham, who were trying to earn a quick buck backing 'Lucky Boy' in the 3.15 at Haydock Park. And, naturally, losing.

The brothers had a few shops around Sheffield, although the betting shop game was not without its pitfalls. I remember that Dad was involved in a fracas with one disgruntled customer. This 'punter' grabbed Dad by his shirt and threw him through the window of the betting shop, ripping off most of his shirt (yes, the window was closed at the time). Somehow unscathed, he went home wearing just the shirt collar and his tie.

180 Moorgate Rd was a single-storey bungalow that had a huge garden at the back, one at the front and a double garage (and another spare garage too, just for good measure), and was bought

for the princely sum of £1,600, which Mum and Dad paid off through hard work and scrimping and saving in about five years. A massive achievement.

I had a pretty typical childhood for a kid growing up in Britain in the sixties and seventies. I remember hot summers, snowy winters and the usual British weather (grey clouds, drizzle, misery) in between. We went on European beach holidays to Majorca, Spain and, a little more exotic, Malta. Dad had a pen friend who he talked coins with (Dad was an avid coin collector – numismatist, if you like) so we went to visit him a couple of times.

First day out by the sea in Malta I jumped in off the concrete jetty into the sea, but unfortunately on climbing out I stepped on one of the numerous black spiny sea urchins that littered the sea floor. I jumped out, several huge sea urchin spikes sticking out of my foot. Cue screaming in pain as they were pulled out, one by one, and any bits that couldn't be removed were left in there to dissolve gradually, according to the Maltese doctor who had a look.

In happier times on that trip, I vividly remember having this bizarre Mediterranean food item that seemed really weird at the time and I felt very brave for trying it (I was under enormous pressure from the parents, of course, not to show them up by pushing it away). It was a kind of dough-based thing with this red and yellow stuff smeared on the top and baked in the oven. My god: I'd just tasted pizza for the first time (we didn't have that kind of 'foreign' stuff back home in Rotherham).

We would play all day in the sand or in the sea, burning viciously under the hot sun. No one ever seemed to think about sun tan lotion or any of that stuff in those days. If the sunburn got really bad some calamine lotion might be deployed in the evening to try and numb the burning pain. It didn't work. Those experiences are probably where I got my preference for shade at all times when travelling in hot places since. That feeling of putting a shirt on at the end of the day, the prickling sensation of sunburnt skin emitting heat like the Ready-Brek kid, and seeing sheets of skin peeling off your back or arms has never left me.

Back at home, I was enrolled at the prestigious Broom Valley Junior and Infants School about a mile up the road from our house. I say prestigious, but the truth is that it was a bog-standard UK primary school, which everyone round us went to. I remember the first day walking through the gates with Mum. I kept my nose fairly clean and, in the Infants, eventually rose to the exalted rank of 'Milk Monitor', all kids being in receipt of a small bottle of milk mid-morning to aid strong bones, good teeth and all-round robust health. Hold on, didn't everyone get a turn at milk monitor? Eventually . . . Anyway, in the early-seventies, Margaret Thatcher (who later became Britain's first female prime minister) snatched this 'perk' off us in a measly penny-pinching example of heartless government cost-cutting.

I distinctly remember being one of the most advanced readers in our school year – however, this did not prevent the odd board rubber (used for erasing the chalk off the blackboard) being thrown, with some force I might add, in my general direction if found to be talking or getting up to some mischief. The heady days of casual teacher/ pupil violence. Bless.

You are probably all thinking that music would have been swirling around us in these formative years, slowly moulding this future drummer. No, not really. Sorry for the bold truth.

The radio was a constant in our house, though, as I'm sure it was all over the UK. There certainly was no morning TV so to speak of; TV didn't really get going until midday or so and then they were mostly little kids' programmes – so I'll have seen plenty of those. At breakfast time, then, it was 'the wunnerful world of Radio 1' and such DJs as Tony Blackburn and DLT – Dave Lee Travis, or the Hairy Cornflake as he was hilariously known. You would have the likes of Noel Edmonds and Simon Bates, and even Jimmy Savile (gulp) on at Sunday lunchtimes. I suppose these shows were harmless, nay vacuous, fun and easy on the ear.

Interspersed between the constant churn of 'wacky' thrills, 'kerazy' jingles and DJ pranks that characterised the Radio 1 of the early to mid-seventies were the latest singles from Marc Bolan, Sweet, Queen, Suzi Quatro, Dana, Brotherhood of Man, Gary Glitter (ahem . . .), Rod Stewart, Elton John and, of course, Abba.

But probably my first musical awakening was the Bay City Rollers. I say awakening, but this is likely a misnomer. I knew who the Rollers were, but never was bothered with the music – it was a glam-rock-lite sort of thing, with harmonies and a large slice of rock'n'roll thrown in. They all wore white outfits trimmed with tartan (good, solid Edinburgh lads, see) – tartan scarves, trousers that ended mid-calf, stripey socks, stacked shoes and had bog-brush hairdos (kind of a proto mullet). The thing about the Rollers is that all the girls were crazy for them. They were the biggest band in teenage girls' affections since The Beatles ten years before. 'Rollermania', they called it. So at school, all the girls were Rollers fans and you could not miss the impact they had. The Bay City Rollers were everywhere. The real Bay City Rollers story is a phenomenal rollercoaster ride of screaming kids, scheming managers and rip-off record companies, but we were none the wiser back then of course.

Someone else who caught my ear – or perhaps eye – was Lynsey de Paul. Lynsey was a sensitive female singer-songwriter who played the piano, was blonde and striking to behold. She had quite the boho early seventies look, with lots of velvet and floppy brimmed hats. She had hits with 'Sugar Me' and 'No Honestly' and represented the UK in the 1977 Eurovision Song Contest with 'Rock Bottom' – probably my favourite – coming in second place to the French entrant. Strangely, I never felt strong enough about Lynsey's music to go out and actually *buy* one of her records, though I'm sure her

17

regular appearances on *Top of the Pops* were enough for the 10-year-old yours truly to get his fix of this beautiful singer, now sadly gone.

One particular piece of music, however, did grab me by the ears: Queen's 'Bohemian Rhapsody'. First released in late 1975, it was all over the radio and TV and ended up hitting number one in the UK charts. It was, and still is, an arresting piece of music, and there's still probably nothing like it. It starts as a gentle ballad, with an over-the-top opera section in the middle and ends with a fab rock 'wig out' at the end. Absolutely nuts. But of course, you already knew that, didn't you? As well as being a rollicking six-minute rock opera, it came with that rare thing for the mid-seventies – an accompanying video, which, of course, was brilliant and over the top, perfect viewing for ten-year-olds and somewhat mind-blowing. So much so that I was moved enough to spend some of my pocket money on the record. I recall getting the bus (top deck, front seat, natch) into Rotherham town centre and buying a 7" copy of the single – black vinyl, on the EMI label, no picture sleeve. I probably purchased it from Woolworths rather than a dedicated record shop, and then played it to death on the stereo in the corner of the dining room. I still have that record today.

We had an ITT radiogram stereo, a huge black thing that had a record turntable, radio and cassette deck all integrated into one unit. It wasn't on legs like you might expect a radiogram to be, but it did seem to be the height of sophistication. I suppose it was more of an integrated stereo system. During the years we had it no one ever seemed to play records on it, or cassettes for that matter, and there was only ever a few LPs stacked up by the side of it: Stevie Wonder's *Songs In The Key Of Life*; The Beach Boys' *20 Golden Greats*; Simon & Garfunkel's *Bridge Over Troubled Water*. There was a cassette of those wholesome Mormon boys The Osmonds ('Crazy Horses' was a firm fave), a Motown compilation, definitely a couple of disco compilations and numerous albums by the James Last Orchestra.★

There would have been a few singles knocking about, too. Those that spring to mind are Ike & Tina Turner's 'Nut Bush City Limits', 'Play That Funky Music' by Wild Cherry, a favourite of mine to this day, and 'Fly Robin Fly' by Silver Convention, which was also a belter. As you can see, disco was big on the ITT sound system.

Mum and Dad held a Christmas party for all the relatives and friends every year, and it was always an event. The vol-au-vents would be filled, the crab (spread) sandwiches would be made, and cheese puffs galore would be deployed in various bowls about the house. Mum made a killer punch with any wine available, fruit juice, lemonade, and copious amounts of vodka and Bacardi, all made respectable by adding some slices of lemon, orange and apple, which would float around in this alcoholic purple soup. Chairs would be moved to the side of the room to make more space. We had a large conservatory at the back of the house that Dad had built – great for occasions like this. He even built a little bar in there, which was a bit odd for a life-long tee-totaller. He never touched a drop; coke or fizzy orange every time was his 'thing', which was quite unusual for men of his vintage.

So, all the guests would arrive and their coats would be piled up in a bedroom for safekeeping and the partying would commence. Eventually everyone would be dancing in the conservatory. The disco compilations would be whipped out and played. James Last would

---

★ James Last was a German big band leader who was massive in the early to mid-seventies. His trademark sound, which he called 'happy music', was big band arrangements of popular hits, and heavy on the bass and brass sections. Often the arrangements would segue into each other to give a seamless run of music. I guess it was the equivalent of the repulsive Jive Bunny from the eighties, or even a DJ mix from today. But obviously way more naff. Still, my mum and dad loved a bit of James Last and at every Christmas party the LPs of 'Hansi' (as he was known in Germany) would be given a spin.

definitely get a spin. (Strangely, I never remember seeing anyone changing the records; there was certainly no DJ manning the ITT, heaven forfend!) I remember dancing away with the 'olds' and throwing my best shapes. Dad loved his soul, Motown and disco tunes and could be quite a nifty mover. Richard and I weren't allowed to drink as we were too young but later we would sneak a few glugs of beer to see what all the fuss was about – oddly, the grown-ups didn't seem to care by this point if we were seen having a crafty swig from a can.

I never had the traditional kid job of a paper round. The idea of getting up and out at 7 a.m. really didn't appeal. Besides, we didn't have a paper shop anywhere near us. However, Richard and I were kind of employed in the family business on Saturdays. Mum had started a pottery business with my Aunt Audrey in 1972 when I was seven and Richard nine. They sold mugs, plates, tea sets, ceramic ornaments, teapots, vases and so on. On Saturdays they would have a market stall in the town of Bawtry, about 15 miles to the east of Rotherham, and later a stall on the market in the centre of the town of Gainsborough, another 15 miles on from Bawtry to the east. So, we had to spend our Saturdays helping out selling pottery to the good people of Bawtry and Gainsborough (I think it was more a case of dragging us along rather than needing to ask someone to look after us). I'm not sure that we were particularly good market traders, as if it was cold – which it seemed to be all the time – we would bunk off for warmth in the Woolworths on the market square. Sometimes the odd sweet would just happen to fall into our pockets from the pick'n'mix section and we'd just happen to forget that it was there. (I bet all kids nicked the pick'n'mix from Woolies. That's possibly part of the reason Woolworths no longer exists.)

Cold and boredom were the main takeaways from market stall trading, but if it was busy the time would fly by quicker and you did get a sense of achievement at the end of the day.

Once we set off for home and there was only me in the cab of the van – no Richard. Audrey said he had gone missing and we weren't to worry about it. I was distraught; how could the grown-ups be so flippant about such a serious matter? Where was he? What had happened? Fool me, he was merely hiding in the back of the van. The laugh was on NB.

Richard and I got on pretty well, I guess, for brothers. It's never easy, of course. Yes we had fallouts, yes he once threw a large chunk of concrete at me – OK, I had been teasing him somewhat. The chunk hit me just above the eye, causing gushes of blood to fly all over the shop (still got the scar). He may have thrown a dart at me that stuck in my shin once (surprisingly, no blood at all this time). The thing that troubled me most was that when we were young Mum dressed us as twins. We both looked the same, even though he was 18 months older than me – we were the same height and had the same hair colour – so I guess it was easier for Mum to buy all her clothes in twos. Made for a simpler life. Can't blame her really – but it really irked me to be seen as a twin. I was definitely *not* a twin, I was my own person, and hated it when people thought we were twins. Richard never seemed to be bothered about this, which again got on my nerves somewhat. So as soon as I could, I would protest about wearing the same as Rich. The foot will have definitely been stamped and some wailing taken place. Eventually I got my way and soon clothes appeared to be bought that were not identical.

We hardly ever had 'brand' stuff at ours. Unless it was specifically asked for, and even then the chances of that particular item being 'got in' was next to never. When I was about 12 or so the new craze was skateboarding (no need for pads, helmets and so on in them days), and all the kids – well, lads – were careering down pavements in varying degrees of control. I needed to get in on this action. As the birthday was on the horizon my eyes were peeled for a suitable 'cool as' skateboard to ask for. Got to be a dead cert for a birthday present. Dutifully, the 'Alley Cat' skateboard, resplendent in black and yellow, was selected at the toy/sports shop.

'That's the one I want for me birthday, Mum,' I said, hopefully.

Come the day, the wrapping was torn off to reveal not the black-and-yellow Alley Cat but a very much inferior 'Flying Pigeon', plywood 'deck' with rubber roller skate wheels screwed underneath – definitely not the state-of-the-art bright yellow polyurethane wheels of the Alley Cat I was so desperate for. 'It's a skateboard, isn't it?' I was told. Technically, yes, I suppose. But so far from what I needed. Almost certainly off Rotherham market. Mum's oft-quoted phrase on these matters was: 'Well. They're all made int' same factory. They just stick a different label on 'em – they're all the same!' No they were not.

Suffice to say, the 'Flying Pigeon' did not fly. It barely moved along the pavement. No amount of scooting along would build enough speed to do anything. The not-state-of-the-art rubber roller skate wheels were rubbish and you ground to a juddering halt pretty quickly. Thus, the requisite skateboard skills could not develop and remained within. As such, the 'Flying Pigeon' never not got its debut run-out with the other kids zooming about. The shame! The horror!

Football was an ever-present feature of growing up. Not, as you might expect, through going along to regular home and away games (we were never much encouraged to support a local team with a stoic fanaticism), or being dragged along as a kid with no interest in on-field events and wondering why you had to stand on a cold terrace when you were too small to even see the match. No, it was all because of Dad's younger brother, Gordon.

To us kids, Gordon was definitely our favourite uncle (sorry the rest of my uncles!). He was a professional footballer – and played in goal for Stoke City FC in the English First Division, as it was then, and later for England. In fact, he was widely regarded as the world's number one goalkeeper and oft cited as the best ever goalkeeper to stand in between the sticks – which I would support, but I suppose I am a bit biased. So to be a young lad in the presence of such greatness, I, as with all the other cousins, held Gordon in awe.

I suppose I first became aware of Gordon's status when Grandma Banks travelled to Mexico to watch him play in the 1970 World Cup Finals. This was a major trip in those days. I can't remember watching any of the games on TV, but Grandma did bring us all a Mexican sombrero back as a souvenir. I remember the hat being huge on my head, although I recently rediscovered it and it's really tiny! Gordon was one of the legendary team of '66 that won the World Cup for England. The final, played on 30 July 1966 at Wembley Stadium, ended in a 4-2 win for England after extra time. I was a year and two days old when that game was played. Both Mum and Dad went to watch, but why, oh why, didn't they take me? It would have been a great tale to tell in future years. What a spectacular lack of foresight from them! Then again, taking two toddlers to Wembley would have taxed the best of us. I guess I was left back in Rotherham with the cousins and aunties.

We followed Gordon's career religiously and it was always a source of great pride that Gordon was my uncle – can you blame me? I would always make sure everyone at school knew that my uncle played for England. When the family met at Grandma's all the kids would have a kickabout in the back garden, with Gordon in goal. It was a great boast in the playground on Monday morning to say that you had put four past the best goalkeeper in the world on a Sunday afternoon in Rotherham. Consequently, what with Gordon playing for Stoke City, we supported them rather than a local team. We had red silk Stoke City scarves that got frayed when they were flown out of car windows when folk went to watch Gordon play. I only got to see him play once, during a First Division tie against Newcastle United in 1972 held at Stoke City's old Victoria Ground (now demolished). I have only fleeting memories of the game – we were in a posh 'VIP' box, if such a thing existed back then. However, I do remember watching some good old seventies football hooligans have a punch up in the stands below us.

Later, in 1972, Stoke City made it to the League Cup Final – their first ever visit to a Wembley cup final. Again, us kids didn't go to the game, but Stoke won and the family were all bursting with pride at the victory. Later that year Gordon was awarded the Football Association Player of the Year award, but more importantly he was given the TV accolade of an appearance on ITV's *This is Your Life*, presented by Eamonn Andrews.

The programme walked celebrities and notable people of the day through their life story with the help of 'the big red book' and guest appearances from significant friends, family members and colleagues. The recipient is kept in the dark until the day of, so everyone was in stealth mode as we were invited to London for the filming of the episode. Dad, Grandma Banks (Grandad Banks died in 1969) and all the Banks relatives were there for the show. Us kids – apart from Gordon's kids, Rob, Wendy and Julia, were all put in a green room with the most enormous colour TV I had ever seen – this was 1972, so colour TV was still a bit of a new thing I guess. We watched the show from there and after filming wrapped everyone piled in for a party. The cup-winning Stoke team were all there and they brought the cup with them. It was duly filled with Coca-Cola for the kids and we all had a drink from it. Later, everyone decamped elsewhere to watch the 1972 European Cup Final between Ajax and Inter Milan. Ajax won 2-0, with both goals coming from the genius that was Johann Cruyff.

Soon after, Gordon's career was cut short after a car crash during which he was badly hurt. His face was all cut up and he lost the sight in his right eye. Rather disastrous for a goalie. We went to visit Gordon in hospital and looked in awe at the card sent to him from the presenters of the BBC kids' programme *Blue Peter* – I think I have it somewhere; it's in a film canister signed by John Noakes, Valerie Singleton and Peter Purves. Gordon's top-flight football career was effectively over. He tried making a comeback in the USA, bringing 'soccer' to the US via the new North American Soccer League. He played for the Fort Lauderdale Strikers down in Florida for a bit, but that was it – Gordon never played pro-football in the UK again.

5

A Comprehensive Education

(Everybody's Problem)

By 1976 I was to make the big step up to secondary school – Oakwood Comprehensive, Rotherham. During the last months at junior school all sorts of rumours circulated about what the other, older kids, did to the new first years: pushing of the head down the toilet and flushing to the 'first year clip', where anyone could bat a first year round the ears for no other reason than they were new to the school and needed reminding of the fact. All very 'British public (private) school', Billy Bunter/Just William-type tropes I guess. However, this was a comprehensive school where everyone was equal. The same. As one.*

The comprehensive school system was designed to replace the previous stratified system of education. It consisted of:

- Grammar schools – for those who could pass an arbitrary exam, the dreaded 11-plus. The object of grammar schools was to illuminate the best and brightest kids and earmark

---

* If you haven't already, go see the 1969 film *Kes* by Ken Loach to get a bit of the flavour of a South Yorkshire comprehensive school of this period. Needless to say, none of the initiation horrors occurred (well, at least not to me) during that first term at 'The Comp'.

them for special treatment, thus prepping them for university and/or careers in the upper echelons of society, but not above those who were privately educated outside the state system – the public schoolboys.

- Secondary modern schools – for everyone else. These were for the majority of kids left to get on with it. Not much in the way of airs and graces for this lot. Many saw the secondary modern as a bit of a dumping ground for the kids who would go on to be the nation's general workforce, and that didn't need too much in the way of fancy qualifications.

So the Comp kids could have the chance of going to university, getting some decent qualifications and perhaps a half-decent career that maybe didn't involve 'high risk of death' every day or back-breaking toil that wore you out by the time you were fifty. Equally so, they never had the chance to daydream their way through their schooldays, getting spat out the other end with a few CSEs (Certificates of Secondary Education) in gardening, woodwork or cooking.

That first day we all filed into the school hall in our brand new school uniforms. This was a novelty – we didn't wear uniforms at primary school. The school uniform was a black blazer with either grey or black trousers, smart black shoes (NO TRAINERS), a white, grey or light blue shirt, a house tie and a grey jumper. Pretty bog standard. Oh, and I had me red Adidas bag to carry my books in. I had to fight for this, as Mum would have plumped for a non-brand bag off the market or from Woolworths that had 'Winfield' emblazoned across it. The social horror that this faux pas would bring. I would definitely be a candidate for the head down the bog treatment with such an 'uncool' bag (things ain't changed much).

At school we were divided into 'houses' – a bit like inter-year teams and a hangover from the British public school system. I was in 'Shackleton' (colour-coded, hence the Adidas bag), named after the famous British Antarctic explorer. The others were 'Campbell' (green), after the pre-war speed record enthusiast; 'Hillary' (yellow) after the famous mountaineer; and 'Bader' (blue) after the legless war hero. All famous British *Boy's Own* heroes, although you could argue that Sir Edmund Hillary, the was first person to conquer Mount Everest, was a Kiwi/New Zealander. But hey ho, I wasn't going to get all pedantic like over that.

In the school hall names were read out and you were allocated your school form. I was in 1S, and all my fellow classmates were in the Shackleton house. We stuck together as a form throughout our secondary school career. Could have been worse, I suppose.

The good news from the first couple of weeks was that the rumours of first-year beastings/hazings were just rumours, and in the end no one got clipped or shoved down the loo. A let-off.

The first two or three years at Oakwood Comp were pretty uneventful. I tried and got into the rugby team (union code) in the first year, and thought I was OK as a scrum half. We had a game arranged for a Saturday morning against a neighbouring school. We duly arrived, changed and got out on the pitch – which, naturally, was freezing. We chucked a ball about a bit until the games teacher told us the other team weren't going to show, so to get changed back. Sod this, I thought – what a waste of a Saturday morning. At least it was a change from going to the market I guess. I didn't bother with the rugby team after that.

My sporting high spot at Oakwood – before music came along – was my crowning as the Oakwood School fishing champion. A coach load of lads (I don't recall any girls going along) travelled down to the River Trent, the idea being to see who could catch the greatest amount of fish by weight. The weather was pretty bad and we all ended up on a lake by the Trent, as the river was in flood. No one was having any luck until myself and the kid next to me managed to pull in a tench each. We were the only people to catch anything all day. At the weigh-in my fish was slightly heavier than the other boy's (approximately 2lb 2oz), so I was crowned the winner. I had to collect the trophy, which I still have, in front of the whole school in Monday's assembly. I held the minuscule thing aloft as if I had just won the FA Cup!

Music didn't come into the equation in those early years; the boys at school were more interested in football than music. I had a bit of bragging rights on that matter with the Gordon thing, of course. There would be games of 20-a-side on the playground with a tennis ball – full-size footballs were banned, as windows were likely to be smashed. With a tennis ball, less so.

I was pretty rubbish at football compared to most other kids and as a consequence of 'the Gordon thing', I was always told 'Banks, in goal', be it on the playground during break times or the quagmire-like school football pitches in games. I had little desire to throw myself around after the ball in mimicry of Gordon and even less desire to land in a freezing cold muddy puddle and thus be left standing in danger of hypothermia for the next hour or so. It usually didn't take long for the cry to go up: 'Banks! Out of goal, you're crap!' Job done. Although that relegated you to vaguely standing around in the middle of the pitch as the game swirled around you, desperately trying to avoid the dreaded thwack of the ball on a cold thigh, a pain too dreadful to contemplate. Time was wasted chatting to the other crap players waiting for the full-time whistle.

As the years passed, music started to play a more conscious role in my life. In 1977, I finally bought my first LP record (a traditional 12" black vinyl, naturally, CDs being a long way off at this point). Jeff Lynne's group Electric Light Orchestra had been putting out some great singles in the mid to late seventies: 'Turn To Stone' 'Sweet Talkin' Woman', 'Wild West Hero', and of course the colossal 'Mr. Blue Sky' – a favourite most definitely. I will have skipped off from the market stall to Greens in Gainsborough one cold Saturday and handed over my hard-earned, purchasing *Out Of The Blue*, a masterpiece double album containing the singles mentioned above. I loved it, played it to death.

Hold on, I hear you cry. 1977? Surely that was YEAR ZERO – the advent of punk, the musical movement that changed the world. Or at least the music world. I should have been plugged into the zeitgeist and spiking my hair up and ripping my T-shirts. Well, remember this is a Rotherham world we are living in. News and revolutionary music movements travelled somewhat slower in those days. Hair remained resolutely home cut (bowl style) and T-shirts un-ripped. Besides, in 1977 I was 12 – hardly ready to 'smash the system'.

In fact, that summer was the Queen's Jubilee, celebrating 25 years of QEII on the throne. Her Maj did a tour of the UK to allow the 'peasantry' to doff their caps in deference and it just so happened that Rotherham got a royal visit around the time of my birthday. We, as loyal subjects, duly went to town. I had birthday money to spend and made a beeline to Coopers Toys in Rotherham town centre. The object of my mission was to splurge the birthday cash on a new Action Man: eagle eyes, gripping hands, realistic beard, all wrapped up in a very fetching sailor outfit (Action Man that is, not me) – why would you not? Afterwards, we got down to the procession route in good time and waited at the front of the barrier for the drive past and regal wave – all the time me clutching sailor boy. Finally, the royal Rolls rolls by and we wave and cheer like good British citizens. I was convinced the Queen looked directly at me as she wafted by, as I'm sure everyone was. How's that for punk rock!

Punk rock, however, was not entirely absent from my radar that year. The news had been full of the Sex Pistols' 'Grundy Incident', during which the band had been goaded by Bill Grundy, presenter of the London regional TV show *Today*. The band duly bit back during the interview and swore profusely live on telly, much to the consternation of viewers. The incident gained nationwide coverage due to the tabloid press and their headlines, including the *Daily Mirror*'s 'The Filth and the Fury!', making grannies 'tut, tut' across the country. No greater publicity could be achieved for any group no matter how 'controversial' they seemed. I do recall the 'incident' being discussed by the family elders and how shocked they were about how 'young' people could want to behave in this way – why would they want to be all sweary and wear safety pins through their noses? These all seemed totally correct and natural views and I too would've wondered why anyone would want to dress 'way out' like a 'punk' and go around being nasty.

The third year at secondary school is seen as quite a golden year. Nowadays it's called Year 9 in the UK. Kids about 13 or 14. You didn't have the expectations and stress of upcoming exams (O-levels, in the seventies, which were traditionally taken in Year 11) and you were not a first or second-year newbie, still wet around the ears.

This was now '78 going into '79. Lots of the other boys were starting to get a lot more serious about music. Loads had older brothers who will have been bringing records home and playing them, influencing younger members of the family. Gradually kids started gravitating to certain genres of music and their 'tribes'.

Some were starting to get into rock, as in 'heavy rock' – Status Quo, Zep, AC/DC, Judas Priest and the like. These kids were easy to spot, as they started sporting denim jackets with patches lovingly sewn on by their mums. The more adventurous 'rockers' would have dabbed a bit of patchouli oil on (we called it gyp juice – it was a pungent scent supposedly to mask the odour of marijuana, which I very much doubt any of the kids at Oakwood Comprehensive had ever tried). The rockers started to try and get away with long hair – only if their Mams let 'em though.

Those that were a bit more 'cerebral', let's say (it is Rotherham, remember), would have a tendency to go for prog, as in progressive rock. These were definitely your 'Set 1' kids, uni material for sure. They had a desire to understand the odd time signatures and complex 'riffing' that bands like ELP, Genesis, Rush, Yes, and the Floyd would employ. Serious stuff for serious kids.

Another conspicuous tribe was the 'soul boys', who were into Motown, soul and chart music. They were starting to adopt a more grown-up look largely consisting of sheepskin coats, smart jackets, slacks and cheap jewellery. These kids were often good at football and keen on attracting (or at least trying to attract) the opposite sex. Usually, they would be the first to get girlfriends, get served in a pub, play footie for the school team and attempt to extort dinner money off the younger kids. And prog fans, of course. Nice.

I remember a few Bowie/Roxy Music acolytes in the older forms, but they were very few and far between. Some older girls were into Roxy Music but they might have been living on Mars as far as we were concerned. As far as I knew, no one in the third year was into such 'exotic-ness'.

Although I had an older brother, he wasn't into music – at all – and so he didn't bring home any records that I could wonder at and thus look cool in front of my mates at school when the music chat got lively. Cheers! I was kind of on my own, left to discover my tribe. I think I was starting to fall into the orbit of the prog crowd, what with my ELO album and Queen single. However, everything was up for grabs. The rock crowd didn't particularly appeal and I hated the smell of the 'gyp juice'. Being crap at footie excluded me from trying to worm my way in with the soul/pop gang. The chances of any member of the opposite sex giving me even a cursory glance were remote. As for getting garbed up like Bowie, that was just a non-starter.

By the time 1978 rolled round the lads with the older siblings were starting to talk about the new punk rock wave sweeping the nation. Rotherham is, as I'm sure you have picked up, a bit of a backwater and so was a bit behind the times. Or so it seemed to a 13-year-old. But by now the straight-leg trousers were coming in big time! A couple of lads in our year had their hair cut 'spiked', as we called it, so that it stuck up, punk style. This was radical stuff. I'd never been to a professional salon. My hair was still cut by me mam in the kitchen. I'd sit on a kitchen stool while she chopped away, convinced that as each hair was trimmed I could feel it happening just as if my fingers were being sawn off. It was genuinely painful. The scrape of the comb on the scalp and the use of 'home hair dressing' scissors that had never been sharpened since the year dot didn't help. I imagine I was a nightmare client at the kitchen barbers. So, an unflattering fringe with greasy collar-length hair was my lot. Tell it like it is: square.

In my year, cool proto-punks were emerging. Dom Wood and Graham Torr to the fore. They had older brothers and thus a ready-made vein of music to mine. We would listen to their regular updates about this 'new music', the Sex Pistols and their records being a usual topic. It was obvious that ELO, Queen et al. were in the 'not cool' bin.

This new direction was the way to go for me. The music we started to hear was exhilarating, the Sex Pistols' 'Holidays In The Sun' being a firm favourite. I needed to start getting into punk in a more serious way to keep up with the other kids at school.

So, back to Greens in Gainsbro' or perhaps the Woolworths record department on the market square to start buying into the punk rock revolution. The Pistols' second album, *The Great Rock 'n' Roll Swindle*, was out by now and the singles from it were hitting the charts. Oblivious to the 'cash-in' nature of this record, I blindly bought 'Somethin' Else', the Eddie Cochran cover sung by Sid Vicious. I loved it. I also bought a copy of 'Silly Thing' – a rather weak effort in hindsight and hardly the punk rock revolution it should have been. Clearly, further exploration of punk's ground zero group (as far as I was concerned) was required. Meanwhile, the two other 'punk' groups that caught our ever-expanding ears were Blondie and The Stranglers.

As part of the musical explosion that was happening to us in '78 and '79, Blondie was much to the front. They'd hit the charts with 'Denis', taken from 1978's *Plastic Letters*, and of course lead singer Debbie Harry was quite the eye candy for teenage boys. They seemed punk to us. We hadn't really heard the term 'new wave' as yet. Market-stall wages were saved and Blondie's new LP, *Parallel Lines*, was eagerly purchased. An easy choice, as Blondie had been all over the radio with 'Hanging On The Telephone' and 'Picture This', so with bona fide hit singles on it, the album was a no-risk purchase. I played it to death on the ITT. It still is a classic record. Punchy power pop at its best. I remember at the time thinking 'Sunday Girl' and 'Heart Of Glass' weren't exactly 'punk' and initially thought those tracks a bit soppy – yikes, disco even. Wot, like me mum and dad like?

My brother Richard was also starting to warm to this new music, and probably around the time of me buying *Parallel Lines* he bought The Stranglers' live LP *Live (X Cert)*, a collection of live tracks recorded in 1977 and '78 – so a bit like a compilation record of their best tracks. It was raw and it was rude. Perfect. The tracks were played with a typical punk velocity, making the studio recorded versions sound a little tame by comparison. The atmosphere was forbidding and it really made the idea of going to a punk gig extremely inviting. It was a great introduction to the band and they quickly became firm favourites with both Richard and me.

However, the Sex Pistols were still seen as the motherlode of punk. We saw them as a mysterious, mystical and mythical group. They were 'out there', far more than all the others. The DJ at one school disco played 'Anarchy In The UK' and we were pogoing along wildly.

However, I needed to show my dedication to the cause and not being able to talk with confidence about the Pistols would be found out in time.

The Pistols' debut album was obviously now seen as THE REAL DEAL, and if you wanted to be seen as 'a punk', this record needed to be in one's collection. Problem. The title. Rude word. We'd never heard such language at home above the gritted teeth of a 'bloody 'ell'. Another trip to Greens in Gainsborough on a Saturday morning was planned. Only this time a strategy was required. The scenario of me returning to the stall with this record under me arm and immediately being frog-marched back to Greens to return the offending item would have to be avoided at all costs. The embarrassment would be just too much. Subterfuge was no answer, or even contemplated – I'd be found out sooner than later. Front it out was the only answer. So, in the van on the way to the market, I brought up the subject of my imminent purchase:

'Gonna buy a new record today. (Nonchalant as you like.) OK?'

'Yes, do what you like?'

'It's got a bit of a rude title.'

'Like what?' with added side-eye.

'Err . . . it's called *Never Mind The Bollocks*.'

(Silence.) 'Hmm . . .'

Phew . . . seems like I'm in the clear. Punk rock here we come! I purchased *NMTB*, probably from Greens but it could easily have been Woolworths. It would have been easiest there, i.e. you'd simply take the empty sleeve to the counter, the assistant would then select the correct disc from the racks behind them, pop it in a bag, slide over your fiver and away you go.

And what a record. Blistering!! Now this is punk rock with a capital OCK! This vinyl slab of adrenaline, excitement and spite was just the ticket. It reached into me like all good music should, and took a hold. It cemented my path. Punk is the way to go.

Chock full of short, sharp, spiky songs – if you think 'punk' is all swearing, spitting and ham-fisted music then you perhaps aren't taking much notice (although admittedly there was a bit of swearing compared to the mainstream music of the day) – *NMTB* is a basically a ROCK record, and a fantastic rock record at that. The musician-ship is brilliant; this lot could really play. Contrary to popular myth, punk rock did not throw out the guitar solo; there's plenty on *NMTB*, served up by guitarist Steve Jones. Paul Cook's drumming is certainly not flash – although there's a couple of tricksy flourishes – but it fits the music perfectly. Direct. Competent.

What set *NMTB* and the Pistols apart from everything else at the time, though, was the vocal delivery. No one had ever heard anything like it. Certainly not 13-year-old Rotherham schoolboys. Snarling, sneering, spiteful. No soppy love songs here. No baby, baby, darling this, sweetheart that. These were nihilistic statements about how your life had, or might, turn out. These were statements on the state of the nation, how it was and how it could be. There were subtle, or not so subtle, instructions on how to live, all wrapped up in a swirling vortex of sound. Anarchy for the UK? Yes please.

Johnny Rotten was the figurehead. The point of the arrow. The future writ before us. We had little knowledge that by now – late '78 or so – the band were, to all intents, no more. Info was much harder to get hold of back then.

NMTB was proudly stacked next to the other LPs by the ITT, and it soon became the most frequently played record in the house. Strangely enough, though, it always seemed to get put to the back of the rack when I came to put it on. Odd that.

That was it for me. I had found my tribe – or did it find me? It didn't seem to concern us that punk rock was two years old and with hindsight the initial rush of punk excitement was over. Punk's Not Dead, they said and we believed them. And there were plenty of 'punks' around. In school we would talk about other groups that we needed to know about: The Clash, Siouxsie & The Banshees, Slaughter & The Dogs, 999, The Damned.

However, one group I could not get to grips with was The Jam, three lads in smart black suits, ties, and black-and-white bowling shoes. They played a punk 'type' music I guess, but certainly with less edge? And they didn't really look the part according to my outlook of what this new movement required. As we moved further into 1979, The Jam paved the way to a new (revisionist) tribe: the 'mod'. A revival started to grow. Kids started wearing big green parkas and talking about Lambrettas all of a sudden. The film *Quadrophenia* was the catalyst for this – the story of a sixties mod played by Phil Daniels, struggling with a dreary day job and dreaming of weekends scootering down to Brighton for dancing, loving, taking pills and battling with the 'rockers'. The new mod was perfect for the lads who were into looking smart, the same lads who were good at foot-ball and getting girlfriends.

Along with the mod revival there was a revival of the 'skinheads' first seen in the late sixties. These were lads shaving their hair off and donning Doc Marten boots and red braces to hold up their Sta-prest trousers or jeans. Altogether far more unsettling.

So, we didn't know it at the time but we were (a very, very small) part of a new cultural revolution. These don't come around very often; you had Elvis and the rock'n'roll explosion in the fifties, The Beatles and Beatlemania in the sixties, and now punk in the seventies. Now, with hindsight, I feel blessed that I managed to sneak in before it was too late with punk. It was a close-run thing, though.

Thing is, those of us being affected didn't *know* that we were being affected. For many years I was of the opinion that music cannot change the world – how on earth could a few taut strings, drums and a bit of singing do that? Much later, I had a flash of inspiration on the matter thanks to the theme tune from TV's *Wonder Woman* – no really, stay with me on this. The lyrics are all about how brilliant and wonderful Wonder Woman is. So far so good, it's what you would expect; but the second verse has the killer line: *'change their minds and change the world'*. That line provoked the light bulb moment. Punk rock *changed our minds*. Just as Elvis changed kids minds in the mid-fifties and thus changed the world, and The Beatles did the same from 1963 onwards. It was not an overnight change but took many years. Punk changed our minds to accept the idea that *you can do it yourself*. You didn't need any 'formal' training to do something unique. You should strive for 'originality' (whatever that may mean). You didn't have to tug the forelock to those who had gone before. Feel free to rip it up. Smash the system, even. New ideas, new rules.

However, it was all well and good talking about punk bands and their records, but one had to start developing some kind of *image*. One of the things that the kids of '78/'79 seemed to be obsessed with was that if you were to be a punk, you had to be a *true* punk. Not a POSER. To be branded a poser was a grave insult. It meant you were not taken seriously in the punk tribe – you were a plastic punk, someone just along for the ride as it seemed *trendy*. No one wanted to be saddled with this charge.

So, problem: how does one go about finding their new 'punk' image? I didn't buy my own clothes. I wouldn't even know where to start. Ditching trousers that had any semblance of a 'flare' was the first thing. This was the easiest step, since we were growing pretty quickly at this age, so new clothes were arriving at home fairly regularly. It didn't always work, though, and there were times when new trousers did not respond to the new regulations:

'What's wrong wi' 'em?'

'Everything! They're too wide!'

'Well, I can't take 'em back. You'll have to wear 'em.'

'Noooo!'

A couple of times a year Oakwood would put on a school disco in the hall on a Friday evening. Attendance was extremely desirable; EVERYONE would be going. It was a highlight of the school social calendar and I certainly was not going to miss out. This threw up the situation that as so-called punks, we would need to dress the part. It's OK talking about it in class, but now you really had to walk the walk too. Some kids seemed to effortlessly transmute into little punks, with their straight-leg jeans and the 'correct' look. I was somewhat fearful of sticking my head above the parapet, so to speak. What would my peers say? Would I get 'it' right? Hold on though: what would the family say? Would I be exposing myself to ridicule and laughter? Probably. Definitely. Maybe. Whatever, something had to be done; I had a decision to make. Peer pressure (self-inflicted – no one was saying 'you need to spice yer image up') kind of won out. I would need some punk threads.

Punks could wear T-shirts, so that was pretty easy. I had a yellow 'Strikers' T-shirt that Uncle Gordon had bought me back from the USA. That was suitable. A skinny black tie was purloined from Dad's cupboard to wear with the T-shirt. But the jacket would be a problem. The regulation punk uniform really demanded a leather biker jacket, where the zip went up diagonally across the chest, but these will have been prohibitively expensive for yours truly. Similarly, tartan 'bondage' trousers covered in zips were out of the question – far too expensive and I knew of nowhere where they could be bought. Certainly not Gainsborough market, that's for sure. To get around the jacket issue I decided, in the truest punk–DIY method, to fashion my own punk jacket. I had an old black school blazer that I was about to grow out of, which seemed a perfect foundation for the plan. I raided Mum's sewing box for some zips, cotton thread and needles. Slight problem: zero sewing skills. Can't be that hard, can it? Good job I wasn't attempting anything more taxing than sewing on some simple zips. I began and soon find out that it seemed you needed three hands to do the job: hold the needle, hold the zip on

39

where it needed to go, keep the jacket still. Eventually I'd affixed around eight zips to the jacket – all different colours, of course, and on the front, back, arms. Must have looked a right state.

Another issue: haircut. Punks needed a suitably punky haircut. Remember, I was still being trimmed on a stool in the kitchen by me Mum. I don't recall asking Mum to attack me with the scissors to create a new style and I certainly wasn't going to hack at it myself. I'd never been to a barber's and barely knew of their existence. The hair would have to stay as it was, and I soon convinced myself that I was sporting a Ramones-style look, with my straight, lank hairstyle. Sid Vicious it was not.

On the night of the disco I felt that I had my 'outfit' sorted. I'll be OK with my mates, I thought, they'd be approving of the 'look'. However, I was fearful of a disapproving family and them all laughing at my risible attempts to 'go punk'. I had a plan.

We lived in a bungalow and my room was at the side of the house. I would have to go past my bedroom window as I walked down the drive to the street. The plan was to chuck my punk-zip DIY blazer out the window. Leave the house cool as you like: 'See you later.' Swap jackets at the window, stroll out to the street, and call for whomever I was meeting before the disco. Worked a treat. I had the requisite punk credentials (possibly) with my fellows and avoided potential ridicule from my nearest and dearest.

Late seventies school discos were odd affairs. Mr DJ would set up on the school assembly hall stage; chairs lined the walls, dancing to take place in the middle. Everyone piled in and immediately the boys would occupy one side of the hall, the girls the other. No one mixed. Yet. Some brave souls would have nicked a can or two of lager from the fridge at home (or even from the offy – off-licence, that is) and necked it in the woods by school, in an attempt to give themselves a bit of a buzz and maybe some Dutch courage to talk to a female.

All done in the desperate hope that a teacher didn't detect the tell-tale beery whiff and deny them entry or, even worse, chuck them out.

The music would finally begin (it's a disco, of course). True to form the girls would be first to start dancing to the pop hits of the day. Those into 'other' types of music would have to wait their turn. The DJ would be badgered from all sides to play this or play that. Eventually he would play a few rock records for the gyp juice-reeking rockers to head bang to, their thumbs firmly wedged into their belt loops.

The music would move onto a few Roxy tunes, a bit of Motown, and then he would play a few punk records for us to pogo to, or, more accurately, to kick our legs up to, aping the dance of Richard Jobson, lead singer in the Scottish band Skids, who were then riding high in the charts with their totally fab single 'Into The Valley' – punk passion with an amazingly catchy verse and chorus. We all loved it. The DJ would even let us flick through his records to select the tunes. I remember us being amazed that he had the Pistols' 'Anarchy . . . ' on the EMI label, an extremely rare artefact even then. Everyone would leave happy, having had their 'moment' in the spotlight. Some might have even got a snog off a girl, but certainly nobody from my crowd.

In early '79 or so the school grapevine really kicked into gear. Some of my fellow schoolpunks had actually been to their first punk gig. How they knew about it I have no idea, but the rest of us certainly got to hear about it in school on the Monday. A group including Dave Spencer and Dom Wood had gone to a mysterious subterranean cellar dive called The Limit Club, located behind the City Hall in the centre of Sheffield, which had put on a gig by the aforementioned Skids. They proceeded to regale us about how amazing it had been, a packed crowd of punky types going bananas. It sounded daring, exciting, dangerous and definitely sweaty. We could only gape open-mouthed at Dom's descriptions of being pressed against the stage – which was only knee height – by the pogoing throng falling all over them in the frenzy. Bouncers had been unable to keep the hordes at bay. This was thrilling punk rock played at maximum volume. Apparently, Skids played their 'hit' 'Into The Valley' several times that night.

Later we learned that they only got in because it was an under-18s gig. Never mind. Impressed doesn't even cover it. We (those of us who failed to get the memo) needed to get to our first punk gig. Thankfully, our chance was fast approaching.

6

Sheffield Top Rank Suite

(Bar Italia)

In April 1979 original punk band The Damned had their first genuine hit single with the track 'Love Song', the lead single from their eagerly awaited new LP *Machine Gun Etiquette*, the band's first since 1977. The band even made an appearance on *Top of the Pops* (the record climbed to number 20 in the hit parade), so reaching a huge audience, as everyone watched *TOTP*, the BBC's primary music show since the early sixties. We watched the band in wonder and all us 'punks' bought the single. It came in a picture sleeve that featured one of the four band members. I got the sleeve with lead singer Dave Vanian on. He modelled himself on a vampire: black cloak, slicked-back hair, kohl-rimmed eyes, dress shirt, black leather gloves, silver-topped cane, that kind of thing (bear in mind, this was long before goth or anything like that came along). A cracking track, it's true, but the biggest news was that The Damned were due to play a gig at the Sheffield Top Rank suite in the centre of town.

The Top Rank was a brutalist purpose-built rectangular concert venue set in a complex that also housed The Fiesta, which at the time was the largest nightclub in Europe (rumour has it the owners almost managed to get Elvis over from the USA in the seventies for a show, but ultimately, of course, they failed). It was more a dinner and dance-type venue, a bit like an enormous, swanky, working men's club catering for the older crowd, with 'chicken in a basket' and 'turns'.★ I remember the parents going to The Fiesta to see The Three Degrees perform their hits. Dad loved them.

On the other hand, the Top Rank held about 2,500 people and was perfect, as it had a balcony on three sides to afford a good view of the stage and a large, wide dance floor directly in front of the stage. It usually held discos through the week (later, we called their over-25s nights 'grab a granny' nights), but lately it had been putting on bands, especially punk-type bands. The audience would cram onto the dance floor and be unencumbered by seats, as in the nearby Sheffield City Hall (which was much plusher but mainly catered to the big rock and touring acts that were definitely not punk). It certainly made for easier pogoing with no seats to fall over, rip out or break your leg on.

About eight of us threw our hats in and said we'd definitely go. We put in our £3 or so and someone went to the box office and bought the requisite tickets. Once we were handed our tickets an immediate problem reared its head. There, printed at the bottom of the ticket, were the chilling words:

OVER 18s ONLY

Right. What are we going to do about this then? None of us were more than 14 at this stage, and we looked it (mostly). We needed to think of a plan. Well, someone did . . . eventually.

Negotiations were opened with parents about being allowed to attend this punk gig. Going out at night to big, scary Sheffield was a

---

★ Working men's clubs were a feature throughout the land, especially in the north of England where they were a social institution. Working folk could gather there and drink cheaply, 'do the bingo', eat a 'pie and pea supper' and 'watch a turn', be it a comedian or a music act.

tricky matter. Town centres were, as they are now perhaps, a bit lairy at night. There was always tension between various different youth factions, especially the fearsome skinheads but also the older rockers or 'Teds', who were feared and demanded a wide berth. The other problem was, of course, that to parents, punks had a really bad PR, and they were expecting their little beloveds to get up in the violence. All of which amounted to a stream of questions:

'Who you going with?'

'How you getting there?'

'How you getting back?'

'What time will you be back?'

The first question was easily parried – Dave Spencer, Dom Wood and others from school. The travel inquisition was probably waffled away with some confident bravado; we knew we'd have to get the 287 bus to Sheffield from the crossroads at the bottom of our road – this bus took us directly to Sheffield bus terminus by a circuitous route that took about 40 minutes for a seven-mile journey. We'd be getting this bus back at the end of the gig. Unfortunately, upon further research, we discovered that the last bus to drop us back at the right stop would set off from Pond Street bus terminus at 10.45, and thus we would have to leave before the end of the show. Never mind; we'd managed to persuade our parents to let us go, and that's really all that mattered.

The date duly arrived and we traipsed off to the bus stop, both equally excited and terrified of the evening ahead. Would we get in? Would we get beaten up? Would we get laughed at? But first the plan: we had to get into an over 18s gig while barely looking 14. Some will have looked a bit older, but definitely nowhere near 18. I suppose we were in our various 'punk' guises to help the cause – Doc Marten boots, leather jackets, straight jeans and so on. Some might have even studded their leathers by this stage. My homemade blazer zip jacket was left behind for this junket.

So, on the bus (upstairs back seats of course – reight 'ard) the plan was formulated; namely, the kid who looked punkiest had to go on point and front us up in case the bouncers were going to give us any hassle. It was decided this would be Graham Torr. He had the studded leather, spiky hair, Dockers and the nonchalant, nay cocky, attitude necessary for this crucial role. The rest of us were to bunch up behind as best as possible so as not to attract any unwanted attention from the door staff and we would be in. No problemo.

Our little gang got to the venue ridiculously early and had to hang around outside with hundreds of others waiting for the doors to open, the crowd growing in size all the time. We spent the time in excited chatter and checking out the other punks waiting to get in. We even saw Rat Scabies, The Damned's drummer, wander by.

As doors time neared, which I reckon will have been about 7.30, the crowd surged and a push started which we were in the middle of. The cry of 'Skins!' went up and we thought that the other end of the crowd was being attacked by skinheads. But in the nick of time the Top Rank doors opened and the door staff started letting the crowd in. It was a real crush going up the stairs and 'The Gang' struggled to keep in formation. Enact the plan. Graham reached the doors with the rest of us in the pre-planned close formation (didn't look odd, since the crush helped us in this subterfuge). The massive doorman who was taking the tickets spotted Graham and said:

'What school you go to, son?'

'Oakwood,' Graham said without thinking.

'Get yer refund over there, son,' the bouncer said, pointing to the box office hatch. 'Over 18s only.'

We used the distraction and thrust our tickets into the bouncer's hand. With a quick wave back at the hapless Graham, we were in and laughing. The doorman didn't bother to try and get us back as he must have realised we were all together and thus underage. I guess he was rather tied up taking tickets. It's fair to say, and rather sad, but no one gave Graham and his predicament a single thought. All that mattered is that we were in and about to experience our first punk gig. Solidarity.

Inside, the Top Rank is dark and full of punks. There are several bars dotted around the outer walls – not that we dared try to get served at the bar. Anyway, it was far too expensive and we really didn't want to bring ourselves to the notice of any staff and risk getting thrown out and joining Graham on the 287 back home. We wandered around, marvelling at everything around us. It was all so *new*. We avoided the scrum at the T-shirt stall – we hadn't budgeted for such frivolities as a T-shirt, probably never even knew that such things existed. We'll know for next time, eh? A badge or two may have been purchased, but that's about it.

The place was filling up, so we found a spot in the middle of the space before the stage and checked out all the equipment, primed and ready for the first band. The glowing amp switches, poised microphone stands and shining drums all looked so exciting. The atmosphere was charged – or so we thought, but this was the set-up for the first band on, a local Sheffield band called Artery.

Artery took to the stage and began to play. We'd never heard of Artery before or their music. We listened intently, not really knowing what else to do. No one was dancing or anything. I don't particularly remember how the music made me feel, but I do remember they had the drum kit set up side-on to the stage, so you could really see what the drummer was doing. The singer, Mark Gouldthorpe, had a real stage presence, though – focused and rather menacing.

Artery played quite 'angular' music, not a punk thrash at all. Looking back, their music would now be seen as very 'new wave'. The best bit I remember, which had us all creased up, was that towards the end of their set, Mark Gouldthorpe brought out a biscuit tin and used it as percussion, shaking it (what was it filled with . . . biscuits? We never did find out) and, furthermore, hitting himself over the head with it. We thought it was crazy. A biscuit tin as a musical instrument? Whatever next?

After thirty minutes of Artery the stage was readied for the next group, The Ruts. This was more our kind of thing: fast-paced, muscular punk rock. The Ruts really could play and had some great songs. They had started to appear on folk's punk radar with 'In A Rut' – not mine though, I had no radar. They rocked us with this and other tunes such as 'Babylon's Burning', which we got to love.

The Ruts went down really well, even though they left the stage covered in the crowds' spit and phlegm. It was a feature of punk gigs for the crowd to spit at the band playing on stage, a throwback I guess to the days when the whole idea of punk was to be as confrontational and antagonistic as possible. Spitting came to be seen by the audience as a way of showing acceptance and as a gesture of gratitude – the punk way of saying 'bravo'. I never spat at a band playing, ever. I must have been brought up proper like. It was pretty gruesome to see players literally covered head to toe in horrible gob, strings and everything dripping with greenies.

We started to notice that the area we were in was beginning to get really packed. The crowd was pushing, menacing, ready to explode. The stage was cleared of The Ruts' drums, amps and guitars and roadies scurried hither and thither, setting up for The Damned. The crowd was getting too much for us. Punk crowds were quite rough, and of course we were only young and dwarfed by nearly everybody around us. We retreated to the balcony upstairs for a better view and to have a better chance of surviving the onslaught.

The Damned eventually came on and really blew us away with their furious live music – hard, hot, sweaty and, of course, loud. I'm sure with hindsight that most competent punk bands would have done the same, but we knew some Damned songs and they had a fantastic look, so we loved it. Along with Dave Vanian's proto-goth vampire look you had Captain Sensible on guitar, who would play in a huge garish furry jumper and trousers get-up, his trademark beret always sported with such style. How he didn't collapse with heat exhaustion is anyone's guess.

Upstairs in the balcony we wormed ourselves a spot by the rail and watched slack-jawed at the scenes before us. By this point the band was going full whack (Rat Scabies on drums was a bit Keith Moon-esque, super-fast, no-frills thrash playing – perfect), the volleys of gob heading stagewards and the crowd pogoing like crazy, falling one way then the other, the crush swaying across the dance floor. The people by the stage looked like they were getting the life crushed out of them, but somehow they were managing to furiously nod along, too squashed to pogo.

The Damned played tracks from *Machine Gun Etiquette* and, of course, their classics 'New Rose', 'Neat Neat Neat' and so on.

Well, I think they will have done. You will remember we had to get that last bus home at 10.45. Missing it was not an option. It was a real wrench to leave before the end. I couldn't really believe what I'd seen in front of my own eyes. I was hooked. Hooked away, that is:

'Come on we'll miss the bus! Gotta go NOW!'

We spat out of the Top Rank and made our way swiftly via the underpass to nearby Pond Street bus station. This was another problem, as it was at this point we remembered the skinhead menace from earlier, when we'd been queuing up to go in. Sheffield town centre was rough at the best of times back then (has it changed?) and the chance of meeting skinheads was very real. Therefore, the chances of a skinhead moon stomp (on your head) was a definite possibility.

Run. Leg it. Sprint. Scarper. The fear of not getting in or the chances of being duffed up in the venue were nothing compared to running this gauntlet. Thankfully we evaded the skins and just made the bus in time, clattering upstairs all breathless and sweaty, both from a hot gig and pelting it to the bus.

Wow. We could not believe what we had just witnessed. Our very first punk gig. Or second punk gig for some. But not poor Graham's . . .

In the following months and years, I went to a few more concerts at the (now legendary) Top Rank suite.

Punk originals The Clash were scheduled to play in January 1980 in support of their new LP *London Calling* as part of the 16 Tons Tour. Someone at school had a ticket they couldn't use. I could though, and so I bought it off them. Trouble is, in our circles The Clash were getting a bit of stick. 'They don't write their own songs' seemed to be the main critique. Oh, how little we knew. This sweeping statement was based apparently on the *Cost Of Living* EP, the lead track being a cover of Bobby Fuller's 'I Fought The Law'. The case for the prosecution was pretty watertight. It was a cover, no question. However, the defence was that this cover was executed with raw passion and a maximum rock'n'roll attitude. At the time I doubt I would have known this. All I knew was that I liked it.

I hit another problem. No one else was going. No one had a ticket. Sold out. So, another decision to be faced. Waste a ticket (hard-earned), sell on (who to?), or go anyway? I chose the last option: I'd go to the gig on my own. With the benefits of hindsight I must have been either crazy or naïve to the point of recklessness. I was still only 14. Gigs at the Top Rank, as we have seen, were no walk in the park. Bravado? Maybe. Heroics? Doubtful.

I will have kept the solo trip a bit of a secret from the old parents. I'm sure I would've received the 'No you're not' talk if I'd have divulged my venture. A little bit subterfuge (we've all been there), and off I went.

Same plan as before: 287 bus from the end of the road, head down there, inconspicuous entry avoiding the bouncers, and we're in. Worked a treat. This time I bought a T-shirt from the merchandise stall (decried sometimes after by Mum as being shoddy quality, especially at that price!) and rather than wander around this time, I got myself a place right at the front. I wanted to be in the thick of the action when it started. Trouble is, the 'thick of the action' started sooner than I desired, as some lads further along the front row leaning on the stage were trying to nick my jacket. Getting thumped was not my idea of a good time. Nonetheless, I stuck it out and held my ground.

Support that night came from Mikey Dread spinning some dub. Punk's musical soulmate was reggae. Before anyone had released a punk record, DJs such as Don Letts would spin reggae to the punks, hence its alliance.

Then, The Clash hit the stage in the usual horrible hail of gob, but with a 100mph version of 'I Fought The Law'. The mad pogoing crowd surge was immense and I was crushed against the stage. It was frightening and exhilarating at the same time. I was positioned off to the left of the stage, directly in front of lead guitarist Mick Jones. Unfortunately, he had a stage monitor sideways-on to the stage, and because of the crowd, my head was pushed against it throughout the gig. Deafening.

Watching Joe Strummer in full flow was truly amazing, full on. He meant it, man. The whole band, of course, were amazing, Topper Headon on drums being a particular fave. I feel so honoured to have witnessed this band at this stage of their career. Lucky me. There's some thought that at this gig Mick and Joe had an onstage scuffle about whether to play 'White Riot' – I have little to remember if they did or not. Maybe it was after I had disappeared before the end to get the last bus home.

Further gigs by The Stranglers and Siouxsie & The Banshees followed in 1980. The Banshees were supported by Altered Images, who went on to be pretty big in the eighties and were, of course, fronted by the lovely Claire Grogan (catch the support band, kids – you never know who you might see before fame and success takes

51

them away). The Siouxsie gig was memorable for the fact that I got to see one of my first drum heroes up close – Budgie. I loved his complex and creative playing. He was/is so original, and to punks originality was fast becoming one of the central tenets of our thinking. I doubt if I knew it at the time, but Budgie's drumming on The Slits' album *Cut* is one of my all-time favourites – not flash in particular, but the way his playing totally complements the music. Notes taken. This gig also sticks in the mind because some of the more lairy elements of the blokey crowd exhorted Siouxsie to 'Get yer tits out!' (unacceptable, of course, but this was basically the seventies still – Neanderthal times). Siouxsie, surprisingly, complied, but to the balcony at one side of the stage – away from the beer boys? – and thus away from me. I was of course only 15 and would have been quite grateful of a flash. Never mind.

Another memorable gig from this period (don't worry; I won't go through every gig I've ever been to, but these early experiences were so visceral and important to me and my musical evolution and adventure that I feel they need noting) was Adam And The Ants. History perhaps has not been kind to Adam and his Ants, who went on to massive commercial success with 'Ant Music' and 'Stand And Deliver', culminating in the fancy-dress pop-style posturing of 'Prince Charming', a track that seemed beloved by little kids all over the shop in 1981.

In 1980, however, the Ants were a firm punk favourites. They had a strong image, based around Native American imagery, pirates and a certain feeling of savagery. Their music – thumping, drum-heavy almost tribal – really stirred the soul in a way I had not felt before. 'Kings Of The Wild Frontier' was a song that reached in and did something to me, just as the best kind of music should.

Again, I was down the front, pogoing along, enjoying the crush and sway of the crowd and that feeling that you were a part (albeit a small part) of something.

Adam was mesmerising on stage, backed by two heaving drummers; he was a real showman and working the crowd into a frenzy. I even managed to grab a bit of his stage costume that fell off, although I'd lost it by the following week. Later, I discovered Adam And The Ants before they went all double drummers and Burundi beats. Their debut album, 1979's *Dirk Wears White Sox*, is fantastic, especially the drumming of Dave Barbe. His playing was so creative and different from a lot of stodgy late seventies punk drummers (like myself?). As I mentioned, a central tenet of punk was to value creativity over technique, which I generally abide by, but Dave Barbe, along with Budgie, had creativity in spades coupled with fabulous technical gifts, which really made for an intoxicating brew. Throw in the passion of Topper Headon (The Clash) and Paul Cook (Sex Pistols) and a blueprint was being formed.

Then there was the U.K. Subs gig. The Subs were a sort of punk phase II kind of band, led by Charlie Harper, age unknown (read that as 'ancient'), who were popular with late-to-the-party punks like me in 1980 or so. I guess we were now searching for groups that we could call our own. Ones that we 'discovered'. U.K. Subs' most successful song around this time was 'Warhead', which even secured them a spot on *Top of the Pops*.

By now, everyone was wedded to their particular tribe (rocker, skin, punk, mod, townie (more on these later)), and so tension between warring musical factions was always a feature of gigs during this period. The Angelic Upstarts were a tough band from the North East who were starting to make a name for themselves around this time, very much in the mode of Sham 69 – a real hard bunch of lads with an even harder following, half punks, half skinheads. They were down to play at the Clifton Hall in Rotherham – a much easier venue to get to than the Top Rank, so I bought a ticket.

Trouble is, during the week or so before the gig there were so many rumours about it all 'kicking off' between the punks and skins at the gig, it was almost like certain death to attend. So I bottled it. Didn't go. Wasted my ticket money. Good job too, as all the reports over the next few days were that it *did* kick off, both inside and outside the hall. Punks and skins going at it hammer and tongs. Clifton Hall didn't put gigs on after that.

The Specials and the whole ska/two-tone movement was really coming to the fore in 1979–81, and I guess us punks saw those guys as kind of rivals. Unfortunately, they attracted a majority skinhead crowd who were not afraid to have a go 'cos they were actually hard enough. Plus, we wouldn't have crossed our tribal lines – that would be seen as a 'sell-out'.

Even so, Rotherham didn't see many (i.e. zero) open-air gigs around this time, aside from The Specials at Herringthorpe Playing Fields. This was almost our local park, so us music-crazy kids just had to be there. And it was free. Result. So, we went along to the gig, but all the time we were worried that rather than experiencing two-tone in the flesh, we'd be getting a good old skinhead 'experience' instead.

On the day of, we ambled up and got to 'experience' an extremely hostile crowd, up for any kind of 'aggro', bottles flying all over. The atmosphere was so foreboding that we had to retreat after a short while to the safety of a mate's house nearby to avoid a good kicking. It was the height of the National Front era and the skins there were '*sieg heiling*' and all that abhorrence. The multi-racial Specials must have been dismayed at the audience they attracted throughout their short career. And again, as far as I know, no other gigs have since taken place on Herringthorpe Playing Fields.

Memorably, around this time I went to see anarcho-punks Crass at the Marples Hotel pub, which had a concert room upstairs. The Marples was famous in Sheffield, as it was the victim of a direct hit by a German bomb in the Sheffield Blitz of December 1940. Over 70 Sheffielders died in the attack.

Crass came to town with a multimedia, multi-band event. They redecorated the room with banners, posters and even TVs, transforming the space, filling the space with screaming punk and poetry. This was an exhortation to 'anarchy' and throwing off of societal norms and behaviours, do-it-yourself aesthetic to the max.

It seemed to be that within the punk movement schisms were now opening up. There was the leather, studs, Mohicans and spikes lot who were devotees of the likes of U.K. Subs, Crass, Discharge, Chron Gen, Infa Riot, Exploited and Cockney Rejects, some of whom later moved towards the skins-yob offshoot of Oi! On the other side you had 'positive punk', followers of which preferred the Banshees, Killing Joke, Southern Death Cult, The Cure, Public Image and The Slits. Some of the positive punks would go on to germinate a new sub-sect: goth. You could even throw in The Damned with this lot, whose follow-up to *Machine Gun Etiquette* was the dark and brooding *Black Album*, which included the 17-minute long track 'Curtain Call', which took up an entire side of vinyl (track it down; it's incredible by the way). These bands and their music seemed less nihilistic than the other lot. By this point, The Clash had also gone all Americana rock'n'roll with *London Calling* and the follow-up *Sandinista!*.

These strands of music were certainly more interesting to me, more thoughtful and creative than the play-faster, buzz-saw guitars and primal screamed vocals of the classic Sid Vicious-style punk, which was a bit of a cul-de-sac musically. Give me a decent tune over that any day.

7

Here's Three Chords, Now Form A Band

(We are the Boyz)

On the inside sleeve of The Damned's *Machine Gun Etiquette* is a cartoon of chord shapes and their names: A, G, F, D minor, etc. This was the next step. One of the central exhortations of punk is to go out and do it yourself. Make your own noise. We did; you can too. It's easy. Lessons are for squares, music degrees are overrated, and you don't need any training. Or even talent it turns out.

Sometime in 1979 the idea of being in a band started to take root. It seems now like a punk cliché that bands were formed simply by kids getting together and saying: 'Right, let's start a band – I'll play the guitar, what you gonna play?' But strangely enough, that's exactly how it happened for us.

A rumour went around that the other punks in my year – Dave Spencer, Dom Wood and Graham Torr – had already formed a band. The rumour was confirmed by simply asking them if they had indeed formed a band. Yes, they had. A punk band, naturally. Revolutionary. Apparently they even had a name: PVC. How fabulously punk. They had even started paper rounds so they could save up and buy their own instruments. It was rumoured that at least two of them could even play a couple of chords.

Us on the other side of the classroom could not be left out of this.

No way. So, we could either become 'the crowd' to that lot over there or form our own band. The former was never going to happen, so it was time for *the* conversation. Initially, it was me and a lad called John Wheaton.

'I'll play guitar,' said John. 'What you wanna play?'

'Err . . . I'll play bass!'

And there you go, a new band is born. It's that easy. It didn't matter that we had no instruments or any idea how to play instruments. Just the conceptual leap was enough. If you said you were a band you were.

It's not true that I had no musical leanings. A very early memory for me is picking out wistful notes on a piano at the church hall in Brinsworth when I was very small. Everyone in primary school had to play the recorder, a child's wind instrument that made the most god-awful noise when in the hands of nine-year-olds screeching and wailing their way through 'Frère Jacques'. I remember being asked to attend further recorder lessons, which I did, and a few of us were ushered into a different classroom. There we were told that the music teacher thought we had 'potential' and would we like to progress on to the violin. My god, they must have been hard of hearing. The violin is even more 'challenging' to the ears when worked by young fingers, no matter how much 'potential' they may (or may not) show. This violin choice was not compulsory. I looked at my mate, Peter Gelder, and we both said: 'Nah, not for me, thanks,' and left. Little did we know that after a few weeks of violin loads of kids moved on to the guitar. Oh well, never mind.

No band is complete without a drummer (naturally) so we had to cast our net around in hopes of trapping one of these rare beasts. Once my brother Richard got wind of this band idea, he decided he wanted in and professed a desire for the drums. No drum kit of course, but that didn't matter at this stage. The singer, though, would be a lot more difficult to pin down. They needed to be a larger-than-life character, bit of a show-off, not afraid to be in the firing line. Unfortunately, no one we knew seemed to fit the bill. Oh well, we'll cross that bridge later, eh?

Hold on. A band ain't no band without a suitable name. We thought long and hard in our attempts to come up with a name to rival PVC across the classroom. I remember loads of kids getting involved in the debates, throwing their ideas into the mix. It's not easy to come up with a band name, especially as 14-year-old know-nothings. Despite all the suggestions, we finally settled on the suitably 'punk' moniker: Fatal Noise. That'll do. Punky enough. All settled. What next? Well, a band ain't no band without suitable instruments. Time to take the lead of the other lads across the room and get saving.

I had my market stall job at the weekends, which supplied a bit of cash, and by cajoling the family to give me money rather than some poxy bad gift for my birthday, I soon had a few quid to spend on equipment.

In Sheffield back in the late seventies, London Road was THE place to go for music gear. There were loads of shops selling guitars, amps, drums and the rest, both new and second-hand. All gone now of course. A buying trip was planned and at Musical Sounds just off London Road (now a swanky Japanese restaurant), I bought my first instrument: a dark-wood bass guitar in the shape of a Gibson SG Bass (no, not a real one – that would have been waaaaay too expensive, but a cheap Japanese copy). It did the trick. It gave a nice, low thump – but then what did I know? I passed over my £30 and walked out of that shop a bass player. I think I got a little amp and a *How to Play Bass Guitar* book at the same time. It would've been a bit sad owning a bass and then not being able to hear anything without the amp.

Practise. And then practise some more. Dum Dum Dum Der Dum was all that emanated from my room for the next few weeks, *How to Play Bass Guitar* open on my knees. I tried to master the 'walking bass' technique à la classic rock'n'roll and blues. It wasn't punk rock, that's for sure. I stuck at it though, enough to provoke the ire of the parents, so I would turn the amp right down late at night and pluck away.

'Shut that bloody amp off!!'

'Sorry . . .'

Our little proto-group would meet at weekends and attempt to play together. We even had a bash at writing our own songs. I'm sure the efforts were awful. I certainly had no idea how the bass and guitar were supposed to fit together. One thing someone should have said to us at this stage was 'Buy a proper tuner!' So, we would've been all over the place, but we were having a great time.

I hadn't had my bass long when another kid had a go on it at one of our get-togethers at John Wheaton's house. Disaster. The strap slipped off its end strap peg and the headstock hit the floor with force, a crack splitting down it where the tuning pegs were.

'Noooo, look what you've done!!'

It was an accident but I was devastated. Dad ended up putting a couple of screws in the headstock to try and hold it together. We carried on valiantly, though getting it in tune was almost impossible. Does punk have to be in tune? Err, yes it does really . . .

Meanwhile, Richard's efforts to secure a drum kit had a boost when a lad at school wanted to sell his. We traipsed round to his house and saw this green sparkle Premier Olympic kit of unknown providence. It was obviously of decent vintage and would not have looked out of place on the cabaret stage at a working men's club. It sounded like a drum kit and looked like a drum kit. It had stands, a cymbal and a snare drum, and so it was purchased. Might have been £100. Quite a lot for the time, I guess. It was duly transported back to the house.

Poor parents: two fledgling musicians struggling with their new instruments. They must have had real patience. It wasn't going away.

They could easily have shut us up after a few weeks to save their sanity but we were lucky that they allowed us to keep trying.

Fatal Noise began in earnest as a three-piece. We had John Wheaton on guitar, who also decided that if no one else was going to sing, he would try, me on bass and Richard on drums.

Problem. Richard really couldn't get any kind of rhythm going. He might be OK playing the bass drum and the snare, but everything fell apart if he tried to incorporate the hi-hat. Similarly if he started off with just the hi-hat and snare and tried to bring in the bass drum, it all stopped or descended into chaos. I found myself sitting at the kit (no dedicated drum stool, just a kitchen chair), trying to show Richard what needed to be done: 'Come on, you do it like this . . .'

Playing the drums seemed to come naturally and I could summon up a basic beat from the kit with ease. The main thing when starting out is to get a sort of 'limb separation' going, where your right and left hands are doing one thing and your legs another, but they're really all linked so the listeners hear a proper drum beat. Some can do it without thinking and others (most, really) cannot.

So here we were: a broken bass and a drummer who couldn't play. Less than ideal, I'd say.

The solution was obvious! I'd migrate on to drums, as it was clearly the way to go for me. Richard then decided playing music wasn't for him and bowed out. I guess I sold the bass and amp (likely at a loss, due to the headstock damage) and swapped for the drum kit.

So, back on course, but we still needed a third member. A kid from school, Adrian 'Cav' Carver, had started learning the bass, and so we roped him in. Dale Richardson, a younger lad, started playing with us too. He could actually play the guitar quite well – one might even venture to say he was proficient. Remarkably, Fatal Noise was coming together.

We'd rehearse mainly in the conservatory at our house. It was big enough for us to set up and we also had the advantage of a big garden

– and so did most of our neighbours, thus saving them from a bit of the aural assault emitting from our mainly glass rehearsal space. I think we only ever had one complaint. Miraculous.

We tried writing our own songs but progress was very slow on that front. Instead we played, or murdered more like, stuff like The Clash's 'White Riot', 'Stepping Stone' (which we thought was a genuine Pistols number rather than The Monkees) and the rock'n'roll standard 'Johnny B. Goode' – mainly 'cos Dale could play it in truth. But the Sex Pistols and The Clash weren't averse to a rock'n'roll classic cover, so in it went.

We sometimes set up in John's front room to rehearse. We had to be much quieter there, though. I used my bright pea green jumper to muffle the hi-hats. It was really Dad's that I'd 'commandeered'. This jumper actually got me barred from school once (and the only time, I might add).

In the fourth and fifth years the boys could swap a grey jumper for a navy blue one to signify their seniority. I decided that a punky pea green jumper was an ideal way to 'bend the rules'. Teachers had other ideas:

'Change that jumper, Banks. Green not allowed!'

'No.'

I had decided to 'smash the system' with the jumper, and all it got me was sent home for the day and a parental grilling. The jumper incident was not repeated. System decidedly unsmashed.

Sadly, if green jumpers are used as hi-hat mufflers, they don't survive. The sticks will eat holes where they collide with the edge of the cymbals, thus a ruined jumper.

Fatal Noise practised whenever we could, and I practised my drumming. Again, the parents must have had cloth ears, as drums solo aren't the easiest to live with. I saved them by hitting cushions instead. Different sized and differently stuffed cushions make different sounds, so they're a sort of alternative kit.

YouTube was nary a twinkle in anyone's eye back then, so the old favourite *Top of the Pops* would have to be my go-to drum advisor. Every kid who grew up in the sixties, seventies, eighties and nineties will have fond(ish) memories of *TOTP*, the music chart TV programme that went out every Thursday evening after *BBC News* at 7 p.m. *TOTP* was a genuine national institution, perhaps the first example of 'water cooler' TV: 'Did you see THAT on *Top of the Pops* last night?'

The programme was fronted, usually, by the 'zany' Radio 1 jocks of the day. The new entries into the pop charts that week would appear in the studio in London to mime along to their hit (although we didn't really understand miming at the time; no thought was given to how the show was made – we just assumed the cameras were dropping into an out-of-this-world pop party). As soon as the catchy theme tune died down and the presenter came into view, the wait would begin. You were hoping the tunes you liked would be showcased on that night's show. In 1979/80 there was a fair chance at least one punk-type group would get on.

Another highlight was the chart countdown. The host would run down the Top 20 (or Top 40 – it varied throughout the show's history): who was a 'new entry', a 'non-mover' or had 'dropped down' from the previous week. It was always a ritual to give a 'thumbs up' or a 'thumbs down' to rate each track as it flashed up on the screen.

Then there was the weekly run-out of Pan's People or, later, Legs & Co – dance troupes of young(ish) ladies who would perform highly choreographed dances to one of that week's hits. Often in skimpy attire. Strangely, dads across the nation would wake from their post-teatime nap just as the girls came on. Odd that.

There were other, more 'serious' music programmes on the Beeb, most notably *The Old Grey Whistle Test*, which aired on BBC Two. This sometimes featured new music of the day but, to our minds, was forever tarred with the decidedly non-punk brush of genial presenter 'Whispering' Bob Harris. This, added to the fact that it was also seen as a mainstay for old prog acts or classic rock in all its hirsute glory, made it a bit of a no-no for us young 'punks'. It's usually late hour of broadcast didn't help us schoolkid drummers either, no matter how keen we were to see some real drummers in action. Watching them mime on *Top of the Pops* would have to do.

No one ever suggested getting proper lessons. I certainly never pushed for them, and there was nothing at school as far as I was aware – the music department was all Beethoven this, Mozart that. Know your semi-breves from your demi-semi quavers in those days; we just thought they were small crisps. You might get the music teacher try and strong-arm you for the choir, but 'rock' music? Don't think so. No one in my family had any musical background at all, so we were just left to get on with it as we saw fit.

Then the miraculous happened. Fatal Noise were offered a gig. Now, this is serious. If you're just mucking about on guitars and drums, can you really allow yourself to be called a 'band'? Well, maybe. If you're gigging, now that's an entirely different matter.

We set up our rudimentary gear in the upstairs function room of The Sitwell Arms, a pub down the road in Whiston, one Saturday evening to play at a family party. Perhaps a birthday, maybe a wedding anniversary, something like that. From small acorns doth mighty oaks grow and all that, but everyone has to start somewhere, so it was here that my live music career began.

We rattled through our 'set' to the bemusement of various relatives, probably wondering what all the racket was about and why they couldn't just get back to their pints of bitter. After probably 20 minutes, we had played all our stuff and it was all over. Folk were complimentary, with pats on the back – 'Well done, son.' – though I would guess more out of good manners than any sort of musical wonder. However, those congratulations felt great. I had elevated myself, no matter how minutely, to the status of 'actual musician'. Well, in my eyes anyway.

However, strangely, or perhaps miraculously, we were offered the chance of *more* gigs. A friend of a relative was there who was on the concert committee of a local working men's club. After we'd finished playing, this bloke lumbered over. 'Good set, lads,' he said. 'Look, if you can learn some pop hits from the charts and some oldies we'll put you on int' club. You can do a couple of yer own if yer like. We'll pay you £150.'

£150? *To us lot?* This was a fortune to us back then. We could do all sorts with that kind of cash. We had a serious think about it. How hard could it be? But the opportunity threw up a bit of an ideological quandary. Potential earth-shattering punk bands don't start off their careers by doing a Beatles medley followed by the latest Hot Chocolate number. It's funny to look back, but we really did have a heated debate about the pros and cons of having a go as a 'club turn' – everyone has their price, eh? Nevertheless, ideological punk purity won out and we never did take up the offer to play at the club. No sell-out, no compromise, no posers. It's amazing to think how quickly we'd been indoctrinated.

Next up was a gig in my conservatory for our schoolmates, alongside Dave Spencer and Dom Woods' band, who had now changed their name from 'PVC' to 'Cute Pubes', which we all thought was a great name for a punk band. Bit of controversy, but hardly the end of Western civilisation. About 12 mates shuffled in to watch us play. Great fun.

So, the idea of being a band member, gigging around the area and touring further afield started to become a very appealing one. Folks at school would wonder about how amazing it would be to go out on tour, playing to like-minded souls across the length and breadth of the country. It all sounded such an incredible way to live; every day could be a great adventure.

The reality, however, was far from great. A friend of Mum's ran a youth club in Darfield, a grim suburb/satellite town of Barnsley.

This was the one time we actually got to play a little further afield. Now, we thought Rotherham was a bit rough but Barnsley was altogether in a different dimension in those days. But, a gig's a gig, as they say. We chucked our gear into the market van and Mum dropped us off at this youth club in the back of beyond.

We did this as a double header with Cute Pubes, I think, Fatal Noise playing first since Cute Pubes were cooler, could play better and had better songs. Both bands played their 'tunes' to a hall of blank indifference but simmering low-level resentment. Kids either sat on the floor or stood glowering, arms tightly folded across their chests. The youth club staff were great, though, and thought it was a successful night. Bit different to the norm, I guess. The 'audience', however, thought the opposite, and as we packed up we could definitely hear snide comments aimed our way.

By the time the van came back to collect us a bit of a crowd had now gathered to watch us getting ready to depart, glad they now had the chance to vent their displeasure at us having the gall to venture onto their patch and subject them to our 'music': 'We don't have punks here!' was the general theme from the 'mod' element of the crowd. Then it started to get more threatening. We jumped in the van pretty smartish, realising that getting the hell out of Dodge was the best policy. The mods proceeded to then 'escort' our blue Transit out of Darfield on their scooters, with a few bricks and stones lobbed in our general direction for good measure. We 'waved' back. A thorough success all round then.

Despite these early false starts, Fatal Noise continued rehearsing and trying to write our own songs, and we played the odd gig to schoolmates along with Cute Pubes. We would also take day trips up to Sheffield to drool at the guitars and drum kits in the many music shop windows, daydreaming about what we'd buy if money were no object.

One time we devised a plan to visit Carlsbro Sound, a vast instrument shop in a suburb of Sheffield. We arrived in the city but never found out which bus to get to deliver us up to Carlsbro, so we ended up walking. It's about two miles out of the centre, up a long hill in an area called The Manor. No fun. What was even less fun was the kicking we got off some local skinheads, who took umbrage at our leather jackets and pseudo-punky haircuts. We escaped on the first bus that arrived at the stop, which took us back to town.

For Fatal Noise, it was obvious the next step on our journey to world domination was to record a demo tape of the songs we'd written. Were we thinking that we'd send it out to record companies, who'd then sign us up in a multi-album mega-bucks deal? I doubt it. I don't think we will have had any ideas beyond making a record of our own music.

Even so, this was a big and expensive undertaking. We scrimped and saved work, birthday and Christmas money to be able to afford a one-day session in an actual recording studio. We knew next to nothing about being in a studio, but it was exciting all the same. We found an 8-track studio in the north of Rotherham, out towards Park Gate. Perhaps the only successful Rotherham chart act (to date) was Jive Bunny who, in the late eighties, played horrible (sorry) DJ mixes of old rock'n'roll tunes. They had a studio in Park Gate. Was it the same one? We will probably never know.

Anyway, we turned up, set up our equipment and recorded six tracks in a single day during August 1981. We had all just finished our O-levels.

We knew little of overdubs or multi-layering, of course. The engineer added a bit of reverb and that's about it. All for about £150. Tracks recorded that day were:

1 'Life On Earth'
2 'Don't You Know'
3 'Get Ready'

4 'No Time'
5 'Nothing Left'
6 'Crime Squad'

I still have a cassette copy of the session, and it does sound a bit like it was recorded with a thick sock over all the microphones, but of course that could be the cassette tape technology. The songs are suitably juvenile and best described as power-pop with a punky/new wave edge. John Wheaton's vocals are, let's say, left wanting for a bit of life to be kicked into them. The playing is OK-ish for a bunch of schoolkids. The guitars are reasonable, but my drumming is awful. I'm OK when playing a straight beat, but the fills are all over the place. Sounds like I'm trying a bit too hard. It's fair to say it would've been a criminal waste of stamps to send copies out; you can't fault the effort I guess, but it's not up to much.

Once the demo was done, Fatal Noise were no more. John and Cav weren't up for the sixth form, as I was, and they embarked on careers with British Steel on, for the time, good money. The band took a back seat and eventually faded away.

8

Kicking About in Sheffield

(Dogs are Everywhere)

Summer 1981 saw the end of my tenure at Oakwood Comprehensive School and the move to the sixth form college next door: Thomas Rotherham College, or TRC, which was housed in arguably the most impressive building in Rotherham. You could easily be fooled into thinking it was a posh English public school, its ancient façade not unlike the dreaming spires of Oxford (if you squinted a bit) and fronted by 'rugger' pitches (cricket in summer, of course). The reality was that inside it was populated by bog-standard Rotherham kids doing bog-standard A-levels.

That summer saw yet more changes. Fatal Noise might have been on the slide but I started to up my game image-wise. Myself, Richard and a couple of other lads went to Margate in Kent for a week's holiday. This was our first attempt at holidaying outside the protective arm of the parents.

Interestingly, our last full family holiday was to communist Romania. I'm sure this was based purely on the fact that it will have been cheap, hot and guaranteed sun rather than any political sentiments. We stayed in a resort near to the Black Sea port of Constanta, built for foreign tourists and their Western money. Richard and me really didn't want to be there and were sulky throughout. The food was awful, it was too hot and the Black Sea was full of jellyfish. There were no shops except for those stocked with stuff us 'Westerners' might want. They were out of bounds to locals and they would only except US dollars. Needless to say there was nothing in them that we would want to buy. It was pretty grim altogether.

One thing alleviating the crushing horror was we could buy beer, no questions asked. So we did. No matter that it tasted like a mouthful of iron filings, it was illicit alcohol. Also, one evening we were allowed a solo venture to the local 'disco', perhaps even a 'nitespot', who knows? It was pretty unmemorable really, other than the chance to drink more Romanian lager.

But on our wander back to the hotel, we noticed the Romanian authorities had hundreds of what appeared to be convicts cleaning the beach, guards watching over them. As we rounded a corner, we suddenly had an AK-47 thrust into our chests and some guttural Romanian shouting at us. Now, I don't know about you but my Romanian back then was not fully developed, so all we could do was point at a hotel and say 'British!' in response to his posturing. This seemed to satisfy his need for interrogation and we were free to leg it back to the hotel. No more nightclub trips.

Back to the Kent coast, I had no idea why we chose to go to Margate either, but we did. We basically mucked about for a week, but the big event, for me anyways, was that I decided to dye my hair black. It was about time. Something needed to be done to spice up my image. Plan: do it away from home, no interference – better to ask for forgiveness than permission, methinks. Boots was visited and the black dye duly purchased. Back to the hotel to proceed to dye my hair for the first time. Problem: half the room got dyed too. The hotelier wasn't too impressed (hope the dye came off the walls – sorry).

Back home, no one seemed particularly surprised or indeed shocked to see my new black do. In fact, the usual comment seemed to be,

'You've missed a bit round the back.' However, it was a life-changer for me: I had reinvented myself in time for sixth form. Well, that might be overdoing it a bit. I had dyed my hair, made it look a bit scruffier. Not quite 'spiked' but definitely 'punkier'.

I had also packed in working on the market stall by this time. However, I still needed some form of income for all the drum bits (they're not cheap), clothes and records. An evening job seemed to be the best fit for my 'lifestyle', so I got off the proverbial and called round a few bars and working men's clubs to see if they needed glass collectors. I was too young to be pulling pints behind the bar, so glass collecting it was.

I ended up getting a job as a pot washer at Ferrari's restaurant on Rotherham High Street two or three nights' a week. Tasks were simply to clean all the customers' plates and the chefs' pots and pans. You got fed and the work was pretty easy, though sometimes a little sweaty.

They were an odd bunch at Ferrari's, though, and I'm convinced – with that old chestnut 'hindsight' – that the owners enjoyed a 'liberated' lifestyle. Desiree, the female co-owner, would sometimes wander around the restaurant in a crocheted top sans bra, nipples proudly poking through the holes. Quite the unnerving spectacle for a spotty 16-year-old. She would often sit on my lap while we were waiting for a lift home after a shift. Awkward.

As my hair got more unruly I had a confrontation with the boss about it. The restaurant was largely open plan, and where I washed the pots and pans was visible to the customers. He said I needed to cover my hair up as it was putting off customers. I countered that no one else had to wear a hat behind the counter (by 'hat' we're talking about the kind of American diner-type hat, rectangular in profile). I held out for a couple of shifts but after head chef 'Skip' had a quiet word, I caved in. I needed the job and shoving my black mop under the cap seemed not to be a hill worth dye-ing on.

Not working on the market freed my Saturdays up for either band rehearsals or getting up to mischief. The latter won out more often than not. Mischief generally meant hanging about in town. Rotherham town centre by day was OK; we'd get up to no good in the market, as all teenagers would, and peruse the record shops. Rotherham only really had one record shop worth visiting for us: The Sound of Music on Howard Street, near the market. The other record shop, Circles, only stocked chart singles. How LPs ever got into the charts if this attitude were replicated the country over baffled us. The Sound of Music, on the other hand, had racks of exotic looking punk/new wave and other genres. And, of course, albums. We'd scan the racks for hours, but I always found it difficult to stick my neck out and buy a record on the name alone or the look of the sleeve. We weren't in the habit of asking behind the counter for the record to be played. You felt honour-bound to buy it then, even if you didn't like it, since the Saturday-hassled staff had gone to the trouble of playing it for you.

More often than not we'd get the infamous 69 bus to Sheffield. It was only four pence to travel the six miles or so.* We'd wander round Sheffield city centre, same as we did in Rotherham but Sheffield seemed so much bigger, so much more cosmopolitan (really!) than Rotherham ever could. For starters, the record shops were much better: we'd head to Revolution, which appeared almost solely devoted to 'our type' of music. Then we'd trek down to one of Sheffield's premiere shopping streets – The Moor – to the outer limit of the city centre and to Virgin Records.

Virgin was a serious record shop. This was way before it was a

---

* South Yorkshire earned itself the nickname 'The Socialist Republic of South Yorkshire' due to the county council's radical left-wing stance and its staunch support for the Labour Party. It funded subsidised housing and transport (and loads of other stuff) for years, hence the buses in the region were easily the cheapest way to get around. So cheap, that even to this day I know folk who never bothered to learn to drive in the seventies and eighties.

multi-business conglomerate running everything from airlines to healthcare businesses. Back then, Sheffield's Virgin was a dark cave inhabited by longhaired hippies loafing about behind the counter. They had well-practised sneers if you asked for anything outside their taste bubble – which was mostly bands like Van der Graaf Generator or Dumpy's Rusty Nuts. However, they had an array of all the singles and LPs we wished we could afford. We window-shopped eagerly.

The Virgin notice board was also a great place to browse – and by notice board, younger readers, I mean an actual bit of wall, where anyone could pin a piece of paper to advertise a gig, or musicians wanted, or gear for sale (musical, that is . . .).

We'd also make sure to hit Rat Records. This was part of the new Leadmill venue development that had recently got up and running. We were even asked if we wanted to help fitting The Leadmill out, so it was ready for punters and gigs. Our building, carpentry and labouring skills were, however, somewhat lacking.

We wouldn't just hit up record stores – we'd take in clothes shops too, at least the ones that catered to our tastes. We were mainly after band T-shirts, leather jackets, studded belts, band badges and other paraphernalia. Another regular stop was checking out the outrageous shoes at Rebina, just off the High Street on High Court. If we were feeling particularly cock-sure, we might pop into X Clothes – Sheffield's top, nay, only 'alternative' designer clothes vendor, which sold proper punky gear, like bondage trousers, mohair jumpers and all that kind of stuff, but for (what were to us) eye-watering prices. X Clothes' staff were notorious for giving anyone who dared enter the shop the disinterested, almost disdainful up-and-down look as they checked out your 'threads', a ritual that everyone went through. No one ever felt that they were worthy of X Clothes. God help you if you actually wanted to try something on!

There were a lot of characters around town. We'd frequently run into an old bloke at the bottom of Fargate, outside Boots, who'd always give you a felt-tip pen. We'd say 'Ta!' and quicken our pace, for we knew what was coming: he'd then jump in front of you with an outstretched palm expecting a 'donation' for his 'gift'. This, of course, would cause an argument and the old fella would always get cross and snatch the felt-tip pen back, causing us to break into gales of laughter. You had to admire his graft, though.

We'd also look out for 'Holding Up Buildings Man'. As the name suggests, this was a man who'd walk around the centre of Sheffield and, every 20 paces or so, would stop and put his hands on the nearest building and appear to try and stop the 'not' falling building from falling down. He'd maintain this stance for five to ten seconds at a time, and then continue his wanderings. Bizarre. I'm sure some kind of mental health issue was in play here, but as kids, especially in the seventies and eighties, we didn't consider that so much and would've just seen it as one of those crazy things to gawk at in town.

As part of our 'rounds' we'd always stop for a snack at a little baker's kiosk at the bottom of Cambridge Street, just down the road from John Lewis (Cole Brothers, as it was then). It was staffed by a girl on her own, who was a couple of years older than us. We flirted terribly with Jane in our naïve little ways and she didn't seem to mind us hanging about and chatting as we scoffed our sausage rolls. We had a good laugh and developed a little bit of a friendship, which I'm sure helped all of us pass the time.

'Oh, wow! Love your jacket, that's amazing! Did you paint it?'

We spun round to see a couple of punkettes around our age, dressed in leathers and tartan and resplendent with spiky hair and bright red lipstick. They were admiring Richard's jacket. Why, you ask? Well, it was the norm to have your fave groups' names painted on your jacket, or schoolbag, or whatever. Some did it in a DIY fashion but sometimes the extra mile was taken. My closest friend by now was a kid called Steve Allott, who was a couple of years younger than us. His mum was quite the talented artist and it was she who painted the back of Richard's leather jacket with the cover image from The Stranglers' second album, *No More Heroes*. It was really good; you could've taken it for a transfer from a distance. He'd get loads of people admiring it. I, on the other hand, not wanting to ape Richard, left the back of my jacket plain save for a couple of red lines on the seams. Bit understated looking back then, but hey ho . . . We chatted with the girls for a little while, quite gobsmacked that we were talking to these otherworldly creatures, who turned out to be really friendly.

One thing we immediately noticed about these girls was that they smelled bloody gorgeous. Like nothing we had ever smelled before. Not like the perfume that big sisters, mums and aunts would wear. Different, somehow.

We made it our mission to try and track these girls down again. It wouldn't be easy, though; we didn't know their names, where in Sheffield they were from (if they were even from Sheffield), whether they worked or were at school or college, or just about anything about them. We mulled over this encounter all week, wondering how we could get to see them again. It seemed like an impossible dream.

The next Saturday we went to Sheffield city centre again, and as usual popped into the little bakery for a sausage roll and a chat with Jane. We mentioned the events of the previous week and Jane was keen to hear all the details. We had to describe the girls a couple of times, and after a bit of thought Jane said, 'I think the blonde girl goes to our school. The description matches and everything.'

Miracle? Fate? Sheffield being the largest village in the world? (Doesn't everywhere claim to be that?) It didn't matter – we had a potential contact. My path was about to take a genuinely new turn.

'Can you get a message to them? Meet up with us one Saturday?'

Somehow, it transpired that we all had tickets to see The Stranglers at the Sheffield Lyceum in a couple of weeks' time (which was, of course, amazing, The Stranglers having long been firm favourites and this being the first time I'd managed to see them live). So, it was decided we'd meet up before the gig to 'hang out' and Jane duly passed on the message. It was on.

Eventually, after our first meet-up went well, I had a scrap of paper with a number and a name on: Anne Murray. But I had a dilemma. I had to pluck up the courage to phone Anne and ask her out on a date – a proper one this time. This was something I had little experience of, apart from a couple of occasions at school. I was about to call someone I thought was much cooler than me and was risking a big put-down.

Deep breaths.

Our phone line was a 'party line' in those days – no, not what you might be thinking; we shared our line with another house nearby and often you would pick up the phone to make your call, only to hear someone else's conversation going on. You had to wait for them to finish. No eavesdropping either!

Eventually they rung off, so with dry mouth and trepidation, I dialled the Sheffield number on the scrap of paper. What made it all the more nerve-wracking was knowing that a senior member of the household would answer (this was always the way), so you'd have to go through the rigmarole of asking if the person you wanted to speak to was actually in and tell them who you were, and all that.

'Is Anne there?'

'Hold on . . . Who is it?' the voice came back, in a gentle Irish tone.

'It's Nick from Rotherham.' (Nervous wait resumes while the lass comes to the phone.)

'Hello?'

'Fancy meeting up with me Saturday?'

'Err . . . OK.'

Mission accomplished. Phew. I had a date with Anne.

We decided we'd meet at famed Sheffield landmark and meeting place: the fish tank in the 'Hole in the Road'. The Hole in the Road was, as described: a roundabout with an excavated middle bit at the centre of a web of busy underpasses. It was almost like a small under-ground city, with shops and entrances to the department stores above. The underpasses went to different parts of the town centre, thus avoiding the thundering traffic above. Along one sector of the open-air central plaza was a fish tank, home to some sad looking fish in some rather murky water, so much so it was quite the challenge to actually see any.

We wandered round town together, poking our noses in a few shops and chatting. We may have ventured to get a coffee, even! And voilà. I had a girlfriend. A cool girlfriend. A not-from-Rotherham girlfriend.

Why's he bleating on about getting a girlfriend, I hear you think? Big deal! But Anne, it transpires, became my way out of Rotherham. A way into the wider circle of Sheffield. I always felt that Rotherham was very parochial and dismissive of anyone who seemed a bit different, or wanted something more. Rotherham had one pub – The Charters, and actually only the upstairs bar in The Charters – where 'outsiders' were accommodated without feeling that it could all kick off at any moment. Sheffield seemed far more welcoming to people who looked 'different', and had many more places and opportunities for people of a similar bent to get together (don't worry: there were still plenty of places to avoid in Sheffield, too).

I can look back now and see that meeting Anne on Flat Street was a pivotal moment in my journey. Plus, Anne was interesting – she had a great laugh and could point me in the right direction, opening up a wealth of new opportunities for me. Oh, and the fragrance? Country Born Hair Gel. As simple as that.

9

Phono Industria

(Looking for Life)

After Fatal Noise stopped I was determined to continue playing in bands. I wasn't about to give up the drums; it was too much fun. Plus, when you're in a band you have a solid gang of mates, striving for a common purpose. So, I answered an ad for drummer wanted. No idea where I saw the advert – it's lost in the mists of time. It was with a couple of kids – well, blokes I guess. They were older than me, that's for sure.

Brian was a keyboard player and a real talker and Hugh, on bass, was very studious. Together, they were wanting to start a new band. Brian was so old he was actually married and had a job, of all things (sales rep, industrial drills). Hugh even drove his own car! This was revolutionary.

I took my kit along to a school practice room and we jammed through some tunes. The band had no singer, so it was all instrumental, but after a couple of hours the other two begged me (literally) to join the band. I easily said yes, as I had no other options at this time. We decided on a name: Phono Industria, Latin for 'active' or 'industrious' sound. Pretentious? Probably. In the early eighties there was a lot of pretension around.

Next we had to put the feelers out for a singer. I mentioned it to Anne, who said she fancied it, so next rehearsal – which we had moved to my convenient conservatory – we held an audition. I say 'audition', but with a definite lack of competition all Anne needed to do was vaguely hold a note and look the part, and she'd be in. Well, she certainly looked the part, but she also showed some potential with the microphone, so audition passed. We had our singer.

The music wasn't punk but rather a more electronic keyboard-oriented sound. Bryan had a big Moog synth and a few other keyboards he played, providing big swashes of synthetic strings all over the place, so it was altogether a more eighties feel. New romantic was really hitting the scene at this time and, of course, Sheffield was *the* place for electronic music, what with The Human League, ABC, Heaven 17, Cabaret Voltaire and countless other unsigned keyboard outfits really putting the city on the electronic music map.

We started to play a few tentative gigs here and there. Anne was wracked with nerves, as she'd never been on stage before, but over time she grew in confidence. We mainly played around the Sheffield pub scene, venues like The Royal, The George IV and The Hallamshire (more of which in a bit).

As Bryan and Hugh had a bit of spare money floating around they had the means to pay for Phono Industria to do some recording. So, we went into a little studio tucked away under the Sheffield YMCA in Broomhall to record a demo, and it actually got sent out. We got a bit of interest from a fellow down in London – possibly Mark Dean? – who ran a label called Innervision. Things looked promising, as this guy was apparently quite into us. Unfortunately, as time went on Innervision lost interest in us, choosing instead to focus on another act: Wham! Well, as we all know, George and Andrew went on to somewhat greener pastures than playing to 25 of their mates in the upstairs room at The Hallamshire on West Street.

Phono Industria's best moment, if you can call it that, was our attendance at the annual Rock and Pop Contest sponsored by the local paper, the *Sheffield Star*. Naturally it was held at the Top Rank suite, and we eagerly entered, playing on 8 September 1982. Competition in our heat included Notre Dame, Pop-Ups, Jayde, Panza Division and Renegade.

These competitions were pretty gruesome affairs, with each band getting 25–30 minutes to play to their 'fans' (really just your mates and maybe a couple of relatives you could strong-arm into turning up). A panel of judges would choose a winner, who would go through to the semi-final and so on. How such a diverse selection of bands could be judged one over the other is anyone's guess. Do they look at musical ability? Song strength? Image? Gimmick choice? Who knows! Anyway, all the other bands, as far as I can remember, weren't up to much, apart from Panza Division – a hard rockin', new wave of British heavy metal-type act. All long hair, tight jeans, waistcoats, bullet belts and facial hair (you get the idea). Their 'gimmick' was that as they went on stage, they pretended to clock on as if at work, punching time cards into a pretend machine they'd wheel on to the side of the stage. Obviously, playing hard rock is akin to a shift at the local engineering works, so it kinda made sense. They were pretty accomplished, to be fair: lots of twiddling guitar solos and bassists pointing into the middle distance.

Then it was our turn, and we really thought we had played the best set we possibly could. Anne was great, the band was tight (well, we didn't cock up any of the songs), so we thought we had this in the bag. Semi-finals here we come!

Not to be. The panel decided the work-to-rule rockers were more worthy winners. Really? It transpired later that Brian, our keyboard-playing motor mouth, had tried to sweet talk the judges to putting us through to the next round. Judges don't like being told who to vote for, so, better band or not, PD went through instead.* Oh well. We still went to the other heats to cheer on mates in other bands. It was quite the social event.

---

* Panza Division went on to be fairly successful, especially after they changed their name to Lonely Hearts in 1982.

10

The Hallamshire And The Limit

(Disco 2000)

The Hallamshire is a pub on Sheffield's West Street, home to the city's most popular bar and restaurant scene. As the name suggests, West Street is the conduit to Sheffield's leafy western suburbs: Walkley, Crookes, Broomhill, Fulwood, Crosspool and beyond. It is also the main student thoroughfare; Sheffield University and its sprawling campus is situated further along as West Street morphs into Glossop Road. All those suburbs are full of student housing and the main halls of residence are to be found to the west of the city centre.

West Street has always been full of pubs and bars. It still is the centre of night-time revelry and debauchery, with Friday and Saturday nights akin to a warzone. Just swap camo for T-shirts and ill-advised short skirts – and that's in winter.

Back in the early eighties, and the fashion may have changed, but the idea was still the same. It was the norm to look 'way out' on West Street. No one batted an eyelid. It's even possible to think that 'straights' or 'townies', as we called them, would feel uncomfortable in the middle of all these weirdos.

Anne knew all these places. She lived in Fulwood, opposite one of the biggest halls of residence, and went to the nearby Catholic high school, Notre Dame. The Hallamshire, then, was *the* pub for 'us types'. It is still there, and has kept its beautiful dark red Edwardian tiled frontage.

In the early eighties it was rather down in its appearance, and the interior was dark and a little foreboding. You entered via a central door and you had a snug to the left with a fireplace within. There was a brilliant jukebox in this part, stocked with great records, up-to-date but swerving the standard 'pop' hits in the charts.

You could turn right and walk into the main room, where the bar was situated. It curved away as you entered, becoming a long, straight traditional bar. There was banquette seating along the alcoves across the right-hand wall. This room ran the length of the pub and the toilets were at the far end. If you went straight on at the entrance you would have passed the entrance to the upstairs concert room on your left and then you would walk into the backroom, which housed the pool table – usually covered up at weekends as the pub would be packed. Overseeing everything was landlord Jim Revell and his wife, Sheila. Jim was spherical, rarely smiled and a man of few words. Definitely a landlord of 'the old school'.

No one ever asked you for ID. If you looked old enough, you were old enough. Bouncers were for nightclubs and they never stood on the doors of pubs. It was never a problem for us 17-year-olds to get a beer, either. Last orders was at 11 p.m. (10.30 on Sunday, don't forget) and there was never any after-hours action.

So, the bar was usually populated with student types and us more local punks, new romantics or alternative types, and not forgetting Doris and Ada (well, they might've been called that); a couple of old regulars from before The Hallamshire became a younger person's drinking den. They looked like everyone's gran and were always sat in the same seats, just inside the door on the right, decked out in all their finery and NEVER without a hat and matching handbag.

Upstairs you'd find one of Sheffield's legendary venues. Well, legendary might be pushing it a bit, but every Sheffield band starting out in the seventies and eighties played upstairs at The Hallamshire. And I mean everyone.

It was basic. Very basic. Just a rectangular room with banquette seating along the walls, a few tables and chairs scattered about and a small stage at one end. The stage didn't even go right across the room, it was just in one corner – the fire escape was in the other corner so couldn't be obstructed. The walls were a riot of busy seventies floral wallpaper. The curtains that covered the six windows which lined the wall overlooking the street definitely did not match the walls, and all this lit by fluorescent strip lights. What else? Dressing room, you say? Please, there wasn't even a nearby toilet to change into your glittery outfit before taking to the stage.

The Hallamshire, then, was the first call for Phono Industria's next gig. We went along one Thursday, early-ish, to ask what we needed to do to get on. Sat upstairs, in the empty room, was the promoter, a fresh-faced young lad by the name of Dave Kurley.

'We're Phono Industria. Can we get a gig here?'

'Yeah, sure. When you want to play?'

It was as easy as that. None of the 'send us a tape and I'll decide if you're good enough'-type nonsense. The truth is, The Hallamshire really was the first rung on the ladder of live music; if you felt you were ready, then that was good enough. You could play.

'In fact,' said Kurley. 'I've had enough of putting the bands on here.'

'We'll do it,' Brian said, no hesitation.

And that was also that. Phono Industria became promoters at The Hallamshire. Brian thought it would be great to use the venue as Phono Industria's base, our stepping-stone to world domination. Or something. If any popular groups, those who could garner a good crowd, happened to want to play there, then PI could be first in line to do the support slot, thus getting our music out to a larger crowd. At least, that was the plan.

How it happened I'm not too sure about, but the main person

who ended up handling all the bookings and bands was good old me. I don't recall Brian or Hugh having anything to do with the day-to-day organisation of running a venue above a pub. Maybe it was too much for them, what with the two of them having jobs. It's not like there was much admin or organising to do anyway. The procedure was this: if a band rang up the pub to enquire about playing, the call was inevitably taken by Jim, the landlord, who'd simply redirect them to my home phone number in Rotherham. The bands would then call me at home. Inevitably Mum would take the call and then I'd be summoned from the TV or my bedroom. Really professional! I had a little blue diary by the phone, where I'd note down all the upcoming gigs. We ended up doing Thursday evening gigs and Sunday evening gigs. Two bands a night – a main act and a support. Following Dave Kurley's example, we didn't ask for demos, or do any kind of 'quality control'; we just took folks' word that they were able to play.

The bands had to really do their own promoting of the gig. We did nothing. They'd sneak about town after dark with a bucket of wallpaper paste and a brush, pasting their own flyposters for the gig. It was a two-man job: one to slop the paste on the wall and then the poster, the other to look out for the police, who took a dim view of the practice. The city centre was liberally plastered with homemade band posters of varying quality. Usually, though, people went to great lengths to try and design an eye-catching poster that might drag a couple of gig-goers down to check 'em out.*

So, as 'promoters' we didn't do the promoting. We didn't provide a PA, either. The bands themselves had to provide their own or hire

---

* The key was not to stick up your poster too early, as it would only get covered by other posters well before the day of your gig. Bands often built up a mythical kind of rivalry around flyposting, especially if one lot's posters tended always to cover another's. Remember: bands are a bit like gangs and, as often male-dominated entities (especially back then) they could get a bit shirty, or at least a bit shouty (or more like just a hard glare across the bar in The Hallamshire).

in. Neither did we have any stage lights in The Hallamshire. Again, we just told bands they'd need to organise their own. Thus, apart from making sure the room wasn't double booked, we did bugger all as promoters. Actually, no that's inaccurate; we did man the door at the gigs on a Thursday and Sunday evening. Anne and me would turn up when the bands did and then merely sit at the top of the stairs, taking the money from the punters. The charge was usually 50p. Bargain. Punters would plop their coins into an ashtray, commandeered as our till. Then a stamp on the hand or a cross from a marker and you were in.

We never asked for any money from the bands. They got everything we took. My dad always thought we were being a bit soft not taking a percentage of the door for our troubles. Not good business, he would say. We weren't at all bothered. If the night had been a success and the room had been busy, Jim the Landlord would slip us a half, on the house. Steady now, Jim!

I found this arrangement to be perfect. I got to have a 'date' with Anne *and* I got to see all the local bands that were about at the time. Moreover, I often got to *know them*, too. I think it's called 'networking' these days.

I only remember one example of us cocking the bookings up and getting four bands turning up on one evening. Problem solved: we simply put two of the bands at the other end of the room, which seemed to work OK. So much so, in fact, that eventually the stage was moved to the other end, thus removing the blockage to the fire exit.

The audience numbers varied a lot. I only ever recall no one turning up once. We'd asked a heavy rock band from Nottingham to play (name now sadly lost to history), who turned up with mountains of gear, PA, lights, the lot. However, as they were from out of town they couldn't, or didn't, do any publicity – and we weren't doing it, that's for sure – so sadly not a soul turned up. Gamely, the band still played and saw it as a rehearsal. The show must go on, as someone once said.

Sometimes a local band could drag in a load of punters – this was quite rare and in truth pretty scary. We had no idea what the capacity for the room was and anything over 100 would be pretty rammed. If anything bad happened, like a fire or some other dire emergency, it would not have been a good outcome, that's for sure. Health and safety hadn't been invented then. Nor the compensation culture that goes with it. Fights would be the main worry if the room was packed, but thankfully I can only recall one time when flailing bodies fell through the doors separating me and Anne from the venue. We shoved them, still fighting, down the stairs and out of our way.

It is also safe to say that the calibre of bands who put themselves forward to play were definitely patchy at best. Electro-pop was a Sheffield speciality and was searing through the charts in the early eighties, so this genre was well represented. Usually it was a couple of guys solemnly prodding synths, perhaps with a female vocalist. Sometimes there'd be a drummer, but often it was another bloke whose sole job it was to start and stop the drum machine at the required moment. This was before MIDI (Musical Instrument Digital Interface) could knit everything together and the tech was still pretty basic. The use of computers in music was still a way off. Nobody could afford a reel-to-reel tape, like the ones Orchestral Manoeuvres in the Dark or The Human League were using. I never recall anyone employing a footswitch to activate the drum machine, but plenty of oddballs lurking in the shadows, swaying to the electric beats their Roland Dr. Rhythms were pumping out, studiously adjusting the tempo and rhythm for the next song. It's fair to say these fellows, and they were always blokes, were usually not your charismatic lead singer types.

Of course, we did have our favourites that played while we sat on the door. Bands like Tsi-Tsa and Siiii. We loved Quite Unnerving, possibly Sheffield's first proper goth band: two basses, drums and atmospherics on tape, eerie Dave Lowkes prowling the stage. There was The Ya-Yas, a group of sixties heads from Notre Dame school and friends of Anne. They were a psychedelic swirl with a 16-year-old Keith Moon-style lad on drums. We had Party Day, a hard, positively punky outfit from Barnsley and a great bunch of lads. Anne and I once went to London for a weekend to shop and look around, and we surprised Party Day by turning up at their Fulham Greyhound gig and had them on that we came down just to see them play. We hadn't, of course; it was a happy coincidence. Party Day got as far as releasing a couple of singles – one I remember had a strange sandpaper sleeve, which the band had done themselves (I'm not sure they quite thought the concept through; the record would get horribly scratched as you pulled it out and pushed it back in the sleeve). Anyway, they even got a few plays on John Peel.

However, our hands-down favourites were In a Bell Jar. They were the oddest bunch of all. They didn't have any real instruments, just a couple of racks of old catering-sized tin cans built onto a wooden stand and various other 'found' things to hit. For example, two bits of wood slapped together made quite an effective handclap sound. They combined these 'instruments' with some really interesting singing, if you could call it that. Songs like 'Lots And Lots Of Yachts' and 'Take It From Me, The Blind Can See' were highpoints, along with 'Steve's Leather Jacket', which took the piss out of Simon Singleton, Steve from ABC's brother, and his choice of outerwear. I guess you had to be there.

In a Bell Jar always went the extra mile to make the gig an event. They would dress the stage in old curtains (that clashed with The Hallamshire's seventies décor) strung across on a bit of washing line, so much so that you could barely see the performers. They would also have their own homemade wooden mic stands. For us 17–18-year-olds it was very different. Impressive.

The two protagonists of this mayhem were Michael Paramore and Tim Allcard (you can see how different Tim looked back then by checking out the back cover of Pulp's second single, 'Everybody's Problem', from around 1983 – Tim's on the left). Tim would often come up the stairs to gigs, but not pay to go in. Not that we granted him a freebie or anything, it's just that he would sit on the bottom of the stairs that led up to the next (spooky) floor of the pub and listen to the bands play while smoking a roll-up. He'd often be accompanied by a tall chap in glasses, with unruly hair that was a bit curly. He was similarly dressed in charity shop clothes, like Tim. His name was Jarvis.

'You two going in t'gig then?'

'Can we sit 'ere?' they'd say.

'Do what yer like.'

The Hallamshire stopped serving at 11 p.m. – as did everywhere else – and by 11.20 you were on the street. If you wanted to continue drinking into the night there was only one real contender where you would hear the kind of music we liked: another Sheffield legend, The Limit Club.

Along with The Hallamshire, The Limit Club was the other half of the scene for us 'alternative' types, be you punk, skin, new romantic, trans, whatever. It put on gigs and dancing throughout the week. It was a real dive, though. It was a few hundred yards down West Street towards the town centre, so a brisk five-minute walk. Just past the Carver Street junction and Co-op bank (as it was then), you came to a door in the wall with a sign above and a notice board outside advertising the upcoming attractions. Through the door you descended about a dozen wide steps to the coat-check counter and the ticket booth on your right. Turn left and through the doors and you were inside.

The Hallamshire And The Limit (Disco 2000)

It was dark. It was loud. It was usually quite sweaty. You could tell that the outer margins of the floor had once had a nice carpet down. However, by 1982 it was a hard crust of spilled beer, guts (vomit) and probably blood. As the evening wore on you often found that if you stopped moving your feet they'd start to stick to this carpet.

To your left were a few arcade games and fruit machines, cigarette vending machines, and some tables and benches. Straight ahead from where you came in was an emergency exit, which was flanked by two bars running along the far wall of the room. To your right as you entered was the main dance floor, with its red sparkly floor covering – yet to be awash with spilt beer and/or bodily fluids. Beyond the bar were the infamous Limit toilets. These were pretty grim, with graffiti all over the place, naturally, and a tendency to flood once an evening. Nearly always, at about 1 a.m., you'd find yourself slopping through an inch or so of water coming from god knows where.

Further on from the dance floor you'd find some more benches or tables and then there was the stage. Approximately 40 centimetres (18 inches) high and not quite the full length of the back wall. The back of the stage was a mirrored wall that was actually stainless steel. At the other end was a hatch, where you could buy chips and snacks, and another bar. This was 'The Wine Bar', mainly because, yep, it sold wine.

On the other side of the dance floor was a raised platform, again with seating, which was an ideal place for observing the goings on in the rest of the club. Also part of this raised platform was the DJ booth, usually manned by Paul Unwin. Paul was happy to take polite requests but these were generally unnecessary, as the tunes he played were perfect for us. Some Limit favourites:

'Planet Claire' – The B-52's
'Lust For Life' – Iggy Pop

'The Passenger' – Iggy Pop
'Bela Lugosi's Dead' – Bauhaus
'Wardance' – Killing Joke
'No G.D.M.' – Gina X
'Liberator' – Theatre of Hate
'This Corrosion' – Sisters of Mercy
'A Forest' – The Cure
'Love Will Tear Us Apart' – Joy Division
'Hand In Glove' – The Smiths
'Release The Bats' – Birthday Party
'I Travel' – Simple Minds
'Stop That Train' – Clint Eastwood & General Saint
'Spellbound' – Siouxsie & The Banshees
'She Sells Sanctuary' – The Cult

The Limit hosted some legendary gigs during the eighties. Famously, U2 played to about 50 people and The B-52's performed their first non-US gig here. I went to neither. There were gigs by The Cramps, The Human League, Echo & The Bunnymen, among many others. Didn't go to any of those either. I did, however, get a ticket for The Jesus and Mary Chain, when they were getting pretty notorious for riotous gigs. Sadly, it was cancelled on the day, with only a little note on the door announcing it was off. Pulp played The Limit quite a few times in the early eighties too. Missed those gigs as well.★

One feature of playing The Limit was that right in front of the stage was a pillar. So if the singer stood stage centre, he or she was basically singing to a bit of wall. Off-putting to say the least. These pillars were dotted about the club, some of them with a TV attached.

★ One memorable gig that I actually did attend at The Limit was The Meteors, a kind of rockabilly/punk hybrid (rockabilly became really popular in the mid-eighties). Unfortunately the 'psychobillies', as they proclaimed themselves, decided to start a riot mid-gig. The entire place seemed to erupt into fists and boots. Not pleasant.

These invariably played videos of *Jungle Burger*, a cartoon that mostly consisted of characters in the shape of cocks running about. Most bizarre.

I recall my first visit to The Limit with Anne. On first impression it seemed so pretentious; everyone posing like mad, trying to appear cool and aloof, casually leaning against the wall like they would do any day. Thing is, it wasn't long before I was joining in with them, what with my black back-combed bird's nest hairdo, à la The Cure's Robert Smith.

We usually always went on the Monday club night; it was free if you got in before 11 p.m., so everyone would leg it down from The Hallamshire at five minutes to, and hopefully beat the queue and slip in before having to pay £1 or whatever it was.

Monday was the main alternative night, when all the 'freaks' would be out. We'd all nurse a pint until they announced the half-hour of cheap drinks. Wednesday was more of a student and nurses night. The music was pretty much the same but the crowd was a bit different. Thursdays was another popular night, but even with the constitution of youth, three nights' a week was a bit of a stretch for the wallet. Not that it was particularly expensive in there. It sounds like a cliché, but back then we could have a great night, drink plenty and end with a bag of chips from Big Al's chippy next door, all for a fiver. You might have to walk home though. That was the pay-off for the bag of chips.

We rarely went at the weekends, when the place was infiltrated by the 'townie' mob – lads straight from Bramall Lane or Hillsborough with their bum-fluff moustaches, burgundy jackets (with sleeves rolled up) and light grey ties. The slip-on shoes were always a dead give-away. They were often all too ready to start a fight with someone, anyone really, so Saturdays at The Limit were where the door staff really earned their wages. One weekend foray there ended with me buried under a pile of fighting skinheads and townies, and comically crawling out from underneath them, trying not to get a shoe in the face. Happy days.

In hindsight, I can't stress enough how important The Limit was in my life. I know it was 'only' a dive club, and it's a stereotypical thing for someone of a certain age to say that we didn't have the internet back in the eighties (well, we didn't – no mobile phones either*), but The Limit – and The Hallamshire, for that matter – were our versions of Facebook, Instagram, Twitter and all the other modern media rolled into one stinky cave with a sticky floor and overflowing toilets. Gossip and scandal was generated and became legend in these places. Alliances were forged and broken. Lovers were found and lovers were lost, sometimes in the same night. It's beyond believing, but everyone really did seem to know each other. All those freaks, congregating every Monday and Wednesday night.

Most of these hedonistic nights out were only possible because by that point I had moved out of the family home.

---

* The first mobile phone I ever saw was when a mate was covering the 1987 general election and the BBC had loaned him one to call in the Sheffield result. It really did come in a suitcase and was enormous. It still boggled our minds, though.

11

Moving on Out

(Do You Remember the First Time)

Anne was working part-time now, as a waitress at a local restaurant. One of the chefs had a room to rent in Walkley, a suburb in Sheffield. We jumped at the chance. I was 18 and had just finished my A-levels at TRC, and had decided to apply to the august seat of learning that was Sheffield City Polytechnic.

'I'm moving out,' I said one day.

'When? Where to?'

'Next Saturday. Sheffield.'

'OK. You need a lift?'

I packed my stuff into the car and we drove down to Fulton Road, Walkley. Simple as that.

I had looked into various university options, including Loughborough and Brunel to study Design and Technology (D&T) with a view to going into teaching. I had no idea if I really wanted to be a teacher, but what I did know by now was that becoming a member of a successful band that released records and toured the world to adoring fans was a much more enticing prospect. Still, as everyone said, 'That's all very nice, but you do need something to fall back on.' Fair comment, really.

I'd thought of other careers during my school days: RAF (I'd even been a member of the Rotherham Air Training cadets for about a month), going to sea as a radio operator in the Merchant Navy, or even going into the family business as a bookmaker (that's a turf accountant, if you want to be posh – a betting shop owner, not someone who actually makes books). But none of them appealed in the end. I was good at designing and making things, and as teachers got good holidays, I thought I should indeed pursue that as my 'back-up' plan. I decided, too, that staying in Sheffield and 'working' on the music scene was my best bet for the 'real' plan. Students in Sheffield were rather looked down upon by us 'natives' and the thought of the same happening to me in a different place didn't appeal. Thus, another brick in the wall of my future path was set.

Eventually I passed the 'promoting' baton at The Hallamshire on to someone else, probably so I could concentrate more on seeing bands, being in bands and generally 'going out'. I joined the Poly's Entertainment Society (Ents Soc), which put on the gigs at the Nelson Mandela Building, otherwise known as the student union (weren't they all called that back in the days before Nelson was freed?). The Ents Soc was a pretty closed shop to a wet-behind-the-ears fresher, but I was called upon to do glamorous stuff, like sit in a corridor to prevent unauthorised access to somewhere. The high point for me was I got to help break down Elvis Costello's gear after a gig at the NMB. Life at the top, eh? We did get some free tickets to gigs if we did an hour's work, though, so it wasn't all bad.

Local bands were becoming more of a focal point for me and a series of gigs were being advertised at Sheffield's top theatre, The Crucible (not in the *actual* Crucible theatre, but in the Crucible Studio, next door to the main area where they hold the World Snooker Championship every year). This was 'Stars on Sundae', featuring the best of the local scene and all put together by our old friend, Dave Kurley.

We went first to see Dave's band, New Model Soldier, who were one of our faves (we'd also seen them at The Limit). They put on a good show, even though they were one of those eighties bands that had no drummer. Heathens! This gig was made special, as the lights were lowered and Dave took his place at the mic stand, stage centre. His other band mates didn't join him. Dave stood there glowering at the audience for what (I'm sure) felt like an eternity. Paul Fern and Andrew 'Miggs' Middleton, meanwhile, had found some fire extinguishers and proceeded to unleash them onto us from the wings. Charming.

A couple of Sundays later we went along again, this time to see a band we'd heard about but were yet to see performing. The band was Pulp.

Pulp had been recording their first LP *It* during the summer and this was, I guess, the grand unveiling of the songs and sound of their debut.

To say I was knocked out by this event is an understatement. Pulp were obviously head, shoulders and torso above anything else on the local scene during this time (October 1982, to be exact). I loved it. Pulp had a sound that was totally in the opposite direction of what I was listening to at the time. It was gentle, very acoustic, wistful even, but also melodic. The band had trombones going off, pianos tinkling away. They even had backing singers, ferchrissakes! And this tall, thin lad at the front with the specs. Jarvis (yeah, him who was too tight to pay 50p to watch the bands at The Hallamshire). You couldn't take your eyes off him, doing his odd little shoulder shuffles and jerky movements and singing in his deep baritone to 'Wishful Thinking', 'Blue Girls' and the forthcoming debut single, 'My Lighthouse'. Jarvis even talked to the audience, which no one else was really doing (all the other singers were either too po-faced, or just had nothing to say), and he had a natural patter. The event was made even more memorable because Pulp went the extra mile and decorated the stage with hundreds of orange paper fish (as per the

'My Lighthouse' cover) hanging on string. It was a very effective look. We came away from that gig totally bowled over.

'My Lighthouse' was released in May 1983. I remember seeing it in the record shop and why I didn't buy a copy has been a mystery to me ever since. Perhaps I was being a bit tight with my money. The most likely reason is that *It* had been released a week or two previous, and I'd bought a copy of that. *It* had 'My Lighthouse' on it, so why bother buying the single? Idiot.

What with being at college and going out, I was soaking up lots of new music. The first half of the eighties was a great time for music. I was still into dark music (OK, let's call it for what it was – proto-goth), but my horizons were expanding fast. Echo & The Bunnymen were big with me and my mates – we can call them 'overcoat bands', as the always wore big overcoats. One of my new course mates at college asked if I fancied going to see a band at the university; they'd come over from Manchester and were really good. I gave it a moment's thought and said, 'Nah, it's OK. I'll pass.' So, I missed out on seeing The Smiths in a tiny bar at the university, just as they were becoming *the* student band of the eighties. Fool.

Phono Industria faded away around this time, so it was time to seek out a new band of players with whom to seek fame and fortune. As previously stated, finding such folks was a case of asking around and keeping an eye out for adverts. On a trip to Virgin Records' notice board, I spied it:

Drummer wanted for new band, ex-New Model Soldier

Oh, this lot have had a record out. Could be good. Little did I know that the record they had put out was self-financed, and Dave Kurley had a pile of about 300 under his bed at home, subsequently to be burned on a funeral pyre some years later as they could not be shifted (look out for it – it's worth a fortune to record collectors, or so I'm told). No bother: I could benefit from the ashes of NMS with this new group.

I gave Paul a call and we arranged to meet and play some music. I dutifully turned up at his house, where I met bassist Miggs and their new singer, Shaun Ryles. A fellow Rotherham-er. Shaun had an amazing Ian McCulloch-esque voice, a rapier wit and a talent for writing songs based on his amorous adventures – of which there seemed to be a lot. Shazam! A new band is formed. We called ourselves God! Where that came from is, alas, also lost in time, and we never discussed whether it was a religious statement, a mild admonishment or an exclamation of despair. God! it was.

We set about rehearsing in Paul's garage with gusto. NMS had been a drum machine band, and I think the lads enjoyed playing with a real drummer, but not the volume of a *real kit* (by this point I'd advanced to a new kit, a black budget Tama, which I'd scrimped and saved to buy. I even sold my fishing gear to help get the money together). It was so loud I ended up rehearsing in a homemade cardboard booth (Paul's family ran a paper and cardboard manufacturing plant so they had plenty of raw materials). I coped, but it's difficult playing without eye contact. It's crucial to learn cues and to see the playing is going in the right direction.

God! gigged, as you do, to little success. Our most controversial moment came courtesy of the Star Rock and Pop competition in 1983. We entered, but a right kerfuffle kicked off once they said we couldn't use our name. God! was seen as far too controversial and blasphemous. Yes, in this day and age. It ended up being a bit of a byline in the local paper, but we really should've made more of it and got some publicity out of it. We didn't though, and despite a lengthy debate, we decided to enter as 'Red'. So much for standing your ground, smashing the system and sticking to your principles.

Needless to say we had a pretty torrid time in the competition. Shaun couldn't hear himself through the monitors, so was hopelessly out of tune. Exit God!/Red.

I had passed my driving test at the third attempt. To save money, I'd taken lessons from my dad, but after failing to pass the first two times it was decided that I should have a few proper lessons. And lo! I finally passed. This meant I got access to the family car – and freedom! It did give us the chance to venture further afield.

Me, Richard, Steve Allott and Anne decided we should drive over to the Pennines to Manchester University, to see Southern Death Cult (they went on to drop the 'Southern' and then the 'Death' bit, ending up as The Cult). We could also double up and drop in on our mate from the bakery, Jane, who was now at Manchester uni. The plan was we'd bunk up on her floor after the gig and return home the next day.

I borrowed Mum's dark green Austin Maxi and off we went. We navigated by guesswork. We knew Manchester Road leaving Sheffield would get us to Manchester, but that was about it. We had Jane's address, so surely everything would be fine, wouldn't it?

We eventually got to Manchester city centre via the circular route, and had a bit of a look around before setting off to try and find Jane's place. Oddly enough, we got hopelessly lost in the hinterlands of south Manchester. Cue the Maxi driving headlong into the side of a brand new bright red Mercedes. I hadn't seen the junction of Chester Road looming up as we were arguing about where to head next. Contact with the Merc was the result. Thankfully, we were all unharmed, probably due to the fact that the Austin Maxi was built a bit like a tank. Even still it, and thus we, were going nowhere. The Merc driver was fine too, and really calm and collected to say we had just trashed his new car.

We pushed the Maxi on to the side of the road and the police took over. It was left to me to break the news back home via the phone box down the road.

'Hi, it's me,' I said nonchalantly.

'Yes?'

'Errr . . . we've had a bit of a crash.'

'Whaaaat!'

Mum was very understanding once we had convinced her we were all unscathed. It did pose the question of what were we going to do now? We had tickets to the gig. Can't waste them. We decided to continue with the plan and still go to the gig; we'd just try to get a late train back to Sheffield that night. We abandoned calling in on Jane and dumping our sleeping bags at her place, and instead jumped on the bus back into Manchester city centre, to get to the university. We'd meet up with Jane there. The Maxi was unceremoniously abandoned at the side of the road, in the Manchester rain, never to be seen again.

Miraculously, we found the uni and got to the gig on time, where we were reunited with Jane. We had no way of finding out about late trains back home (remember – no internet, no phones), but Jane was our saviour. She was going to a party nearby after the show and suggested we could crash there that night. So another phone call was made and we could watch Southern Death Cult without worrying about running for the train.

The party was in Hulme, close to the uni, and we ended up having a grand time and being made most welcome by the students. Crashing out later was no problem. We slunk home at some point the next day, full of apologies for the demise of the Maxi.

A Red Talbot/Chrysler Alpine replaced the Maxi, and Anne and I decided to borrow it and take ourselves off for a holiday in Cornwall. Mum and Dad had a little holiday place there. All went tickety-boo and we had a great time, that is until the seven-hour drive home. As we passed Exeter, the Alpine's engine started to make a terrible noise. Not good. We rolled to a stop on the M5 hard shoulder and were eventually towed off the motorway to the nearest garage, which was just outside the Devon town of Cullompton. The prognosis for the Alpine was terminal. The mechanic gave us a stark choice. Junk the car or pay him to fit a new engine. Oh god! Here goes another difficult phone call.

It was decided to get a new engine fitted and get back to Sheffield ASAP. Trouble was, it would take the garage about four days to source and fit the engine. I had no money for a room and Anne needed to get back for work the next day. The solution, we decided, was that she'd taxi to the nearest train station and get home that night, and I'd stay with the car until it was fixed and I could drive back home.

The mechanics suggested I sleep in the car for a few nights until it was ready. It was my only choice, so that's what I did. I spent the days in the little café attached to the garage, nursing a coffee and reading the paper. In the evening I walked the couple of miles into Cullompton town to find a pub and have a drink. It really was like walking into the Slaughtered Lamb.* As I entered, everyone stopped their conversation and watched as I walked to a seat. Pretty unnerving. Needless to say, I settled for just a half and walked back to my automobile billet.

The car was fixed as per the schedule, and I eventually made it back home. It took me ages to repay the garage costs for that bloody engine. It really bit into my pitiful wages.

I'd been working Saturdays quite regularly by now in the aforementioned X Clothes. I'd made a few contacts there via The Limit and The Leadmill, and when a vacancy came up I asked if I could do it. My style credentials must have been up to the mark, as I was accepted.

---

* As seen in the 1981 horror/comedy film *An American Werewolf in London*.

'65: Myself and all the cousins for brother Richard's second or third birthday. I'm being held up the top of the picture.

'71: At some posh do with David, Brenda and Richard.

Six years old: got the attitude right from the off …

Below: 1980: Fatal Noise. L-R John Wheaton, Adrian Carver, Nick Banks, Dale Richardson, background, Darrell Huggup.

DALE RICHARDSON

Above: 1980: this was from Fatal Noise's first gig at the Sitwell Arms in Rotherham. I'm in my new 'punk' mohair jumper.

Right: 1981, me at 17: be calm, ladies. Hair has been dyed black (badly) and is starting to take on a life of its own.

The Stranglers jacket: this started everything. Richard's jacket that Anne saw that Saturday in Sheffield.

t a family party. The foundation goth years firmly taking hold – posing with my uncle, Jack.

982, Phono Industria: battle of the bands event with Anne. She swooped the best female ocalist prize. Phono Industria didn't place.

1984, God Live: from Sheffield's Hofbräuhaus. Peak big hair days, out of sync with Sean, Miggs and Paul. Time to lose the hair.

1986, Jass: Dave Thompson (right) and Matt Smith (left). TV Centre. DAVID BOCKING

987: first photo shoot with Pulp. L-R Steve Havenhand, Jarvis Cocker, Candida Doyle, ussell Senior and yours truly. DAVID BOCKING

1988 at Burgoyne: complete with lobster and nurses.

All I had to do was to perfect my X Clothes 'sneer' for the customers. The assistants saw this as a bit of sport. Sorry to anyone who felt intimidated; we only did it to entertain ourselves, as shop work can be a bit dull. The best bit about working there was the staff discount, and we could get first dibs on any new stock that arrived. It was also another great way of networking with folk about Sheffield.

12

The Dole Stroll

(Deep Fried in Kelvin)

Sheffield was founded on heavy industry, and steel-making was still very much at the heart of the city's identity during the eighties. Of an evening, and if the wind was blowing in the right direction, you could hear the fall of drop forges and hammers shaping billets of hot metal over on the other side of town. However, this traditional way of life was slowly dying and a lot of the workshops were being repurposed as rehearsal spaces, and so they ended up ringing with the new sound of fledgling bands. Some of the ghosts of the old metal workers must have seeped out of the walls and into those bands, as 'industrial funk' was starting to take hold. This was a harder, more industrial sound with a funk edge, a no-compromise type of approach that melded dance-y rhythms with found instruments, and even industrial machinery, to produce it. Industrial funk was gaining traction in indie land via groups such as 23 Skidoo, Test Dept, Einstürzende Neubauten and SPK. But the prime exponents were Chakk – fierce, danceable music that was really starting to make waves. Chakk signed a mega recording deal and, with the dosh, they set up a state-of-the-art studio in a former metal workshop in the east end of Sheffield: FON.

I was keeping my options open music-wise around this time.

Consequently, I was roped in to playing drums with some other Limit ne'er-do-wells, One Stop the World, who were aping this new trend of northern industrial funk groove.

Two Limit lotharios who shared vocal duties fronted the band. We had a suitably twangy slap bass and keyboards provided by Dean Honer, who went on to some chart success with various Sheffield projects such as The All Seeing I and I Monster. Also part of the group was Bill Pritchard, a quiet lad who soon went off to do his own thing and become strangely popular in France of all places.

The funk influences on the music we played enabled me to explore a deep-rooted guilty pleasure, which I'd harboured since those long-ago family Christmas parties: disco. The punk mentality meant that, no matter what, one could always venture down different musical avenues under the guise of 'smashing the system'.

OSTW followed the usual well-worn path: rehearsing, writing, hustling for gigs. Our high point was a gig at Sheffield Poly's Psalter Lane site, where we played to a good-sized crowd but all trying to out-cool each other. I can't recall anyone getting on to the good foot that night.

Around the same time I was also roped into a more experimental group called Jass. Led by the enigmatic Dave Thompson (you could always spot Dave in The Limit because he'd always be on the dance floor doing a very odd dance that never seemed to vary, whatever record was being played). Dave always had a head full of great schemes that should be pursued with fanatical zeal. He created hypnotic tape loops from cut-up recordings nicked off other records and the radio, very much in the style of *My Life In The Bush Of Ghosts*, the 1981 collaboration between Brian Eno and David Byrne. He layered all this with guitar and bass, and Matt Swift on percussion. This approach did, however, throw up some technical conundrums: if there's a tape playing away while the band is playing, what does the drummer do? He's not required to keep time, since the tape is doing that. The keyboards and guitars can lock into that rather than what the drummer's doing. Perversely, the drummer now has to keep time with the tape! And the tape cannot move with the drummer's tempo, as human musicians do with ease. It's fixed. Immovable.

Now, as I've already mentioned, the drums have a tendency to be the loudest thing in the room, which is good when everything else has to lock in with them, but if the tape needs to be heard to allow synchronicity then we have a problem. The members of Jass didn't have anything to hand to build a drum booth, like my NMS cardboard one. If we'd had limitless resources (i.e. money), of course, we could've found a solution involving headphones and separate feeds for the drummer to listen to. Failing that, it was really just a matter of turning up whatever was on the tape to ear-splitting volumes and hoping to not get too carried away when playing, still being able to stay in time with the tape.

Unsurprisingly, it didn't always work. The band would tend to follow the tempo of the drummer as opposed to that of the tape. It's like when a DJ gets the beat matching wrong when mixing and you get that horrible grating beat as the two records fight for supremacy. Now imagine that being done by four or five blokes, none of whom have the faintest idea how to regain control. Not pretty, that's for sure. This is what I had to work around.

During the Jass/One Stop the World era, I moved house again. The romance with Anne had fizzled out, so I started sharing with Dave Thompson, one of his old school mates, Paul Infanti, and a lad called Paul Richards. Paul Infanti was the singer in the up-and-coming band Treebound Story, who were starting to put records out via Dave Taylor's FON Records, an offshoot of the FON recording studio set up with the Chakk money. Treebound Story had started playing together at school and were blessed to have a Mr Richard Hawley on guitar. I'd met Richard previously, one night in The Leadmill after he'd approached me in a somewhat 'refreshed' state, slurring,

'Youthatdrummmmer?' Paul Richards was an unbelievably good looking lad (Trevor 'Howcha' Jones called him 'Yum Yum') who I think did some work in broadcasting and journalism.

The Burgoyne Road house soon became a centre of mayhem and merriment. As I'm sure you can imagine, four creative types in a house meant that household chores generally took a back seat. We got around that by ensuring we had a house party every three months or so, as the only time the place got a thorough clean was in the aftermath. I've no idea how the neighbours got on with all this carry-on, but the time we built a six-foot tall snow penis (in great detail, I might add) in the backyard certainly did bring out their ire. One neighbour chopped it down with a huge sword, shouting: 'I've got two kids back there, I don't need this shit!'

More often than not there was a body or two crashing out on a sofa or floor at any given time. Often that body was Hawley, who could usually be found in a state somewhere between slaughtered and hungover.

We also experimented with mind-altering magic mushrooms quite a bit at Burgoyne. Come September or so, we'd get a bus out to Derbyshire, where we knew certain 'productive' fields were, and wander around with a carrier bag, hoping to fill it with the 'correct' type of homegrown psychedelic mushrooms – and hopefully not the type that could kill you. Don't try this, kids. (Something quite odd usually occurred when we were out picking mushrooms. We once noticed a very large aircraft heading straight for us as we were foraging. An RAF Hercules proceeded to fly directly over us at what seemed not much more than head height, though I suspect it was a bit higher than that.) Once we were satisfied we had a good amount, we'd head home and boil up the mushies to make a disgusting 'tea' that really had to be forced down. The show then began, taking us all off into a time- and mind-bending psychedelic trip.

★

Jass played a few gigs around and about, most memorably putting on a party in an old warehouse, where we could play to a captive audience who could then go on and party proper.

Dave was especially adept at getting the name out and drumming up interest, and he eventually heard back from US industrial alternative label Wax Trax Records. It finally looked like I was going to appear on an actual record. Little me, on a piece of vinyl for the first time. Success at last. I could call myself a recording artist and listen back as I grew old, reminiscing about the day I drummed on that record.

Hold on. Not so fast. When I eventually got hold of the record, which was titled *Theme (W.R.)*, I eagerly gave it a spin to hear how it had worked out . . . and what am I not hearing? Dave had mucked about with it so much since we'd done the actual recording that any 'real' drums had been replaced by machinery. I could just about make out a cymbal strike that may have been saved from my contribution, but that's about it. You could hardly call it a sparkling debut. However, *Theme* had taken so long to emerge, by this time I had moved on to another project. And this one was so very different.

13

The Advert

(Woodchip On The Wall . . .)

There it was. A simple little handwritten note pinned to a wall.
Probably half the size of a postcard. It stopped me in my tracks. I
stared at it. I was not expecting to see this that afternoon in The
Leadmill café. I was not looking for it, nor had I heard that the
position was up for grabs. But there it was. My heart actually did
seem to skip a beat and catch in my throat. This one was tailor-made
for me. I couldn't miss this opportunity. I could barely believe it:

Pulp Want Drummer
Call Russell/Jarvis on XXXXXXX

It's not so often in life you get these genuine heart-stopping moments.
I knew that I could do this. I knew that I wanted it. I knew that it
had to be the next move for me in my band career.

It was now mid to late 1986, and since seeing Pulp at The Crucible
studio, and loving the *It* album, I had become a real fan. I tried to
attend every Pulp gig I could, be it in Sheffield's Library theatre –
where sometime Pulp member Tim Allcard spent the entire gig atop
tall stepladders centre stage – or at The Limit, or anywhere they were
playing. It was always an event. The band seemed to have a gift for

doing everything differently, which certainly appealed to me. For
instance, they'd use toilet roll to decorate the stage. And I mean a lot.
They'd drape it over everything, stringing it up all over the place. As
the performance intensity grew, the loo roll would increasingly disin-
tegrate. Cheap, but very effective. Or they'd decorate everything in
tin foil, thus altering the stagescape to something totally surreal. Again,
cheap, but very effective.

Jarvis was still very much someone who grabbed your attention
on stage. You never seemed to know what was going to happen next.
Writhe about on the floor? Berate the band for getting something
in the song wrong and starting a tune again? Around 1985, he famously
appeared at a number of gigs in a wheelchair. He'd tried to impress
a girl by attempting to climb out of the window of a first-floor flat
above a sex shop and re-enter via the next window along. He failed.
He didn't have sufficient strength to haul himself back in, so he
decided instead to let himself drop to the pavement below, broken
wrist, ankle and fractured pelvis being the result. Again, don't try this
at home, kids. Some contemporary reviewers thought the wheelchair
was some kind of Morrissey 'disability chic' schtick* but it was
genuine. Even when he walked off stage after the last song.

The music of Pulp had changed somewhat from the acoustic
fey-ness of *It* that I'd fallen for. That early sound had now hardened
to a darker pitch. The musicians that had shaped *It* with Jarvis had
also scattered, almost immediately after the record had been released.
This meant Pulp going back to square one. Time to regenerate into
the next incarnation. New band members were duly assembled: Russell
Senior (guitar, violin and vocals), Candida Doyle (keyboards, backing
vocals), Peter Mansell (bass) and Magnus Doyle (drums).

This new lot put a whole new slant on Pulp. Russell had a very
steely, severe, almost unfriendly, angular stage presence – oft likened

---

* Morrissey, as singer with seminal Manc band The Smiths, often sported a hearing
aid and specs on stage, even though he needed neither.

to Sparks' Ron Mael, who sat motionless, staring bug-eyed at his keyboard. Russ brought out a confrontational side in Pulp, never shirking from the desire or possibility to shock. Even if it was only tongue-in-cheek.

Candida is someone that appears incredibly fragile. Don't be fooled. She has an incredible toughness. She played, to the untrained eye, what appeared to be an old kid's toy organ, with bright, multi-coloured switches and grey and white keys where one would expect the normal black and white. It was not, in fact, a toy but a Farfisa Compact Professional 222 organ of late sixties' vintage. A thing of great beauty, made even more intriguing as Candida would play it tilted away from her so the audience could see the top of the machine. This, however, was simply to raise the height of the keys, so she didn't have to play sitting down. It also made a great noise that was central to the new Pulp sound.★

Peter Mansell was Candida's boyfriend at the time, and definitely injected the 'yob' element into this version of Pulp. He certainly balanced out Jarvis and Russell's more artistic leanings with a more down-to-earth approach, let's say.

Magnus, though, was *out there* – really quiet but a real misfit oddball. He and Tim Allcard seemed determined to out-weird each other and often appeared together in the most outlandish outfits. Magnus would cut his hair in the style of a medieval monk with a bald tonsure, even wearing the monk's habit, if I remember correctly. It was light years away from what anyone else was wearing (apart from Tim) in the mid-eighties. Magnus was Candida's brother and a fantastic drummer. He had a great 'feel' and complemented the songs wonderfully, with a rather florid style of playing. He was technically very good and added a layer of percussive creativity that totally fitted in with

---

★ You can see a Farfisa Compact Pro being used by Sly & The Family Stone on the *Woodstock* documentary (1970). I think that's the only other time we ever saw one in action.

the sound. He'd often add a large, tarnished copper kettledrum to his kit to great effect, believed to have been given to Jarvis by Jim, The Hallamshire landlord. Watching Mag play certainly spurred me on to try different things in my own playing.

It took Pulp two years to release *Little Girl (With Blue Eyes)*, their third single (actually an EP) after 1983's 'My Lighthouse' and the follow-up 'Everybody's Problem' – a track that has since been roundly denigrated by Jarvis as a poor effort, done as a stab at a pure 'pop' song. It is definitely a chirpy track and more up-tempo than the songs on *It*. However, you can see why Jarvis has since tried to forget about it (my tip is to check out the B-side, the delicious 'There Was').

Anyway, *Little Girl* came out on London indie label Fire Records, who Pulp had signed with in mid-1985. The title track on the EP caused a bit of controversy with its chorus lyric, 'little girl . . . there's a hole in your heart and one between your legs', then asking if the girl had thought about 'which one he's going to fill'. Seems pretty harmless these days, but not in 1986.

It certainly prevented Pulp getting any local airplay. Not that they got much national radio play, despite being asked to do a John Peel session way back in the early days of 1981. (Pulp should have been a quintessential eighties Peel band; they were indie, quirky, unusual, with great melodic tunes but an acerbic edge. Alas, they seemed to be one of those bands he missed out on. Peel made up for it later.)

Needless to say, I loved *Little Girl* and was one of the few who actually bought a copy when it first came out. The title track was a gloriously melodic affair, with scything lyrics. A bittersweet ballad. Plus it's an EP, so you got three other tracks that indicated deeper waters at play: 'Simultaneous', 'Blue Glow' and 'The Will To Power', that last track gamely sung by Russell. (That song was to forever follow him around, generating accusations of him skirting with fascist imagery, with its talk of 1933 and fanaticism. Russell was no fash; he was a fervent leftie who'd been on the picket lines at the miners' strike a couple of years before. His favourite sticker was 'Coal Not Dole', for god's sake.) The record got some great reviews, but as Jarvis was in hospital and then wheelchair bound after the window incident, Pulp had to miss out on some important promotion. Consequently, *Little Girl* didn't sell well.

Sadly, the follow-up to *Little Girl* sold even fewer copies. *Dogs Are Everywhere*, another EP, this time of five tracks, was released seven months later in mid-1986. The title track was another uneasy ballad with dark undercurrents and commentary on the tendency for humans to descend to the level of animals, easily observed in any UK town centre on a Friday and Saturday night (see West Street as mentioned earlier in the book). You know the type.

The lead track was, for me, nice as it was, overshadowed by the other tracks: 'Mark Of The Devil', '97 Lovers', 'Aborigine' and 'Goodnight'.

'Mark Of The Devil' had an unusual drumbeat that was possibly the most dance-floor friendly Pulp had managed to date. Rumour has it, it was developed by Jarvis in a 'let's swap instruments' session. It's a great track and could've been single material if the 4/4 beat was a bit more consistent throughout. But it has a few sections where the beat drops out and the tempo changes, which would've foxed dancers in my opinion. Still, it's a fabulous song.

'97 Lovers' and 'Aborigine' showcase the breadth of creativity that was forthcoming – it's not often that 'Roger Moore in a short towelling dressing gown' is mentioned in song. Listen out for Russ's violin scrapings. (We'll hear more from '97 Lovers' later.)

'Goodnight' is a beguiling, atmospheric and hypnotically quiet piece, and one of my all-time favourite Pulp tracks. Jarvis sings in a whisper about going to bed and whether the objects in a room come alive when you sleep, with nightmare connotations. It's quite disconcerting listening back to these records as to how low Jarvis sings. It's a real low-down growl.

111

What hooked me about both these EPs was that they were so full of *melody*. Each track is easily hummable and memorable. Even 'Aborigine', which took a while to bed in, was infectious. It was a mystery to me why this lot were not getting anywhere on a national level. 'Dogs Are Everywhere' was *Melody Maker*'s Single of the Week, an accolade any band would die for and a fantastic springboard to getting some radio play on the BBC. Not a peep, though. Pulp couldn't get arrested, as the saying goes. It mattered not a jot to me, as Pulp were my favourite local band by a country mile. It could even be said without overstatement that they were my favourite band full stop.

And here I was now, staring at this gilt-edged opportunity. My chance.

I'd been trying for a while to get into a band that looked like they had more of a chance of getting records out and playing to more than 30 mates in the back room of a pub.

I tried out for Vendino Pact, a band that really looked like they could go somewhere. I auditioned somewhere near The Leadmill but was overlooked, as they didn't think my timing was quite right. Bloomin' cheek!

Floy Joy were another Sheffield group with a definite soul/pop groove. Not really my thing, but if it proved a pathway to playing on records, then what the hell? Bernie, one of my colleagues at X Clothes, was seeing Desi, the singer, so they put my name in the hat. I practised along with the Floy Joy record 'Weak In The Presence Of Beauty' – later a hit for Alison Moyet – for ages, to make sure I was ready for the audition. Which in the end never transpired. I always wonder how my life would have diverged from its eventual path had either of those opportunities come off. Narrow margins.

I scribbled the number down from the Pulp ad on a scrap of paper and promised myself to call later. I've often wondered why I didn't remove the paper from the wall to prevent anyone else seeing the ad and responding. Best to try and nobble the opposition as best you can, eh?

It came to pass that I didn't have to call the number. I was in The Leadmill (possibly that very evening) and who was in the queue for a beer but Jarvis.

'I hear you're looking for a drummer,' I ventured.

'Yes, that's right.'

'Can I have a go then?'

'Alright.'

Phew. First hurdle overcome. We had a chat and it was arranged that I should go up to the rehearsal room that Sunday afternoon coming up.

Sunday arrived and I packed up my snare drum into its case and got on the bus up to Jarvis's house. He lived in Intake, a south-eastern suburb of Sheffield. It's pretty rough up that way – Intake's just beyond Carlsbro Sound instrument shop, where I got a kicking from those skins a few years earlier.

Jarvis lived at his mum's house, which was attached to his gran's house, just behind a row of shops and the now demolished Woodthorpe pub. For Intake, their house was quite grand, with a big yard out front and some garages, one of which Pulp rehearsed in. The garage wasn't a double-size or anything like that, but a single old tin garage that looked like it might possibly collapse at any moment. It was cramped in there – mostly full of junk – and crammed deep within were a couple of amps, the Farfisa organ and a little drum kit. There was hardly any room to stand. Or sit, as I would be doing.

I approached the front door, a bit nervous as you might expect, ready to give it my best shot. I could hear from inside the house this almighty commotion. Dogs were barking and snarling most alarmingly, and it wasn't just one. What was I stepping into? I knocked on the door and it opened a fraction.

'Quick, get in,' said Jarvis through the door crack, just audible over the noise.

The door opened into the kitchen, where a smallish white pit bull-type dog was going apeshit. The door to the rest of the house was shut, but it was obvious there was another dog on the other side going equally mental. This was Bonzo, the aptly named Cocker family dog.

'It's followed me 'ome and won't go away.'

'What y'think we should do about it?' I said.

'Well, we can't do anything with it here. We should try and get rid of it before we go into the garage.'

The problem white bulldog needed sorting, that's for sure, so we decided our best tactic would be to take it for a walk and hopefully it would run off home. So, off the three of us went, strolling around the streets of Intake. The bulldog showed not one sign of toddling off to find its rightful owner. We tried waiting for it to stop and sniff a lamppost and then we'd run off round the corner, giving Fido the slip. Nothing seemed to work; the dog always caught up with us. It really wouldn't leave us alone. We must have walked around Intake for an hour before we realised we needed to launch the nuclear option. We had to find a suitable house and drive. Once the best candidate was found, we could put the plan into action. We'd pick up the dog and put it on the other side of someone's fence, and that would be the end of that. Then we could finally play some music.

So, with plan firmly etched out, the bulldog – we didn't go as far as naming the beast – was carefully placed over someone's driveway gate and we made off. The dog was last seen with his head between the bars of the metal gate, watching us disappear up the road. Tragic.

With the dog finally out of the way, it was time to have a go at some songs. Unfortunately, as we got back to the house, Jarvis realised he'd ran out of time, so that was that. I got back on the 95 bus and went home.

What we did glean from this strange audition was that we had a few things in common and got on well. Being in a band and getting on – trite as it sounds – is rather fundamental. Things can get quite fraught when you're trying to change the world and stuff, so getting on is a good thing. Jarvis has subsequently said that if he'd heard me playing it could have turned out very differently – I'm thinking this is tongue-in-cheek-type stuff, but you never know . . . I have no idea if Jarvis had ever seen me play in one of my other groups but I suspect so.

It was decided I should come back later in the week when the others, Russell, Manners and Candida (drummer Magnus having left the group to go travelling, his enthusiasm having waned), who were expected to be there for weekly rehearsal.

I knew Russell a little. He was a Limit regular (as was Jarvis, of course), and he'd also done a bit of violining with Jass. Often you'd be in The Limit and realise Russell was standing by you. 'Alright,' he'd deadpan, but that's it. Nothing else. Next time you looked he would be gone.

I returned in the week and we started to play some tunes, and all went smoothly. Nothing was ever confirmed as to whether I'd got the seat, nothing as easy as that. It was more a case of 'see you next week?'

Pulp didn't rehearse every week, though. There were still some upheavals going on. I did another couple of rehearsals with Pete and Candida, but they too went on to leave the group.

Was my new path any clearer now? Pulp were in pieces. Still, I seemed to have wormed my way in. By luck? Maybe. Fate? Definitely. It could all have been down to there being no other candidates on offer to fill the drum seat. I certainly don't recall any of the other members talking about auditioning other drummers, so it could well have been a case of 'we need a drummer; he'll have to do'. My gain, as they say. But, I had worked (?) and played myself into the position to the point where I knew I could take on the role. I knew it was for me. Excited about the future? You bet.

Jarvis had sunk a whole load of time and energy into Pulp and didn't seem to be packing it in anytime soon. Plus, he had a raft of new stuff to work on.

14

Debut

(So It Started There . . .)

Well, typical. You join your favourite band and then nothing happens. Well, not nothing per se – just a few garage rehearsals, working on the new sound. Pulp had some outstanding gigs but with the fall-outs with Magnus, and the fact that I had no time to sit in and learn the new set, the band did a couple of shows with Simon Hinkler in the hot seat. Simon had been a long-time collaborator, playing on the *It* LP and producing the last two EPs. His usual musical output was with Artery (who we've met previously), and he was just on the cusp of joining goth merchants The Mission: his road to the charts.

During this phoney war period Magnus, Manners and Candida (who as we know had also left by this stage) were lobbied to re-join the group, with limited success. Only Candida was persuaded. For now.

The rehearsals eventually picked up pace and Pulp were working on wholly new material, even though the next LP, *Freaks*, was already recorded and ready to go. Or so it seemed. The question of bass duties still remained. Pete Mansell was gone for good, so enter Steve Havenhand. Steve was a Limit enigma (wasn't everyone?) and he'd been a major force in another local band, Lay of the Land, who'd just imploded (members Steve Beckett and Rob Mitchell went on to found Warp Records and later Gift Records – more of which later).

117

Steve was very quiet, thin, smoked voraciously and wore suits. Perfect for Pulp's image. He was also definitely not a yob and, like a lot of us in the mid-eighties, rejected the macho, football, beer and fighting culture that was rife back then. As far as I know there was no audition, he just sort of turned up and started to play.

By November, Pulp had been booked to play at The Adelphi Club in Hull, and this turned out to be my live debut with the band. The Adelphi is a tiny, ramshackle affair fashioned out of a humble terrace house. The front room was a kind of taproom, with a pool table centre stage. The back room was the venue, with a bar in the middle that served both rooms. Naturally, the toilet was the dressing room. Outside was a small car park that was a Second World War bombsite. Still is. The Adelphi has gained a well-earned reputation for being one of those venues where everyone who's anyone has played at some time in their career.

The set we played that night was devoid of recently released Pulp material. No 'Little Girl', no 'Dogs' and no 'My Lighthouse'. Everything was brand new. The only track we'd rehearsed from the upcoming *Freaks* album was 'They Suffocate At Night', another lush, beautiful ballad produced on a shoestring budget.

That night, The Adelphi was packed. It was certainly the best crowd I'd ever played to – probably 120 souls came to see us. I was impressed and nervous.

We played our set of new songs that no one had ever heard before and finished with 'They Suffocate At Night'. I recall quite vividly ending the song about eight bars too soon (whoops). I think we (I) got away with it and thankfully no one got on my case about it. Yet.

The Adelphi was one of the few venues that put Pulp on with any frequency outside Sheffield, and we played there half a dozen times in the late eighties. Not always to packed houses, I should add; sometimes only 20–30 hardy indie types.

Our usual routine for gigging in Hull was to make a day trip of it. Set off early enough and there should be time to visit the seaside: pop over the Humber Bridge and visit Cleethorpes or go beyond Hull, to Withernsea. Muck about on the slots or down by the sea. Russell was a bit of a gambler and we once played a game to see who could walk out to sea balancing on one of the groins that jut out into the surf. All chuck a quid in and furthest to venture out scoops the pot. Wary of falling in, most were quite tentative in their efforts (Candida wisely declined the invitation altogether). Jarvis, on the other hand, went for it and made it the farthest. However, on his return to terra firma he lost it, and went in. Most folk would just go for damage limitation and surrender their dry lower limbs to the water. Not Jarvis. He threw himself fully off, landing with a great splash in the freezing water. Much mirth. There was less mirth on the drive to the venue, with a soaking wet Jarvis in the back, his charity shop suit giving off quite the wet dog pong. No spare clothes, of course.

Another time at The Adelphi, after the sound check, we repaired to the pub down the street. The Mainbrace was a largeish pub that had a small, low wall running along the front with a gap for the path to the entrance. In my eagerness to taste a sweet pint I decided to go for the shortcut over the wall. The next thing I know, I'm in a crumpled heap on the floor, having tripped over the stupid thing. Luckily no one had seen me, so a quick wipe down and into the bar. Trouble is, my finger really started to hurt. I had to keep it moving to be able to bend it. If I stopped, I couldn't bend it. Solution: keep bending the finger. In true trooper style the gig went ahead, although I was in quite some pain from this sodding finger. A trip to A&E the next day revealed it was broken. Don't take the shortcuts, kids.

As for the songs that so far only the denizens of Hull had heard, they were a stylistic swerve for Pulp, being Eastern European Balkan with a dollop of disco. Sometimes both together. While Jarvis was recuperating from his run-in with the window, he'd borrowed a little Yamaha Portasound keyboard from his grandma. This had a palette of fairly basic sounds and an even more basic rhythm generator, so you could play along. From this inauspicious instrument Jarvis was inspired to write a couple of songs that started off this new era.

First up was 'Separations', a melodramatic number (aren't they all?) featuring probably Russell's finest moments on the violin. It's sweeping intro leads into a dark and glowering verse, which leads to the introduction of the Portasound and its very tinny, but effective, rhythm. Drums and bass flesh it out further. I decided to employ brushes on this track for two reasons: first, the tempo in the mid-section is actually quite fast in 6/8 time, so in the rehearsal garage real sticks would've made a right clattering racket. And second, keeping time with the Portasound would be very difficult with our rudimentary equipment. Playing brushes allowed me to hear what the Yamaha was doing, so sticking to the rhythm. Overall, the brushes really lend the song a different quality to the others in the set.

The other song born in this era was what I consider to be *THE* greatest lost Pulp track ever: 'Death Comes To Town'. It's a Pulp disco classic; pure pop magic. We considered it to be the best song we developed during this period. Based on the disco setting of the Portasound, it has a killer melody added to some fantastically dark, yet tender lyrics from Jarvis, seemingly about desire, and all topped off with an uplifting chorus that you could imagine setting the pop world alight. We really thought it could be a winner.

Playing 'DCTT' live was always a pleasure, but not without difficulties. That difficulty was staying in time. A drummer will not, and perhaps should not, stay to strict tempo throughout a song. Human musicians can adapt to the drummer's tempo vagaries (thank god) without even noticing. This tempo movement can give added excitement to the music and a real human, live quality. However, machines don't do that, and the Portasound was a strict disciplinarian; it would not deviate from its 120bpm or so. As I've said, Pulp's equipment was very rudimentary back then, so we'd put the keyboard rhythm through the vocal PA and try our best to stay in time with it. If we went out, the rhythms would clash and it would sound terrible. This was especially nerve-wracking in a live situation, when you didn't want to have to stop and start again. So unprofessional and such a vibe kill. The solution, I discovered, lay in the Portasound itself. On each first beat of the bar a little LED light on the keyboard flashed, and so I worked out that if I was at my first beat of the bar on the bass drum at the same time as the Portasound, I – and the rest of 'em – would be in time even if I couldn't actually *hear* what the Portasound was doing. Not easy to do, but it was the best we could get at the time. Just to add another problem into the mix, a little slider on the front of the keyboard controlled the Portasound tempo. A tiny difference in slider position could result in a wildly different tempo. It needed very careful setting up.

'Rattlesnake' was another track developed in those early days that really helped stamp this new Balkan beat into 'new' Pulp. Russell was a real Eastern European and Balkan aficionado (he was even banned from Albania, I believe, around this time). I'm sure his influence really pushed this Balkan-beat disco phase. 'Rattlesnake' featured me playing the timpani that Jim from The Hallamshire had donated to Jarvis and some visceral fuzz box Farfisa, leading to a massive Balkanesque disco chorus. Bizarre. Yet fabulous.

These songs, along with others that ended up coming out on the *Separations* LP (more on that later), were mostly started or developed during rehearsals in Jarvis's garage and on stage at various early gigs of this version of Pulp.

Candida was still unsure whether she wanted to be in the band, and once again decided to leave. The net was cast to find a replacement – as if any old keyboard player could replace the irreplaceable Ms

Doyle. She has such a unique playing style; possibly in part due to her almost debilitating arthritic fingers. She is unable to spread her fingers like a 'normal' player, leading to her developing her own style, which was perfect for Pulp. Technical proficiency was always way down the list of requirements to be in the band. Candida brought something indefinable to Pulp, way beyond mere Farfisa player. She would be greatly missed.

The cast net for a new keys player dragged in a most curious creature: one Captain Sleep. A small, gnomeish figure, still to this day no one knows his real name. As per Steve Havenhand's non-audition, the Captain just turned up one day and was in (in fact, I don't recall him ever having been at a single rehearsal).

Pulp had an important gig coming up at the world-famous 100 Club on London's Oxford Street. The 100 Club is the oldest continually operating music venue in the world and has been putting on shows since 1942. Everyone, and I mean *everyone*, has graced the boards here: Sex Pistols, Rolling Stones, Paul McCartney, Jimi Hendrix, Muddy Waters, Siouxsie Sioux – you name it. We were to be part of a Fire Records night along with Colenso Parade, our labelmates.

We picked up Mr Sleep in the van and headed down the M1 to London. The Captain immediately, and true to form, got his head down in the back and didn't surface until we had arrived at the venue. Once there, we ran through our sound check and I believe the Captain then topped up his sleep quotient.

We did the gig to a smallish crowd, with Captain Sleep sat on the edge of the stage and the Farfisa on the floor. Perhaps the stage was full of our ramshackle gear, along with Colenso's.

Back into Kirky's van straight after for the return to Sheffield, recumbent keyboardist snoozing in the back. That amount of sleep can't be good for you and I must admit Captain Sleep did look a bit pasty. After the event we never saw the Captain again and thankfully

Ms Doyle was persuaded to return to her rightful home as our keyboard queen.

Strangely, the show garnered quite a good review from *Sounds* Roy Wilkinson that week:

Strolling on with all the visual impact of a bar mitzvah band from the Depression, Pulp are getting over a dormant interlude based around singer Jarvis Cocker's decision to free fall out of a window and spend the early part of the year in a wheelchair. They are just about to release a single and a long player – their first vinyl output for over a year. This, their first appearance in the capital in a similar period, would indicate that this newfound proliferation could see them as quite a force in the year to come.

Determinedly low-key in appearance and sound, they're now mining a lugubrious Eastern European vein. It's a Balkan beat without the cosmic overtones of 3 Mustaphas 3 and you could well imagine them breaking into the 'Harry Lime Theme' if they owned a zither and it wasn't a little too cheerful. Cocker's awkward yet mannered Scott Walkerish voice and his baiting of the audience, combined with Russell Senior's morosely busy violin, set an intensely melancholic mood which recalls any low-life tableau from Weimar Germany onwards.

The strength of this band was emphasised when they turned in a consistently compelling set without including their brilliant one time single 'Little Girl (with Blue Eyes)'. You should put this lot on your best-sellers list and that's no pulp fiction.

Kirky was our affable roadie/van driver/sound man, a great bear of a bloke who would always wear a rabbit-skin jacket that seemed to have bits falling off it. His Transit wasn't much better, appearing to be held together with gaffer tape. Luxury it was not. However, that was all we had. It's a bit of cliché, bands travelling up and down the country in battered Transit vans playing the 'toilet' circuit, but it's true.

Knackered vans and changing in toilets: that was the way it was. We'd fashion seats out of the amps and equipment boxes, and throw a couple of sleeping bags on top for added 'comfort'. We'd then hunker down for hours as the van made its creaky way to the next show. Strangely, Russell nearly always ended up front in the real seats, and not in the back with the rest of us. And I can tell you, it's no fun pushing a fully laden van at 2 a.m. in the pouring rain to get it going, but this was an all-too-frequent occurrence when it came to the wonderful Jonathan Kirk and his blue Transit (with added go-slower gaffer-tape stripes).

15

Freak's Fallout

(Don't You Want Me Anymore?)

Even though the group that recorded *Freaks* was essentially no more, it didn't stop Fire Records releasing singles in support of the soon-to-be launched LP.

'They Suffocate At Night', the first single from the album, is another mesmerising Pulp ballad, full of melody and yearning. You can easily imagine the song being drenched in luscious string treatments and really benefitting from a shot of 'glam'. Well, you don't get that when the entire album is recorded for the princely sum of around £600, as *Freaks* was.

Sadly, 'They Suffocate At Night' came out to the usual indifference, securing negligible airplay and thus sales. It was obvious the relationship between Fire and Pulp was faltering. What really put it into the shade was that *Freaks* was taking a long time to come out, especially for an album that was recorded in a week. Furthermore, I appeared to be in a band that had already moved on from the *Freaks* material. They'd recorded the album the previous June, and most of the tracks had been in Pulp's live set for at least two years by this point. It took the best part of a year to hit the shops. You could imagine a major label liking a good run-up with a major worldwide release, but a tiny UK independent? Bands want their stuff out there as soon as possible;

they can't afford to sit on material going stale. Such delays would come back to haunt Pulp.

Still, Fire continued with the releases. Jarvis and Russell insisted 'Masters Of The Universe' be the next single. Fire weren't overly keen but they agreed, possibly to placate the band.

'Masters Of The Universe' is perhaps the best indicator of Pulp's future sound. A harder rock/disco affair building to a towering crescendo, it always went down well when played live. Well, that was the plan. The track possibly suffers from a lack of 'oomph' in the recorded final version. It does indeed rock, especially compared to the more ballad-esque releases to date.

But, you guessed it: 'Masters Of The Universe' failed to master *any* universe, its release generating even more indifference than the first single. I was an avid buyer of all of Pulp's output, and even I didn't see a copy of 'Masters Of The Universe' for some years. Jarvis claimed to have never been sent a copy, or seen one in a shop. In Fire's defence, distribution is the Achilles heel of small independents: if you can't get shops to stock a few copies, then folk can't buy it. Simple as that.

Freaks was finally released in May 1987. Reviews were mixed, generally along the lines of 'great songs, but god it's glum'. But April's edition of *Sounds* was more positive:

> *Freaks is a bit mad, a jagged collection of cruel words fastened to frequently enthralling music, the voice of Jarvis Cocker reciting the lyrics with a dry, almost mockingly tuneless nonchalance. More often than not he hits home and you realise what you're hearing is the truth.*
>
> *Sounds*, April 1987

I, of course, loved *Freaks*. I knew the songs from seeing the band live and devoured the vinyl with glee. It wasn't a case of 'I wish I was playing these songs' though, even though I was in the band by now, for I knew the new material currently under development was even better. Plus, I don't think I could've done Magnus's drum parts justice. They were his.

With the release of *Freaks* the Fire deal was essentially over. Jarvis and Russell didn't have many kind words to fling in Fire's direction. No budget = ham-fisted recordings = under-par releases = no airplay = no success. Throw in crap distribution and zero marketing and it's not a very good recipe for success. Jarvis had been Pulping for nearly ten fruitless years by this point. He couldn't waste any more time.

Enter FON Records. (What's FON stand for, you ask? F**k Off Nazis, of course.) They had started gaining real interest with their releases around this time. Plus, despite its dingy, backstreet, rodent-plagued location, FON was state-of-the-art for the mid to late eighties; a *proper* recording studio. And it was attracting some *serious* artists (Cabaret Voltaire, Sly & Robbie – even David Bowie, I kid you not!). Now label and studio manager Dave Taylor had Pulp in his sights. And with no desire to repeat the horrors of Fire, we were all ears.

It was decided the best course of action would be to go into the studio and record some tracks, the end-result being said tracks would be released on the FON label. Hindsight suggests this was clearly a tactic to see how it would go, since we didn't sign anything – it was more a case of 'let's see'.

FON studios were just off The Wicker, right along from where Jarvis had lived (sadly, it's now all gone, buried under the Sheffield Inner Ring Road). We were aiming to record a couple of tracks which, we hoped and prayed, would be good enough for FON to release. We knew the new material was so much better than *Freaks*: poppier, punchier, less morose, but still with some serious depth and drama. Oh, and some killer hooks.

FON was hardly Sarm West or Abbey Road, but to us it was fabulous. We got such a buzz from being in a great studio for the first time. Finally, we were making a Pulp record that was bang up to date. The plan was to record 'Rattlesnake', 'Don't You Want Me Anymore' and 'Death Comes To Town'. There was no great pressure to get everything done as quickly as possible, before the money ran out, which was a huge relief.

The strategy for recording was to simply set up and play 'as live', then each instrument would be listened to for errors, bum notes, out of time events and so on, of which there are always plenty of examples. It's especially hard for us drummers, as the initial takes tend to centre on the drummer's performance and whether the 'take' is up to scratch – if the others are off-key, they can usually redo their parts later and get them spot on. Not so fast for us drummers. A 'take' needs to be captured 'error-free' in its entirety, as it's much harder to redo a drum section later on. This certainly was the case with technology in 1987.

We toiled away under the watchful eyes of Alan Smyth, who we got in to help record the songs. He'd been doing a bit of live sound for us around this time and was perfect for helping out on these vital recordings that could shape Pulp's future. Al's a patient chap (needs to be) and an old Sheffield music type – his band was Don Valley & The Rotherhides, no less. With Al's guidance and FON engineer Rob Gordon manning the mixing board, we managed to make Pulp's best recordings to date *by far*: polished, professional and ready for release.

'Rattlesnake' is a dramatic piece, with timpani and layers of acoustic guitars, that explodes into an Eastern European Polka-type chorus, not unlike Boney M.'s 'Rasputin' in a strange way. You could certainly hear the Pulp evolution from 'Mark Of The Devil', which you could argue is 'Rattlesnake's nearest musical cousin. But the difference in recording, playing and songwriting is crystal clear.

The pearl of the session was 'Death Comes To Town', which, as I have touched on before, was a bona fide, radio-friendly pop classic. If this didn't propel Pulp onto the airwaves – and hopefully the charts

– then there was no justice and we might as well give up. We all believed this was our best chance to date.

The version Al recorded leant heavily on the Portasound and its plinky-plonky rhythm, my drums taking more of a back seat, which I was perfectly happy with. Jarvis isn't much of a fan of drums cranked up to the fore in recordings, which goes back to the *It* days. Listening back to the track now, the Portasound rhythm gives it a kind of disco/ska feel, plus Russell's twangy guitar riff really drives the song along. One part that surprised us, when we were invited to listen to the final mix, was that Al had inserted a little break after the first chorus, right where Jarvis says, 'Do it'. It was never there during live performances, but its creation was inspired, the break adding a new twist and a delicious pop moment to the track. We were ecstatic about how it turned out.

Studio manager Dave Taylor loved the recordings, too; he could hear they were easily Pulp's best to date. Trouble is, FON was getting too successful for its own good. They'd scored their biggest hit to date with Leeds band Age of Chance and their reworking, let's say, of Prince's iconic track 'Kiss', which reached number one in the indie charts in 1986 and even scraped the Top 50. The following year saw FON hit the charts big time with Krush, and their single 'House Arrest', which hit number three in the Official Singles Chart right around the time Pulp were in the FON studio, working on 'Death Comes To Town'. Subsequently, Taylor was left running around like a headless chicken dealing with the fallout from this (unexpected) hit, and it's fair to say Pulp couldn't really get much of a look-in, nor the all-important answer to the question: are we in, or not?

Time dragged on. And on. The more it dragged on, the less likely it seemed that FON would release the tracks. Taylor later confessed that he couldn't really see how Pulp would 'fit in' to the music scene of '88, and so he decided not to risk it. Our chance had gone. No

FON release meant nobody would get to hear the pop masterpiece that was 'Death Comes To Town'.

To say we were deflated was a bit of an understatement. I had joined my favourite group and was convinced we would be releasing fabulous records and reaping vast success on the back of it. With the FON mirage fading, it looked like my chance of appearing on vinyl was slowly slipping away. Pulp went critical. 'What's the point?' became our motto. Russell was fed up and was all for quitting the band. Jarvis was starting to look at other options besides music. Ten years at the Pulp coalface was enough even for him.

To me it seemed a great tragedy that this group and these songs didn't receive wider exposure. We'd made our most accessible recordings and had shown with 'Death Comes To Town' that we could write killer pop. Pulp had a track record of releasing some very interesting music, and could again. More to the point, we had the best, most intriguing, interesting and enigmatic lead singer anyone could ask for. If someone like Jarvis was allowed to slip through the cultural net of the British music scene then there really was no justice. In the mid to late eighties we were assailed with a slew of vacuous pop stars, and even the indie scene was devoid of characters; aside from the brilliant over-the-topness of Morrissey, no amount of Wedding Present, The Jesus and Mary Chain, House of Love, Dinosaur Jr., Pixies, Primal Scream and even New Order could produce pop star-grade characters for us, and the record-buying public, to worship. They made some great records, for sure, but weren't they just Third Division cloggers compared to our star forward?

Jarvis could write a tune. Jarvis could mesmerise an audience. Jarvis was unafraid to go out on a limb. Jarvis was a walking music encyclopaedia. Jarvis was, and still is, funny as. Trouble is, Jarvis also doesn't have an 'off' switch. He's in a constant whirl of daft voices and acting out scenarios that only he can see in his head. Which can all be incredibly hilarious, and yet irritating . . .

frequently all at the same time. Jarvis lives by Jarvis time, and that 'time' is not necessarily the same as for us mere mortals. Don't expect punctuality.

By the end of 1988 it was looking more likely that British music culture would be denied the chance to see Pulp and Jarvis in full flow. We were slowly entering the dark ages.

16

The Dark Ages

(Separations)

In January 1988, Pulp fractured. The first crack appeared when Steve Havenhand disappeared. It came to pass during the FON sessions that Steve just wasn't cut out to be Pulp's bassist. He's a nice bloke and all that, but Jarvis ended up redoing the bass parts, as Steve tended to tickle the strings somewhat, not giving them the welly they required. Pete Mansell was a forceful player. Steve was not. Pulp needed forceful.

Steve Genn was a quintessential Sheffield bandsman and all-round Limit character. A sometime Jarvis collaborator on various side projects, he'd been around the scene forever and was also larger than life, a hear-him-before-you-see-him type of personality. He had a way of sailing through life minus the encumbrance of gainful employ, yet somehow managing to run his own band, Mr Morality.

Steve's much younger brother, Antony, was fast becoming a regular sofa surfer at Burgoyne Towers, and despite little previous experience he ended up taking the Pulp bass reins. Ants would not appreciate the comparison but he, like Steve, had an unerring knack of somehow getting what he wanted, when he wanted it. Ants was a voracious ingester of mushrooms and acid, and could talk himself into and out of just about any situation he found himself in. This, combined with a fierce intellect and sense of humour, was good fun to be around.

Ants and I worked together off and on around this time. A couple of lads had a business selling music and film posters to students in universities and colleges throughout the north of England. Business was booming, especially around September/October time when the students arrived in their halls of residence or were fitting out new flats for the academic year to come.

The job involved picking up a van at an ungodly hour in the morning and filling it with your stock of posters for that day. You were allocated a college to visit, and off you went. Ants wasn't much of a morning person, so I'd pick him up en route and he'd usually decamp his bed to the van to get a couple more hours' sleep in as we drove. You'd then set up, usually in some student union hall, and run around the campus, pinning adverts for the sale on notice boards and lampposts. Business was usually pretty brisk for the rest of the day, and you'd return to HQ in Sheffield, rather knackered. Best thing was, no one ever checked the amount of stock you took out in the morning, so they had no way of knowing how much money, and unsold stock, should be returned. If it all looked about right, then it was. You thus pocketed your share of the day's take plus quite a lot more for those additional unaccounted-for-sales. Not that they minded much; the posters were all 'unofficial' anyway. No regard for copyright or anything like that.

I had a couple of other poster-selling adventures, too. Another seller, Stubbsy (first name superfluous) asked me to be the driver for a weekend trip to London to sell posters outside a two-day Damned gig in Finsbury Park. Load a car up with hooky Damned posters and a sleeping bag, and head south. We'd sell to the punters going into the gig, but that was always pretty rubbish as no one in their right mind would pay to carry a poster around all day at a gig. The real action, then, was as the punters streamed out. We'd have a stack of huge posters cradled in the crook of one arm — yes, they were heavy — and the other arm was for taking the money and handing out a poster off the stack. You couldn't drop the posters on the floor as they'd get trampled on (or, even worse, nicked), plus the best sales were always done in the middle of the crowd. And boy did we work it. Posters were flying out and our pockets were rapidly filling up with cash. The only real downside was the 'rougher' elements of the crowd, who'd try to steal stock or rob us of our takings. Thankfully, the crowds were so thick they usually couldn't get near us.

We bunked down in the car, rather than spend hard-earned on a B&B. Repeat the next day and return to Sheffield with a car boot full of money. Me and Stubbsy got on well, so next we were tasked with a poster-flogging tour of Ireland: Galway, Limerick and ending up at Trinity College, Dublin. The Irish kids' taste in posters was pretty much the same as the UK kids': the film poster for 1986's *Betty Blue*, Mickey Rourke and, of course, U2.

This was more like it, having fun in far-flung foreign lands. I loved travelling around, seeing all these towns and getting a taste of the 'craic'. We had our first taste of 'exotic' overseas nightclubs in Ireland, too. It was all very strange: in some place in Limerick, we were gobsmacked to find that at the end of the night, everyone stood up to sing the Irish national anthem (we didn't, of course, as we had no clue what was going on). In Dublin, they didn't bother with the national anthem malarkey, but they did throw open the doors at the end of the night and put on a looped recording of an old man, saying: 'Thank you for coming to O'Neills. Please make your way out.' Over and over, at ear-splitting volume. Job done; no one hung around.

We stayed at a lovely old hotel in Dublin, The Clarence, which I believe is now owned by U2. We had a friendly way with the concierge and one evening as we headed out for more 'craic', 'Be sure you're here later, boys' he said with a wink. Intriguing. We arrived back later that night, to our man saying, 'Take a seat. They'll be here soon.' Double intrigue. We sat for about 40 minutes, all the while our chap giving us the knowing wink.

Suddenly we could hear cars pulling up outside – lots of them.

Out from the cars poured loads of young kids in ballgowns and tuxes. 'Debs ball!' said our man with obvious delight. The Debs (that is 'debutantes', as in young well-to-do Irish kids having a tear-up) all poured into a side hall in the hotel that was set up for the do, and proceeded to dance the rest of the night away in all their finery. Naturally we joined them. Much 'craic' was had.

Jarvis was in need of new lodgings around this time and a place at Burgoyne came available, so he moved in. Well, technically he moved in, but the reality was the rest of the house moved *him* in.

Jarvis is a keen 'collector' – of any old tat. To the untrained eye it might look like hoarding. Needless, to say he has a lot of stuff. So, on the moving-in day Jarvis appears with Kirky's Transit absolutely filled beyond the brim with all manner of trash – sorry, my mistake – carefully curated curios and antiques. We all chip in and start helping unload, only for another car to pull up at the kerb.

'That's my driving instructor,' says Jarvis. 'I've got a driving lesson booked.'

Jarvis promptly abandoned the unloading, jumped in the Ford Fiesta and kangaroo'd off down the road.

'I've got a band to shift and a gig to do in about 20 minutes,' said Kirky. So, it was left to the rest of us – actually, mainly me – to empty the van and fill Jarvis's room with his 'stuff'. This included:

Joe 90 annuals (many)
Seventies ceramics
Plastic fruit
Millions of records
Bin liners full of jumble sale clothes (far fewer charity shops
    back then)
Two life-size cut-outs of cartoon nurses from the fifties
Dressmaker's mannequins, at least two

This is just a sample of the torrents of 'collectables' we decanted. You could barely get in the room once everything was in it. Still, Jarvis brought yet another layer of odd to Burgoyne. Which was starting to feel more like a bit of a scene, I guess – well, at least to us, I suppose. There was always something going off, often creative, sometimes surreal.

By early '88 we'd reached our nadir, and Pulp gigs had started to dwindle to a trickle. We piled in the van to go play the 20th Century Club in Derby, a bit of a chrome-and-black eighties disco-style affair. We arrived, promptly, set up and sound-checked as usual. A car load of mates made the short journey down the M1 to the venue, but the only paying punters that night were two girls that clearly had no idea who Pulp were. They sat politely at the side and watched us cavort on stage to our odd Eastern European indie-disco sound. I would love to know if they remember the gig. You would, wouldn't you? And if they enjoyed it. Perhaps it's a closely guarded secret, to save one another from eternal shame. Maybe. We will never know (if you're reading this, though, do get in touch!).

Thankfully, we could always rely on a home concert to pull in the crowds. And 1988 saw Pulp performing two landmark home-town gigs.

The first was at Sheffield University's Lower Refectory. This was a good'un, as the Refectory was quite a large room with a high ceiling, and played host to 'proper' bands. It had a good PA and a decent-sized stage to allow certain people to prance about on.

Pulp were still wedded to decorating the stage as wildly – and cheaply – as possible, and this time it was decided to take the 'plastic bags full of coloured water fixed to rope idea' (which we'd put to good use at one of my earliest Pulp shows) to another level. The stage was festooned with all these bags and assorted 'stuff' clipped on to them. It was amazing. When the lights hit the bags, it produced a somewhat psychedelic effect.

It was a great feeling to be part of such a creative set of folk, making magic from bits and bobs that cost pennies (we didn't count the hours it took to get it all together and construct it, but hey ho, we were doing little else).

We played a brilliant gig that night. Everyone was on top form and we were playing better and better together. You could really see the audience (and there was plenty of 'em) were really getting into it as well. I sensed that we were finally on to something. The Sheffield kids loved it and if they were into it, why wouldn't kids all over the place be into it too? If only we could release some goddamn records so folk could hear them.

Rob Mitchell joined us on stage that night, dressed in long johns and armed with his viola, adding additional strings where necessary.* But my most cherished memory from this triumphant night is playing away at the encore with my eyes transfixed on Ant's naked bottom, jiggling away as he played his bass. Ant's never had any problems about stripping off anytime, anywhere, so why not on stage? It just so happened that where he stood was right in front of a conveniently floor-placed light, which was aimed right up his fundament.

'The Day That Never Happened' concert at The Leadmill in the summer of 1988 was a different story. It was supposed to be a wild, full-on sensory extravaganza, or, as Russell put it, 'A multimedia cosmic tangerine experience'. Well, that was the idea anyway. Alas, it didn't really go to plan.

Pulp were well known for trying to put on a bit of a show – decorating the stage, ambitious props and all that jazz – but this time we wanted to go for the full monty. So, the plan was to wrap everything with tinfoil, as per usual, and hang the coloured water

---

* Rob went on to form Warp Records with Steve Beckett not long after.

in bags, festooned about the stage. Jarvis also wanted to use dry ice for a song or two, as seen on *Top of the Pops* where the performers' legs would be shrouded in the fog. We were also keen to add film projections, using the band as the screen. Russell then had the idea to pair each song with a different scent, and had devised the chemicals necessary. If that weren't enough, there were trees sprayed with white spray paint and a plan to have fake snow fall as a dramatic climax. So, quite the 'multimedia cosmic tangerine experience', as I'm sure you would agree.

Now, if you had a decent budget – and I'm talking thousands – and phalanxes of experienced theatre technicians to make it all work, this would all seem very doable. Only Pulp had a budget of about £100 and two daft lads from Chesterfield to operate and corral everything into place. Doesn't bode well, does it?

Naturally, things started to go wrong from the start. The video projector broke down in the sound check, so that idea had to be scrapped and instead a TV was plonked on stage as a (poor) substitute, so at least the visuals might get seen. Russell's 'smell-o-song' idea was a non-starter, as the scents dispersed so quickly that not even we on stage could detect them (probably for the best, looking back). No one knew anything about dry ice and how much frozen carbon dioxide was needed to produce the required foggy effect. Unsurprisingly, the carrier bag's worth of icy chunks we had could barely produce fog to fill a bucket. Best, or probably worst, of all was the snowfall. Blowers (read that as big hairdryers) were to blow out white particles, simulating the aforementioned snowfall. But again, no one knew how much white stuff – or 'blow', for that matter – was needed for it to work (now, now; these were more innocent times). Suffice to say we didn't have enough of either, so we ended up with one Mark Webber and his mate, Greg (from Chezzer), running about the stage, trying to cajole the white particles (tiny polystyrene balls?) into some, indeed any, kind of semblance of snowfall using the oversized hairdryers. Nothing of the sort transpired. Instead it was all-round farce.

I suppose you're thinking that at least the music will have been spot on. Well, no, it wasn't. Antony Genn's attention span wasn't the best around this time and he spent most of the time pre-gig mucking about with something else that was of no consequence to the event, and subsequently I took it upon myself to tune his bass. Which, by the way, had to have coloured stickers all over the neck to remind Ants where to put his fingers for which song. The lesson here, kids? Don't get the drummer to tune your bass. I had no idea what I was doing, so his first note of the first song was horribly out of tune. This is not conducive to a good show.

Coupled with the stress of all the other stuff not going to plan, it meant Jarvis was not happy. Not happy at all. No one was. The entire event, while with the best intentions, seemed to sum up Pulp at this stage. We were trying for the grand statement and attempting to be as entertaining as possible, but on almost zero budget. Trying to do everything ourselves because who else would do it? Reaching for the stars from the depths of the gutter? You bet. A spectacular failure? Certainly. But it further cemented my notion that this was the only band to be in. There was such creativity! OK, so perhaps it did detract from the music at times, but the ideas! Again, if we could only get someone to help fund these escapades (like a major recording label, perchance?) more folk might actually get to see them and, in turn, so would we. I was convinced that once people got the chance to see us, hear us, be entertained by us and this lanky 'get' in brown trousers, then we would inevitably be successful. If not, we will at least have had a proper go at it. However . . .

Pulp fractured again. Ants found God. Yep, God.

In Sheffield during the late eighties there was a religious sect going off. It was all cool, young, hip-looking things having a rave every Sunday under the banner 'The Nine O'Clock Service'.

Severe-looking girls with identikit black bob haircuts and red lipstick would 'love bomb' the emotionally vulnerable into going along 'just to see what it's like', and once in they would have their claws into you. Ants, who'd perhaps been indulging a little too eagerly in the old hallucinogens, was thus vulnerable to their attention and was lured in. Pretty soon he found he couldn't do both, so he left the band.

Plenty of folk had tried to drag me and my bestie Steve Allott along to the NOS, but we always said no. Religion means nothing to me and is something I despise. The nearest we got to it as kids was attending Sunday School, but that was probably to get me and Richard out of the house so the parents could have some peace. Thus, all NOS advances were vehemently repelled.

Also, around this time Candida moved from Sheffield to Manchester, where she found work in a toy shop in Didsbury while we all figured out how to move forward as a band. Who can blame her? Pulp seemed to be hitting a brick wall and everyone was hedging their life bets by exploring other career avenues rather than wasting their time on a band seemingly on its last legs.

I had finished my degree by the summer of 1987 and left with a 2:2 Bachelor of Education certificate (low swot rate, in my humbler opinion). This enabled me to start applying for posts in secondary schools teaching D&T. However, I was rather reticent to embark on my teaching career. I had experienced some rather sobering events in the classroom at my last teaching practice at Chaucer Comprehensive in Sheffield.

Chaucer was on the Parson Cross council estate, which at one time was one of the largest council estates in Europe. Council estates in Britain can be pretty rough places and this was no exception. The kids at Chaucer gave me a right run-around as the trainee teacher, and it was more like survival training rather than a chance to hone my teacher skills. I didn't want to jump back into the classroom anytime soon. But, we all needed an income, so instead I took on jobs of varying degrees of mundanity during this period.

I enrolled with the local newspaper, the *Sheffield Star*, as a display advertising executive – a fancy title for a crap job, all told. The day-to-day involved hitting the phones, cold-calling local businesses and trying to persuade them to buy space in the paper to advertise their latest offerings or services. You were paid a pitiful 'basic' that was topped up should you hit your space target for that month. I never did. Not once. The reality was, I didn't believe in the selling power of the *Sheffield Star*. I just could not see why anyone out there would respond to an advert in the paper. I certainly wouldn't, so why would others? Thus my powers of persuasion were somewhat limited. Plus, I was sat around folk of a similar age who all saw themselves as thrusting eighties businesspeople, acting like Gordon Gecko while cajoling a Bridlington guest house into spending £80 on a little ad to hook South Yorkshire readers into spending a weekend in their establishment. Pitiful. The lads and lasses were generally an OK bunch, some smart, some thick as pudding. I just could not fathom how some of them could effortlessly sell sell sell, whereas I couldn't sell a thing. The final straw was when we were tasked with selling ads to 'support' a charity push by the paper, but ostensibly using the charity to push the ads. The idea was that the charities would get free publicity. As if they run off 'publicity'. No thanks. Resignation, I'm off. Thank you. Goodnight.

I had been working in clothes shops on Saturdays for what seemed ages, X Clothes, of course, then later at a shop called 20th Century with Rich Hawley. So when I saw a new shop was opening in town, I applied in hopes of becoming manager. For this one, I had to travel down to Radius HQ in that fancy London, whereupon I was hired . . . but only as shop-floor staff rather than anything more elevated. Never mind, job's a job. It wasn't long, though, before I could feel myself dying inside. Being on a shop floor day in day out is soul-destroyingly boring. It's OK just doing a Saturday, since that's the busiest day, but a wet Tuesday morning with one or two punters is a different matter. Dull. Dull. Thrice dull. Couldn't stand that for very long.

My mate Steve's girlfriend had opened her own florist shop and needed folk to make wreaths in the cellar. I can do that, I said, never having any experience of wreath-making, and myself and Steve Genn jumped in.

The run-up to Christmas was obviously peak wreath time, and we'd take the van down to the local cemetery to 'liberate' the trees of some holly to help make the wreaths, possibly tip-toeing along the margins of legality. We'd also be tasked with delivering floral bouquets and I'd have great fun teasing all the girls in the offices where you'd be delivering the flowers, as they all wanted to be the recipient, of course.

At 20th Century I worked with a brilliant lad called Brian Johnson, who started a new job at a local jeans shop, Bankrupt Clothing Company, delivering stock to their stores around the north. They needed help in the warehouse, taking in the stock and redistributing it out. So I got a job there. I mostly spent my days in the warehouse, emptying and refilling boxes and stacking them in vans.

I got along great with all the other lads, it was genuine camaraderie. Once I helped Brian with a delivery up to Leeds. We packed the van and set off, but by the time we'd reached the Meadowhall area we realised that for the last 200 yards the back doors had opened and denim had been flying out. We could see loads of vehicles coming to an abrupt halt on the road, their occupants jumping out and grabbing whatever garments they could before zooming off. We stopped, retraced our tracks, and retrieved what was left, half laughing like drains, half worried that this would be our last day at Bankrupt. It wasn't, thankfully.

It seemed that I was putting off embarking on a 'serious' career in teaching by taking these other jobs. Being a teacher was a proper vocation, and I was holding on to the fanciful idea that I could still make it in the music biz with Pulp. That big break could be just around the corner. Isn't it always? Thing is, was it going to be with Pulp?

Not yet. Pulp fractured yet again. This time it was much more troubling. 'The Day That Never Happened' concert was Jarvis's last Pulp gig as a resident of Sheffield. He'd been at Sheffield Poly doing a course in filmmaking, and had accepted a place at the prestigious Central Saint Martins, University of the Arts London, to continue his studies. This was a serious event for us other members of Pulp. How could we keep the band going when Jarvis was 167 miles away? Would this be the end of Pulp, once and for all? Jarvis had been toiling away at the group since 1978 and, as we have seen, there'd been precious little success. Yes, records had been released, but no one had really bought them. Jarvis was definitely NOT a pop star and Pulp seemed to be going nowhere. The band had been toiling away for ten years with nothing to show for it. And now we had no record label, no bass player, and no singer. This really did look terminal.

17

London Calling

(Death Comes To Town)

Pulp was in bits. Scattered. But, we never sat down and said, 'That's it, the end, see you later.' There was still a dimly flickering ember under the rubble. There was still a desire to try and keep things going – somehow. We didn't know how this was going to happen, we just thought the songs we had were too vital to let die. We still had the personnel invested in trying to make it work, aside from a bassist.

Then I had a rare brainwave. I had cast my mind back to a gig we'd done a few months earlier in a dingy back room of the Camden Falcon, North London (a gig one Bob Stanley, later of Saint Etienne fame, had reviewed for the *NME*). The show had been sparsely attended, which was not unusual in these dark times, but one attendee stood out, with his long, luscious, curly brown locks, whooping and hollering and really getting into it. That guy was an old Sheffield compadre who'd de-camped to London a few years earlier. Namely, a Mr Steve Mackey. He'd played bass in a couple of Sheffield noise bands, one of which was the curiously monikered Trolley Dogshag. It seemed an avenue worth exploring. Steve was obviously into the music, so we might as well at least approach him to see if he was interested. Also, having two-fifths of the group down in London (plus two-fifths in Sheffield and one-fifth in Mancland) might be a good way of keeping Pulp together in some small way. I suggested this to Jarvis, and he agreed it was a good idea.

Steve didn't need asking twice. He jumped at the chance. A flicker of life returned to Pulp's deathly corpse. We had now a full band – at least on paper.

Steve was a great addition to the cause. He could play with the requisite 'oomph', was on the same wavelength as everyone else and was a consummate organiser. Pulp, or more correctly, Jarvis needs organisers. Russell had been doing plenty of Pulp organising to date, but now distance was involved it was really fortunate to have another organiser down south.

Not that there was much to organise. Pulp had one gig left in 1988. We had been invited (god knows how) to perform along with The Membranes at *Sound's* Christmas Party, *Sounds*, of course, being one of the three major music paper weeklies, along with *NME* and *Melody Maker*. This was a great opportunity to get ourselves in front of a load of London journos who might, if we are lucky, take a bit of note of us rather than concentrating on getting leathered at the bar. Reports suggest our performance was a bit on the shambolic side, but this didn't seem to have a detrimental effect on proceedings, as after the gig we were reintroduced to Fire Records.

Looking back, these events could be seen as the start of the upturn in Pulp's fortunes. The band was finally stable and there was perhaps a chance that Pulp may start putting records out again. (Is a band really a band unless it has actual recorded output? No matter how dismally received or successful? Without getting the songs out there, it's just five people making a racket in a dingy room, ankle deep in beer cans (as most rehearsal rooms tended to be). The record gives a band *legitimacy*.) However, I'd proffer something else as being the first step on the road to fame and fortune: contact lenses.

What, I hear you say? You heard right. Contacts. Jarvis decided to ditch the glasses for live shows. This one simple move had a definite effect on Pulp's fortunes. Previously, Jarv had been rather defined by his donning of the chunky NHS-type specs (although I don't think they were actual NHS ones; those were usually reserved for poor kids) and, more often than not, commentators would focus on the specs, leading them to believe Jarvis – and by extension, Pulp – were not to be taken seriously. But these new lenses had a transformative effect; they seemed to infuse Jarvis with the confidence to appear like, behave like and, more importantly, believe he could become a bona fide pop star. Even more incredulously, some started claiming that onstage Jarvis was *sexy*. Now, hearing this for the first time was met with gales of laughter. *Jarvis? Sexy? Really?* But why not? New converts to Pulp don't have to know about the previous 'nerd' version of Jarvis. If we could move forward with this cool, sexy, pop star version of Jarvis, it might just work in our favour. (Please bear in mind that this whole thing was completely unpremeditated, and progress was slow while Jarvis cultivated this new version of himself. But taking off the glasses in favour of contacts was, in my eyes, the first step.)

Back to Fire Records, and Dave Bedford, who'd taken over A&R, had the job of trying to persuade Jarvis that the relationship could be rekindled and there was the distinct possibility that Pulp could start recording and releasing records again. And Jarvis needed some persuading. The previous Fire experience had scarred him and was not to be repeated. So, Dave dangled the carrot of a greatly improved record budget: £10,000. This was a phenomenal increase on *Freaks* and not to be sniffed at.

A plan was hatched. Maybe if we did the record at FON in Sheffield, but spent the Fire money on it, once FON heard the finished album they'd want to sign us. We just needed to be able to make the record without signing a contract with Fire. Tricky. But this was probably the only way Pulp was going to survive. If everyone could cling on to the hope of this new LP and a proper release, our desire to become a successful band might just live on. I'd had a glimpse of a non-Pulp future as a teacher, office worker, poster salesman, whatever, and it did not fill me with joy. Please, anything but that.

We duly booked FON studios and asked Alan Smyth to produce this sink-or-swim album. Al was given the brief to make Pulp sound like a cross between the 'Walrus of Love', Barry White, and those arch electro-poppers The Pet Shop Boys. Quite a departure, then – no pressure.

It was plain to us that we needed to utilise this studio to its full potential. We wanted to max out every bit of technology on this album. No ideological straitjackets here; we'd do whatever it took to make this as good a record as we knew it could be. We had lived with these songs now for at least two years, and we knew how they need to be recorded to do them full justice.

This approach threw up Al's first conundrum.

'Err Nick . . . what would you say about doing the drums on a drum machine?'

'You what?'

Now, I could have been forgiven for getting straight on the blower to the Drummers' Union for this heresy (spoiler: there isn't one). After all, I'd been playing these tunes for a while now and knew how to play them inside out. That, however, was not the issue. To run the tracks through the new(ish) MIDI digital tech, everything needed to be knitted together with extreme timing accuracy. This meant the drums. Me. As I mentioned before, drums and tempo aren't necessarily a fixed thing, but with the metronomic tech stuff clattering away, the drums needed to be spot on. Hence Al's little 'chat'. If we'd gone down the route of using real drums on all of the tracks, we'd have eaten through our studio time far too quickly, not to mention the entire budget, just getting them into the right state to do the songs justice. Although we had three weeks and ten grand, it still would not be enough to accommodate real drums.

The reality is I had no qualms whatsoever in getting to grips with a drum machine. I was willing to do anything, and if that meant subverting myself to the demon drum machine, so be it. Truth be told I was a bit miffed that a drum machine was going to be doing a lot of my parts. What drummer wouldn't be? I had to swallow that pride and get stuck in.

So, with pride now firmly swallowed, I was given an Alesis HR-16 state-of-the-art (for 1989) drum machine and the instruction manual. I was then shut away in a tiny broom cupboard in FON, first to work out how to program the damn thing and, second, to get accurate versions of my drum parts on the songs for the album.

I spent most of the first couple of weeks in FON in that cupboard. I had some cassettes of rough demo recordings we'd had done of the songs, so I at least had a template to work to. Slowly, I began building each song, hoping to get all the right parts in all the right places. Once I thought I was about there, I'd get Jarvis to play along and sing away in the broom cupboard, to check the verses and middle-eights were all the correct length and the drum fills were in their proper spots. Once we agreed it was right, and I was happy with all the twiddly bits I would've played on a real kit, the drums were then laid onto tape in the main studio control room. I then got on with the next one while the others started adding their bits. Sounds easy, yeah? Nope. It was *so* frustrating. I'd had little experience of programming drums, so this was literally learning on the job. Drumming was something I found easy(ish) to do. It came so naturally. But here I had to surgically dissect what I was physically doing and rebuild the robo-drummer, all by peering into a tiny screen atop the Alesis HR-16. Many a time I wanted to chuck the thing out the window and be done with it, but the broom cupboard had no window so I just had to soldier on. Plenty of times Al had to reassure me that the end product would justify the hours and hours of head-banging horror I was going through.

But, as the tracks started to be fleshed out with bass, guitar, Farfisa and so on, I could appreciate that Al's approach was right. The songs were sounding amazing, far better than if we had toiled away getting drums miked up and capturing that one brilliant take. Having said that, we did do at least one song with all real drums. 'Down By The River' was a gentle waltz-time doom ballad that needed to be recorded with all of us together, playing in the same room. So, at least we (I) had a bit of a break from Alesis hell.

Once all the drums were done I could sit back, relax and marvel at the textures now being added to the record. As the tunes are originally written and played by five people, you can only get five things (six, if you include the voice) happening at any one time when you play live. In the studio, we had the freedom to add multiple layers to the music, and to hear these songs fleshed out with choirs, strings and synth lines was just brilliant. Experimenting with swinging microphones and incidental sounds are always the things that make a record so special. Jarvis is also king of adding odd little vocal ticks to tracks, while his 'drunk-sounding' backing vocals brought vivid atmospherics to the recordings. It's things like that which really brought the songs to life for me. I added my own embellishments, too – cymbal swooshes using softheaded mallets, tambourines and so on.

Most of the songs ended up sounding radically different from the live versions, some more than others. The reliance on technology drove the sound in a very electro way.

'Love Is Blind' is a pretty straightforward reproduction of the live performance, albeit very much beefed up with the addition of choir and strings at the start. Jarvis's drunken yelps at the start give the song an unearthly feel and set the tone for the record, giving you the feeling you're in for something different. As it drops for the verse, the chunky treatment of the Alesis drums and Steve's bass really come to the fore. Jarvis added some acoustic guitar here to give it some drive. The sound is so solid, and it would've been very time-consuming and expensive to achieve this with real drums. The stereo call and answer of Candida's fuzz-treated Farfisa and Russell's violin melody is very effective. The song in its entirety is a grandiose statement of intent for the whole album. (Spoiler alert number one: Check out 'Sunday Sunday' by Blur and see where they got the rhythmic idea for that song.)

'Don't You Want Me Anymore' is, again, another fairly straight rendition of the live tune, and one of the oldest on the record. We added some extra keyboard lines added and again the Alesis drums give the track a solid feel. Russell's violining is augmented by extra strings. The acoustic guitar in the chorus was a lovely touch; it really brings that section to life.

'She's Dead' is a real tearjerker. (Spoiler alert number two: Listen to 'Honey' by Bobby Goldsbro after reading this, and check the, err, 'influence'.) Jarvis was always brilliant at a bit of balladeering and this is no exception. Both FON and Al's capabilities allow the keyboard layers to build and build so that they really pull on the heartstrings. The oboe – or what sounds like an oboe – towards the end is the real pay-off line for me. Love this song.

Is 'Separations' Russell's finest hour? Certainly in his violin repertoire. It's also perhaps the only one of the Eastern European disco-type songs that fully made it on to the record. The high drama is encapsulated by the extra strings going for it with Jarvis's singing, beautifully counterpoised by the almost pathetic-sounding Yamaha Portasound. I'm actually playing real drums on this track, albeit with brushes to give a softer sound, and then going for it on the cymbals at the end for dramatic effect. It's probably the most overwrought track on the record.

'Down By The River' is another song of a decent vintage. It's more doom balladeering and drunk-style background vocals from Jarvis. It's a lovely song, though. Once again, I played real drums with brushes on this one for that softer tone. There's some fab slide guitar from Russell, too. You could easily hear Nick Cave doing a treatment on this one.

Side 2, for the vinylistas, opens with 'Countdown', originally called 'Death 3', as it was our third stab at a disco number using the Portasound after 'Death Comes To Town'. 'Countdown' is an almost totally synthetically reconstructed song, but it's a faithful(ish) version of what we played live, only on stage it was done with loads less keyboards and certainly lacked a lot of the flourishes we hear on the record. We made a radically remixed and speeded up version for a single release later on, but we'll get to that in due course.

The centrepiece of the record is 'My Legendary Girlfriend'. This was a real stomper when played live and one of our favourites and, I think, one of our (small) fanbase's favourites too. Jarvis had asked me to play a 'Barry White' beat when this song was written. Now, this could be taken to mean a number of things. I knew Barry's stuff from his hits in the seventies, and from him being played at the parties of my youth, so I had a fairly good idea of where Jarvis wanted to go. Essentially, it needed a beat where each snare hit is on each beat of the bar, as opposed to every second and fourth beat. Very much as you might hear on a lot of Tamla Motown records from the sixties. Live, it was more often than not the set closer, as we could stretch out the start and allow Jarvis to tease out the squeaks and squeals, the whispering and the panting, Russell weaving some ghostly feed-back from the Rosetti guitar, ratcheting up the atmosphere so that, on a given signal, perhaps an arm being dropped, we'd drop into the full verse, bringing in the bass synth and bass guitar. This was always a great moment – the pent-up frustration and atmosphere boiling over the top and then going even further into a crashing chorus. The Alesis drums were perfect for this, as played live the song was (is) a really hard work out, and as fatigue creeps in, tempo and control are the first casualties. Thus the machine's control allowed the scene and pressure to inexorably, and seamlessly, build. Jarvis is ad-libbing in the background again, as if shouting in the street after an evening in the pub, but it's great at providing an emotional punch, the yelps and twitches really drawing the listener in. It somehow has passion and meaning. (Jarvis had used this technique to a limited degree on earlier Pulp records, but this time it was different: more pronounced, more deliberate, more effective.)

We knew 'My Legendary Girlfriend' was a winner as we were recording it. It seemed to have the same effect on me as all those formative records from my youth. An ability to reach inside you and do something to your emotional state. Music as a way of opening your head and heart and whisking it around somehow. So, if it was doing that to me (and, after all, I'd heard the song as a live entity for ages now), what could it do to a *new* listener who'd never even heard of Pulp?

'Death II' was really a working title that never went away. It's another live stormer that gets the full-on electro treatment here. Having said that, there's some real drums present mixed in with the Alesis. It's great to hear 'Ottawan' and even 'Gene Pitney' get oblique mentions, but, with hindsight, I feel the electro treatment was a bit over the top on this one. But what a fab pop track. Any notions that Pulp were a mere band of indie glumsters, epitomised by the *Freaks* era, were well and truly dashed with 'Death II'.

'This House Is Condemned' is, well, rather a seismic musical change in the Pulp world. The latter part of the eighties had seen the emergence of house music and later acid house. These dance movements seemed like the start of a new era; it was totally different music seemingly from another universe.

Our first exposure to this kind of thing was Steve 'Silk' Hurley's 'Jack Your Body', originally released as a single in 1986. It was a regular spin in The Limit, and always divided the crowd. Steve (Mackey) had discovered a legendary club in London called Shoom, and he and Jarvis started to explore the rave scene with gusto. It seemed everyone was experimenting with house-type tracks around this time, as it was everywhere, and once you'd been to a couple of rave 'events' you'd eschew 'normal' guitar-based music to listen to the new electronic, hypnotic house beats. We were no different, I guess. This track was borne out of this experimentation, and is the last Pulp song to feature a Russell vocal (ironically, I don't recall Russell ever going to a rave at all during this period). His lyrics and vocals add a surreal element to the track yet in a very 'Pulp' way. Not surprisingly, there's very few actual instruments played on this track; it's almost all machinery, apart from some cut-up guitar from Russ.

Now it sounds terribly 'of its time', and it is.

I'm not sure why this track was included on the album when 'Death Goes To Town' was not. Maybe 'Death Comes To Town' was seen as an ancient track, what with songs like 'Countdown' and 'Death II' being fresher takes on the Portasound disco vibe we'd been exploring. For me, though, 'Death Comes To Town' would've been a far better song to include on the album, and maybe 'This House . . .' could have been released under a different guise. Probably wishful hindsight thinking from me, but it's still a mystery why we abandoned 'Death Comes . . .', which only saw the light of day as a B-side, and then only the extended 12" mix.

So, that was it. We came out of FON convinced we had created a fabulous album and record companies would be falling over themselves to sign us up. And if not all record companies, then surely FON Records would see that we'd produced a piece of work to make waves on the music scene. A different kind of pop music that had real depth and breadth, delivered with modern panache, scathingly sharp lyrics and killer melodies. It was obvious to us. BUT, was it obvious to anyone else?

No. It was not.

FON still could not see where Pulp would 'fit in' at the present time. No other record company wanted to know. Except one. Fire of London.

18

Return to Fire

(Going Back to Find Her)

A stark choice befell us: sign back to Fire or stump up the ten grand we'd spent at FON and keep hawking the new record around. Russell, Jarvis and Candida *really* did not relish the thought of having to deal with Fire again. But, once more, does a band really exist without releasing records? *Freaks* had taken what seemed like forever to be released. The same couldn't happen again, could it?

For myself, I'd not had any dealings with Fire and really just wanted to have a record out with my name on. And I knew this was a great record. Eventually, and with no alternative presenting itself, everyone was talked round to re-signing with Fire so that *Separations* – so named as the band were separated to the four corners of the land – would get a release. Russell was the most reluctant. He'd been the foremost Pulp organiser and so the one to deal with Fire. He was ready to quit Pulp rather than do Fire again. Thankfully, he didn't go that far, but this was definitely the last throw of the dice as far as he was concerned.

Thus, we made the leap. 'My Legendary Girlfriend' was selected as the lead single off the album, with the expectation, of course, that the single would be released followed by the album, then another single. All pretty standard stuff. But what did we get? Nothing. *Nada.*

History appeared to be repeating itself. Pulp had a record to go and Fire were holding off on releasing it. The frustration was incredible. Had we just done all that work of writing and recording for it to sit on a shelf somewhere, gathering mould? I thought the way things worked was bands got together, wrote a dozen songs, recorded them, someone released them and you went on to go on tour and have a degree of musical stardom. Not necessarily playing Wembley, but making a living at least. So this seemingly unnecessary wait was awful. We did hear that Fire and a whole swathe of British indie record companies were having terrible problems getting their releases into the shops, as both The Cartel and Rough Trade distribution organisations were going bust. But this held little water with us. We had signed a record deal and wanted our record OUT.

The upshot was that Pulp stopped playing live, pretty much. Why put your energies into gigging when you had no record to plug? Getting Pulp in the same room was now also logistically difficult, us being so spread out.

It was around this time I upped sticks and headed for the big city lights. Steve was living in a 14th floor squat in Camberwell, South London, and mentioned that there was a room coming up. I jumped at the chance. I was working in Bankrupt Clothing Company's warehouse in Sheffield and asked them if the London store needed any assistants. Yes, came the reply, so I had a job to go to straightaway. Sheffield was becoming a bit stale and lots of folk were seeking their fortunes elsewhere, mostly in London. I really fancied the idea of living in the nation's capital and this seemed an easy way of giving it a go.

I paid Steve's outgoing flatmate £50 for his key to the flat – actually, it was journalist, Barbara Ellen, who gave me the key, as she was his girlfriend at the time – and lo! I was a resident of Crossmount House, Sultan Street, SE5.

Crossmount House, just off the Walworth Road, was a sixties tower block, typical of the type found all over the UK – council run to provide low-cost housing to all manner of people. It wasn't particularly pretty from the outside, but the flat was perfect for our needs: two bedrooms, a small kitchen, a tiny bathroom and a living room. What made Crossmount so desirable was that the living room was north-facing, meaning the view was breathtaking. One side of the living room was all glass, meaning an uninterrupted view across central London. At the extreme right you could see St Paul's Cathedral and to the extreme left was Battersea Power Station (of Pink Floyd's *Animals* fame). In between you had a panoramic view of the Houses of Parliament, Big Ben and all that. You could spend many an hour just gazing out of the window onto the cityscape below. At night the room would be illuminated every couple of minutes by the headlights of Heathrow-bound aircraft as they turned to make their final approach to the airport.

However, some of the fellow residents of Crossmount were less indisposed towards us squatters. I really don't know why. We didn't bother them very much. We only had a couple of parties over the years, our music wasn't any louder than anyone else's and we certainly never pissed in the lift like some folk obviously did. Note to potential high-rise residents: If you find yourself getting into the lift and someone's abandoned fridge is already in there, DO NOT OPEN IT. Like I did once. The horrific smell does not leave the lift until you do, 14 floors later. Also, if when you get in the lift and someone has decided that was the best place to leave a rotting piece of meat, get out and see if the other lift is working (which is hit and miss). Riding a slow ascent up 14 floors accompanied by a rotting piece of meat is less than optimum in my book. Oh, and walking up 14 flights is no picnic, either.

Each morning I would get on the number 12 bus into central London to work flogging jeans just off the famous Carnaby Street, the swinging fashion centre of town. Or so it was in the sixties:

even by this stage it was morphing into a tourist trap. Still, it was employ.

I also met up with some old Limit mates from Sheffield, Mick and Laura Deeley. They were running a small pub just off Shoreditch High Street, the Ship and Blue Ball. So I signed up to do a few shifts a week pulling pints, to supplement my meagre shop pay. Also, it was a great way to interact with some friendly faces from back home.

Working in a pub, especially if it's busy, is usually a good laugh if you have good colleagues, which the Ship had. The locals were a good bunch too, and we could have some good north/south banter. This was when Shoreditch was dog rough, before it became hipster heaven. Even the pub up the way would still have strippers 'performing' on Sunday lunchtimes (I went once and it was really grim).

I'd often travel to my shifts at the Ship by bike. Cycling in London was a pleasure compared to Sheffield. No hills, you see (or certainly none of the vertiginous type found up north). One time I was cycling back to Camberwell after my shift. It was about two in the morning, and I was pottering along the almost deserted city streets when a policeman jumped out in front of me and indicated for me to stop – Dixon of Dock Green-style, the palm of his hand facing me.

'Where you goin' son?'

'Home. Camberwell.'

'You ain't got no lights on. That's an offence. Where you been workin?'

'Pub in Shoreditch.'

'You look like you've just come from Spitalfields.' Spitalfields was still a wholesale meat market back then. I was wearing a white smock-type top that I suppose you could imagine a Spitalfields butcher wearing.

'You bin drinkin'?'

'Might have had a couple of halves,' I lied. Not that I was sloshed, but if I'd been driving a car he'd have carted me rightly off.

The policeman drew himself as tall as he could. 'You do know it is an offence to be drunk in charge of a pedal cycle, don't you?'

'Really?'

'AND to be riding at night without suitable lighting?'

'But I only live the other side of the river, and it's well-lit all the way.'

'Hmmm,' he said, relaxing his shoulders. 'On yer way son. And get some lights.'

And off I scooted, scot-free. Smashing the system, one crack at a time!

Socialising in London was a lot more difficult than in Sheffield. Definitely a lot more expensive, but everyone knows that. In Sheffield you just wandered down The Hallamshire or The Washington with no particular plans, and you'd always bump into someone and end up at a mad house party or two (my record was five in a night, but I don't like to brag). In London this was just not the case. If you wanted to meet up it needed military-style planning. With folks being spread out across the city, a suitably equidistant area would have to be selected, and then did anyone know of a suitable place to meet that was decent? Nowadays, everywhere in London has a good selection of trendy, chi-chi pubs and bars open 'til late, but this was simply not the case in 1990. It was exhausting. Remember: this was before everyone had a mobile phone in his or her pocket. But what we did have was pagers. Yes, like the things doctors in hospitals have. You'd call a central number from a phone box, dictate your short message to the operative on the other end and to whom the message was destined for, the operator would then repeat your message back and then they'd send it to said recipient. Usually the message would simple, like a pub name and a time. But sometimes we had to talk in code if discussing something a little more . . . let's say, dubious.

It was a serious palaver, so we tried a different tack. We decided we should explore a bit closer to home (i.e. Camberwell), the idea being to see if there was a local scene or crowd we could infiltrate. The best, most amenable option would be our *chosen pub*. And that pub was The Grove, on the other side of Camberwell Green. The clientele there didn't seem to growl at you as you went in. However, we went there as often as our pockets would allow, but try as we might, no one would acknowledge you as a regular face. Vic Reeves and Bob Mortimer were regulars at The Grove, and we couldn't even break into *their* crowd.* Back to the drawing board.

One pub we gravitated to in Central London was Shuttleworth's. I'm not sure that was the actual name of the place, but it was the cellar bar for the Phoenix Theatre on Charing Cross Road. You sort of had to be a member but could often blag your way in. It was a quaint and calm place to have a drink in the middle of town, and it subsequently became a bit of an indie musicians' hangout into the mid-nineties.

Having said that, in 1989/90, the M25 rave scene was at its height. Steve had become an advocate after having some revelatory experiences at Shoom, and he and Jarvis had been to a couple of early clandestine raves and were evangelical about the atmosphere and vibe going off. It was like nothing they'd ever experienced before.

This needed checking out. Steve managed to get hold of some tickets for an event called 'Sunrise', to be held at an old film studio in West London. Just getting in the place was pandemonium. There was no semblance of a queue, just a mad scrum of many hundreds all trying to get through the massive metal gates as quickly as possible.

Once in, we regained our composure so we could move on to the next part of the evening: score an 'E'. The entire house and subsequent acid house scene was built on the energising and euphoric

---

* Vic and Bob were all over the place at this time, with their hit Channel 4 TV show *Big Night Out*. Our paths would cross again later.

effects of ecstasy. Drop an 'E' and dance like a goon all night. Fab, I'm in. I had never had an 'E' before but had heard tales from as far back as the early eighties. Back then, the soul groovers took it to enhance their night out and get all touchy-feely with their partner.

Anyway, we managed to find our 'man' and all necked our 'Es' at the same time. Thirty minutes later we were all in a euphoric state, hearing the music in such a new way that it was literally blowing our minds. Everyone around was similarly affected and dancing with abandon. It was incredible. What was most unusual was that every other person there would be giving you a hug or just saying, 'Nice one, geezer!' Ecstasy really was a potent 'love' drug: you just couldn't stop grinning, high fiving and dancing. Soul II Soul's 'Keep On Movin'' was *the* track to play, and when it dropped, everyone just went off even further. You really did feel like this was something that could change the world.

Once we made it back to the flat sometime the next day, it was difficult to comprehend what we'd just been a part of. Was this our generation's 'punk' movement, ready to rip up the rule book all over again? Maybe.

Pirate radio was the best place to hear the sounds we'd been raving to a few hours before, and acid house became the sound of Crossmount. What I loved about it was that you never knew, or cared, what the track was called or who was the composer or performer. I loved the idea that it was all totally anonymous. If the track moved you in the moment, that was all you needed. This anonymity didn't last, though; names started appearing to attract the punters, as if at a gig, which, to me, seemed to go against one of the central tenets of this 'new way'.

It wasn't long before the authorities began clamping down on these illegal parties, and the venues had to move further afield and become more clandestine. It became that you had to buy your ticket for the event without knowing where it would take place, leading to a mad cat-and-mouse chase of calling various numbers to eventually get the right address, and off everyone would go at full pelt, zooming around the M25 to find the rave.

The most notorious event for me was held in an enormous aircraft hangar at White Waltham Airfield, near Maidenhead, Berskshire. Thousands attended, most of them suitably 'E'd' off their heads. We had scored ours in the chaotic car park and they were a bit of a dud: no euphoria, like at Sunrise. But still, you could see this thing that was happening was something very special. There was never any trouble at raves. You'd get more aggro down the local pub.

We readjusted after by crashing out on Brighton beach, all of us burning the side of our faces as we slept on the pebbles. Next day the party was all over the tabloids. Pics of ravers all wide-eyed and gurning and doing the 'big fish, little fish, cardboard box' dance were accompanied by headlines such as 'Ecstasy Airport'. Alongside the heavy police tactics and the increasing difficulty of finding an event that was not about to be closed down, this took the shine off going to these raves. 'Ecstasy Airport' was the last big rave I went to.

★ ★ ★

The idea that you didn't have to go to a nightclub or disco to get yer rocks off had been fermenting in the mid to late eighties, eventually coalescing into a new type of night out: the warehouse party. These were real do-it-yourself events. Thatcher's deindustrialisation had left loads of big empty spaces all over the place, Sheffield being no exception. They were in desperate need of being rented out. So, a few of us got together and decided to throw our own warehouse party.

We found a building in the centre of Sheffield and rented it for a pittance (the party would help to cover the rest of the rent). All totally illegal of course, since the owners didn't have a clue what we were planning on doing there, but you could get enough punters through the doors through word of mouth in the hope you didn't get raided by the fuzz.

We set up the place with decks and a PA, stocked up with loads of beers from the cash and carry, and booked Sheffield's premiere warehouse DJs, Parrot and Winston, to officiate. Everyone would take turns on the door taking the £5 or so entrance fee and keeping an eye out.

P&W went down really well and I got to meet loads of new people, most notably a bunch of lads who turned up when I was minding the door. They had an older guy in tow, who wanted to haggle with me to get in on the cheap.

'Come on mate, we've just been playing over at Take Two.' (Take Two was a music venue in the east end of Sheffield outside of the city centre.) 'It's late and we can only stay a couple of hours.'

'OK, £15 for all of you,' and in they went, caps pulled tight on their heads and collars turned up.

The older guy came back out about ten minutes later for a smoke and we struck up a conversation about how the gig was. The chap turned out to be called Gareth, the band's manager. We talked about music for a bit and I told him I was in a band called Pulp and how we were quite popular locally.

'Why don't we swap gigs? We could support you lot in Sheffield and you can support us in Manchester?' said Gareth.

'Err, dunno about that.' I mean, who was this bloke? Could be a right chancer. I don't think I had enough confidence with the other Pulpers at the time to say yes and commit us to this possible Mancunian folly. Anyway, I bet his band is shit, I thought. 'I'll pass. But what did you say your band's called, Gareth?'

'The Stone Roses.'

19

Waiting for Everything to Start

(Forever in my Dreams)

I could hear the glass smashing in the distance. The air was thick with excitement, a fervour I'd rarely experienced before. It was 31 March 1990.

Thousands had descended on central London to demonstrate and march against Thatcher's hated Poll Tax (where citizens would pay a flat fee towards local services, independent of income, meaning a pauper would end up paying the same as a millionaire). Unsurprisingly, the police had turned violent towards the marchers and the event had descended into a full-scale riot.

I'd been present (kind of) at a similar event in the Miners' Strike of 1984–85, during which the National Union of Mineworkers, led by Arthur Scargill, attempted to prevent the mass closure of collieries across the north through picketing and protests.

The Battle of Orgreave was a violent clash – the worst of its kind – between picketers and South Yorkshire Police. Mum's pottery business was based in Catcliffe, between Sheffield and Rotherham, and was just down the road from the Orgreave Coking Works, which had become a central flashpoint in the dispute. Miners had been picketing the works to stop the production of coal into coke for use in the steel industry (remember our lesson on mining from earlier?). It was

18 June, a roasting hot day, and I had to accompany Mum down to the pottery, and you could just feel that something was going to go off. Again, the air was charged with it. Plus, hundreds of striking miners were milling about, enjoying a pint at The Plough, getting ready to march on Orgreave.

My sympathies, as with just about all my contemporaries, of course, lay with the miners, who were fighting for jobs and communities and heroically sticking it to the horrific establishment figure that was Margaret Thatcher, who'd been deindustrialising urban northern England at a frightening rate, throwing millions on to the dole. She was everything we hated about the political class and the holier-than-thou posh folk that have forever seemed to govern Britain (certainly in my lifetime). My Mum, however, was a Thatcher sympathiser with a deep-seated hatred of the left. Quite how or why this was the case, given her working-class, poverty-stricken background, is a bit of a mystery. I, however, grew to despise those who'd support such entrenched capitalist ideas.

Russell was a keen anti-establishment fighter and would stand on picket lines and rattle a collection bucket for the strikers. He'd also adorned his guitar with 'Coal Not Dole' stickers. A curious disconnect, however, was that the kind of folk who worked the industrial jobs now being dissolved by the Tories would often be the kind to ridicule us oddballs. Steel work and mining folk were tough, no-nonsense, straight-talking people. They usually had no truck with us 'artsy' types, especially those with a burning desire to ponce about on stage, trading daft disco music.

I didn't see any of the actual violence that day at Orgreave, but watched avidly on the (twisted) news, marvelling that I too had been there that day. Sort of.

Same thing with the Poll Tax riot. That day, I finished my shift at Bankrupt Clothing and got out onto the streets to see what was happening. I headed on to Regent Street, which was packed with people all moving towards Piccadilly. I could hear shouting and sporadic glass-breaking, but couldn't see any action (which was so frustrating). I got as far as Piccadilly Circus, where the crowd was so thick I could go no further. We were surrounded by mounted police and the vibe was intimidating. The air was still thick with expectation, and it seemed like all it would take was one small spark for it all to kick off. It was so odd to be in that big a crowd that couldn't go anywhere, but that also had no destination. Everyone was just kind of milling about, not really knowing what to do. I later learned that all the action was in Trafalgar Square and none of it ever reached as far as Piccadilly Circus. I hung around for a few hours and eventually made my way back to Crossmount.

★ ★ ★

The months continued to tick over with no sign of Fire releasing, or getting anywhere near releasing, *Separations*. Pulp had pretty much stopped doing gigs by this time. In the years 1989 and 1990 we only played two, and both of those were at The Leadmill back in Sheffield, the latter supporting Manchester-based current weirdos du jour World of Twist. They'd been getting loads of press in the weekly music papers and we were of the notion that they must have seen us in action before and decided to rip us off wholesale. It was galling to see a band ploughing a similarish furrow as us, yet we could barely get a look-in at *NME* or *Melody Maker*. BUT, a gig's a gig, and we had, for us, been away a long time, so this was our way of jumping back in the saddle and maybe even securing a positive bit of press by hanging on to World of Twist's coat-tails, no matter how much it stuck in the craw. Suck it up, folks; it won't be the last time.

At least as support we had no way of doing an over-elaborate, homemade stage set, and so had the mind space to concentrate on actually *playing* the songs rather than worrying if there was enough dry ice around our legs. This turned out to be a good thing, as we were killer. The time away from the stage had given us even more of a desire to make it work.

The only positive movement from Fire during this time was, of course, that 'My Legendary Girlfriend' had been chosen to be the lead single off the LP. And rightly so. We got Parrot and Winston to do a 'remix' of 'This House Is Condemned' for the B-side*, and Jarvis designed the sleeve while he and Steve got to work sorting out how we could make a video for the princely sum of £200.

To make a music video on a shoestring budget it's handy to have two filmmaking students in the band. This gave us access to a studio to film it in, plus all the gear from Central Saint Martins and a smattering of video-making knowledge. We also managed to secure the help of some of the other students, mainly Martin Wallace, the only other northerner on Jarvis's course.

After an aborted attempt filming in a room above a pub in the East End (way too dark), we set up in a film studio at the uni, where we would mime to the song while we were filmed from various angles, then we'd cut it all together.

Problem: we didn't have a drum kit in London for me to use in the video. It wasn't feasible to get a van to bring mine down from Sheffield and we didn't know anyone we could borrow one off (or that drum kits can be hired by the day). Instead, Jarvis and I made a pretend kit out of cardboard, black paper and tinfoil for the cymbals. How very Pulp.

We wrapped filming in a day (probably an afternoon) and Jarvis, Steve and Martin Wallace edited it. Looking at it now, with some distance, it has a certain homespun charm; everyone looks like they're

---

* The remix on the flip side is a real dance-floor head-scratcher. Well, could you dance to it? Only maybe. Different? It divided opinion, that's for sure.

trying a bit hard, except Jarvis, who seems rather inanimate (for him). It is very much of its time, I suppose: Pulp desperately trying to do something grandiose but with a budget of pennies. I thought it was fabulous. It was, of course, the first time for me in a pop video. One step closer to the Promised Land? Yes, but it was still a long way away.

So far away, in fact, I had changed jobs. I decided that working in shops was a deadbeat career and I should use my teaching degree. Pulp were no more likely to make it than I was to become an astronaut (or so it seemed). So, I enquired with Wandsworth Council Education Department to see about any D&T posts in the borough.

Wandsworth was only a few miles down the road from Camberwell, and seemed as good a place to start as any. I'd already decided it wasn't a good idea to teach at the comp local to Crossmount House; didn't fancy seeing my weekday charges at the weekend or wandering around in my local shop. Thankfully, Wandsworth said yes, come for an interview. London comprehensives were always on the lookout for fresh meat; new teachers are cheap compared to grizzled old hacks with elbow patches.

My interview was a success. The council bods said they'd find me a teaching position to do my probationary year (all new qualified teachers must do one to complete their training). 'Great, but I have one request,' I said. 'Can I only do three days' a week?' I knew teaching was tough and I wanted a bit of freedom for other stuff, mostly Pulp-ing, and/or getting my 'shit' together for that week's teaching. Or so my plea went. I didn't have any rent to pay (I was living in a squat, remember), so I figured losing two-fifths of my pay was acceptable.

This was clearly an unusual request. The panel conferred and came back with 'What about three and a half days?'

'Done.' This meant I'd complete my probationary year by just doing it part-time. Result.

Subsequently, I was appointed to Burntwood School for Girls to teach D&T. Gulp. If anyone thinks teaching at an all girls' school is an easy option, they are deluding themselves. It was hard, and I was glad of the one and a half days' 'rest' I had negotiated. Even still, each evening as I got back to Crossmount, a good hour or two's head down on the sofa was required. To say the girls were 'high-spirited' would be an understatement. Having said that, I only had one pupil fall out of the window. Good job/ Unfortunately (delete as appropriate) we were on the ground floor and not any higher up. I was also talked into doing an hour a week of Computer Technology, despite hardly ever having sat in front of a computer. Needless to say, it was not a successful venture. Still, there were a couple of youngish new teachers there, and we all got on just great.

One conundrum I faced during my time at the school was when one or two of the classes went through a phase of making what would now be called crack pipes, only these were for smoking pot, as crack hadn't been invented then. Should I confess to knowing what it was they were making, perhaps leading others to wonder why I knew exactly what they were for? Or should I just ignore them and feign ignorance should it ever come up? I decided that rather than draw attention to the pipes, I was best served letting it go. Didn't want the grief. This kind of summed up my attitude to teaching: couldn't be doing with all the fuss and bother. I never gave out homework, as I'd only have to mark it, so why bother? Teaching requires dedication, which I really don't think I had. There was no 'calling' for me, as such, and of course the best bits were the holidays.

In March 1991, 'My Legendary Girlfriend' finally got its release: the first Pulp record of the new era and featuring my good self (well, drums programmed by me at least). It was also the first Pulp record for almost exactly four years. It seems like the hiatus did us the world of good. The single garnered fab reviews in the inkies and was awarded the coveted Single of the Week in the ol' *NME*, courtesy of all-round good egg Stuart Maconie:

Hold the front page! Stop the presses! This is what I thought working for the NME *would be like. At the fag end of a very ordinary singles column, we grudgingly sling on one last disc . . . and it is fantastic! Do you hear me, you dropouts! Fantastic! A throbbing ferment of nightclub soul and teen opera. World Of Twist play the theme from* Shaft *with Cathal Coughlan on vocals. Mysterious and grand. Maybe we could have done without the rude noises, but let's not carp. Steve Lamacq tells me that this is the worst song in their set. Which means that Pulp are the greatest rock 'n' roll band in the world. I think.*

Wow, that's some review. Thanks Stuart. The World of Twist thing was still a bit grating, though, but never mind – at least it gave the reader something to grab on to; something that was seen as NOW.

From this moment on things became different forever. This was now Pulp's year zero. The ascent began, imperceptibly so at first, but there was no doubt we were on an upward trajectory.

Pulp's stars had finally aligned. Since Magnus and Manners left, Pulp had struggled to retain a stable line-up. That had been solved with Steve's and my introduction. Jarvis was moving away from speccy rake-thin geek in a charity shop suit to a smouldering sex-god in contacts and a natty line in seventies-inspired garb that demanded attention rather than ridicule. We had the songs in the can ready to go and they were unlike anything else at that time.

At the end of the late eighties/early nineties, music was pretty much dominated by a meld of rave scene and indie in the shape of 'baggy' and 'Madchester', which spawned bands like Happy Mondays and The Stone Roses, the latter of whom, in '89, had released one of the most earth-shattering debut albums ever heard. The early nineties were also a bit of a transatlantic battle between the plaid beshirted Americans like Nirvana, Pearl Jam, L7 and other grungeniks, and the fey British indie kids of 'shoegaze', who hid behind their fringes and played fuzzy sound textures coupled with vague shimmering vocals. Bands like Ride, Lush, Chapterhouse and Slowdive. It's safe to say, Pulp didn't fit in with any of these contemporaries. Any student of British rock music will know that the industry tends to be cyclical, and that whatever and whomever is riding high today can be easily washed away tomorrow. The fickle finger, moving on to the next big thing. Would it be Pulp?

It's all well and good getting rave reviews in *NME* and *Melody Maker*, but what did the people out in the real world think? Looking back over radio and club DJ reaction sheets, collated by Rough Trade Media Promotions, it was a real mixed bag:

I don't feel it's a radio track. Will not be playing. – Paul Flower, BBC West Midlands

I don't like that one, I think it's shit! Saw them supporting World of Twist at The Leadmill, they were better live but this was still pretty dirgy. – Piccadilly Radio (Manchester)

Played it four times last Friday and people coming up to me asking what it was. Totally mind absorbing, one of the few records to make the hairs stand up on the back of your neck. – Tim Everett, Vapour Club, Telford

What a start, what a let down. When the bubble burst it sounded like The Human League, the spoken word is brilliant! The B-side sounds like someone has died on a drum machine. – Jeff Jackson, Radio Brunel

Waiting for Everything to Start (Forever in my Dreams)

After seeing the band live a number of times I found the record lacking in their sense of humour & strange dislocated rhythm. – Morgan, The Leadmill, Sheffield

Really kind of good, kind of brooding, menacing then building into an almost funky chic-esqueness and Wolfgang Press. More than above average. – Karl, Club Culture, Liverpool

Sorry I couldn't be more positive but I really can't stand this! It's like The Human League demo from '82 or thereabouts . . . Maybe I'm missing the point. – Angus Beaty, Paraphernalia/Independiente club nights, London

Yep, there was still work to do.

With more members of the band in London than out, the logical idea was to play more gigs in the capital. Try and build on the positive press reviews and keep winning people over. If those people just happened to be influential press, TV/radio folk or folk from other record companies, then all the better. That was the only tactic available to us. We knew we had the power to turn a crowd into fans. We just needed a bit of exposure.

It's around this time that Pulp made their TV debut, on *The New Sessions* – a programme that showcased up-and-coming bands and was broadcast to various ITV regions, though not all. In March 1991, they filmed (and broadcast) us playing four or five songs at a gig at The Leadmill, where we were once again supporting World of Twist. This was just the kind of thing we needed to get the message out there – trouble is, it went out on a weekday middle-of-the-night slot, so hardly ideal fuel towards our attempt at pop-world domination. Still, it's a start, and we were all so very chuffed we'd been the telly playing our music.

What Pulp needed now was someone to pursue leads within the

music biz, someone to help us in our quest to *get heard*, be it on the radio, TV or just to get better and bigger gigs. Russell had been doing a lot of behind the scenes stuff for the band. I'd also had a go at trying to drum up gigs in London. I recall doing something a bit different and sending a videotape of 'My Legendary Girlfriend' to The Venue, rather than an audio cassette tape, to try and get the booker's attention. It worked, too. He remembered the video. I think eventually we did get a gig there on the back of the videotape. All well and good, but what Pulp needed was a proper band manager to undertake all the day-to-day hustle it takes to become successful.

At one of the Leadmill gigs around this time old Pulp head and The Mission guitarist, Simon Hinkler, finally managed to get his then girlfriend to actually see Pulp. For one reason or another, she'd always missed our previous gigs, and Simon had been badgering her for ages to do something to help Pulp. He'd seen Jarvis's – and by extension Pulp's – potential for many years, and knew that the band could only take so many false starts. Hence his persistence in persuading Suzanne Catty to see us. Suzanne was a record executive with Hollywood Records, and had previously been employed at major record label Phonogram. She had the contacts within the British music biz and thus was perfectly placed to give us a leg up.

Thankfully, Suzanne was completely bowled over when she finally saw Pulp in action. She could see us on the biggest stages, playing to thousands, our name in huge lights. Pulp finally receiving the adulation that we certainly thought we warranted. And it came from the oddest of places. Suzanne was the complete opposite to Pulp. She was Canadian, and like many from the North American continent, was full of confidence, bravado and attitude. She knew what she wanted and she was prepared to push and push until that goal was achieved. If she had to break some balls to get there, then so be it.

Suzanne wanted to become Pulp's manager. As I've already mentioned, Pulp needed a manager, so this seemed like the perfect opportunity. Another example of just how the wheel of fortune was turning, finally, in our favour for once. I thought that the arrival of Suzanne was a sign that progress was going to be made. I hated phoning folk up, trying to persuade them to put Pulp on at their venue. It was a thankless task. Pulp's self-promotion definitely had an amateurish flavour and clearly it was not succeeding.

Suzanne Catty was the first person from the record industry to say Pulp could be a success. And not only a success, but a *massive* one. She could see the star quality in Jarvis, and that the band had everything it takes to make it BIG. What had we to lose having Suzanne fight our cause for us?

Russell lived around the corner from Simon and Suzanne's place, so they started working closely together to plot a course for Pulp to burst through the seemingly impregnable British music scene defences. But was it our time?

20

What Just Happened?

(Joyriders)

I thought the lad had a knife, the way he kept moving his hand towards his back pocket as if looking for something. I really didn't fancy being found lying in a pool of blood in a dank stairwell in South London.

'Gimme some money,' he slurred.

I had got in the lift on the 14th floor, on my way to a shift at the Ship and Blue Ball. This lad (he wasn't old enough, or nice enough, to be a 'bloke', too old to be a 'boy', and definitely not genial enough to be a 'fella' or a 'geezer') was already in there, propped up against the wall. As all British people do in lifts, I completely ignored the other person and silently wished the lift would move quicker. The atmosphere in that lift, though, was not good. The lad looked as though he'd either had a skinful or a massive spliff session. Hard to say which, but either way it was menacing. As the lift descended he moved towards me, looking at me with that glassy-eyed look we all know.

'You got any money?'

'I'm off to work mate, I've got me bus fare, that's it.' I probably had a few quid on me, not much, but I wasn't about to hand over my dosh just like that.

As the lift slowed to its stop at the ground floor, we waited for the doors to open. The lad managed to get himself between me and the door so he would exit first. Bad move on my part. We both nonchalantly started moving towards the door, and my escape to the outside world. I didn't want to push past, so hoped he would slope off as we got outside and I could go the other way and get to the bus stop. As we neared the opening, he suddenly turned and said those words: 'Gimme some money.'

I repeated my line about only having my bus fare, realising this was now officially a 'situation', since he was now blocking the exit door of Crossmount House. My mouth was now rapidly drying out as various unsavoury scenarios ran through my mind, particular when I noticed his hand movements. Two blokes entered and I took that as an opportunity to get out the door and get away. Bang! I was side swiped in the ear and grabbed by my assailant. We swung round on the concrete outside Crossmount, with me protesting about my undeserved treatment. Bang! Another strike on my head, thankfully not as hard as the initial hit. 'Gerroff!' I heard, as the two blokes who'd just passed us returned and dragged my assailant off me, who made his way off. They enquired if I was OK and went back inside. I sat on the wall and tried to catch my breath. What had just happened? An attempted mugging, that's what. Unpleasant. I contemplated continuing on to the bus stop and getting on to do my shift at the pub. But I didn't fancy encountering my attacker again, so I went back up to the 14th floor and rang Mick to tell him about the attack and that I'd not be coming in. I sat down in the empty flat and sobbed.

It was shortly after this incident that I decided London was not for me and I should return to Sheffield once my year at Burntwood Comprehensive was done.

Pulp were starting to gig more now that 'My Legendary Girlfriend' had got us a bit more positive exposure. 'Countdown' was earmarked as the next single and we had *Separations* ready on the launch pad.

The hope was that music journalists would want to check us out at one of these gigs and write about us. And we were confident they'd only write positive things when they saw our worth, thus leading to ever more folk wanting to check us out and starting a virtual circle.

In May of '91 alone we hit Subterrania, The Mean Fiddler, the Camden Underworld, the Borderline and the University of London. These were all good gigs that were decently attended. OK, we were low on the bill, but never mind; we were in the mix, as they say. The music weeklies even started using Pulp's name in bylines for the up-and-coming gigs we were involved in. This was all good stuff.

More concerts means you rehearse more. More rehearsing means more songs get written, and if they seem good enough they get inserted into the set. This is what was happening prior to the adventures of '91. 'Live On' quickly became a live favourite (it really rollicked along). 'Space' was an acid-rock wig-out that had a typical Pulp atmospheric spoken word beginning, building to a Stylophone solo, courtesy of Jarvis (he had it attached to a guitar strap so he could play it as such – you know, behind his head, foot on the monitor, ostensibly taking the piss out of 'real' guitarists. We often started sets with this. Guess you had to be there). Songs such as 'O.U.' and 'She's A Lady' will have been started and possibly debuted around this time, the Stylophone being prominent in all these songs too.

Jarvis was a bit of a Rolf Harris fan (long before all the unpleasantness emerged many years later), and Rolf had been a big advocate of the Stylophone, a pen-operated synthesizer about the size of a portable transistor radio. 'Synthesizer' might be stretching it a bit, as it really only makes a vague buzzing/whistling sound. Even so, David Bowie no less used one to great effect on his masterpiece 'Space Oddity'. Good enough for Dave, good enough for Pulp. Stick one through a decent PA, add a bit of reverb, and the Stylophone could sound fantastic.

We'd heard of a mythical deluxe Stylophone that had *two* pen styli, and with more sounds and features. Jarvis made it a quest to track one down and, of course, he managed it. The 350S. A rare beast indeed, about the size of a laptop with a bigger 'keyboard', selectable sounds, a reiteration function that was a bit like a rudimentary sequencer and a thing called 'photo control', where you could add vibrato to the played sound by waving your hand above the 350S to change the amount of light falling on it. Very, very odd. Whenever a new instrument was brought to a rehearsal it nearly always resulted in the writing of new songs, the sonic novelty sparking creation (as we will see).

Summer 1991 saw us play some odd gigs, one of which, I feel, was a massive turning point in Pulp's history, and two others that convinced us *something* was happening.

We were asked to play in the West Yorkshire town of Halifax, about an hour and a half north-west of Sheffield. The venue was a room in the North Bridge Leisure Centre normally used for badminton and exercise classes, but once a week they put on bands. So, we turned up in Kirky's battered blue Transit as usual, hoping that we'd get a good crowd, although we weren't sure as we'd never played Halifax before. Set up, sound check, get something to eat, muck about to pass the time, pre-gig drink to settle the nerves, and then step out to play.

But then something astonishing happened. The audience, who seemed quite young, started going mental. Moshing, dancing, trying to get on the stage – it was mayhem. We weren't prepared for this! But it was exhilarating, seeing kids going crazy for your music. It spurred us on in to even greater heights of fervour in our playing, as we tried to get the kids to go even more mental. We came off stage all sweaty, as usual, but this time we all looked at each other and wondered – what just happened? Whatever 'it' was, we wanted it to happen again. We'd been so used to playing to the 'semi-circle of indifference', audience watching with arms folded, at a respectful distance from the stage, rarely getting up close and personal and never too involved. From this date onwards the semi-circle of indifference never appeared again. Thank god!

On 25 July 1991, Pulp played their last ever shows at the tiny upstairs room in The Hallamshire on Sheffield's West Street, more as a thank you to The Hallamshire, than anything else. We knew we could fill the room many, many times over by this point, but we only had enough time to do two shows in one night. Get one audience in. Play. Have a break. Get another set in. It was a great night.

Then, for the first time, Pulp were asked to play overseas. France, to be precise. The French music mag *Les Inrockuptibles* hosted a series of gigs every year to showcase new, often British talent. They had got wind of Pulp through our burgeoning profile in the British music press and invited us over to play in Lille and Paris with established acts Lush and Blur. Yes please, and thank you very much! The excitement level was off the scale. This was huge for us. It's what joining a band is really all about, travelling the world, winning over the hearts and minds of the great unknown.

First we had to get there. Kirky's van, with sleeping bags thrown over amps as makeshift seats, would just not do. We couldn't afford a real tour van, so we had to make do with a standard Transit minibus with proper seats, although no separate compartment for all the equipment. We just piled the drums, amps and guitars in the back atop the seats. No special treatment for the irreplaceable Farfisa, but at least it had its black vinyl case to protect it. And, at long last, the humans all got their own seat!

We knew this was a fantastic opportunity to make a really strong impression – not just with overseas audiences, but we knew these gigs would be covered extensively in the music press back home. How would we do that? Through a new stage set, of course! This time we needed something cheap (as usual), but not too elaborate as we'd need to transport it and assemble it before each gig, and of course take it all back down before the next band went on.

Jarvis had an idea. Balls. Silver balls, in fact, suspended from a kind of child's mobile. It wouldn't take up much space in the van and it would be cheap. OK . . . We managed to get hold of a job lot of cheap plastic footballs from a wholesaler – the type that when you kick them they go anywhere except where you wanted them to go – and some cans of silver spray paint, and spent an afternoon spraying the balls silver. A whole load of bamboo canes and fishing line later, and we had two 12-foot tall silver-sphere mobiles. We piled our stuff into the minibus and set off like a gaggle of school kids on a surreal school trip.

We turned up at the first concert, in Lille near the Belgian border, parked up next to the other bands' swanky tour buses, looking like the Bash Street Kids. We started assembling our decrepit gear, while the other groups' minions looked on with a mixture of bemusement and pity. We didn't have the luxury of 'roadies'. One of Blur's roadies was assembling their drum kit with white gloves on, for god's sake, as if it were some priceless artefact!

Being the first band on, we would sound check last, if there was any time left (this is standard stuff: the main attraction gets the lion's share and the lowliest gets whatever is left). We did manage a quick sound check, but there was, of course, the small matter of hanging the homemade mobiles we'd carted across the Channel. Minutes before the doors opened, we ended up precariously balanced on each other's shoulders, getting these silver balls to hang from the lighting gantries while the French audience, now ambling in, looked on in bewilderment. It was literally a case of finish hanging the mobiles, dash backstage for a quick change and refreshment, then back out to play our first ever gig outside England.

The French kids had never seen or heard anything like it: a stick-thin singer engulfed in a huge rabbit-fur coat, yelping and twitching through ten desperate songs about love, lust, desire and fag ends, surrounded by four oddball misfits cranking out some schizoid disco at a frenetic pace best described as feverish. Plus, Jarvis had a secret weapon: a reasonable grasp of the French language and enough confidence to communicate to the kids in their mother tongue. OK, perhaps not fluent, but certainly enough to be understood. This went down a treat, and after the first few songs we seemed to have the crowd firmly on our side. More than that, we had Blur and Lush on our side, too. We retreated to our confines after the set and clinked glasses at a job well done: Sheffield 1, France 0.

After Blur closed the night everyone partied away with abandon. Our hosts were most forthcoming, with fantastic praise for us, and we immediately became good pals with the Blur party and the Lush mob.

Of course, everyone moved on to Paris for the following day's gig with bone-crushing hangovers. It's only 60-odd miles from Lille to the French capital, so we got there with plenty of time for a snoop around the Pigalle district, before sound-checking at the fabulous venue, La Cigale – a beautiful, balconied theatre that had been welcoming acts for over a hundred years. The Hallamshire it was not.

Pretty much the events of Lille were repeated but in a Parisian setting. The crowd reaction to Pulp was (to us, at least) off the scale. Jarvis's A-level French got the crowd onside from the off. Fair to say, the folks from *Les Inrockuptibles* were deeply impressed, too. It was the start of our love affair with France.

The British music press were also in attendance, and here a sea change seemed to have occurred, *NME*'s Gina Morris commenting that 'Pulp are seriously serious'. There was no Pulp are 'wacky' (a term we all hated with a passion), and we'd also managed to escape comparison with World of Twist, or any other *NME* darlings, for that matter. We'd trodden the same stage as two cool, established bands and matched them every step of the way. Sheffield 2, France 0. We partied the night away in a place where topless girls descended from ceiling holes to dance on the bar, before moving on to several très chic French discotheques, all the while shadowed by our new French fans.

Even though 1991 had been Pulp's busiest year to date it was still very much a part-time adventure, and we desperately needed an album release to keep the momentum going. The second single from *Separations*, 'Countdown', had been released in August, again to some very positive reviews and (for Pulp) decent sales. The single was heavily reworked after the FON sessions, and is quite different to the album version – a bit faster with a definite beefier treatment, laser-guided to hit the indie club dance floors across the UK and beyond.

'Countdown' was the culmination of the Yamaha Portasound experiments that had started with 'Death Comes To Town'. Pulp were fast gaining new fans, at home and abroad. Now all we needed was to get *Separations* in the shops. Trouble is, Fire had other ideas.

21

Salvation?

(Being Followed Home)

Jarvis and I, meanwhile, decided to go on a bit of a French jaunt that summer. Jarvis's mum had a little place in Brittany, so Jarvis, his sister Saskia and her boyfriend 'Reg' piled into my Blue Mk1 Ford Escort estate and I ferried us over to France. The Escort's gear lever had a tendency to come off in your hand as you changed gears. Thankfully, though, it stayed in the right place for the entire trip.

We lolled around in the sun for a couple of days and then decided to take a road trip down to Bordeaux, just for the hell of it. My favourite memory of this trip is the two of us (me and Jarvis) belting out Maria McKee's smash power balled 'Show Me Heaven' at the top of our lungs as we barrelled down the tree-lined French roads. We slept in the back of the Escort in a car park in Bordeaux, neither of us in possession of the funds necessary for even a cheap hotel.

One day we found a deserted stretch of beach and flopped there for a few hours. I recall teaching myself to juggle while sat there in the sun. A few figures appeared in the distance and began walking towards us, the only other souls visible. As they neared Jarvis called out: 'Alright, Uncle Steve!' It only turned out to be his actual Uncle Steve! Jarv claimed he had no idea they were in France, let alone in the same vicinity. How strange.

Adventure was never far away. One day we stumbled across a large, beautiful lake with an island in the middle. 'Wow, wouldn't it be great to get over there?' we both wondered. And lo! A rowing boat and oars appeared. Well, after we'd looked around a bit ('No one's about, so they'll not miss their boat for an hour or two . . . ?'). Next thing, we were making good progress, rowing out to the island.

One thing us landlubbers don't appreciate is just how far away things are across water. It ended up taking us about 30 minutes of hardcore rowing to reach the island. When we finally made it, we explored the woods and marvelled at the views. Sadly, there didn't seem to be much wildlife about, though it was incredibly peaceful.

After an hour or so we headed back, and after more hard rowing began to near our departure point, now occupied by a rather irate Frenchman with a suntan that could only be described as 'mahogany'. I didn't need Jarv's French language skills to know he was pissed off.

'He's not happy,' I over-simplified.

'I bet it's his boat,' Jarvis agreed.

Jean-Claude was on his much bigger boat and really was hopping mad. I reckon the rowing boat was his method of getting out to the yacht, as it was moored about ten metres off the shore. He gestured to us that we should draw up alongside the yacht. Here's where Jarvis's French skills surpassed mine:

'He wants us to get out and swim ashore.'

We had little choice, as he now had hold of the boat. We stripped off and dropped into the water, desperately holding our clothes above our head so as not to drench them as we kicked our way ashore. We gave Monsieur DuPont a bit of good old Anglo-Saxon once we were on land, as a bit of face-saving recompense.

We mingled with the locals down the town disco, obviously wowing them with our cool English moves as we skittered across the dance floor. So much so, in fact, that the French kids thoughtfully provided us with our own space, right in the middle. The pointing and laughing was a little strange as Jarvis perfected his jerkin' moves and pointy finger expression. I'm sure this was all cross-cultural signs of sartorial approvement. Or something. A great night was topped off by Jarvis saving my life; as a typical Brit abroad, I looked the wrong way while stepping out across the road and almost got wiped out by a speeding Citroën. He pulled me out the way in the nick of time. Ta, Jarv.

The France trip now complete, on our return to Blighty HM Customs wanted to give the Escort the quick once-over to check for illicit contraband. None was found, naturally, but they decided to search each of us just to make sure. Reg, Saskia and I were done pretty quickly, so we could sit back and watch the spectacle of Jarvis turning out his pockets. Nothing to see here, you say? Oh no, far from it. It was like watching Inspector Gadget at work. The pockets and their contents seemed never-ending: key rings, pens, furry gonk, numerous bits of rubbish and about 30 ancient condoms, which kept appearing from all the different pockets as they were emptied. Now, Jarvis was slowly turning into this UK music media indie sex god, but at this point he was either very discreet in his romantic liaisons or not scoring at all. I fear the latter.

'What's wi' all Johnnies, Jarv?' we asked.

'You never know,' came the cryptic reply.

Back at home, it looked like *Separations* would never be released. We kept hearing there were problems with the sleeve, problems with the pressings, problems, problems. We took that to mean Fire were sitting on the record, hoping a major label would sweep in with a lucrative offer for Pulp. Surely Fire wouldn't want to waste the opportunity of this growing momentum to miss out on record sales?

With hindsight, Fire were a victim of the collapse of the independent record distribution that happened at this time. Cartel, Rough Trade and a large slice of the UK's indie labels were struggling to get records out to the shops. I would imagine they were as frustrated as us at the lack of a Pulp release. Still, Fire had managed to get a few other bands' products out there, which didn't much fill us with confidence that they were telling us the truth. What little faith we had in Fire treating Pulp with a bit more respect was rapidly eroding. History was most definitely repeating itself: sign to Fire, and wait. This was an utterly depressing state of affairs. The momentum we'd built would start to evaporate, and fast, leaving us back at square one as had happened so many times before.

Our new manager, Suzanne, had not been quiet. She'd been working her contacts to get record company execs and A&R bods to see Pulp. A&R has always been a thankless task, since most major labels are based in London, and it's notoriously difficult for them to get beyond the M25 to see acts. As such, it transpired that there was only one label who seemed interested enough to see us, and that was Island Records. Nigel Coxon had seen us at a couple of the '91 London gigs and his scout, Dave Gilmour (no, not that one) had even travelled up to Sheffield to watch us perform in our natural habitat. We started seeing Dave at more and more of our shows, and he was reporting to Nigel that we were getting better and better. Dave was like an over-eager puppy and was therefore very enthusiastic about us. He instilled a very real sense that we could kiss Fire goodbye, sign to a major and have a proper shot at a stellar music career. Heady stuff.

Despite having an album written and recorded and gathering dust, Pulp were still mining a creative seam. By now we had moved to a secure rehearsal space in a railway arch in the space above my Mum's pottery warehouse in Catcliffe. It was typical Pulp. We had to cram into a quarter of the available space, as the rest was piled high with old pottery and junk. Trains would rumble overhead as they went to and from the Tinsley Marshalling Yard about two miles distant. Local kids would shout obscenities at us in breaks between songs. 'You're shit!!' 'Yes, but we're louder,' Jarvis would reply.

The arch was actually perfect for us: no heavy metal band next door giving us all a headache, no need to share with any other bands making the place untidy (we could be untidy as we like and there was no one else to blame), we could leave our gear set up and it was pretty secure. The downsides were that we could only use it after 4 p.m. weekdays and it was best accessed by car. Somehow Jarvis had passed his driving test (he must have had a very lenient examiner) and had acquired a bright yellow Hillman Imp, something of a classic. So, Candida, Steve and I would meet at a café in town and Jarvis would drive us all to rehearsals in the Imp (this was, of course, when everyone was up from London for a spot of writing and rehearsing).

Jarvis had an 'unusual' driving style, let's diplomatically say: he seemed unable to keep his foot steady on the accelerator and kept lifting it off every five seconds or so, the result being a very on/off style of motion. We'd eventually get there, though (even with knuckles semi-permanently whitened through sheer terror). Russell would invariably meet us there; he had a much flasher old Rover SD1, as I recall, and was strangely reticent to give us all lifts.

The Imp was frequently in the garage and once did break down in Catcliffe. Some local lads came to Jarvis's rescue and the lyrics to 'Joyriders' are based on that event. Sadly, it ended up being crushed into a cube at a wreckers' yard and given away as a Pulp fan club competition prize. It was last heard of still rusting away in a back garden somewhere.

★　★　★

We were starting work on the next tranche of Pulp material, much of which would provide the backbone to tracks on the *Intro* mini-album and, a bit later, *His 'N' Hers*.

The two most pivotal tracks to originate in this era were 'Razzmatazz' and 'Babies'. As previously mentioned, Jarvis loves finding stuff in junk shops. And he loves nothing more than finding some ancient piece of discarded music equipment. So, one day he turns up with a little Korg synth – possibly a Delta – and, as usual, this new instrument sparked new music. This was how the opening chords to 'Razzmatazz' came to be. A pinch more tinkering and a splash of some of the most biting lyrics ever written about lost relationships, and we had another belting pop song in our armoury.

'Babies' was, arguably, the song that changed all our lives (for the better) and it was written in about 15–20 minutes. We had a tea break one evening and as Jarvis and Russell went out for a smoke downstairs in the yard, I picked up Jarvis's Hopf guitar and started strumming. I'm certainly no guitar player but knew a couple of chords and enjoyed noodling around with the limited knowledge I had. These chords sounded nice together, so I kept playing them.

Jarvis came upstairs and said, 'What's those chords you're playing?'

'Err, one's G and I've no idea what the other is but my fingers are here.' (It was Dmaj7, apparently.)

I handed the Hopf back and got behind the kit. We all started playing round the two chords, then Jarvis added an Emaj to give us a chorus, and there it was: a fully formed hit record. The classic three-chord, three-minute pop song.

With this whiff of (potential) stardom in our nostrils, the idea of sticking with Fire was laughable. Trouble is, we *were* stuck with Fire and an extremely onerous five-album contract. Oh. But with *Separations* seemingly stuck in limbo we needed a way out. A plan was hatched.

Suzanne was of the mind that we had signed to Fire under duress, what with the big studio bill and no way of paying it except by signing the deal. Besides which, we hadn't had proper legal representation. So, she ventured that we could put out records with a different label and kind of challenge Fire to sue us and/or the other label. But what label in their right mind would go ahead with that kind of crazy idea? Our old mates Steve Beckett and Rob Mitchell, that's who. They had formed the Sheffield dance/techno label Warp Records a couple of years before to almost instant success, and were now ready to branch out with a more indie-based label. And even better, they were dead keen to launch Gift Recordings with Pulp material.

Even though Suzanne had been making headway with the London A&R bods and Island Records, we'd made up our mind. Let's bung Gift some money through the back door, finance some Pulp singles to challenge Fire, and if they start getting shirty, the Island Records 'muscle' could wade in. Pulp would be free of Fire, Gift would get a solid start for the label and Island would get first dibs on Pulp to push them to superstardom and fame. Perfect! What could possibly go wrong?

22

Gifts for All

(Fairground)

Nothing. For a change, nothing went wrong. This was uncharted territory for Pulp. We knew we were taking somewhat of a risk and could get sued by Fire and destroy our chances of ever releasing any records. We were walking a tight rope. Again. But what else could we do? The plan went ahead.

We managed to secure some money from Island to ostensibly record a bunch of 'demos', but of course used that money to record 'O.U. (Gone Gone)' at FON. By this point, FON had moved out of the rodent-friendly Wicker space to a new, super-swish place in the centre of Sheffield.

The idea was to do a much more live band-type track and not lean so heavily on the electronics, as per *Separations*. This was the new Pulp. Another new era.

Simon Hinkler was drafted in to man the controls, assisted by our live sound guy at the time, Mike Timm. The sessions were tough; it was so difficult to get a good drum sound and I really felt under pressure. The song needed to sound strong but it was coming out weedy, as if I was hitting the drums with a rolled up newspaper. I can assure you, I was giving it my all. It just sounded nowhere near robust enough.

189

The rest of the instrumentation was great and the song was a rollercoaster ride, driving along with breathless abandon and a nagging violin riff, Stylophone solo, the lot (even some old Pulp chord progressions made it on to the track – recycling at its finest). However, we were still unhappy with the sonic result, so we got a young producer in called Ed Buller (former keys in The Psychedelic Furs) to give it a remix and, thankfully, he rescued it. We also got our mate from Sheffield, Martyn Broadhead, to do the sleeve, as he'd previously done for 'Countdown' and *Separations*. This one depicted a page being turned. How very apt.

Being our first release on Gift, it was decided we needed a bit of a splash upon release to drum up publicity and get the music rags talking. So, it was decided we should do a balloon release and a prize for the label returned from the farthest place (I think someone in Norway won. What, I don't know). If you had once of these labels, you got in to the Gift Records' launch party at The Leadmill after the gig. This ruse seemed to work as we did get music journos up from London to do interviews and take photos of this rather odd event.

It wasn't just the event that got people on the train heading north. Suzanne had been beavering away in the background, working to get record plugger Scott Piering on board to help push the record to radio programmers across the country. We also secured the services of music PR Best in Press, again an outfit whose purpose was to get acts into the papers. Here we had been helped in no small way by Miki from Lush, who we had wowed in France. She was the girlfriend of John Best, Best in Press's main man. Fortunate, maybe. Deserved, yes. A lot of this was negotiated on a 'work for us for free now, and when (if) we sign to Island, we'll employ you properly' deal. It worked.

These were things we'd never really thought of. To get a hit record, Suzanne drummed it into us, you needed radio play. The more the merrier. The people who decide what goes on their 'A', 'B' or 'C' playlist needed courting like shy teenagers. If you had someone pointing them in Pulp's direction, all the better. If said radio producers had been reading all about some hip and happening new group – say, called Pulp – in the music papers, then your chances of hitting the charts were skewed (hopefully) in your favour. All this is, of course, predicated on you having a great single to push. It doesn't necessarily happen overnight, but often via a drip, drip, nag, nag technique. The addition of Scott the plugger and Best in Press PR, then, were two vital bricks in Pulp's construction.

We never got round to doing a video for 'O.U.' – Steve and Jarvis had one planned but there was probably no money left to do it. Never mind, we didn't need it. 'O.U.' was scheduled for release in May 1992, but we got wind that Fire were going to finally release *Separations* in the same month. Cads! They would piggyback on the good publicity and press we had garnered without any of their help to release a record that was now three years old, and very, *very* different to our current sound. This could really muddy the waters and throw a spanner into Pulp's new era. It was also the perfect illustration that our relationship with Fire was, indeed, dead.

There was nothing we could do about it but forge ahead with the plan and, incredibly, 'O.U.' came out to fantastic reviews across the board. 'This is colossal,' said *Melody Maker*. 'The glam-shackle Pulp make you think of spaceships and tower blocks and trains. Marvellous,' said *NME*.

'O.U.' moved Pulp a couple of spaces further across the music-success chessboard. More publicity, hey even a tiny bit in the greatest teen music mag of all time, *Smash Hits*, more good reviews, more notices that Jarvis and Pulp were *THE* new kids on the block (never mind the previous 14 years, though). Pulp even got their first radio session in 11 or 12 years* thanks to Mark and Lard (Mark Radcliffe

---

* Pulp had done a John Peel session back in 1979/80 when first starting out, and precisely zero sessions since then.

and Marc Riley) and their Radio 5 show *Hit the North*. It was great to be busy, or rather busier, with the band and we knew it was only a matter of time before we could go professional.

I had manoeuvred my working life (we all still needed to buy stuff, remember, and at this point we were receiving no money from Pulp activity), so that I could devote as much time as possible to Pulp matters as they arose. I became a supply teacher in Sheffield, working mostly at King Edward's Comprehensive in the west of the city. Supply meant you could be called first thing (very first thing, at that) and asked to cover an absent teacher in any subject, PE through to Physics. Subject knowledge was not essential, as the absent teacher would usually leave the lesson's work behind, and all I had to do was try to stop the kids from a) killing each other and b) falling out of any windows.

Doing the set work was not necessarily the goal. I usually started each session by gently reminding the kids that we could endure the next hour or so most agreeably together by simply quietly getting on with any homework they needed to do, completing the set work or just chilling and avoiding either a) or b) (see above). King Ted's kids were generally a decent bunch, so my tactics nearly always paid off: I got no grief; they had time to complete stuff they otherwise would have to do at home. The only time the set work ever caused me any 'moments' was doing an hour of Biology on human genitalia. Oh god, I'm going to have to field various questions on knobs and fannies. Not quite what I'd signed up for but, hey ho, all part of the job. I found it rather amusing telling the kids they'd know more about it than me.

Still, the future was tantalisingly close. Turning professional with Pulp was almost within our grasp. We just needed Island to sign us. However, didn't someone once say the darkest hour is just before dawn? Well, I was seemingly on the cusp of being a paid drummer when I found myself homeless. I was renting a room in a nice flat near Sheffield's Botanical Gardens but Emily, the owner, was moving her boyfriend in. As they say, three's a crowd, so I was given my marching orders. With nowhere to go I had to move back in with the parents in Rotherham. My god, this was torture. I lasted about three days when Leon, who was driving the band around at this point, said I could housesit one of his rentals until it was done up or I found something better. The house really did need doing up and I had hardly a stick of furniture to kit it out with – literally, a mattress on the floor and a microwave oven. Some rooms looked like they had suffered a recent fire, too, even though it was freezing in there. There was no central heating and the front room gas fire was so feeble it was hardly worth lighting. I ended up heating a dinner plate in the microwave and putting my feet on it while I watched TV. Grim. Thankfully this purgatory didn't last too long and I managed to get back into my old mate Julian's house down the road, just off Sharrow Vale Road.

Meanwhile, we went on our first UK tour. Well, with 11 dates spread out over a month it was hardly 'tourmageddon', but for us it was a first, and we could take our Pulp evangelism to new ports of call in exotic locations such as Norwich, Oxford and Birmingham, and even our last hurrah at the good old Adelphi in Hull.

We knew we would be winning hearts and minds wherever we went. We still wanted to put on a show. Entertainment was always the goal. By now we had done away with the silver balls mobile idea and gone for something a little easier to transport, set up, take down and generally live with: a six-foot-tall star made out of plywood, painted black and with coloured fairy lights set around the outside. The glamour. It was constructed by Sheffield freak Chris Wilson, who was a bona fide sculptor. A general oddball, he tended to communicate by whistling, rolling the eyes and giggling. He would sometimes decorate the stage with gold-coloured mechanical heads that would revolve or push a switch and the brain would pop up. We couldn't afford to take Chris along with all his gizmos, so the wooden star would have to do. It was easier to handle than the ball mobile, that's for sure, but it was still a right pain. The lights were always going out and you had to constantly fiddle with them to get them to fully light up. Plus, of course, lugging the thing on stage (it was usually propped up at the back behind the kit) was a nightmare – and all this, of course, before setting our own gear up and sound-checking.

While we weren't yet in the position to employ roadies, we did get a tour manager to help everything run as smoothly (!) as possible: get everyone to the gig on time, make sure the band was paid properly at the end of the night, and everything in between. Mark Webber had been helping Pulp out on the side lines for a while now, since 'The Day That Never Happened' fiasco (y'know, the gig that had failed dry ice, failed arty projections, failed fake snow – that one). Mark helped out with a bit of instrumentation on stage, too. It was a problem for Candida to play the Stylophone at the same time as the Farfisa, so Mark was initially called in to play Stylophone on 'She's A Lady' and 'O.U.', which he handled with aplomb.

We'd been getting better gigs around this time due to Pulp's much-improved music press profile, but also because we'd gained a proper booking agent. Steve had met with a bloke who he thought was a real East End wide boy; all slicked-back hair and a no-nonsense attitude. The perfect person to handle your interests when getting you onto a multi-band bill or festival stage. Enter Jeff Craft: another vital cog in the machine that was going to, with luck, propel Pulp up the slippery slope of success.

As well as setting up the modest 'O.U.' tour, Jeff would get us on to support slots at bigger venues, opening for other, more successful acts. On one such gig we supported The Fall, eighties Mancunian post-punk/indie legends fronted by the irascible and unique Mark E. Smith (Jarvis had a bit of the Mark E.'s about him at times) at the Cambridge Corn Exchange as a one-off. It was illuminating to observe Mark in his natural habitat – this was before he really went off the rails and Fall gigs seemed more 'care in the community' than a music event. He had great presence as a front man, with his uniquely Mark E. Smith mannerisms and his use of the mic stand as a stage prop. I'm sure Jarvis learned a lot.

The reason this gig in particular stood out was that afterwards in the bar, Candida and I spotted the legendary indie/alternative DJ, massive Fall fan and music guru John Peel. We cornered him and asked if he'd caught the Pulp set, which he had and claimed to have enjoyed it immensely (he must say this to all the bands). We advanced that it was about time we did a Peel session, and gently reminded him that the last – and only – Pulp Peel set was way back in 1981. John dutifully checked this in his sessions book and was rather astonished there'd only been the one session in all those years. Pulp would appear to have been the ideal mid-eighties Peel session band: deeply 'indie', unusual material, rather ramshackle, oddballs, characterful. But somehow we had slipped through the John Peel net. Not now. In February 1993, we were duly summoned to the BBC to record our first Peel session in over ten years at Maida Vale studios – I'm sure still a record for the longest period between Peel sessions ever.

Doing sessions was a win-win. We'd get on the radio – which was always good – and we'd also get some free demo time in a decent studio with decent engineers at the controls. Though, the Beeb was a bit unusual in that there was a definite 'work' vibe among the staff there: proper break times scheduled in, everyone had their specific role and could not deviate from it, and if the session was to end at 6 p.m., it did. Strictly no overtime. We were much more used to doing marathon studio sessions, the type where you went in and came out when the recording was done. If staying in all night was necessary, then so be it.

We'd get to do another couple of Peel sessions later in our career, one in 1994 and the other in 2001. Pulp were honoured to be asked to play at John's 40th anniversary party (40 years of DJing, that is), while Jarvis and I were invited to Peel Acres to do a special radio show where we listened to the other 'Pulp' – a band from the seventies who released one record, *Low Flying Aircraft*, of which John had a copy (natch). We'd never heard or even seen a copy of this mythical record. Sadly, it wasn't much cop.

Pulp and John's relationship grew over the years and we became firm Peel favourites. Was he making up for lost time? We will never know – it was a sad day when we heard that John had passed away.

To the casual observer, it would seem Pulp had now overcome the bad times and were on their way to success in some form or another. Rave reviews of recorded output and of live performances were fast becoming the norm. The idea that Pulp were the band to watch was not too drastic a concept, all said. We had been chipping away for so long and now the Promised Land was just over the next hill.

It was, however, somewhat galling to see other bands zip past us on to the front covers of the music mags after what seemed like only their first steps. Suede had an *NME* front cover before ever releasing a record. We ended up supporting them at the Camden Underworld. We were shocked. Here was a whippet-thin front man with some very Jarvis-esque stage moves, all whipping the mic lead and slapping his arse, coupled with a band behind trying to make grandiose music that was very much at odds with the current musical climate. Personally I didn't think they were up to much, compared with us, and I was completely flummoxed as to how they were getting front-page splashes as *'The best new band in Britain'* when we weren't. I know I'm biased, but I knew they could not hold a candle to us. Perhaps it was their major label masquerading as an indie label that had something to do with it? This model was becoming rife in the early nineties. Indeed, we were looking at a similar model ourselves, what with the Gift/ Island pairing. Maybe Suede had just beaten us to it.

Pulp and Island Records were getting very pally by now, Nigel

Coxon and Dave Gilmour were invariably always at our shows and were gearing up to give Gift some dosh to be able to release another Pulp record as soon as possible.

Thing is, in true Pulp fashion, the plan was about to hit the rocks. Big time.

23

More Problems

(Goodnight)

It's true: Suzanne Catty had instilled a spirit in Pulp that we could be up there with the best. We were though, an incongruous fit: northern oddness versus North American brashness. It was not long before the cracks started to appear.

As I've mentioned, Suzanne lived round the corner from Russell in Sheffield, and they'd meet regularly to plan and organise Pulp's day-to-day and future existence. Trouble is, Russ was soon coming to rehearsals with tales of Suzanne's crazy plans. She was starting to drive Russell nuts.

Russell can have quite firm beliefs of how things should be, and can be rather stubborn if needs dictate. So could Suzanne. She'd go round to Russ's place, ranting and raving about how the band should be doing this and that. Pulp had been going for a long time now and were used to doing things a certain, northern British way – the Pulp way. Often with Russell at the helm. This clash of personalities was becoming all too clear.

As often with fallouts, it mainly centred on the kind of management contract we should have with Suzanne. A band manager can expect to receive 10–20% of a band's earnings. After all, they should be working to get the band better-paid gigs and more financially lucrative contracts. Everyone wins. We had this notion that a manager should be seen as a kind of 'sixth member', and so should be rewarded financially as such. The band only gets any money after all the expenses are paid, and these expenses can be quite substantial. Our stance, then, was that Suzanne should be on a par with the band and get paid after expenses, as we did. This did not go down well. Within the band there was a debate; one camp wanted to sack Suzanne, the other to stick with her, since currently we had no one else fighting in our corner. Could our potentially glittering future founder without a manager? The music biz is notoriously fickle and I was certainly worried that if we ditched Suzanne we'd be risking everything.

In the classic Pulp way, our relationship with Island also started to look very precarious. Island were going to bung Gift some money to help them release the next couple of Pulp singles, to help with building our profile and gaining fans and momentum. Slight problem: no one seemed to have told the top brass at Island that we were still contractually obliged to little old Fire Records. HOLD IT, they said; we could get our arses sued off by Fire if we seem to be inducing Pulp to break their contract. Suzanne tried to fob this off with her claim that we'd signed to Fire under duress (which we took as correct – we essentially signed without proper legal representation. But sign we did). Was Island getting cold feet? You betcha. It was so depressing to be that close to a major recording contract and yet past mistakes/events were coming back to bite us.

The turn of the screw was not over – yet. We had been using Island's own recording studio in West London, The Fallout Shelter, located in the Island office basement, to record our follow-up to 'O.U.' – and it was sounding glorious. 'Babies' is a heavenly slice of pop served up with yet more intriguing lyrics; Jarvis's pervy story about hiding in a wardrobe and doing a bit of casual voyeurism. Ed Buller was once again drafted in to twiddle the knobs. He'd recently done the Spiritualized record, which we all loved. He'd also been working with that band Suede, so must be good?

I was shoved into the stairwell to record the drums, which gave a fab, natural reverby effect as the drum sounds bounced up and around the cramped space. I'm sure the office bods enjoyed that. I was really annoyed with myself with the take that actually made the record, though. It has a mistake right at the end. I should've done the last three hits of the song around the toms, but on that take I did them on the snare. I wanted to redo the pass but everyone else thought it was brilliant, so it stayed put. Might seem trivial to you, but to me I was kicking myself – I really enjoyed the tom ending. Never mind, it wasn't worth spoiling the atmosphere for.★

Time was, as always, tight and everyone wanted to press on with doing their bits. Listening to the squelchy synth sounds being added in the studio was a great privilege: these were never present when the song was played live at this stage, and I really thought they added a whole new dimension to the track.

It was also the first time we'd properly heard the lyrics. Jarvis tended to mumble in rehearsals, the words being indistinct – you just got an idea of the tune, and perhaps the lyrics on the chorus. So, to hear them in all their glory was fab.

We all really thought we had a potential hit on our hands. It was easily the most catchy, accessible song we'd recorded to date. It's a song that really seems to soar, especially when you get to the pay-off line: 'I only went with him 'cos he looked like you . . .', and has any song not benefitted from some good old 'Yeah yeah yeahs'? It's a song that can make the hairs on the neck stand up – just as all good ones should – and have you jumping round your room like a deranged kid. Pop perfection.

★ I make up for it live now anyway – I always finish the song going round the toms, unlike on the record.

Here we go again, familiar Pulp territory: an amazing record but with no means to release it. Island had put the brakes on funding *Gift*, and there was no way we were giving it to Fire to fuck up. It boiled down to two options: Suzanne would put up the money, but we'd have to seal the deal by signing her management contract on her terms, or find £5,000 to finance the release ourselves. Oh dear, what a to-do?

Jarvis ended up borrowing the five grand off his grandma to facilitate the 'Babies' release. This meant that Suzanne had to go. It all happened in a blur. Candida and I had travelled down to London in Suzanne's car to a Fallout Shelter session. We knew the relationship between Russell and Suzanne had got really bad, and that there was the problem of how to release 'Babies', but we had no inkling the axe was about to fall. Once we arrived a quick band meeting was called and we were informed that Suzanne was to be sacked forthwith. Could we have voted to stop the sacking? No. Jarvis, Steve and Russell were for it. I was ambivalent at best – it seemed we were taking a big leap into the dark. But Steve wielded the axe and Suzanne was gone.

So, that left us manager-less. We had a record company we didn't want to be with, a major who wanted to sign us but legally couldn't, and another record label that wanted to release a record but couldn't afford to. Jeez. It seemed only Pulp could get themselves into such a mess.

Still, legal knots aside, we did still have a record to release. 'Babies' came out in the October of '92 to, again, almost wall-to-wall amazing reviews and Single of the Week accolades all over the shop.

Steve and Jarvis did another lo-fi, low-budget video, ably abetted by Jarvis's Central Saint Martins college mate, Martin Wallace. I vividly remember us doing the band scenes and Martin wielding the camera while being pushed round in a shopping trolley (there was no money for sophisticated tracking. The shopping trolley worked just fine). Two friends of Saint Etienne's Bob Stanley were roped in to play the two sisters, and they were filmed in a bedroom in Tufnell Park. That was it.

It was the most complete Pulp package to date. Even the B-side, 'Sheffield Sex City', became an iconic Pulp song. Let's be clear: Sheffield is a rather dour northern English city that had its heart ripped out like so many others during Thatcher's process of deindustrialisation that started in the eighties. Sexy it really isn't, in any kind of classical sense. New York, Paris, Cannes are sexy, but it's a bit of a stretch to add Sheffield to that list.

BUT, as Jarvis observes, sordid goings on can happen anywhere. Sheffield being no exception. And this track is a great example of Pulp building an atmosphere; it seethes with a slick heat and heady expectation. To the uninitiated listener you could perhaps imagine Sheffield actually being Sex City. Candida getting in on the action with some explicit readings at the start certainly helped. Great to hear Greasy Gordon's get a shout-out, too; an ancient all-night café in Sheffield and one of the few places you could get something to eat late at night back in the day.

'Sheffield Sex City' is a song that could never have been written if you actually lived in Sheffield. The remove seemed to play a big part in the romanticism. You gain a different perspective once you get to look at a place from afar, rather than drowning in all its sorrows. I found that when I had left Sheffield to try my hand in London, the change could often amplify one's 'Sheffield-ness'. Sure, you could adapt a mockney-type accent to try and fit in, or you could stubbornly keep your natural accent with all its flat-cap connotations. I, of course, chose the latter, revelling in that small feeling of otherness it conveyed.

The release of 'Babies' presented us with another opportunity to hit the road again to capitalise on the ever-increasing Pulp profile. This was our second national tour of the year, but we were hitting loads of new towns and cities: Glasgow, Bristol, Brighton, Cardiff, Leicester and so on. All pretty low-rent venues, though, and we were still cramming ourselves into the back of a Transit van. We'd sometimes crash out on fans' floors after gigs to save on hotel bills, and such was the case after the Bristol show, where we were all up early(ish) to catch our first ever video appearance on Saturday morning TV on ITV's *The Chart Show*. We were so excited to see ourselves and the 'Babies' video being given such fabulous exposure – on national TV, no less. It was a great coup for a band that was essentially self-funding record releases without the backing of a major label. Safe to say, these were heady times. It really felt as if we were all in a tight gang now, united with a common purpose and totally devoted to giving it all our energy and commitment. We rarely, if ever, fell out; laughs – especially with Jarvis's comical turns – came easily. It now seemed we had left the 'old Pulp' way behind and the future was so bright we needed shades.

But we still needed to get Pulp out of the Fire/Gift/Island legal quagmire. And we couldn't do it alone. We needed help from music industry insiders to sort it all out.

We met with various managers with a view to them taking us on. Most thought Pulp were an amazing prospect, but once they learned of the legal tangle we were in they just couldn't face the struggle. Our PR, John Best, put us in touch with indie music legend Geoff Travis, who'd founded Rough Trade Records back in the early days of punk and gone on to release such iconic bands as Sheffield's Cabaret Voltaire, Stiff Little Fingers and The Smiths. Rough Trade became the backbone of the UK's independent music scene, helping bands and tiny labels to get their records into record shops across the land.

Rough Trade had branched out into band management and Geoff, along with Jeanette Lee, his partner in crime, came to see a show we did at Sussex University in Brighton on that 'Babies' tour. Jeanette had been at the forefront of the nascent punk scene in London right from the start and had been a member of Public Image for a time (that's Jeanette on the cover of PiL's *Flowers Of Romance* LP, by the way). Needless to say, both Geoff and Jeanette were blown away by our performance and could see the vast potential held within. They were definitely interested in representing us. So, we met with Geoff to outline the horror of our situation. Now, Geoff's either a glutton for punishment or a wide-eyed idealist, but the situation didn't seem to faze him – or Jeanette – and they wanted to take over management duties.

Looking back, this was another key pivotal moment in Pulp history. Having bona fide professional people behind us who 'got' Pulp and were not put off by the massive challenge ahead, extricating us from the legal wranglings, was a major boon for us. Plus, they were real human beings that loved and relished Pulp's oddness (a real reprieve from some of the other 'beings' we'd come across in the biz). They both had a genuine love of music in all its quirky forms, which was perfect for us. Finally, we had found our kindred spirits who would help us navigate the shark-infested waters of the music industry.

A meeting was set up between the band and Fire to see if we could overcome the contract problem. We were faced with what I can only describe as a huge, greasy slob of a lawyer in his offices to discuss the situation.

We sat down and he asked: 'Have you changed your position? Wanting to leave Fire, that is.'

'Err, no,' we replied.

'Well, there's nothing to discuss,' and he promptly got up and showed us the door. So much for constructive 'talks'.

We ended up leaving Geoff and Jeanette to negotiate with Fire, as we were out of our depth. Finally, after a few months or so we got Fire to release Pulp from the erroneous contract and leave the way clear for us to sign with Island Records – the home of such towering artists as Roxy Music, The B-52's, The Slits, U2, Tom Waits and, err,

Hoobastank. To get us out though it cost us a slice of our future earnings for the next four albums. That ten grand that Fire put up for *Separations* and the subsequent contract repaid them back many times over.

No matter. Pulp could finally breathe a collective sigh of relief. We could put the 'Age of Fire' fully behind us now and forget it ever happened. Pulp was eager to get on with being Pulp, and seeing just how far we could go. We signed to Island on a beautiful sunny day, resplendent with clinking champagne glasses and an advance cheque printed, à la Football Pools winners, on a massive piece of cardboard.

Phew.

24

A Little Bit Of . . .

(Razzmatazz)

Why do young people join bands? Is it to become more interesting and thus more popular at school? Perhaps as a way to start meeting like-minded folks in hopes of making a connection with them, and maybe even one of a romantic nature? Is it to chase a dream of fame, fame, fatal fame? Maybe it's the lure of luxuriating in a lifestyle unencumbered by monetary woes, flashing the cash at all and sundry and tossing coppers to ragamuffin children? Or perhaps there's a more serious dream: to be remembered for producing great 'art'? Putting a marker down to say 'I woz 'ere'? Or, more simple desires: to save oneself from having to get a 'proper' job? Maybe just a great way of having a laugh with your mates?

It's probably a mixture of all of the above. I think it was for me. Certainly, being in a successful band was a much better prospect than an actual 'job' and miles better than being a teacher back in the classroom. Being in a band definitely got you to meet a wider range of people than you could normally expect. Girls? Sure. Did we want fame for fame's sake? Not so sure about this. No one can really know what 'fame' feels like until you get it. Plus, there's always someone more famous than you lurking nearby. Just as there's always someone richer, better looking and thinner than you are. As a drummer the fame thing is always going to be a bit tenuous anyway – you'd need to get into Ringo territory to really feel it. However, Jarvis was starting to get a bit 'famous' by now, and we were starting to see a few more devotees worshipping at the Jarvis altar. Who wouldn't? We'd known for yonks he was destined for this.

We, well, certainly I, didn't crave to make Elton John-style piles of cash. Don't get me wrong, it's always helpful to be financially stable, but Pulp were not the kind of folk to run off with our record company advance money and blow it on Ferraris and lap dancers. Not to start with anyway. Just being able to pay ourselves a weekly wage was a massive triumph after what seemed a lifetime of struggle. So we did: £100 a week each. Not much change left to throw to the starving ragamuffin children, I'm sorry to report.

Did we want to be remembered for making great 'art'? Sure. It wasn't the be all and end all, but to get this far, after such circuitous travels and *not* set the music world alight would be a crying shame. That was the plan anyway. Anyway, music is 'art' whether it be the bubblegum pop of 'Barbie Girl' or something a little more taxing, say, Scott Walker's avant-garde album *Tilt*, or a bit of Steve Reich. I'd bet Aqua couldn't come up with musical 'art' on a par with La Monte Young, but then could Scott, Steve and La Monte conjure up a subliminal earworm that gets to number one worldwide? It's a lot harder than you think.

We had kissed Fire goodbye at last. We had embraced the double-edged sword that was 'a major record company'. We had the management support mechanism to help us sail the uncharted waters ahead. We had press momentum and a fledgling but expanding following of fans. The future, for once, looked rosy. But the best bit was that, on top of all this, we were writing more and more material that we knew was going to sound epic once recorded. And like a Transit van going uphill, we needed to keep the pedal to the metal to maintain this forward momentum.

'Razzmatazz' had been earmarked as the next single release, the song having been born out of experiments with the Korg Delta keyboard scavenged by Jarvis from a junk shop. It was decided that even though we were now on Island, it would be better to put this single out with Gift Records – a way of saying thanks to Rob and Steve for helping us get out of the Fire (and into the frying pan?) and with the added bonus of still keeping Pulp's indie credentials suitably on point.

Finally throwing off the Fire straitjacket felt fantastic. We had wanted Pulp to be able to be seen and heard by as many people as possible for years now and at last we started to believe this may actually come to pass. With major labels I suppose it's easy for the initial novelty of a new act to wear off, the result being that an act can get lost in the 'system' and disappear. Or, they're forced into producing insipid, watered-down music that has the life sucked out of it. A sell-out, you might say. We'd seen it happen before. And we were not going to let it happen to us. Hopefully.

After what had seemed years and years in a kind of wilderness, we were so very excited and thrilled to see what the machine of Island and PolyGram Records could do for us. We would know once and for all whether we were on to something, or not. If the latter, we could finally get on with the rest of our lives knowing that we'd had a go, tried our best and if folk didn't like it, fair enough. Back to scrubbing crabs.

Ed Buller was again at the controls for the recording of 'Razzmatazz', which turned out a bit fraught and again it was decided that the drums were sounding feeble and needed more 'punch'. I've no idea why. Was it the old kit I'd been using since I joined the band? Was my playing somehow deficient in the studio? Was it a combination of these things? Maybe Ed needed to take more time over coaxing a better sound out of my kit. I dunno. The solution was to have a go at re-recording the drums at another studio. I duly traipsed off to do this in East London with producer Phil Vinall. The initial recording was reused, this time with me playing again over the backing. As all the backing was played to a click track to keep the tempo steady, it was pretty straightforward. I think we used a different kit to the one I used for the original recording, so in that case let's blame the old kit for the subpar sound. Once we'd got that sorted, Ed did a remix and eventually everyone was happy: me, the rest of 'em, Geoff and Jeanette, and, probably most importantly, Island. The finished track was easily the best-sounding Pulp record to date, the extra effort put into getting the drums right definitely paying off.

For the video we stuck to our trusty formula: Jarvis and Steve come up with a rough idea; Steve plans how it's going to work; Martin Wallace is drafted in to actually make it happen. We were off to France once again to play a couple of gigs, so it was decided we'd use the trip to do a video at the same time. Cuts costs, see.

Steve secured permission to film inside the historic Moulin Rouge for the day. The owner even suggested we could use his pet crocodiles . . . err, OK. Unfortunately, when we got to Paris he reneged on his promise and said 'Non!' The Moulin Rouge was off. So, not to waste the time, Jarvis did some lip-syncing to the song on the street outside the Moulin Rouge and we used the rather grotty hotel we were staying in for the cutaway scenes. We came away from Paris with half a video. We needed a band performance bit so, back in London, Steve contacted Sunset Strip in Soho, London's oldest strip club. They gave us a four-hour window to shoot the band scenes we needed before the 'punters' arrived to be 'entertained'. The Sunset Strip was about as seedy as you could imagine. Perhaps it looked more glamourous with the lights down low, but during the day you didn't want to look too closely at the carpet.

We . . . erm . . . finished just in time. Martin filmed some more scenes with Jane, one of the PRs at Best in Press, stuck it all together, and job done.

Released in February 1993 to yet more Single of the Week accolades – or 'nearly' Single of the Week – 'Razzmatazz' skimmed the lower reaches of the UK Singles Chart. Another Pulp first. Our radio plugger, Scott Piering, had been evangelical in his Pulp promotion, even going the extra by having the band's name shaved into his head to try and help the cause. Thanks, Scott.

This was all further proof that we were on the right track, and a lot more like what being in a pop group was supposed to be. Releasing great records – as soon as possible after recording them of course! – shooting videos in exotic(ish) locations and playing breathless gigs to adoring fans. And naturally, more releases = more press.

We were doing more interviews now. Well, I say we – we soon noticed they were becoming more 'Jarvis-only'. This was understandable, as all five of us gabbing away could perhaps dilute the message with confusion. I certainly didn't mind as we all benefitted from the extra press. Jarvis is a natural; he can do depth just as easily as frivolous frippery, and he's always in 'Jarvis mode'. There's no off button – manna from heaven to music journos. And Pulp interviews, compared to those with most vacuous nineties music-makers, seemed a revelation: informative, entertaining, yes sometimes ridiculous, but certainly never boring.

In February and March 1993, we went on a national tour in support of a bigger band, Saint Etienne, early nineties arch pop gurus who were making waves with their wry electro musings and led by Bob Stanley, who had been championing Pulp for some time. This was the first time we'd been on tour as the support act. We did ten shows – mostly universities – all around the UK.

It was a great tour. It put us right in front of the kind of kids who would love us. And they did. I'm sure plenty would've heard of Pulp by this point, and they were clearly pleased to get to see us in the flesh. Playing support was always a chance to try and upstage the main act, and naturally we tried our damnedest to blow them off the stage every night. Saints were great, but they did seem to rely on a lot of backing tapes to reproduce their studio sound, and to me, backing tapes are no substitute for a full band going at it full tilt – Saints had a full band as well as the tapes but I think we had a harder, more robust sound.

Were Saint Etienne a bit London wishy-washy? Maybe. They had the beautiful Sarah Cracknell upfront, who certainly caught the eye, but we had Jarvis and his 'eccentric' dance moves and often surreal between-song 'patter'. I may be biased but audience reactions after the gigs was usually that we did indeed 'blow them off the stage'. We gained many fans during this tour, and we could sense in the air a feeling that there was a growing section of British indie music fans who were rejecting the down-at-heel American grunge look, or, indeed, the good old British 'crusty' look. Now, feather boas and glitter for all were the order of the day, and glamour and fun were to the fore.

Around this time the music journalists who were documenting events seemed to be vying with each other to coin a suitable name for this slowly emerging scene. They all love a tidy pigeonhole to bung bands and their fans into, so they were trying out a few different names for this new 'movement', things like 'Lion pop' and the 'Crimplene scene' (though contrary to popular belief, Jarvis is not a fan of manmade fibres). No one had heard of 'Britpop' at this time.

Despite the friendly competition on stage, we had a great time with the Saint Etienne mob, and they themselves became fans of Pulp (even though Bob would often bemoan us for, indeed, blowing them off the stage every night). No one was even put off by the puking incident of the first show in Glasgow; we all piled into the Saints' dressing room to help liberate their 'rider', which we attacked with gusto. Unfortunately, Jarvis went at it with a little too much gusto and ended up puking behind the sofa. He retreated into a ball under his black furry coat, gently moaning while we all laughed at his predicament, knowing that the tables would turn and at some point in the future the same fate would no doubt befall each of us.

To be fair to Jarv, we'd had a traumatic journey from Sheffield to Glasgow. Our sound man, Mike Timm, had hired a van to get our gear and us to the gig. A van that was slightly, and only slightly, better than the Transits we were used to. It was supposed to have one row of real seats behind the driver and passenger bit. We were all stood in a freezing car park waiting for it to arrive, but it got later and later with no sign. Eventually Mike got a message that the van had broken down before even reaching us. There's no way we were going to miss the start of the tour. Luckily, Sheffield has the UK's premier tour vehicle company within the city boundaries: Stardes. So Mike was despatched forthwith to get a new van. He returned about an hour later with a real, proper, brand new, nice-smelling, purpose-built, all mod cons tour van. It was one of the best Pulp moments ever. We were all jumping for joy at the sight of this beautiful vision. It even had a table surrounded by seats inside. We had arrived (before we even set off). You may be thinking – so what? It's just a van? But after years and countless miles of sitting in the back of a cold Transit on amps and sleeping bag cushions, this tour bus was heaven. You could even hear the sound system! Led Zep was jammed on the cassette deck and turned up L.O.U.D. Now, *this* was the way to travel. Hang the cost; we'll sort that out later when the Island cheque arrives.

Around the same time we went back over the Channel, to Nantes, France, to play a gig with Suede. I guess we were the support group again, all the time biting our tongues at seeing this group overtake us once more. But, we gave it our all as per usual and afterwards where we were all 'celebrating' backstage, there was a window down this corridor with loads of French kids sticking their heads through. They were shouting at Suede singer Brett Anderson. Unfortunately

212

for him, though, they didn't want him. They wanted Jarvis. 'Where ees Jarvees?' I observed this with a wry smile, before Brett turned to me and said, 'Do you know where Jarvis is?' I shrugged my shoulders in the best Gallic tradition and laughed. I loved this turn around. The French kids weren't bothered about the ne'er-do-well, blow-in Brett. They wanted the real deal.

Folks out in TV land were also getting to see a lot more of the real deal, as we started appearing on more and more TV shows in 1993. These were generally 'as live' in the studio-type affairs, which, for us, were pretty much like doing short gigs. The pick of the bunch from around this time was a trip up to Glasgow to perform a few numbers in a beautiful old church for a BBC Two show called *No Stilettos.* The venue was impressive, but what really sticks in the memory was watching all the TV bods panicking as they waited for the other bands on the show, The Dubliners and Shane MacGowan of Pogues fame, to appear. Time passed and all we heard was that they had got waylaid in the airport bar somewhere, and subsequently got held up/ too pissed. What a surprise. They eventually made it and we watched agog, wondering how all these men could stand, let alone sing (sort of) and play any kind of instrument. Suffice to say they were a bit the worse for wear.

Elsewhere, I remember one bizarre time performing in a cramped corner at the end of comedian Sean Hughes' show. Quite why, I still don't really know. Around this time we also took our first trip over to Ireland, for a gig in Dublin and an appearance on RTÉ 2's 'yoof' show *JMTV Rocks the Garden.* This was different, as we were all interviewed separately having some of the old Irish craic. Needless to say, a rather uproarious night out with the presenters was to follow in Dublin's fair city. It's part of the contract, yeah?

All these were still very much late-night, niche sort of programmes. But any TV is better than no TV, so it was all very much appreciated.

★

Once we had the Island cheque in the bank it was time to go shopping. It was obvious that the recent recordings had shown my drums to be below par for the stage we were at. A new kit was required. I have never really been a drum geek, slavering over the latest gear from Pearl, DW, Premier and the like, and I certainly never bought any drum magazines or anything like that. I was never really bothered about the equipment per se, so much as what could be done with it. Most of the drummers of the day seemed to be playing Yamaha kits, so I headed up to Carlsbro Sound in Sheffield and ordered a black Yamaha 9000 kit with all the trimmings, a classic Ludwig Black Beauty snare drum and a set of beautiful Zildjian K cymbals. Everything sounded fantastic. At the same time, Steve got a complete new bass rig and Russell chucked his antiquated (definitely not classic) amps for new stuff.★

We were now fully ensconced in Island's bosom and we could start to think about the rosy future ahead of us. Success, like hit records, is never guaranteed, even if you're signed to a prestigious label. You still need the songs as ammunition to fire out the guns.

We were now professional musicians, paying ourselves via the Island money. This meant we were unencumbered with having day jobs and could concentrate on writing material and doing gigs. We still used the upstairs at the Catcliffe pottery to write and rehearse, though. It seemed like home. Yes, we could still only use it after 4 p.m. and at weekends, and getting the equipment up the stairs after a gig was a real ball-ache. But it was up those stairs at Catcliffe that the songs that would become *His 'N' Hers* were born.

★ During this period some guitars had been stolen from the van – Steve's white Fender bass and Russell's Rosetti guitar, obviously pinched by thieves who knew nothing about guitars as the Rosetti was rubbish. The bridge was at the right height only by the addition of a wooden chip fork under it. The thing had a very cheese grater-style action, in that it shredded your fingers and was the tinniest sounding instrument on God's Earth. I guess it suited Russ's and Pulp's needs at the time, but we were sailing off into new territory now.

After the release of the Gift singles, Island's Nigel Coxon wanted us to keep the momentum going. So did we. We'd come through the legal hell with Fire and we were desperate to get in the studio and record what would essentially be our debut album. OK, *Separations* had come out the year before, but the songs on that were 1987–88 vintage, and *Freaks* was from 1986, which seemed a lifetime away (which it was, in pop music terms). The plan, therefore, was to release a 'mini' album of the Gift stuff as a kind of stopgap before the real 'debut' Pulp LP. This would be a way for the new fans to get into Pulp on vinyl (or CD), as the singles perhaps hadn't received a wide enough distribution and were very hard to find by now. Plus, they'd get to revel in the murky depths of Jarvis's B-side musings, all in one handy package.

Safe to say, *Intro*, released in October 1993, was reviewed with gushing praise by all the weeklies. However, there was one caveat: we can't wait for the real thing – Pulp's first LP with Island.

25

Blast Off

(Space)

'What you doin'?"
  'Shush,' she said.
  'You can't do it like that!'
  'Fuck off. Watch,' she said again.
  A group of us – Ants, Nige from Liverpool, and me – were drinking in The Porter Cottage pub in Sheffield one Saturday night, seeing what the evening would bring. We stood and watched two rather delectable girls play The Crystal Maze pub quiz machine. Hanging round the quiz machine was often a good place to spark up a conversation by helping players (especially girls) answer the questions posed, on the premise that we'd get a chance to chat them up. But this time it was different: the girls needed no help from us. The game required the players to solve various puzzles onscreen to be able to have a go at playing for money in the finale. These two were brilliant at it. Hence the admonishment for us lot to 'Eff off and watch'. They proceeded to pull money out of the machine as we watched, slack-jawed (it was a shock to see anyone win at The Crystal Maze). We chatted briefly as the pub was closing and we told them we were moving off to a place called The Tufty Club. 'See you then. We're off home,' came the response.

Fast forward 30 minutes, and the girls had followed/stalked us to The Tufty. This was a good sign. They claimed to have got back to their flat and decided that going out was a better option than wasting a Saturday night in front of the telly. Anyway, we all got to talking, as you do, and everyone was getting on very well. I ended up talking to the Crystal Maze master, Sarah. Our conversation turned to the songs we'd chucked on while getting ready for the night out. I'd been listening to The Smith's *Hatful Of Hollow*, their compilation album of Peel sessions and other bits (which I consider to contain superior recordings of The Smiths' earlier stuff). Sarah talked about a song about some bloke hiding in a wardrobe while spying on others shagging. Hmm . . .

'I wrote that song,' I said with the supremest of confidence, because I had, ostensibly, written the song. I was thinking – I've hit the jackpot here, this kind of situation never occurs. I can really impress her, I just need to sound believable, or even just cocky. Either way, try not to sound like some egotistical knobhead too full of himself.

'Yeah, right,' was the correct sarcastic response from Sarah. (Note: If anyone claims to have written the song that you listened to while putting your lippy on, run. He's a nutter, obvs.)

'But I did,' I protested, while informing her of my new(ish) musical career. Ants and Nige backed me up, but even I could see that no one in their right mind would fall for such trickery. Sarah had never heard of Pulp.

The night ended with all of us back at mine watching Glen Campbell live on the TV – 'Rhinestone Cowboy' and all that. Somehow Sarah left her bag and had to retrieve it the next day with her brother. Sid/Jim was a music nut and did indeed confirm to her that I was who I said I was. Result. We started dating a couple or three weeks later and at the time of writing (2021) we have been married 25 years. See, 'Babies' really did change our lives.

★ ★ ★

Between gigs and tours we were pretty seriously rehearsing, our new equipment and wages spurring us on to more writing. Lots of new songs were being formed in late '92/early '93 in preparation for our next record. Looking back, *His 'N' Hers* was our debut LP. The majority of our new fans had little knowledge of our previous releases. Why should they? They were from a different era. A different band even. I think a lot of them knew Pulp had got a past and they explored the back catalogue records. But most were coming to the band afresh, and were getting excited about the future, as were we.

Songs developed in this period included 'Pink Glove', 'Acrylic Afternoons', 'Lipgloss', 'Happy Endings', 'Do You Remember The First Time?'. 'She's A Lady' was probably the oldest of the bunch. It had been a live fave for seemingly ages. The newer material also was quickly adopted by our ever-growing fanbase of devotees as 'bangers'.

Accruing 'fans' was good. A bit odd, I suppose, after years of playing to the 'semi-circle of indifference'. Now it was all folk asking for 'autographs' (selfies were years and years off). Very strange. I have never asked a pop star, famous or not, for their signature. Couldn't see the point really. So, I was always saying, 'Why do you want my autograph?' when anyone asked for it. I can understand people wanting their records signing, but you would often get a scraggy bit of paper thrust at you – and don't get me started if they didn't have a pen.

Anyway, we now had a coterie of dedicated fans who we started seeing regularly, especially at London gigs. They'd be swinging their feather boas about and generally looking very 'glam' – not as in Marc Bolan or some costume copy of early seventies fashions, but shimmering, sparkling, looking like fans and band belonged together. Seeing *NME* cover stars at our gigs was super gratifying, too. It was great to see Miki from Lush down at the front in the thick of the action, moshing away with the kids. Chatting with Damon Albarn backstage at our gigs was always interesting, although I did get to thinking that he'd taken a big slice of Pulp back to Blur during this period. I recall him saying he was going to use a Portasound template for Blur. Soon after we heard 'Girls And Boys', which did sound very familiar. Hmm. It could be argued that stuff like that would only benefit Pulp in our quest for pop glory.

While getting our shit together for the upcoming recordings we were asked to contribute a track to a French album, of bands doing covers of the French singer Michel Polnareff's songs. I'd never heard of Monsieur Polnareff at this stage, but Jarvis was somewhat of an aficionado, naturally. The track 'Le Roi de Fourmis' ('King Of The Ants') was selected and it was suggested we try out Stephen Street as producer for the track, and as a bit of an audition for the forthcoming album sessions.

Stephen Street had done nearly all The Smiths' stuff and was Blur's producer. He seemed to be everywhere in the mid-nineties, so it seemed like a good idea to see what he could do with Pulp.

So, Mr Street turned up at the arches of Catcliffe and sat there in his pristine white trousers, positively grimacing at the surrounding dirt and Pulp-esque squalor. We worked together on the track, and I for one was pleased with the results – which took the French six years to release by the way (sound familiar?) – as Stephen gets a really clean sound where all the instruments are heard good and loud. I would have signed him up on the spot for the album, but Jarvis was more of the opinion that his approach was a bit *too* clean and nice. A bit too straight, even. So, Mr Street was politely declined and, in the end, Ed Buller was asked to man the controls at the next session.

Britannia Row Studios in Islington, owned by Pink Floyd no less, was chosen as the place to record this new album. It had helped birth records by Kate Bush, Joy Division and Kylie Minogue, even (among loads of other notables, of course). What was most entrancing was that at last, at long last, we could make a record that had the potential to be whatever we wanted it to be. There were no constrictions, apart from the desire to make the absolute best record we could. Budget? Spend whatever's necessary. Time? Get it right rather than rush things. After all, we had so much experience of tight budgets and timescales. To say we were excited would be an understatement: we had the material and we were not studio newbies. Our equipment was now top-notch and Ed was at the top of his game. We could even safely say that the record-buying public were genuinely waiting for our new record. The stage was set . . .

We worked getting the basic rhythm tracks down pretty quickly – after all, some of these songs had been in our live set for ages, so we could play them inside out – with a confidence only live exposure can give. We spent a fair amount of time on drum sound, always an expensive and time-consuming process. Plus, it really puts the pressure on as this is usually the first thing to be done so everyone else is chomping at the bit to get their tracks and parts down. Ed's simple, and only, instruction was, 'Hit 'em hard, yeah?' Righto Ed. For most songs we would've used a click track a computer-generated timekeeper to synchronise the various parts of a track, or tracks. I had been practising with click tracks the previous year and had developed my own particular type that worked for me. Most drummers I talked to about it just played along to a noise/click that was steady on the snare beat. When I tried to use this method I found that when you are in time, you effectively cannot hear the click, as the snare sound masks it, so it was fairly easy to wander off the tempo/beat. Solution: set the click so it's *between* the beat and so you can play to it easier. Put a different sound on the beat and you can lock in. Once I had settled on that system, playing to a click was pretty easy.

Once we had 'The One', it was time for the other instruments, starting with the bass, then guitars and keyboards, and finally the vocals. We'd record all day with a break in the evening, when the in-house chef (oh, how we had changed!) served up our tea. Sessions would often go on well into the evening as required (studio work never has set finish times; things just keep going until whatever's done is done). Plus, we all lived together during these sessions, at the

Britannia Row house just around the corner from the studio. It was certainly nicer than our actual houses.

Once the main instrumentation was complete we moved on to, in my opinion, the best bit: the addition of all the extra little things that would complement the music. Stuff that folk had heard in their heads all the time we'd been playing these tracks live and that could now be committed to tape. Parts that really made the songs burst with life, like Russell using his violin bow on his guitar or a bass, or Candida adding little keyboard tricks.

But the bulk of these special bits came from Jarvis. It was almost like the floodgates opening. Along with the typical yelps and groans, he'd add lots of guitar parts and odd synth textures.★

I had a couple of tricks up my sleeve to bring to the record, including lots of percussive shakers (see 'Lipgloss') and tambourine parts to fill out the rhythm sections. (For what it's worth, playing the tambourine is harder than you might think; you need strength and concentration to play in time and with the same fluency for three and a half minutes.) Elsewhere, I used a trick I'd pinched from an old jazz drummer, Christian Garros, who I knew from The Jacques Loussier Trio (they specialised in jazz versions of Bach compositions; I'm no jazz fan by a long way but this lot were doing some interesting stuff). Monsieur Garros would hold the drumstick at 90 degrees to a cymbal, and kind of scrape it along to produce strange, out-of-this-world sounds, my attempt at which you can hear on the breakdown section of 'Do You Remember The First Time?', among other tracks on the album. Ed stuck a bit of echo and reverb on top of the sound, and it really adds atmosphere. On 'David's Last Summer', Ed wanted a metallic clanging towards the climatic end, so we decided

---

★ We had a huge seventies vintage synth set-up for ages, which we used for some really unearthly sounds on this album. At one point, Jarvis and Ed thought the synth was starting to produce its own 'Tones of Evil' that went on to jinx part of the recording: tapes broke, the desk threw a fit, odd bits got wiped.

I should play along by hitting a fire extinguisher we wrenched off the wall. Works well.

The old Pulp stalwart, the timpani, were wheeled out for one last time on the song 'Someone Like The Moon' – probably the one track I wouldn't have bothered with, even if it does sound very Pulp circa 1985. Still, never did anything for me and seemed like a bit of filler somehow on an otherwise barnstorming record. The kettledrums were never heard on a Pulp record again. End of another era?

You often hear about inter-band disagreements that can emerge in the studio, the high-pressure atmosphere and egos coming to the fore producing an explosive mix, but I don't recall any times of disagreement at all. Apart, that is, from the session for mixing 'Pink Glove'. This had been a live fave for quite a while and I saw it as a real uplifting dance song that had a way of building the tension, only for it all to be broken as the chorus comes crashing in. To me, the chorus on the finished version was a bit of a washout, the beat being drowned out by a fat acoustic guitar and losing all its 'oomph'. Live, this was the moment the crowd really went for it, but I could not hear this release in the track. I brought up my concerns in the control room only to be drowned out by the others. A case of back in yer box. Later Adi, the Brit Row engineer, confided that he agreed with me, and the track dips when it should have soared. Maybe I should have shouted louder and stamped my feet, but I doubt it would have made the slightest difference; drummers don't have much clout in these matters. Never mind, eh.

As if Jarvis and Steve weren't busy enough with the recording, they decided that they'd also make a film during our time at Britannia Row. 'Do You Remember The First Time?', a short film funded by Island, would be a companion piece to the official 'DYRTFT?' video and featured celebrities revealing the story behind their own 'first time' along with Jarvis talking about his. Steve talked the celebs into taking part, Martin Wallace filmed it, and Jarvis directed. The ping-pong room at Brit Row was cleared and turned into a film set, and folk like Vic and Bob, John Peel, actress Alison Steadman, fashion designer Pam Hogg, The Specials' Terry Hall, Vivian Stanshall of Bonzo Dog Doo-Dah Band fame and even Candida's mum, actress Sandra Voe, traipsed in and said their bit. Guitars would be put down while Jarvis, Martin and Steve filmed.

It was a great distraction and confirmed to me that we were doing stuff that no one else seemed to be doing, or had done before or maybe even since. The film was even 'premiered' at the prestigious Institute of Contemporary Arts, where we also played a few numbers. Pulp: piercing the heart of the art establishment.

By February 1994 we had a record we all were very, very proud of, and we all knew we couldn't have done it any better. We had an amazing clarity of purpose and confidence. Everything came together very quickly. We were happy, and just as importantly, Island were happy.

However, as the record was being readied for release it was time for our first argument with our new label. Island wanted 'Babies' on the record; we didn't. We considered the song to be an elder statesman of the set and, besides, it was on *Intro* – why stick it on *His 'N' Hers*? Plus, we didn't want to be seen to be potentially ripping off our fans by expecting them to buy the same song twice. Island's argument was that it was a hit record in waiting. It just needed re-releasing at the right time and with the right push, and it would be a Singles Chart shoo-in. With those kinds of words, our resistance soon cracked and we agreed to let them include the track on the LP.

Jarvis had been into airbrush art for a while and decided he wanted that kind of look for the cover, so the master of the medium, Philip Castle, was commissioned to create it for us. He worked off a photo shot previously, and when the finished piece was unveiled I was rather underwhelmed to be honest. Sorry, Philip. Can't say I've ever been a fan of band paintings as cover art; they don't do much for me, and anyway – why not just use a photograph? Again, I wasn't going to rock the boat and flounce off in a huff over what was, after all, a well-executed painting.

One other major difference with this record: we wouldn't be stuck in limbo, waiting for its release. 'Lipgloss' was cued up as the first Island single, and it was released before the recording for *His 'N' Hers* was even finished. Cue the usual rave reviews, and we filmed a super colourful video in an odd structure called the *Eggopolis*, a series of interconnected and inflatable primary-coloured eggs that you could walk through. Once inside, the light from outside filtered through, making those colours seem very intense.

So, another great song and another great video in the bag, this time with major label push. In November, Pulp played a blistering live version of the song on Channel 4's *The Word* – our highest profile TV appearance yet. Pulp were finally entering the record-buying public's consciousness in a big way. Would they like it?

26

Slow Boil

(Don't Lose It)

'Lipgloss' scraped into the UK Singles Chart – in with a bullet at precisely number 50. This was in no way seen as a disappointment. It was higher than 'Razzmatazz' and in the teeth of everyone releasing stuff for Christmas (this was late November 1993, remember), so number 50 was very respectable indeed. Let's face it, we had been scrabbling along the gutter for long enough.

Thing is, with hindsight it was still a bit like the analogy of a frog in a pan of hot water: it will not jump out until it's boiled to death – the growing temperature creeps up on the frog until it's too late. Pulp were in a similar state. To the casual observer, it looked like we were zooming along to stardom at a fair lick, but inside the bubble it was far more genteel. It may have seemed like Pulp went from indie backwater also-rans to sleazy, sleek pop machine in one fateful bound, but you've heard the story; you now know what really happened. The fickle pop searchlight was sweeping the landscape, and moving in our direction, that is certain. The UK youth were also looking for something more glamorous to spend their cash on. Britain had not seen a new youth cultural movement since the late eighties with acid house. Indie had overall been a bit worthy and dull (although, in my opinion, Pulp essentially came from indie).

Nirvana's Kurt Cobain was found dead at home, seemingly by his own hand, on 8 April 1994. Grunge's poster boy was no more. The British, and to a certain extent European, youth were ready for something new: a homegrown set of oiks, flouncing about in garish shirts, shiny trousers and glitter, and storming into the space left by indie and grunge.

★ ★ ★

Along with recording, video and filmmaking, we were still out treading the boards, doing what we did best: playing live. After the Saint Etienne tour, we went out on our own headline tour of indie venues up and down the country, taking along Sheffield group The Longpigs, featuring our old mate Richard Hawley on guitar and fellow Rotherham drummer Dee Boyle (formerly of Chakk and one of my all-time favourite players). To complete this 'proto-Britpop-fest' of a line-up, we had Elastica and Echobelly support us at some of the gigs.

This series of shows proved to us that there was a very real upswell of support for Pulp. Folk were getting to hear our music and by the sight – and sound – of it they were liking it. A lot. We played to packed venues every night, everyone seemingly dressed up (in a Pulpy, individual way) for an event, and all of them hanging on to Jarvis's every word, flick of the wrist, crotch thrust and yelp. This was what joining a band was all about.

One particularly memorable night, after the Bristol gig, we were chucked out of the venue and quite a large gang of us, with fans in tow, went in search of further 'refreshment'. Unfortunately, like many far-flung cities outside London, Bristol in the nineties was absent of late-night party venues for thirsty indie rockers, so we ended up bribing the night porter at a hotel we passed to allow us to use one of the rooms for an impromptu aftershow party. Trouble is, he insisted we must not make any noise or upset the 'real' guests. So, being a nice bunch we sat in near silence for about 40 minutes, passing around a couple of bottles of tepid wine, trying to party hard while whispering. Riotous gigs should be followed by riotous hotel room trashing rather than polite conversation – or so that's what the rock'n'roll manual would suggest. But we were always more interested in ignoring rock'n'roll clichés. All part of the desire to be different. We left the room as we found it and never did upset the other guests.

The venues we were playing during this period were still very much part of the 'toilet' circuit, or maybe a cut above but definitely less than 1,000 capacity, and some a lot less. The dressing room walls were usually seen as a canvas for bored band members to try out their (non-existent) graffiti skills, and they'd deface them with their badly drawn band logos or poor humour. We found these places a little depressing and fantasised about bringing some white paint and making the rooms more palatable.* Though that's not to say Pulp, or more realistically I was not opposed to a bit of mischief.

By Christmas 1993 we were considered sufficiently 'cool' to be invited to *NME*'s seasonal bash. It was 'sponsored' by a famous brand of vodka, which basically meant free vodka bar. Oh dear. Us northern souls had never been exposed to such hedonism and could scarcely believe the bar would be operational the whole night: surely they'd shut it after an hour or so? Well no one told us, so we thought the best policy was to line up a load of shots just in case. The bar stayed open so we kept up ordering the shots. At some time hence, the room started taking on a life of its own, and down became up. Best leave, said my legs, so I went to get a cab back to the Islington house, but slipped in a pile of fresh vodka vom and fell over, fracturing my wrist – which is bad news for a drummer, of course. Still, I somehow got the cab back to the house and ended the night chasing Mark

---

* We never went ahead with that, but I believe ex-Fire Records inmates Teenage Fanclub actually did on one tour. And I can say, hand on heart, we never graffitied 'Pulp' on any dressing room wall in any venue. Keep being different, see.

around the house with an assortment of kitchen utensils. Rock'n'roll ain't dead, eh? At least that's what I remember . . . Thankfully I had completed my parts for the album and there was enough time before the next tranche of gigs to heal up.

They often say don't meet your heroes, but at one gig in Portsmouth we got wind that one of our heroes was on the guest list. Richard, my brother, was part of our growing road crew by now, and he rushed into the dressing room to exclaim that Joe Strummer of The Clash would be coming. Lawks, this is big news. We were pretty much stunned. Like all the gigs on this tour, it would've been a corker, and afterwards Joe popped in to see us; and for him to say we were destined for the top was the ultimate compliment. He was so gracious with us, it was heart-warming. We crossed paths with Joe several more times over the years before his passing and he was always fun to be with. Joe's endorsement was such a vindication of our direction. We were on the right path.

Island Records' mantra was that we needed to release two singles before the album came out proper. 'Do You Remember The First Time?' was unanimously chosen as the follow-up to 'Lipgloss'. It was destined to be a single as soon as it was born. It's all tense atmospherics leading to an uplifting chorus, despite the somewhat sneering yet unrequited lost-love lyrics, all wrapped up with a thumping beat and melodic hooks aplenty. Phew!

A dizzying promo video was filmed – for once not by Steve and Jarvis, who were too busy making the album, but by a fellow with the heady name Pedro Romhanyi. If you look closely you may just make out my be-corduroyed legs. That's about as much of me as you can see in the video. I believe some of the interior shots were filmed in the old Yugoslav Embassy in Kensington. Yet again, Philip Castle provided original airbrush art for the sleeve, keeping the theme going in readiness for the LP.

Released on 21 March 1994, 'Do You Remember The First Time?' became Pulp's first Top 40 hit when it crashed into the charts at number 33. Usually a new entry at 33 would win you a slot on *Top of the Pops*, but sadly the powers that be, namely *TOTP*'s producers, decided to air another up-and-coming band, who subsequently sank without fanfare. *TOTP* was a big deal; we'd just have to bide our time and keep our fingers crossed that we'd make it next time around. Still, 'Do You Remember The First Time?' went on to be a massive hit in all the indie disco clubs and a bona fide Pulp classic.

The pressure was building. No rest for the wicked, we needed to cue up another single release. Here's where Island's foresight came into play. As mentioned, we'd had our reservations about including 'Babies' on the LP, as it was an old track by now. Thing is, it had been elevated to 'one of our best songs' status. It was often the highlight of a live set, as it really seemed to set the crowd alight. We had to bow to Island's experience here, so 'Babies' was lined up as the new single.

As a nod to fans who had bought it previously as part of the *Intro* mini-album, we decided 'Babies' should be wrapped up with three other quality Pulp productions that didn't make the cut for *His 'N' Hers* – 'Your Sister's Clothes', 'Seconds' and 'His 'N' Hers' – to form *The Sisters EP*.

'Your Sister's Clothes' continues the story of the same girls in the narrative from 'Babies'. 'His 'N' Hers' – a rare Pulp track, as I play congas on it – was strangely left off the LP of the same name, though I would argue it's actually stronger than some of the other tracks on the album. (I can only imagine it sounded too similar to 'Acrylic Afternoons', since it too had a long(ish) quiet bit in the middle.*

---

* When played live, these sections meant Jarvis could ad lib to his heart's content. It was not unusual to find him singing from atop the PA speaker stacks or from under the drum riser during these parts. We'd have a secret signal so we'd know when to bring the song back to the main theme.

I suppose what went against its inclusion was that we were trying to cram as much variety on to the LP as possible. (I do recall voting for it for *His 'N' Hers*, but again I was in the minority. Hey ho.)

Had we demanded 'Babies' be left off *His 'N' Hers*, which song would we have chosen as the third single, if at all? One of the slower numbers, perhaps (a typical record company strategy, designed show off the band's more 'sensitive' side)? So, maybe 'Happy Endings'? Trouble is, we'd been turning out upbeat pop classics, so to continue that theme there would've been only two choices: 'Pink Glove' and 'Joyriders'. I thought 'Pink Glove' had suffered in the final version and a remix would likely happen. 'Joyriders', on the other hand, was a harder, rockier Pulp track, in which we'd tried to flip the traditional song structure, going for a quiet chorus and a barnstorming verse rather than the more conventional calm verse, soaring chorus. So, that might have been a bit radical for the conservative radio programmers.

By this point in our career, one thing was clear: we needed as much exposure as possible, and that meant TV, and that meant we needed a proper HIT RECORD. Top 20 at least. All signs were good, based on our recent success, but I must doff my cap to Island for their uncanny foresight.

27

Pop Stars – Official

(The Day After the Revolution)

I could see the windscreen by looking down the aisle of the plane and directly through the open cockpit door. The horizon was moving up and down at an alarming rate – too alarming for some, and hands were gripping armrests and faces were pale with worry, especially Russell's, who had a morbid fear of flying. The small plane was taking us over the English Channel for our first ever appearance on *Top of the Pops*, something that would've been unheard of for us only a few years before. We considered *TOTP* the gateway to stardom: get on that stage, even just once, and you could call yourself a pop star. Before that you were merely a wannabe.

But it was now official. Pulp were pop stars.

* * *

The Sisters EP was released at the end of May 1994 and 'Babies' got plenty of decent airplay, meaning it soared to number 19 on the charts. *TOTP* could no longer ignore us, and we were finally invited to perform (well, mime) at the holy grail of British music television. This news was met with whoops of joy from us all – it

231

really was a massive ambition of ours to perform on the show, ever since we started being in bands and making music. It only took 14 single releases and 16 years of toil at the musical meat grinder to get there. Trouble is, we were in the midst of our French tour in support of the album. We had to get back to London pronto to appear on the show that week. Hence, the small plane, which was hired so we could do our Reims gig then hop over to London in time to record *TOTP*.

This plane had just enough space for the band plus tour manager Richard Priest and chief roadie Roger Middlecoat. The weather was bad. A typical early summer storm was a-cookin' up. It threw our little craft all over the place as we made our way through the maelstrom. Oh the irony if after all this time our rightful place on *TOTP* was to be snatched away by poor old us being thrown into the Channel and lost to the ocean like dear Glenn Miller. Well, we survived and made it to the studio* in a fleet of posh cars laid on by Island (but charged to Pulp, of course).

As we were on tour, we were now used to a certain level of pampering when doing a gig – and this felt a bit like doing a gig: we were together all day, waiting for stuff to happen. However, the BBC didn't provide the traditional 'rider' you'd expect backstage at a gig. We were surprised. This was a prestigious TV 'do': wasn't there a well-stocked green room with big TVs and plenty of refreshments? Nope. We were shown to a somewhat dowdy room with a few desultory chairs and were left to it. Any chance of a tea? Bottle of water? Nope. BBC canteen opens in a bit, was the response. At least the BBC food was cheap and cheerful.

What also surprised us was the amount of 'run-throughs' required. There were camera rehearsals, dress rehearsals, band rehearsals. We

---

* Not at TV Centre, as we'd imagined, but a studio in a non-descript suburb of north London called Borehamwood. Not far from Pinewood Studios, where we'd filmed the 'Lipgloss' video.

had been gigging solid for the last two months, so we could play 'Babies' in our sleep (and probably did). The BBC could have put five sacks on stage and pretended we were there, but no. We had to go through miming the song several times. 'Rock'n'roll' it was not.

Miming the drums is not as problematic as you might think. Chuck some cut-out lino onto each drum to deaden the sound and put two cymbals together to stop the crashing when they're hit, and you're good to go. You can play away, hitting the drums in sync with the track, and it looks genuine. It's actually quite fun: there's no pressure whatsoever, no chance of cocking the song up no matter how nervous you might be. Hey, you could even muck about.

One thing I did need to think about prior to this possibly once-in-a-lifetime experience, though, was how was I going to deport myself on the most influential music TV show of all time. Do I 'play' as if I'm Animal from *The Muppets*, all gung-ho, wild, craziness? Or do I approach it like Charlie Watts (one of my all-time favourite drummers), and go for understated brilliance? Watch any Stones *TOTP* appearance and Charlie always looks like he'd rather be anywhere else. He's completely bored with proceedings. I'm not a particularly demonstrative player anyway, so Watts it was.

But first we had to ask the BBC technicians to actually turn up the playback from the level of a transistor radio playing ten feet away. The Beeb were very keen to protect everyone's hearing, but music performance is about passion, and you can't get into it at low volume. Eventually, they turned it up.

The rest of the time outside rehearsals you hung about a bit, watching the other performers go through their rehearsals. The biggest star on that particular episode was Mariah Carey (who is surprisingly tall), and she seemed to be excused of any 'run-through' duty. Odd that.

Finally, it was time for the make-up ladies to trowel a bit of slap on us, and to do the show for real, with the traditionally bemused teenage audience looking on. Once we stepped on to that (rather tiny) stage, we could officially call ourselves POP STARS.

I never set out with an aching ambition to be a 'pop star'. A working touring musician would have done me fine. Travelling round the world with my mates playing our daft songs and getting paid for the privilege would have been more than fine. This 'pop star' malarkey was fun, though. And it stopped the relatives joking about 'When you getting a proper job?' Of course, they were all dead chuffed to see me on the telly, BBC One, 7 o'clock on a Thursday.

This particular *Top of the Pops* was a bit different, as it went out live. We were miming, of course, but the camera action was being beamed straight into living rooms across the nation. No editing, no redos, what happens, happens. Opportunity for mischief was thus high.

The show began with the redoubtable Radio 1 DJ Simon Mayo at the head of proceedings and we watched as the acts went through their thing: Beautiful South, Big Mountain, The Grid, Salt-n-Pepa, and then it was our turn. The playback began and before you knew it Simon Mayo was already introducing the next act – Pink Floyd, no less. The show finished with the schmaltz fest that was Wet Wet Wet and their version of 'Love Is All Around', which had indeed been around in the charts for a then record-breaking 15 weeks, and Pulp (and, we hoped, the nation) were sick of it. As we returned to our dressing room we learned that at the climax of 'Babies' Jarvis had revealed the inside of his jacket to the camera, which had a note pinned to it that said:

I Hate WET WET WET

Oh how we laughed at the pettiness and the beauty of such a simple yet provocative statement. The Wet's singer Marti Pellow certainly had a smiley style that many, including us, would find detestable. Putting ourselves on the other side of the fence to the Wets was a great way of getting all those kids watching on our side. Or so we hoped. It was the start of Jarvis's leap into the public consciousness that he seemed destined for from the first time he got up on stage to front a band. I had always thought he was made for it.

This push for national recognition was given another boost a couple of weeks later, when Jarvis appeared on the BBC's Saturday teatime show *Pop Quiz*, hosted by Chris Tarrant. Well, it wasn't really a push for national recognition; it was just one of those odd things he got asked to do, and if you'd been in the wilderness for as long as we head, wouldn't you jump at the chance? Thing is, Jarvis is a deep well of pop knowledge. Anytime we did an in-the-van quiz he'd usually wipe the floor with us. Despite that, he got his first question wrong on the show, and looked rather shell-shocked to be there at all. But he went on to single-handedly triumph in the final quick-fire round, showing the other contestants (including Des'ree, Chesney Hawkes and Marcella Detroit) how it's done. We were cheering Jarvis on from the other side of the TV screen and once it had finished, we knew his appearance had done Pulp a world of good. The casual observer would want to see more of this character and what he would get up to next. One thing's for sure, he was never boring.

Never mind all these TV shenanigans, it was time once again to hit the road for more gigs in support of *His 'N' Hers*. This time round we hit mostly university-type/sized venues (definitely no more 'toilet circuit'). We even did some our first 'in-store' gigs, usually at a branch of HMV: you turn up and play a few numbers 'acoustically', which really meant stripped-down versions. I'd play tambourine or maracas, Candida would have a little electric piano set up and so on. Once we'd done a couple of these, along with the obligatory signing sessions, we decided it would be good if the band could get some HMV freebies. So, we began asking if we could do a 'supermarket sweep' of the shop floor. Let's face it, if you don't ask you don't get, and

HMV would let us have five or six free CDs as a thank you for coming into the store.

I enjoyed these sessions, as you got a chance to meet the fans who were, generally, really nice. Everyone was always excited about the show that night and some would even be added to the guest list if they claimed to be ticket-less and we had space.

On one of these trips around the UK we were offered a promising new band from Manchester as support. A bunch of rough-diamond scallies called Oasis. They were already somewhat notorious due to a drunken brawl on a cross-Channel ferry and for the 'volatile' relationship between the band's mainstays, the Gallagher brothers. Jarvis declined them, possibly on the premise that Pulp – and by extension Pulp fans – would rather reject any notions of 'hard' or 'machismo' or 'giving it large'. Oasis looked like the kind of lads who would have chased any of us down the street to give us a roughing up for being 'weird looking'. Still, would have been entertaining that's for sure.

At the end of May we returned to France to headline a national tour. We were quite amazed to be so popular in France – the kids there were really into us.

The most memorable moment from this tour was playing an amazing venue in Toulouse, south-west France. It had a swimming pool backstage, which, of course most of us ended up in after the show. Russell, meanwhile, had bought a load of fireworks and proceeded to start a display. Unfortunately, the Catherine wheel failed to revolve and ended up setting fire to the owner's prized palm tree that he'd nurtured for years. We tried to extinguish the flames with vodka, which patently a bad idea, and eventually a few buckets of swimming pool water did the job. The owner was less than pleased.

We managed to add a few new countries on our European jaunt, including the Netherlands and Belgium. But our first visit to Sweden resulted in a gig that is in my top ten Pulp gigs of all time.

The journey over was memorable. As we know, Russell is not a good flyer, and this time he decided to 'self-medicate' so he could make the trip without freaking out. Needless to say, by the time we landed in Stockholm he was zonked and could barely walk straight.

We were met at the airport by our record company 'minder', a most pleasant young lady, who would be on hand to help. Russell proceeded to ask her for some 'herrrn' repeatedly. She looked most troubled and shocked and said she would see what she could do. We were all in stitches watching Russell in his altered state (no one gets a free ride in a band!). The rep was looking most worried and asked us if Russ was all right. Yes, he'll be fine in a bit . . . 'Does he need *something*?' she said, looking concerned. 'Herrnnn,' said Russ. We were none the wiser. He wandered off to his room and the rep admitted that if Russ needed some heroin, it would be very, very difficult in Stockholm, almost impossible. We very much doubted that was what Russ wanted and indeed he confirmed later that he was really after some pickled herring, the Swedish fishy speciality.

The next day we were booked to play at an outdoor venue in Stockholm, almost a mini-festival that seemed, oddly, to feature just us. The sweet Swedish summer had turned into the Swedish summer deluge, with rain coming down like stair-rods. The stage was barely covered and it was obvious we could not play outdoors. Never mind, said the practical Swedes, just play indoors. The outdoor stage had a small room behind it that to us resembled a scout hut. It was tiny, but the only solution.

So, Roger, Mike, Justin and Priesty (chief roadie, front-of-house, sound, monitors and tour manager, respectively – yes, we really were pop stars now; no more humping heavy amps about) set up the gear on this tiny stage. Typically, as soon as they'd finished, the rain abated and the sun came out, but inside it was to be.

The hut could probably hold 150 max, but about 400 mad Swedish kids crammed in and proceeded to go literally apeshit. Roger and

Priest had to physically hold the PA to prevent it falling on the crowd, and I played with several kids' heads poking through the windows right next to the kit, so close we could have a conversation between songs, and most pleasant those kids were. The stage seemed to be in a constant situation of crowd invasion and the walls of the hut were just dripping with kids hanging off the rafters for a better view of the chaos. It really was astonishing. Sweden immediately became one of my favourite places to play.

We did a couple of British festivals that summer, too – the gloriously Scottish T in the Park, and the kind of music biz away-day that is the Reading Festival. We debuted a couple of new tunes at Reading that pointed to the direction of the next Pulp album, namely 'Pencil Skirt', 'Underwear' and a half lyrically finished number called 'Common People'. We were rather new to the festival game. We had played outdoors before, though. One of my early pulp gigs was in Sefton Park, Liverpool, playing a free festival. I recall the stage being set up so that the lake acted as a kind of moat to keep the hordes at bay. In truth there was no hordes to keep back. Pulp had been on stage at Sheffield's Dole Busters festival before my joining, but these seemed like events run by enthusiastic amateurs. Reading and T in the Park were proper grown-up dos that signified how we were slowly climbing up the stairway to success.

But before any more new material could be conjured up we were due our first visit to the Good ol' US of A. Blur had asked us to open for them on their eight or so dates there. This idea of playing in America was a different gravy. It was quite mind-boggling to think that this bunch of misfits had got so far as to attempt to woo US audiences with our tawdry disco foppery. Pulp had come a long way from playing to two bemused teenagers in Derby to boarding a plane bound for Boston, Massachusetts.

So what would the US make of Pulp? We had no idea, and neither did the Americans. We had hooked up with a US-based manager to help things along over there, one Peter Rudge. He'd been an old booker for the likes of The Who and The Rolling Stones, so he seemed perfect for the job.

Not that we had any fancy notions of 'breaking America'. Music biz folk always seem to push bands into this notion that your aim should be to get to number one over there, despite the amount of ball-breaking work it takes. Unlike the UK, there is no national radio, and even then the market is so fractured and competitive it's almost impossible to get yourself noticed. I think we just went along for the ride and with a 'see what happens' approach.

Our first experience of the US was a heady mixture of joy and pain. And clichés.

Well, first off, on the plane Russell was again full of nerves, and this was somewhat compounded at take-off when the air-conditioning system above us decided to spill its watery guts onto Russ's head as the aircraft tilted to climb into the air. We laughed, he screamed.

Still, we were feverish with excitement about playing in America. Being on tour is a bit like being on a very, very long school trip. Everything is organised by someone else and you just have to turn up with snacks and sandwiches for the journey. Any problems en route are sorted by the tour manager, who is a bit like a trendy teacher who has to keep straight with the kids but secretly enjoys their mischief. And yes, the pupils – the band and crew – do get up to mischief. You even get pocket money, known as PDs (per diems) to spend on whatever takes your fancy, ours being doled out by our tour manager Richard Priest each day. So, on our way across the Atlantic everyone (except Russ, who was too damp) was in high spirits.

Our first show in Boston seemed to go down well with the Anglophile yanks in attendance, not that the venue was really very big. Obviously they'd come to see and hear Blur; perhaps they'd only just heard of us on the way. Safe to say, this was not a check shirt and mullet crowd, Boston being possibly the most European-feeling (if that's possible) US city. As they say over there, 'it's a big college town'.

We picked up our tour bus the next day for the long drive to the next show in Chicago. Now, this bus was a major step up – a beautiful, streamlined, silver coach that was so clean it was unreal. Bob was our genial driver who would pilot us across the States for the next two weeks or so. We marvelled at the vastness of the country as it rolled by, and also at Bob's stamina at the wheel. Drivers in Europe are governed by law to take breaks at regular intervals for everyone's safety, not so in the US. Bob's limit was about 28 hours of driving non-stop, which was crazy. The drive from Chicago to Atlanta is a loooong way, but it was what the schedule demanded. At least it got us to do a bit of tornado chasing, as the flat landscape allowed you to see for miles and wonder at the towering weather systems spewing lightning all around.

Atlanta was interesting, as the basement venue seemed to be home to a rather strange S&M sex dungeon. Disclaimer: this was discovered while waiting around either to sound-check or for the doors to open. There's a lot of waiting around on tour. Russ and I were heckled from passing cars when we went out for a wander – possibly to go to the Coca-Cola museum in Atlanta. 'I want some cream in my coffee' was lobbed at us by a young black girl. We responded with some suitably appreciative sounds. Everywhere we walked in America we felt like we were on the set of a film. US imagery had permeated our lives from day one, so actually being in these familiar scenes is, at first, rather surreal.

The most bizarre event occurred when we went on a detour to New Orleans. There was a gap in the Blur tour schedule, and Peter Rudge or some-such said Pulp were getting 'traction' in the Louisiana city (maybe a college station had been playing us a bit), so a gig should be slotted in. OK, we said. New Orleans is about halfway from Atlanta to Los Angeles (our next port of call), so why not?

So, our enormo tour bus pulls up outside this small bar that really was like something out of the *Blues Brothers* film – it just needed the chicken wire across the front of the stage to protect the performers from flying objects and it would have been just the same: a couple of mulletted rednecks shootin' pool and suckin' down some suds was what we were greeted with. The place was clearly not ready for a band like us: for starters, we had European spec gear and it didn't like the US 110-volt system, meaning it only took a short while to blow all the electrics for the place and it couldn't be sorted without us getting a generator in to run all our gear – of which we had far too much for such a small place. Anyway, as they say, the show must go on, so eventually we hit the stage and it was like going back in time: There was a pitiful audience forming the semi-circle of indifference again. It was obvious that Pulp had in fact, not been making any waves in New Orleans. The slide guitar player who we were supporting went down surprisingly well with the good ole boys, though. Still, we got to mooch around Bourbon Street and the French Quarter, which was what touring should be about.

It's always good to try and get out and about while visiting new and exotic places on tour. It's far too easy to get trapped in the pattern of staying up way too late after a gig and sleeping most of the day away until sound check time, becoming almost nocturnal. I always tried to find time to get out and have a look around: going up the Sears Tower (now the Willis Tower) in Chicago, the CN Tower in Toronto, cycling round San Francisco Bay (not all of it, it's massive). I passed on going up the World Trade Center building in New York, instead choosing to hop on the ferry to the Statue of Liberty (don't bother, it's rubbish). When future events came to pass, of course, I really wished I'd chosen differently. This solo sightseeing started to become a thing for me.

We heard that another British band were in San Francisco the night we hit town, the night before our gig there with Blur. It was those pesky Mancs, Oasis. We decided to call in before we got to our hotel so, again, our huge tour bus pulls up outside this tiny venue and Priesty pops in to see if we can all get on the guest list for that night's show. The answer that came back was that Jarvis had to go in and see them before they made their decision. No idea what was said – he probably had to grovel about turning Oasis down earlier in the year – but we all went along later, and they were electrifying, menacing and mesmerising in equal measure. It really would have been some tour.

28

And the Winner is . . .

(Mis-Shapes)

And the winner is . . . M People!

Cue swearing under the breath yet putting on a brave and cheery face as we see our 25-grand prize being swiped from under our noses. *His 'N' Hers* had been nominated for a Mercury Music Prize as one of the albums of the year 1994. We were at the swanky Dorchester Hotel on Park Lane in that London, and had been highly tipped to win. Pulp had never been up for as prestigious an award as this, so we were keen to scoop the prize. Let's face it, the money would've been very welcome. We were still on smallish wages compared to most, and royalties were just a trickle. Plus, getting that kind of recognition from the 'industry' would have been a nice British two fingers up to the naysayers who had failed Pulp in the past.

The buzz on the day was palpable and we made sure we enjoyed the 'hospitality' in full. A panel does the awarding of the prize on the night, and the rumour mill was seriously working overdrive in our favour. In the end, they announced M People's 'shopping centre' soul as the album of the year, putting us second by a measly point. Never mind. However, there was more than a little schadenfreude as we watched M People's popularity start to wane almost immediately upon lifting the trophy. Hmmm, take note?

We'd recently been nominated for another award, an *NME* Brat – a kind of indie/alternative take on the UK's largest music awards, the Brits. The *NME* Awards is a somewhat boozy affair and after ligging around voraciously with all and sundry from the indie and emergent 'Britpop' world, everyone retreated to some swanky night-club-type place to get further trolleyed. It was here that our Brat statue got smashed into a million pieces by me. Oh dear. My intended, Sarah, and myself had got into a bit of a 'disagreement'. My displeasure at this ended up with me throwing the statuette at the wall in frustration. Somehow, just before I was unceremoniously thrown out by the bouncer, the end of the statue's finger was picked up and saved. It's the only bit that survived (I still have that finger end to this day). It was possibly the most rock'n'roll clichéd thing that happened to me during that period. Not much to be proud of, I suppose.

In the mid-nineties, Quentin Tarantino was *the* hotshot filmmaker, and we were asked to play at the party to celebrate the premiere of his new film, *Pulp Fiction* – seems obvious now, I guess. We jumped at the chance, but as long as we got to go to the premiere ourselves – we wanted to see the film, so this seemed like a fair swap. After all, oiks like us would never get an actual invite in a million years, and it sounded like fun.

The premiere was no red carpet affair of swanky frocks and popping light bulbs: more of an undignified scrum. It was to be held at the Curzon Cinema on Shaftesbury Avenue, so we prepared, like a lot of the attendees, at the pub across the road. And predictably, everyone left it to the last minute to evacuate the pub for the cinema, hence the almighty crush at the door, as everyone wanted to get in at the same time. As I edged towards the gatekeeper, a large hand appeared and without a word created a space in the queue ahead of me. The hand was attached to a rather large gentleman, who proceeded to insert a rather diminutive lady ahead of me in the queue: Kylie Minogue, the Aussie pop songstress, no less. Who was I to argue about this blatant bit of queue jumping as the crowd pushed me and Kylie together, to the point where certain bits of me were touching Kylie where perhaps they had no right to be. I had zero control of this situation; I just had to grin and bear it (the things us drummers have to put up with). This 'collision' only lasted a brief minute or so as we gave our names on the door and were ushered into the foyer, me now in rather a flustered state, as events like what had just happened don't occur very often. We made our way to our seats and again boggled at the fact that we were sat behind Björk, who was making steady progress through a large box of popcorn, and immediately in front of Mick Jones of The Clash. After the film, we made our way to Ministry of Sound, where the aftershindig was being held, and we played a few numbers, including 'Girl, You'll Be A Woman Soon' from the film's soundtrack. The audience were probably inconvenienced by our presence, but at least we had fulfilled our side of the bargain.

We finished off 1994, which had been by far our most successful year to date, with another zip around France and some of our largest British shows up to that point, playing, again, with Blur at Aston Villa Leisure Centre and Alexandra Palace in London. With the addition of Supergrass, the bill almost represented a festival of this new(ish) scene folk were blabbing on about: 'Britpop'.

The term didn't really mean much to us. We had seen enough putative scenes come and go with our name attached as to become meaningless. All it was to me was a collection of British indie bands that were making the most sparkling and exciting guitar–ish pop music the UK had seen for ages. There was no draping ourselves in the Union flag for Pulp, oh no. Well, I suppose Russ was quite fond of wearing some Union Jack socks, but that is about as near as we got.

Elsewhere, we got to almost ruin one of London's grandest theatres: The Theatre Royal, no less. Pulp had done a Christmas show for years, and naturally as we had achieved greater popularity the venues had become somewhat fancy. This year it was decided to top the lot by doing a show at the famous Theatre Royal, built in 1812. It was a great way of capping off a momentous year and we went balls out to make it as grand as possible. A vertiginous staircase was set up centre stage in front of an enormous starry night back cloth, so Jarvis could prance about to his heart's content – either that or look a right knob falling off them. He had got into the idea that at 6ft 3 or so he wasn't tall enough, so he'd taken to wearing shoes with three-inch heels on to increase his tall-ness even more. He really was asking for trouble. The place was packed out with all the new devotees in their shimmer and sparkly garb, the air full of feather boa fluff.

It was a night that really did live up to its billing: a thrilling celebration of the weirdos and misfits getting to the front of the queue. Pulp had got there (wherever 'there' is) after all this time. The crowd were rewarded by getting to listen to some real Pulp oldies and rarities, Jarvis calling out the years that they were released just to highlight to those who were 'new' to the party that Pulp had history. Some of the old ones played here were never played again, namely 'I Want You', 'Death Comes To Town' and 'Love Is Blind'. They also got what they wanted hits wise and naturally went mental.

We only heard afterwards that there was so much dancing on the balconies that the theatre staff were seconds away from halting the proceedings and clearing the theatre. Cracks had begun to appear in the supports that fix the balcony to the structure, and they feared an imminent collapse. At least Jarvis never did fall down the Hollywood stairs or off his high-heeled boots, so that's something.

By now, we were ready to start writing and recording again. We already had a few new songs to work on that we'd written over the past year since the *His 'N' Hers* sessions had completed, and we were eager to get started on them.

29

Surprise!

(You Are the One)

Jarvis often recorded ideas on a crappy old seventies cassette recorder and would play back the efforts to us to develop the idea further. One day he comes in (always late – it's like his concept of time is far different to everyone else's. We'd often tell him a meeting started 30 minutes earlier than it did to get him there on time. Rarely worked). He pressed play on the machine and the distorted noise of him playing the old Portasound – badly – drifted out, but you could just about discern a tune amid the distortion and crackling. This was not unusual. He hadn't really bothered to get the hang of recording his musings with any great clarity, so the recordings were always like this.

After we'd stopped laughing at the ham-fisted attempt, we got behind our instruments and started working on this new idea. We would play around with it for hours, trying different bits. I thought it was OK but perhaps a bit one-dimensional. There were no stops or even a chorus as such, but it had a nice 'driving' quality and a shade of 'Mr. Blue Sky' about it. Nothing wrong in that. There were no words at this point, mostly a kind of mumbled tune. Again, this was nothing new; we were used to not really hearing the words clearly in rehearsal as they were being formulated in Jarv's brain.

During yet another run-through of the song, possibly the millionth one (it was quite rare to devote such a lot of time to a new song; often if it wasn't working, we'd move on), I was getting rather bored of doing the same old drum beat, so I just started mucking about with a super heavy bit. Jarvis liked it, so we incorporated parts of it into the song, just before the chorus lifts off, giving the song dramatic essence.

'What's this called Jarv?' I asked

"Common People".'

'Oh right.'

Seemed a daft title for a song to me, but that's the way it is sometimes. Back in Sheffield, being 'common' was rather an insult and being one of the 'common people' was worse. Remember, we only heard little snatches of lyrics at this time, so had no idea what the song was about. What we did know, though, was that it was starting to rock. It needed recording ASAP.

★ ★ ★

We were feeling pretty confident at this stage. *His 'N' Hers* had been a massive success for us and the run of singles since 'My Legendary Girlfriend' had seen us reaching higher and higher in the charts. We had gained a serious following and were getting to be regulars in the music press and on TV. We knew that the new record had to be good, hopefully better than *His 'N' Hers*, but we didn't feel under any pressure while formulating the songs for it. Everything seemed relatively easy. We were coming up with plenty of new ideas (still mostly upstairs at the railway arch in Catcliffe), and things were sounding very promising.

It was suggested that we needed a hotshot producer to shape the new Pulp record. Someone who might make people sit up and think, making them even more eager to hear the new Pulp album. Ed had done a grand job with *His 'N' Hers*, but we needed something different.

Stephen Street was again banded about, among others: Stephen Hague (Pet Shop Boys/New Order), Trevor Horn (ABC/Frankie Goes to Hollywood), Jeff Lynne (ELO) . . . even Benny from ABBA was mentioned. But one name really stood out: Chris Thomas. He's been involved in, or at the controls of, tons of legendary recordings. Here's just a small sample (it's a rather good roll call):

The Beatles, *The Beatles* (aka 'The White Album') (1968)
Pink Floyd, *The Dark Side Of The Moon* (1973)
Roxy Music, *Country Life* (1974)
Bryan Ferry, *Let's Stick Together* (1976)
Sex Pistols, *Never Mind The Bollocks, Here's The Sex Pistols* (1977)
The Human League, *Hysteria* (1984)
INXS, *Kick* (1987)
Elton John . . . errr . . . *The Lion King: Original Motion Picture Soundtrack* (1994)

The other names on our list never really get a look-in.

Thankfully, Chris was keen to help. He came to see us perform at the Theatre Royal (he watched proceedings in shades that had weird refracting lenses, so that everything looked 'far out'. Brilliant). Once Chris said he wanted to work with us the reality started to kick in that we were about to enter a new music-biz stratosphere. Chris would provide an elemental link back to some of our many music idols from when we were kids. Perfect. He even looked a bit like Mick Fleetwood. Double perfect.

We didn't have enough material ready for an album, yet this song seemed to be screaming at us to get it recorded and out. It was so 'now' that to wait for an entire record could easily dilute its impact.

Cue Townhouse Studios in West London to record the track, and a couple of others that were ready to use as potential B-sides. The Townhouse was a serious studio, packed with all the latest mid-nineties equipment and the buzz of amazing records having been produced there. We settled right in and recording began in earnest.

Alas, we hit a hurdle almost immediately: tempo. Now, as the drummer this was definitely my area of (in)expertise. After all, it's the drummer's main job to keep the tempo and speed of the song for everyone else to lock into so the whole thing stays together. We had been playing 'Common People' for a few months now, so it was well road-tested and we considered it just right. However, once it came under the studio microscope it was clear the song's tempo goes from around 130 beats per minute (bpm) at the start to about 155 bpm by the end. This is a huge difference. I acknowledged the discrepancy was down to the dynamics of the song: as it builds, the you get the feeling you're being swept along with the excitement of it all, and thus the drummer brings the tempo on to reflect the developing drama. This all happened completely naturally; we never discussed this as a method for ramping up the feverish quality of the tune. It just happened on its own. And we all liked it. But, in the sterile world of record production, it becomes a bit of a problem. Remember – modern techniques rely on click tracks, so that any electronic additions can be added and synched to the track that I, and thus everyone else, would play along to.

So, we tried playing the song with the click track set to the start tempo, but everyone was bored stiff halfway through. It was as if the song was being played in slow motion and dragging through mud all at the same time. OK, so that was a non-starter.

Next we tried playing it at a tempo that matched the end speed, and it just sounded comical. Even a mid-tempo between the start and the end tempos was ridiculous – it sounded stupidly fast at the start and dismally dull by the end. It was obvious the song relied upon the subtle tempo changes to make it work.

In the end, programmer Matt Vaughan had the painstaking task of constructing a click track that mirrored my natural playing, increasing in tempo by a few bpm every few bars. Thus the dramatic feel and energy the tempo change creates could be replicated *exactly* every time, allowing us to add the electronic trickery down the line. My drums were also samples, so that any straying from the strict tempo framework could be massaged in the computer, making sure everything was spot on. Once that was done, we could build up the many and various layers to get the staggeringly thick sound we achieved on the finished record.

I had to put me foot down at one point when the programmer put in a fancy doo-dah drum fill to herald the part where everything crashes in and the song really starts. I had always done this without a fill, as I thought it just needed to *get going*, everyone coming in together. Impact. No! Get rid of that drum bit, it's crap, was my finely honed argument, and for once I won through and it got binned.

Once the drum and bass backing was finished, which, once the tempo framework was done, didn't take very long, it was the time to start adding the rest of the instrumentation. And there's a lot. Recording studios in the mid-nineties generally had 48 separate recording tracks to fill up with whatever you like, and we crammed all of them with the ingredients that go towards making the record.

During the *His 'N' Hers* sessions, we had started to realise the potential of working in a properly good studio, and Chris Thomas was the key to unlocking that potential in droves on the new album. Jarvis wanted a much 'thicker', 'wall of sound' approach this time round, and 'Common People' is a prime example of that. As the song was coming together, it was obvious something special was happening. Often in the studio folk wander off when they've done their parts to play pool, watch TV and so on. Anything but listen to endless playbacks of the track. Not this time. Everyone was sticking around, soaking in the track as it grew and grew. Chris had the unenviable task of harnessing these 48-plus tracks into a coherent, exciting, single entity that was primed to launch Pulp to the next level.★

In the studio was, of course, the first time we'd all heard the lyrics in full. We'd hear snapshots here and there, but now they were finally unveiled to us in all their vicious, spiteful, vituperative, vengeful glory. This was a wonderful commentary on wealth, the class system so unique to Britain, and the people that inhabit the world around us. A tale of rich kids slumming it for the hell of it, safe in the knowledge they can escape any time. It was a lyric very much born out of Jarvis moving from Sheffield to London, and experiencing for the first time folk who could escape a life of drudgery with a simple phone call home to a rich parent. You didn't get many of those in Sheffield, but you did in London. We loved it. And we weren't the only ones.

Everyone from Island, Rough Trade, Best in Press PR and Scott Piering adored it too. However, Island needed some persuading to get on with releasing it as soon as possible. The job of a single is to enhance album sales, which is where the real profits are. After all, the record company is a money-making business – or, at least, that's the idea.

If you've read this far, you'll be well aware that Pulp's history was littered with delays, excuses and frustration while waiting, hoping for companies to release our records. Too many times the hold-ups meant the 'hot new track' was now stale, and we'd moved on by the time it finally came out. This time we were adamant that wasn't happening. 'Common People' seemed so very relevant and hard-hitting, we *had* to get it out there, even if the rest of the record wasn't even written yet. Thankfully, Island and Nigel Coxon relented, and I guess they decided to take a risk with it. The record would be released as soon as possible.

★ The reality that we were making something really, really special hit home when Chris was struggling with the mix one morning. The cleaner was hoovering away in the corridor outside the control room, and Chris exploded: 'Will someone shut that fucking door . . . we're making a hit record here!' Note he didn't say 'trying' – it was almost as if he knew we were on to something, and that something was a hit.

Right, all down to Frank's caff in Maida Vale to shoot a cover and rope in Pedro again to do a video. A bunch of kids who looked 'interesting', punters (like us) of the Smashing nightclub on Regent Street, were drafted in as dancers. Jarvis made up a sequence dance routine virtually on the spot for him and the kids to perform, and bona fide film star Sadie Frost was snared to play the role of the girl from Greece who had a thirst for knowledge.

Recorded in January 1995 and released on 22 May, 'Common People' was, of course, Single of the Week across the board and received blanket airplay everywhere, although with an edited version that clipped off the last verse so it was more radio-friendly than the six-minute LP definitive version. (Sell-outs!)

It was clear it was going to be our biggest hit to date and we really did dare to think that it could make it to number one. In the charts. Number one. You can request 'mid-week' sales to give you an idea of how it's going, but we didn't want to know in case we jinxed it.

That week some bright spark at Radio 1 had decided that they should do a live rundown of the charts at a Radio 1 roadshow event in Birmingham, where the acts featured in that week's chart would appear as their position was revealed and they could then mime the tune to the kids amassed in front of the stage. Yes, mime. On the radio.

We milled around excitedly in the green room. We had a good inkling that 'Common People' had done well and was going to be a high new entry. Exactly where we were unsure. Gradually as the afternoon progressed, the green room emptied as folk went out to do their funny little dance and then once the chart rundown had got to number four or so there was just us lot left in the room. Baby D had left to mime to her hit 'I Need Your Loving', then we heard that Perez 'Prez' Prado's 'Guaglione' was at number three and then . . . and then . . . (adopt annoying Radio 1 jock voice):

'It's a brand new entry on the chart, in at number two . . . PULP with 'Common People' . . .'

Fuck.

Fuck! We're actually at number two in the actual charts!

And . . .

Fuck! We're not number one, as we'd all secretly hoped and perhaps expected.

We ascended the steps onto the stage, which looked like the back of a flatbed lorry truth be told, and proceeded to mime to our number two hit with a strange mix of elation and disappointment. 'Common People' had failed to dislodge a couple of jobbing TV actors (Robson & Jerome) singing a lovely, but schmaltzy, old song ('Unchained Melody') from the top spot, where it had been firmly wedged for the past couple of weeks and would remain for a few more.

We soldiered on gamely, even though by this point the Birmingham rain was slashing down at a fair rate. We started prancing and goofing (there's no fear of the musical cock-up when miming, remember). Jarvis, however, was in ocular agony, as he'd failed to rinse his contact lenses properly so his eyes were bright red and streaming. As the playback of 'Common People' hit its climax, our front man leapt off the monitor in his dramatic style and promptly fell on his arse, the three-inch heels not helping much on the downpour-drenched stage. The rest of us enjoyed the spectacle of Jarvis, still miming, lying flat on his back, soaked through, staring up at the grey sky through smarting eyes. A fitting, incredulous moment in what should have been a crowning achievement. Oh how we laughed.

Were we that bothered about missing out on the top slot? Not really; to get to number two on the UK Singles Chart after all we had been through was an incredible achievement. It was affirmation, at long last, that the record-buying public liked it. The years of struggle had not been in vain. Yes, getting to number one would have been fantastic, but we now had the momentum and platform from which to build who knows what the next single may bring. It wasn't written yet, but the omens were looking good.

While all this chart malarkey was going on, we had squirrelled ourselves away to write more material for the as-yet-untitled forth-coming album. New ideas seemed to almost flow effortlessly out of us: Pulp-type ballads, upbeat pop stuff, glowering dramatics and even a bit of ska. Lots of the LP was written upstairs at the arches in Catcliffe, but we would also head down to London every now and then too (one of these sessions was at a similar place in Waterloo, only here the cockroaches were the size of cats – something Catcliffe couldn't boast).

We never felt any pressure to write more songs in the vein of 'Common People', even though it had been our biggest hit to date. That was just one side of our varied capacity to develop different kinds of music. Once again, we undertook spells of instrument swapping as a way of generating ideas without getting too technically proficient. Pulp are not master musicians, if you must know. Actually, I think that's part of our charm: no (or not much) guitar or keyboard noodling, and certainly NO drum or bass solos. One new song did need a drum break, though, and I was struggling to get something down that I was happy with. Mark suggested, 'Do a "Ringo" roll!' and that was enough to spur me on to the drum fills in 'Live Bed Show'.

Jarvis was mucking about with a vintage Roland Juno synthesizer one day and started playing a simple two-note 'riff', saying we should build something around it. So we tried (all ideas are valid – you never know what could come out of them), but then we stopped. We can't use it, it's too blatant a rip-off of the main riff from the Laura Branigan hit 'Gloria'. No, Jarvis insisted, this was different. Or, let's say, different enough. So, we persisted and I gave it a thumping 'four to the floor' disco beat, and 'Disco 2000' was born.

★　★　★

During these writing sessions, we were asked to take part in the BBC Radio 1 annual Sound City event from Bristol. We also made a surprise appearance at Sheffield Arena with Oasis.

Oasis had thrillingly lit up the music scene like a banger casually thrown by a couple of tracksuited delinquents, and had booked the 12,000-capacity Sheffield Arena for a one-off mega show. I fully admit we looked on with a bit of jealousy; yet again, a band had come seemingly from out of nowhere and overtaken us in the popularity stakes. The Verve had been picked as support, but the day before the gig their guitarist bust his wrist in a bar fight in Paris (such exploits would never befall the members of Pulp; we couldn't fight our way out of a wet paper bag), so they were forced to pull out (the first time another band's bones gave Pulp a break).

Geoff and Jeanette got the call from the Oasis mob and we jumped at the chance, more as a way of actually getting to go to the gig – which was being touted as a major event – than any attempt at building a 'scene' or gaining new fans. In 1995 we were entering a new era. Bands that a few years before would have occupied the 'indie' charts were now penetrating the mainstream consciousness. Plus, it would be a good laugh to play as a complete surprise to the assembled legions.

No one was any the wiser as we assembled by the side of the stage and Jarvis, unseen by the crowd, started picking out the notes to start 'Babies'. The gasp of recognition from the audience was delicious and the raucous cheer as we strode out was glorious. I ended the night swapping band stories with Oasis drummer Tony McCarroll, who was a really nice kid but only a few weeks away from getting unceremoniously, and in my opinion, wrongly, sacked from the band. Just goes to show, drummers hold a precarious position within bands.

Despite these distractions we had managed to assemble a collection of songs. We re-camped back to the Townhouse with Chris Thomas to finally get this new record on.

30

Raaaaajput!

(Life Must Be So Wonderful)

'OK, stick it through the Fairchild.'

This was Chris Thomas's stock phrase during the recording process for *Different Class*.

I'm not a studio twonk in the slightest, but 'the Fairchild' seemed to be some mythical amp from the sixties that must have bestowed some magical effect on Chris to facilitate his record-producing powers. My cloth ears could barely discern any noticeable difference but it kept everyone happy, I guess.

Progress on the new album was swift. The drums and bass went down seemingly in a trice. At one point I played the drums on my own for a couple of days as Chris and the engineer, 'Chipper' Nicholas, fiddled with mics and twiddled knobs to get the best sound possible – even at one point fitting two bass drums together to form a really long, deep drum and covering it in heavy cloth to tickle out that deep thumping sound.

Once again, modern technology and computing really helped us to get the 'perfect' take and, as usual, everything was played to click tracks to enable us to fit it all together. And so it didn't seem long until we hit the stage where different layers were being added and the magic truly started to emerge. But first Jarvis had to do some singing.

Jarvis ended up writing the majority of the lyrics for *Different Class* over a period of two brandy-soaked nights sat at his sister Saskia's kitchen table, when we had a break from recording up in Sheffield. I think we can all agree that those were two rather productive writing sessions, during which time Jarvis was probably at the peak of his lyrical powers.

The lyrics on *Different Class* cover the usual romance, sex and revenge, but in a way folks didn't really ever get to hear. They were funny, subversive, incisive, eccentric. As Barry Walters would write in *Spin* magazine, these were 'songs about naughty infidelities, sexless marriages, grown-up teenage crushes, twisted revenge fantasies, obsessive voyeurism.' 'Something Changes' is all aching longing for how life pans out (perhaps borrowing from a similar theme in Abba's 'The Day Before You Came'). 'I Spy' and 'Mis-Shapes' focused on revenge, a chance to stick two fingers up at all our detractors over the years who'd ignored or derided us. Drugs and going out are superbly illustrated in 'Sorted for E's & Wizz', 'Monday Morning' and 'Bar Italia', although certainly not glorified: we of a certain bent or age are well aware of the pitfalls of over-dabbling. And I include alcohol in this, kids.

Once my parts were down, the days would usually start about midday and go on till about nine in the evening, and we'd lounge about in the control room listening to the different parts as they were laid down and reading the paper. Candida and I would often do the crossword. We'd make good use of the pool table in the upstairs lounge and settle into a kind of excited torpor, waiting for the inevitable, usually unprintable, anecdote from Chris about Elton, Bowie or perhaps Bryan Ferry (he had an almost inexhaustible supply of top-grade stories from his long and illustrious career, and was great company). Sessions often ended with Russell and me retreating to the Townhouse flat above the studio, where we were staying, and ordering a delicious curry from the Rajput next door. We loved how as the waiter took down the order, he'd always repeat it back to us, only in reverse.

Listening to the same track for a few days can soon get a bit wearing, but your ears would often prick up as a new, unheard part developed. 'Live Bed Show' really came along in this regard when some beautiful organ parts fleshed out its sumptuous vibe. 'Monday Morning' benefitted from some deep sub-bass, adding an almost 'dub' vibe to the verses.

But one of the most startling changes came during sessions for 'F.E.E.L.I.N.G.C.A.L.L.E.D.L.O.V.E'. The song had started, once again, with a piece of junk-shop equipment brought in by Jarvis, a Synare drum synth from the early eighties. This was a round, fat disc that had a few knobs and switches to one side and a black rubber pad on the top, ready to be struck. It was rather limited in its sonic scope and similar machines would have graced many a seventies disco tune with a falling pitched sound – see Anita Ward's 'Ring My Bell', a real favourite of mine from that era. Needless to say, the Synare was a bit shagged, and it needed fixing up, but once brought back to life Jarvis started mucking about and made it play a kind of low, crashing sound.

'Give us a bit of a beat Nick, something a bit mysterious,' was my instruction in the rehearsal room. So I came up with the odd, jerking beat that's on the start of each verse in the song, punctuated with two hits on the Synare (I think played by Jarvis in the studio, so I could concentrate on the drums; live, I always played the Synare – or later, at least, a sample of it).

Our old band mate Anthony Genn was a frequent visitor to the Townhouse during the recording of *Different Class*. By now he was trying to make his way as a DJ and suggested that along with the jerky drumbeat, we add a bit of jungle-esque machine drums and skittering percussion. Who'd have thought it – Pulp and jungle? But there we go. Jungle was massive on the dance scene in the mid-nineties, and we were intrigued to see what he could come up with.

259

I must admit to being a bit sceptical, but it really fits, and gives the stark intro a unique flavour. That bit of studio magic we all craved.

Island Records never once baulked at the idea of spending big to make this record the best it could be. A real orchestra for strings and things? You bet. Anne Dudley (ex-Art of Noise and composer of countless movie soundtracks) was drafted in to work on additional scores for the orchestrations. When these are grafted onto the track mixes in the control room it is always a genuinely moving moment. 'I Spy' and 'Something Changed' are easily the best examples of orchestration turning these tracks into stand-outs. 'Lush' is perhaps an overworked term when it comes to describing indie/disco/pop bands adding orchestral arrangements to their records, but it's hard to think of a better fitting word here.

With most of the songs now in the bag, it was time to name this album. Cue one Anthony Genn. One of his sayings was if something was good, it was a 'different class'. He said it all the time, and I guess it rubbed off on us. Once Jarvis had completed the lyrics to all the songs and he realised commentary on the British class system ran through them like a guided missile directed at the heart of the estab-lishment (or summat like that), the penny dropped and he wanted to use the phrase as the album title. I remember asking him about it over a game of pool and as soon as I heard the title I thought it was absolutely perfect. It really summed up the record and, more im-portantly, even Pulp itself. We had felt 'different' for years, and with the papers full of Britpop stuff, which we didn't really connect with, it really emphasised our 'differentness'. Furthermore, we knew the music on this record was easily our best yet. Truly a 'different class'.

Perhaps to labour the point, once everything was done it was easy to see that 'Mis-Shapes' needed to be the opening track, with its storming statement of intent, telling the world that it's our time now, just as the British music scene seemed obsessed with UK-based indie guitar bands taking over the charts. Move over you 'townies', move over you 'straights': all those times you mocked our otherness are coming home to roost and, indeed, 'Revenge is going to be so . . . sweet'.

The mood in the Pulp camp was buoyant. Mostly. I must confess that some cracks of dissent did appear around this time. When you start out in a band I think folk have a notion that it's a kind of a benign democracy; all ideas can have the same weight as anyone else's and decisions should be agreed by the majority of the band. In the studio, it does get tricky, however. On the whole everyone was pulling in the same direction, the goal being to make a great record. As time went on, certainly Russell and I felt we were getting sidelined. Jarvis and Steve seemed happy to direct things with Chris without consulting anyone else. Were we being paranoid? Maybe. They always seemed to be in a huddle together, talking about ideas. This was noticed by us, and we had to have a 'discussion' about it in the pool room. I'm not sure much got solved with that chat, but for me it was good to get things out in the open. Perhaps this affected Russ more than me.

It was also a time when Jarvis was becoming almost a ubiquitous face about town (London, that is) at any old gig/shindig/event. We went to plenty of events too, but nothing like Jarvis. Who can blame him? After so long with his face pressed up against the sweet shop window, it was his turn to be allowed a trolley dash around the delights within, and he certainly filled his boots. The star status he'd achieved was certainly becoming evident, and who would want lowly drummers cluttering up the place? I don't blame him for getting out and among; he'd been kept out for so long that no one could begrudge his exploration of this hitherto unseen life. One of the album's central tenets is observing life as an outsider. Now Jarvis was getting to observe it all from the inside. Good on yer, I thought.

These ripples in the Pulp universe were just that, ripples. We were forging ahead with our project and knew it was going to do really well. We were happy, Island were happy. So what does a band do? Get a new member of course.

Mark had been helping us out more and more over the preceding years, from assisting with realising unrealistic stage presentations, to setting up the Pulp People fan club hub, to playing Jarvis's guitar parts on stage and assuming various keyboard duties for Candida. He'd also had a hand in producing and writing some of the parts that made up *Different Class*.

There was little in the way of discussion between the five of us as to whether everyone was 100% OK with asking Mark to join the band as an equal member. Geoff Travis mentioned to us separately that Jarvis was keen on the idea as a way to reward Mark for his endeavours. It was fine with me, as I could see it was a fair way to proceed. We could've simply paid Mark for his contributions, I suppose; perhaps given him a small percentage of the album royalties. What I would've preferred was all of us to have had a proper sit-down discussion on the matter. At times, Jarvis wasn't particularly forthcoming about sharing his ideas and thoughts with the rest of us. Of everyone, I think Russell was the most resistant to Mark's addition. I was OK with it in the main. Welcome Mark Webber.

Then came the phone call that changed everything.

31

Rod Can't Make It

(Ansaphone)

'Nick? It's Geoff. Glastonbury want Pulp to headline the Saturday night.'

'You what?'

'Glastonbury. You up for it?'

'Err, fuck. Yeah, of course. Oh god . . . Shit . . .'

This was big. *B.I.G. big.*

Lady luck had fallen in Pulp's favour for once. Glastonbury was – and still is – the UK's – arguably the world's – biggest and best music and arts festival. Taking place on Worthy Farm in Pilton, Somerset, since 1971 it has attracted growing audiences upwards of 100,000 music fans to wallow in (usually) mud for a weekend in midsummer, and listen to thousands of acts from niche to mainstream, small to mega. Landing a Saturday slot on the main stage at Glastonbury – the undeniable highlight of the live music year – is a momentous event in anyone's career.

Originally, The Stone Roses had been down to headline the Saturday night main stage. Since I had inadvertently crossed paths with them on a dingy night in Sheffield all those years before they had gone on to produce one of British music's best debut albums of all time (the 1989 classic *The Stone Roses*) and spawn countless imitators during the early nineties 'baggy' and 'Madchester' scenes. They had taken ages to make the follow-up to their brilliant debut and had finally emerged to do mega-gigs like Glastonbury, which would've been their first UK gig for yonks. Or not, as fate intervened. Guitarist John Squire came off his mountain bike in Marin County, California, breaking his collarbone and thus making it impossible for the band to play (making it the second gig in a row that we were drafted in to replace a band due to a guitarist's orthopaedic misfortune).

The good old rumour mill kicked into gear immediately. How come we were asked? There must've been loads of bigger bands that could have done it? Someone said Rod Stewart had been up for it, but Glasto said no: we want Pulp. This, nerve-wracking though it was, was something you did not turn down. The news instantly gave us a dry mouth and a churning stomach. We knew we had to turn in a performance to remember – for whatever reason, but hopefully the right ones.

Problem: we were in the midst of mixing *Different Class*. This was a time to concentrate, as we didn't want to muck it up. We especially didn't want to decamp from the studio to a rehearsal space to work on our set; we needed to be around to make decisions about the album's evolution. Fortunately, the Townhouse has several large live rooms, and it was decided we'd repurpose one of them for rehearsals while Chris laboured with the latest mixes. Every now and then we'd traipse through to the control room to hear the latest progress and suggest changes over a cup of tea. The live crew were also recalled: Roger, Scotty, tour manager Richard Priest, and, of course, my brother Richard, who was central to the Pulp live juggernaut as general helper and dressing room technician. We had about two weeks of rehearsals before the big day to get our act in order.

Next problem: there's nowhere to stay anywhere near Glastonbury. All the hotels for many miles around had been fully booked for a year. That's OK, we can book a sleeper tour bus and stay on that. Nope. They're also fully booked out, throughout the UK. There was only one solution left: Roger was despatched to the nearest camping shop and instructed to buy several big tents and a load of sleeping bags. We'd have to camp out backstage and make a weekend of it.

I'd first been to Glastonbury in 1990. I went along ticketless with my girlfriend at the time and her mates. Security was a much more lax affair back then, and the plan was for the girls to go in, get their wristbands, but not properly put them on (you were just handed them to put on yourself in those days), and I'd loiter outside the main gates armed with double-sided sticky tape. Julie would then come back out of the site with one of the other girls' wristbands in her pocket, meet me at the rendezvous point, where I'd put the spare wristband on with the tape, and we'd nonchalantly return to the site, me waving my correctly applied wristband to denote I was a bona fide ticket-paying customer. On the inside, I'd return said wristband to its actual owner and just hope security wouldn't notice and kick me out. They never did, thankfully.*

Strangely enough I have few memories of that Glasto experience, save for watching Happy Mondays from the tent and wandering around in a high haze. That's what festivals are for, yeah? I do remember being deeply struck by the scenes across the campsites akin to a filthy medieval army encamped before a battle, muddy faces lit by campfires as far as the eye could see. Evocative or what? I remember bumping into Steve (Mackey) at this Glasto. He had gone armed with a load of homemade daisy or sunflower pendants to hawk to the daisy-age festivalgoers. He sold out on the first day.

Pulp had played Glastonbury the year before (1994) on the *NME* stage on a sunny Sunday afternoon, wedged in between Leeds anarcho-popsters Chumbawamba and Oldham's finest, Inspiral Carpets. That just shows what a meteoric rise we'd encountered in

---

* As far as I recall, there was no Plan B for how I would get in if Plan A failed. Hitch-hike back to Sheffield, probably, or maybe join a feral gang of crusty fence jumpers, of whom there were quite a few, and chance my arm with them.

265

the last 12 months. From mid-table Championship strivers to top of the Premier League. You could say.

We began honing our Glasto set at the Townhouse. Jarvis would usually decide on the running order, but more often than not sets kind of write themselves. You want to include songs you know folk love, but throw in the odd curveball and perhaps a couple of new tunes to blood them in front of real-live human beings. However, headlining Glastonbury ain't no 'normal gig'. Did we have enough 'big' tunes to pull it out of the bag? Could we live up to the dashed expectations of 100,000 Stone Roses fans? Tricky. We had an album full of new material that was crying out to be played live, and we'd had a couple of bona fide pop chart 'hits', plus our last album had been a triumph. In the end, Jarv decided we should debut three unreleased songs out of a set of 12. Great if you're facing your beloved fans but, as I've mentioned, we weren't. This was a risky strategy on two fronts: first, playing unknown songs to a new and possibly less-than-enthusiastic audience risks mass indifference, and second, practising new songs in a studio or rehearsal space setting is very different from playing them in the turbo-adrenalised arena of the live stage. Cocking up any – or all – of the new ones was a very real and very possible scenario. No one wanted to mar this most auspicious of events with an almighty balls up. It's a strange reflection of the musician's mind that you dwell far too long on mistakes made in the heat of a gig rather than the amazing moments you can see and hear all around you. Screwing a song up on this stage – Glastonbury Saturday, yeah? – would haunt you forever. So that's a couple of hefty bits of jeopardy to throw in the mix.

In no time at all, the festival was upon us. We set up Camp Pulp backstage on the Friday: two large-frame tents and a couple of smaller tents arranged in our little area. It's not the Hilton, but we were happy to be there. In fact, Glastonbury is best seen and experienced under canvas. Even an onsite posh sleeper tour bus is 'selling out' somewhat. We were down 'wiv da kidz', so to speak.

Soon, we were exploring the site and checking out some of the bands. Who? Well, that's lost in the mists of time, but we certainly would've caught Oasis on the Friday night. More than likely we spent the days – like most people – wandering round and taking in all the weird and wonderful sights, sounds and smells on offer. I could certainly wander about unmolested by fans (hey, I'm the drummer – bottom of the food chain band-wise), but Jarvis probably couldn't by this time without being overwhelmed by well-wishers, autograph hunters (this was pre-selfie, remember) and general lunacy. Plus, we had the escape route to the backstage bar areas and, of course, the posh(er) loos.★

Saturday dawned with fuzzy heads and dry throats after a bit too much backstage bar on the Friday. This was the day of days. We dined on Glastonbury's artist hospitality and tried to fill the time as best we could. All the time, though, the nerves were starting to build. By mid-afternoon we were allocated our Portakabin dressing rooms, after they'd been hosed out from the Friday night debaucheries. Richard helped get them into shape and we settled into dressing room torpor – japes to pass the time and joshing with visitors from other groups. Didn't Brit bad-boy actor Keith Allen spend some time holding court with his kids in tow for a couple of hours? Maybe. I guess one of them will have been a young Lily Allen, but they could all swear like navvies, that's for sure.

I mainly spent my afternoon popping over to the main stage to see how the other artists were getting along. I could get right up on to the stage using my Access All Areas (Saturday) pass anytime. The 'undercard' for Saturday was thus:

★ Glastonbury is famous for its, let's say, 'basic arrangements'. Think First World War latrine and that's about as near as you'll get this side of time travel.

Dave Matthews Band
Indigo Girls
Everything but the Girl
Jeff Buckley
The Boo Radleys
Jamiroquai
PJ Harvey
Orbital

And lastly:
Our good selves

To see the massive crowd during the afternoon was a sobering sight: it just goes on and on as far as you can see, before gently morphing into a sea of tents to the horizon.

We knew, and had played loads of gigs with The Boo Radleys, so watched a bit of them. Never appreciated Jamiroquai and his hat-based cod-funk, so we gave him a miss but reported back to the gang that PJ Harvey (in her pink patent jumpsuit, no less) was going down really well with the crowd. I watched a bit of Orbital, who also were going down a storm – I'm still a bit concerned that two blokes poking knobs and twiddling samplers is great entertainment, but whatever floats yer boat. Seeing the other acts, even for a couple of minutes doesn't help with the rising nerves (please refer back to Chapter 1).

Excessive nerves were not just the reserve of the band. My girlfriend Sarah was out in the audience waiting for us to come on and admitted to being so nervous she could only keep them at bay by repeatedly plaiting and unplaiting her friend Heather's hair. She knew how important this event was for us, and how wary we were of the audience's reaction to us coming on instead of the Roses.

Eventually, it was time to hit the stage. Sadly, not the world-famous Pyramid Stage; that had burnt down in 1994. So, this was a standard festival stage of the type seen throughout Europe. Never mind, that was the least of our worries; we had to somehow win over a crowd that had bought tickets to see Ian Brown and chums.

Jarvis had decided the set should run as follows:

1. Do You Remember The First Time?
2. Razzmatazz
3. Monday Morning
4. Underwear
5. Sorted For E's & Wizz (debut)
6. Disco 2000 (debut)
7. Joyriders
8. Acrylic Afternoons
9. Mis-Shapes (debut)
10. Pink Glove
11. Babies
12. Common People

Yes, *three* song debuts plus 'Monday Morning', which had perhaps been played once or twice before to real humans. No biggie then.

Once I started 'Do You Remember The First Time?', we were off. I had decided NOT to look out into the audience if at all possible. Just the thought of the vast multitudes was enough to put you off. My strategy was to concentrate first and foremost on what I was doing. Bit of a no-brainer, you might say, and I would agree, but it's your base level: focus on how each song develops; how you're hitting each drum; where the stops are; how the fills are done. It's amazing how if you let your mind wander mid-gig that's where the mistakes are made. Complacency.

Monitors are crucial. They're there to help you hear what you, and the others, are playing so that everyone locks together. I liked a lot of drums in the monitors, along with a lot of vocals and then a general mix of other instruments. If the monitor mix is good, then it helps to put you at ease as the set develops and you can start to relax a little.

The other major area of concentration is being able to see the others. Especially Jarvis. We had developed over the years many odd little cues that he would use to signal where a change during a song needed to happen; bring the main theme back in or go to a chorus. 'Monday Morning', for example, has a break towards the end that we wanted to draw out (the 'Stomach in, chest out' bit) – we loved having bits like this where Jarvis could hype up the suspense and drama. We needed to bring it back in though, and come in at the right time. So it was decided that Jarvis would tease the audience and the cue to crash back in for the last chorus was that Jarvis would do a jump and as he landed I would hit the snare and the hi hat, which was the cue for everyone else to come in. I had to be on it for this to work, and work it did. Every time.

Playing music in a band live is very much about eye contact and knowing and trusting your fellow players to know where they are in a song. Even simple things like bringing in the next song require timing. Jarvis liked to talk to the audience a lot between songs and you needed to allow him time to waffle on. Plus, Candida often needed time to alter the settings on the Farfisa, Russell or Mark might need a guitar change. There's no point in trying to start a song without knowing if everyone is ready.

We had perfected this in-band communication over the many years of studio sessions, live gigs and rehearsals, and every song we played that night at Glastonbury went perfectly (well, perfectly in as much as we can say with years of hindsight that there were no major cock-ups). Focus was maintained. And Jarvis's between-song banter hit new heights at this, the biggest gig of our career. He was able to appeal to the sense of occasion, which it undoubtedly was, everyone there together as one, experiencing a once-in-a-lifetime event and creating a lifelong memory. Banish thoughts of reality and revel in the other-worldliness of the Glastonbury experience. He talked to the audience about Camp Pulp, and how we were in tents just like them. The new song, 'Sorted For E's & Wizz', was introduced almost as if it had been written for the Glasto occasion, when it was really about raving. It was all really rather special, and Jarvis had this ability to reach out to the audience and inform, amuse or just connect with them. He engaged with jokes, chatter and woe betide anyone fancying a heckle. He did it from on stage easier it would seem than in 'real life'. It had been a feature of Pulp gigs since day one, and had always set Pulp apart from other bands. Another one of those things that made us 'different'.

The zenith of this between-song banter occurred on the stage at Glastonbury, right before we launched into our biggest hit:

'You can't buy feelings, you can't buy anything worth having. If you want something to happen enough then it actively will happen . . . and I believe that. That's why we're stood on this stage today after 15 years. So if a lanky get like me can do it, and us lot . . . you can do it too, alright? . . . So, on that positive note, this is the last song. 'COMMON PEOPLE'.'

It was almost as if this was the Pulp (and even perhaps a punk) manifesto writ large and preached to the masses. We had stuck at it for so long: overcoming numerous obstacles and doubters to find ourselves on the biggest stage in the UK. We had 'made it'. And to be able to impart to the 'Common People' that this dream is achievable and possible was so poignant at this time and at this place that it was almost too much. It was perfect.

By now we knew that the gig had been an unbridled triumph. No one had chucked a bottle of piss at us or even a chunk of mud. The audience had loved it, in fact. We launched into 'Common People' with gusto. What struck me immediately was the sound of that enormous audience singing the lyrics back at us. Even myself at the back with some very loud monitors going full pelt, could hear them almost as loud as Jarvis, and it was so exhilarating. It was totally unexpected, too; we had never heard a crowd sing one of our songs back at us like this before. Mid-song the lighting engineer illuminated the crowd and at this I managed to allow myself a quick look. There was a sea of faces disappearing into the night, flailing limbs, crowd surfers, the lot. And all singing along to our song. I could do no more than scream at the top of my lungs while playing with the sheer euphoria of this moment. From playing to two paying guests at Derby a handful of years before to 80,000–100,000 souls screaming their heads off in a field in Somerset . . . what a ride.

We streamed off the stage in a haze of heightened adrenaline and hysteria. Wow, we had done it. We had pulled it off and we all felt 100 feet tall and instinctively knew something very, very special had just occurred. It was back to the Portakabins, where we would have a brief moment, just the six of us together, to wonder at the amazement of what had just happened. We could barely believe it. Almost immediately, though, the dressing rooms were thronged with crew, guests and well-wishers, all marvelling at the gig they had just witnessed.

The evening melts into a fuzzy out-of-focus mess from here, but it was certainly different listening to a recently gone-solo Robbie Williams reciting his poetry to a (sort of) rapt Jarvis and Liam Gallagher. It seemed like everyone who had been on stage at Glastonbury that year was now in our dressing room, congratulating us and slapping our backs on a job well done.

32

Different Class

(Something Changed)

Different Class was released on 30 October 1995. The time between the triumphal Glastonbury appearance and the record's release was full-on busy with getting the LP ready for release, namely finishing mixing the thing and stuff like deciding on artwork for the sleeve and all that entails, plus the little task of putting more tracks from the LP out as singles to whet the appetite for the forthcoming release.

Sleeve design was always something that hampered previous indie Pulp releases, so we – well, Jarvis really – was dead keen on getting it sorted in good time. He'd bought a load of *Nova* magazines (a beautifully designed women's mag from the sixties) and had taken inspiration from a series of photographs contained in one of the issues. They showed an 'observer', watching mundane activities happen. The observer was in black and white and the action in colour. We roped in Donald Milne for design and a then little-known photographer called Rankin to take some solo shots of us to use as the basis for the sleeve.

A date was set and I arrived at the studio to pose away as necessary. Trouble is, the night before I'd decided to go out rather than take the opportunity to catch up on my beauty sleep. Where I went I cannot recall, but I do recall the brain-crushing hangover I had throughout the session with Rankin. Despite the hangover, though, I was in high spirits – probably the residual drink still coursing through my system – and after the usual deadpan posy shots we always did, I started trying to ape the move Michael Jackson makes (someone must've put a bit of Jacko on the stereo), where he momentarily stands on the tips of his toes. Believe me, it's not easy.

We left Rankin to choose the best pictures – I certainly don't remember sifting through loads of contact sheets deciding which ones make you look best; leave it to the professionals, yeah? Two or three were selected and made into black-and-white hardboard cut-outs that could be placed in whatever situation Donald wanted. Again, we trusted Donald to find the perfect places and locations to photograph along with the cut-outs, to give us a suitable image for the sleeve reflecting the brief thrown up by the *Nova* template. Donald certainly came up trumps and we all loved the images he presented to us a few weeks later (the image of me in front of a bus, dancing with Russ and Jarv at what looks like a crap house party, is the Jacko-style pose).⋆

These images perfectly summed up the thrust of *Different Class*, an album very much about outsiders looking in on the mundanity of real life. We were six observers, quietly watching the goings on all around us. With so many great images it seemed sacrilege to waste 95% of them, since, of course, only one could be the actual front cover, set in stone for eternity. So, the idea was floated: could we use all of them by producing a number of different sleeves, the LP being printed up with one of, say, four or five different covers? Definitely possible, if a tad more expensive, to print, although it was eventually rejected as perhaps making Pulp seem a bit too mercenary, as our

---

⋆ Bizarrely, Russell took his young family for a break in Scarborough on the Yorkshire Riviera and one day noticed something odd going on down on the beach. Turns out it was Donald and a cut-out of Russ himself being photographed amid a herd of beach donkeys. Completely coincidental.

faithful fans might feel under pressure to buy every one. We didn't want to be accused of profiteering off the kids.

So, a compromise was reached where we decided the first run of vinyl albums would come in a sleeve that incorporated six LP-sized cards that had a different image on each side, while the outer sleeve had a cut-out hole so that the purchaser could select their favourite image to use as the cover, and change it over at will. Now, anything outside the norm in record manufacturing ramps up the costs, so this 'aperture' sleeve was just for the initial pressings – we just wouldn't be able to afford to do it for every copy (bands tend to get lumbered with these 'extra' costs, as they're over and above the standard). Tip: if you have one of these pressings, keep it somewhere safe – they're going for hundreds these days.

While all this was going on we were also preparing the next single release. As I've said before, it's all about momentum in the pop world, and although we'd released 'Common People' in May and we knew the LP was going to be out in the autumn (Christmas sales, anyone?), we still needed to get a single out just prior to the release of *Different Class*. Trouble is, we had so many single-worthy tunes that it was difficult to choose. 'Mis-Shapes' was an obvious choice. But we also wanted 'Sorted For E's & Wizz'. Solution: a double A-side. If DJs found the subject matter of 'Sorted' a bit too controversial they could just flip the disc and plump for the barnstorming rally cry of 'Mis-Shapes'. Everyone's a winner. Or so it seemed; little did we know that controversy was just round the corner.

'Mis-Shapes' was a call to arms for all the weirdos, outsiders and, indeed, 'mis-shapes' who didn't quite 'fit in'. Originally titled 'Broken Biscuits', this was the idea that us 'not like everyone else' types were like the packs of broken biscuits you'd buy in the market, mis-shapen seconds that weren't quite good enough to be packed and sold as perfect.

The song itself is a rollercoaster ride, rattling along at a fair pace, the razor-sharp lyrics calling on all 'mis-shapes' to rise up and claim our place, in charge at last, and finally, beautifully getting our revenge on the louts, with their bum-fluff 'taches and white baggy-booted girlfriends who'd mocked and intimidated us all these years. Two fingers to the 'old guard': it's *OUR* time now.

The video is a glorious affair in which the 'townies' get their comeuppance down the local disco, in front of a backdrop of the band mugging our way through the track. Lots of the kids appearing in the video were the same lot from the 'Common People' vid. Jarvis, playing both the leader of the 'mis-shapes' and the head townie in the guise of his sometime alter ego, one 'Darren Spooner', is resplendent in skinny tie, requisite bum-fluff 'tache and repulsive grey leather box jacket. The climax comes when Jarvis machine-guns the townies, *Billy Liar*-style. My word, did that gun firing blanks make an enormous racket.

The 'Mis-Shapes' sleeve (although we were releasing a double A-side and the record was the same for each, we put out two different sleeves) was a slightly more serene affair, being based on a sewing pattern your mum might have bought back in the seventies to make a new frock, complete with cutting patterns and diagrams and so on. Early versions did actually come in a pack with a pattern for you to make your own Jarvis-style jacket (I'll bet someone did make the jacket).

OK, I can see what you're thinking: 'All rather benign so far, and you said controversy a few lines back. Where is it?' Well, one word: SORTED (For E's and Wizz).

Maybe not the actual *music*, for that was a rather gentle acoustic-y number, which was certainly a detour from all our previous barn-storming singles going back to 'My Legendary Girlfriend'. A touch of ravey synth-squelching and baying crowd noises (nicked from Mark's ancient Casio keyboard he'd had since he was a teenager in Chesterfield) gave the track a different edge to our usual stuff. I even use quiet drumsticks (called Hot Rods), to keep it on the 'soft' side. So, if it wasn't the music, what was it?

It all comes down to those strangely British arbiters of taste, the tabloid press. The lyrics were the problem. See, they're all about raving and drugs. It's not much of a revelation to say that folk who went to raves took recreational drugs. Not all, but a fair chunk. The song talks about scoring tickets rather than scoring drugs, but it's a nuanced, balanced viewpoint: there's the rave experience (be that the 'E', or the music, or just the otherworldliness of the event) and then afterwards there's always the comedown – the price to be paid for your 'good time', so to speak. It's the realisation that all those folk who seemed to be your new best mates, bonded through acid house and strong ecstasy, were just ordinary folk in the end, and probably not the sort you'd want to hang out with again. Plus, there's always the nagging thought that you and your brain had been permanently altered by the experience. So, far from a clarion call to Britain's youth to say, 'Hey kids, take drugs, they're great.'

Still, that's what the tabloids – in their lazy ignorance – picked up on: 'They're saying "E" and "Wizz", so it must be an advert for wild drug-taking and thus corrupting the morals of our innocent children!'

What really got the tabloids frothing, though, was the sleeve. It depicted a drug wrap, the kind passed from hand-to-hand throughout the land and round the clock. Inside the booklet there were step-by-step instructions on how to fold the 'drugs' wrap from what looked like a magazine page from a Pulp interview. Quite how these origami instructions were going to send UK youth into the hell of drug debauchery was never quite explained (the sleeve does not say that this is a wrap where you can conceal your drugs).

'BAN THIS SICK STUNT!', thundered Kate Thornton in the *Daily Mirror*. Just in case you misinterpreted, the article went on to include quotes from parents of kids who had died after taking ecstasy, to really get the message across. In a subsequent follow-up piece some hack had doorstepped Uncle Gordon for a quote, in which he expressed his dismay that his (favourite) nephew was pushing such narratives. Gordon was no fan of the tabloids and had been approached with a typically skewed question.

This furore was a massive surprise to us. We saw no controversy in the release; we thought it was a great song that summed up our rave experiences coupled with a sleeve that told it like it is. We had even desired for the CD to come actually wrapped in a drug-style wrap, but Island kiboshed that, as the production costs would've been astronomical. Still, what band has not prospered after a bit of tabloid outrage? It almost goes back to the dawn of rock'n'roll: Elvis, The Beatles, the Stones, the Pistols, Frankie Goes to Hollywood, Madonna, and now little old us! Personally, I thought the storm was brilliant – it gave us masses of promotional acreage, which could only do us good in the long run: Pulp, the bad boys of '95! (As if.)

But, and it was a biggie, Radio 1 were considering banning the song (they'd been giving it loads of airplay until now). We wanted to build on the success of 'Common People' and it had been drummed into us that you can't have a hit without airplay. So, reluctantly, we had to say that the sleeve would be withdrawn once that pressing had sold through. I don't know whether a different sleeve was ever made in the end, but no bother; Radio 1 were placated and the airplay continued. Needless to say the hoo-ha blew over pretty quickly and we were in the clear. We'd got all the publicity of a ban without actually being banned. Result!

We were confident of a high chart placing the week after 'Mis-Shapes'/'Sorted . . .' was released. Could we go one better than 'Common People' and hit the top spot? Sadly not; Mick Hucknall's Simply Red were unmovable in the top spot with their hit 'Fairground', so we had to be content with stalling at number two again. Were we disappointed? No. Pulp at number two in the hit parade was still amazing to us. Perhaps that elusive number one was just the next single away. If Pulp had anything after all this time it was patience. Besides, us bunch of misfits were now chart regulars and Jarvis was rapidly becoming a national institution.

Different Class was obviously going to be a BIG DEAL, too. We had two, nay, *three hits* already out there in the UK's consciousness, so Island and Best in Press organised a raft of print, radio and TV interviews, and photo sessions for publications far and wide as part of the promotional circus that precedes such a big release.

However, now there really was only one person the journos wanted to speak to. This was no surprise to us. Jarvis gave good copy: never formulaic, always interesting. If I was obliged to do a piece on Pulp at this time I would concentrate on Jarv and forget the rest, no matter how interesting the rest may seem, for each member of Pulp was capable of an interesting take on events and could provide good quotes and 'lively' insights. However, the rest of us were now firmly on Second Division duties. Was this a problem? Did we have egos crushed by this cruel twist? I think a lot of bands could find this a problem, especially after so long being denied the limelight, but for us I don't think it was. Yes, it was nice to be asked your opinion on the state of things, musical or otherwise, but we knew we had the best there was fighting in our corner. Let Jarvis do all that – why get in a twist about it? We still did plenty of fun TV stuff as a band, such as the *Big Breakfast*, messing about with puppets Zig and Zag (BIG favourites in our house back in Sheffield) and lots of music shows and other mundane TV bits and bobs. Either way, it was still a novelty for the time being, that delicious feeling of being injected into the mainstream.

★ ★ ★

Needless to say, *Different Class* came out to rave reviews, the general thrust of which being this is the album Pulp had been threatening to make for the last ten years. Can't really disagree with that. The record sailed into the album charts at number one. Yep, numero uno. We had kind of done it. Just taken the best part of 15 years. I don't recall any great champagne clinking celebrations when we hit the top spot, no big party or whatever. Getting the album to number one was probably not as big a deal as having a number one single. Plus, we'd been on the road now since the start of September, on a nationwide tour to support the record, and during release week we were on a break before heading on to Europe for our biggest tour yet, which would take us right up to Christmas.

Being on tour was something I always looked forward to. I loved playing live and now we had been playing to fanatical fans for some time, so it was great to be back out there. It's one of those odd things that when you're beavering away in the studio the thrill of playing live again is a nagging draw; you just want to get out there and play. Perversely, the opposite is true too. After a couple of months on the road the quiet sanity of the recording studio has a definite pull.

Now we'd sort of 'made it', we would travel in a sleeper tour bus, usually piloted by the wonderfully affable Neil from the north-east of England. These double-decker affairs would have a lounge downstairs and perhaps a little kitchen and then another larger lounge upstairs, all kitted out with lavish seating and tables, plus a section of sleeping bunks where after gigs folk could get some kip as the bus trundled along to the next venue.

There was something oddly comforting about sleeping in the bunks. Although they were rather small (lying on your back, you only had about six inches between your nose the bunk above) and you only had a curtain for privacy, the thrum of the engine and the gentle rocking of the bus were rather soothing.

Having said that, the bunks were often empty until the small hours of the night. Every gig was a massive high. Thousands of kids, many new to Pulp, were really going for it every night and after such an experience we'd come off stage exhilarated and high on our own adrenaline. This takes time to recede and so we'd party every night after our gigs, usually in the venue afterwards with fans, guests and well-wishers. Then Priesty would drag us away to board the bus, making sure that Richard (who was still working for Pulp as general assistant and dressing room vibe technician, which meant setting up the illuminated make-up mirror and making sure some suitable tunes were on and everything was cosy – what a bunch of divas!) had put any remaining booze rider onto the bus so we could continue pillaging the drink stocks as we started off to the next place. The bus was kitted out with video games consoles, so we'd usually hit the Virtua Golf games during these journeys, preferring the vicarious thrills of whacking a virtual ball rather than watching James Bond on repeat.

The British leg of the *DC* tour did throw up a couple of curious events.

While playing at the Cambridge Corn Exchange (a beautiful venue where a few years previous Candida and myself had collared John Peel), to kill a little time while the stage was being set up a few of us went out for a wander and were rather surprised to find ourselves in a bit of a Beatlemania-type scenario, in which hordes of screaming fans were running full pelt down the street at us, so we hightailed it back to the comfort of the dressing room. This was the only time I remember such a thing happening.

But even stranger was that Russell went out later, once the screamers had gone, and on his way back to the venue he was approached by a young kid who struck up a conversation. Being a genial(ish) chap – like us all – Russ was happy to chat. But then the kid offered Russ a wrap of what looked like drugs. You may think that this must be an everyday occurrence to us 'pop stars', fans showering us with illicits, but it really was not. Russ gently asked the lad about why he was giving him drugs when he spied the unmistakable glint of a long photographic lens poking out of a bush on the other side of the road. Russ immediately saw this for what it was: a sting. The 'Sorted . . .' furore had just about died down at this time, and this was clearly a way for the tabloids to besmirch Russ – and Pulp by association. 'Hypocrites sing a song about how drugs don't do you any favours but here they are, happily walking off with a stash in their pocket.' Russ politely declined and made off. We had a lucky escape there, as the image would have put us in a rather poor position. Now if the kid had approached a different member of the band, the outcome could well have been very different.

We were a young(ish) bunch and in a now-successful group. It's really no stretch of the imagination to assume that drugs were easy to come by and, yes, even offered free if you wanted them. Some of us dabbled a little; mostly white powder that will have had varying degrees of actual cocaine in it. I don't think anyone got into difficulties or dependence, but it became a little more prevalent for a while as time went on. I know it's such a cliché, but bands often turn to the old 'Bolivian' to keep the buzz of the live experience going. Plus, the London music and club scene in 1995, the zenith of 'Britpop', was really quite well lubricated with the stuff. Obviously the Gallaghers quote 'We snort a line every 20 minutes' was, in hindsight, a strong advert for folk to have a go themselves. But lots of people tend to go through phases when it comes to exploring the world of narcotics. We had, in previous years, enjoyed a spliff after gigs, experimented with LSD at Burgoyne Road and raved our tits off on 'E' in the late eighties. Now the world of coke was open to us, we had to see what it was like. You became talkative (often about yourself), find that you can drink like a fish and not get drunk, and become an all-round good-time gregarious individual. But, as foretold in 'Sorted . . .', then you come down. The piper had to

Different Class (Something Changed)

be paid with an almighty hangover and that empty feeling of dread
as your brain tries to recover from the twin assault of alcohol and
coke. Don't do it, kids . . .

Another curious event from the UK *Different Class* tour was our
triumphal hometown show at Sheffield City Hall. Back in the dark
days, Sheffield was just about the only place we ever played to any
kind of audience. Not now. We hadn't played Sheffield since the
previous April, 18 months before (this is not counting the Sheffield
Arena show with Oasis), and let's face it, a lot had happened since.

So, this being a rather momentous occasion, it was the ideal gig
to invite the parents to, show them that this 'band thing' is the equivalent of *a real job*.

Sheffield City Hall, a beautiful, neo-classical concert hall, was opened
in 1932 and is arguably the finest building in the city. So I asked my
mum and dad along, and we invited Uncle Gordon too, and of course
he was happy to attend. The City Hall has a large bar downstairs,
underneath the main auditorium, and I left the sanctity of the dressing
room to see the relatives there before we went on. The bar was, of
course, packed with the audience enjoying pre-gig drinks, but there
was a different atmosphere, a weird buzz. I soon realised it was the
long line of people waiting to politely shake Gordon's hand as he
and my mum and dad sat at a table. Indeed, the whole room was
buzzing with folk agog that one of 'the boys of '66' was in attendance.
No one wanted anything to do with me; no autographs or nothing,
which I found rather hilarious.

Sometime before, I'd explained to Gordon how I thought goalkeepers and drummers were somewhat similar:

• They're both put at the back, but also sort of in the middle.
• They're both pretty exposed – if you make a mistake, everyone
  knows about it. And will tell you about it.

- A band can't be good without a good drummer. Same goes for a football team and a goalie.
- Both drummers and goalkeepers are usually a bit on the crazy side.
- Goalkeepers are often the loudest in a team, shouting instructions to the defence. Obviously, drummers annoy their band mates to death with all that loud banging . . .

In fact, we can take this analogy even further and add the rest of the band to this 'musical football team':

Lead singer = hotshot centre-forward, grabbing the headlines with each new goal.
Bass = sturdy central defender, reliable, dependable and works well with the goalkeeper.
Lead guitar = midfield maestro, pulling the team strings and making the magic happen.
Keyboards = mercurial winger dodging the tackles and serving up the right ball for the striker.

Or something like that . . .

We did our set, which for us ended up being a bit subdued – Sheffield City Hall was all-seated, a situation we had very rarely encountered, and it discourages the audience from really letting go. A gig should be a virtuous feedback loop between band and audience, the band's playing stoking the audience's fervour to greater heights, this in turn spurring the band on to reach as yet undiscovered levels of playing, and so on and so forth.

Plus, the main hall is built as an elliptical shape, and you will remember from your geometry lessons at school that the two foci of the ellipse are at each extreme of the oval, roughly where you would place a drum kit. So in the oval hall I'm sat at just the right place where each snare hit would be followed milliseconds later by a slap back echo as the sound rattles around the hall's walls and comes straight back to me. This was somewhat off-putting, so that also affects your performance. We never played Sheffield City Hall again after that, and in fact actively avoided seated halls.

For a hometown gig it's obligatory to have a proper aftershow party, and we had a massive guest list to invite along to such a prestigious place. The City Hall has a gorgeous underground ballroom with an illuminated dance floor, the centrepiece of a colonnaded room.

Sarah was in charge of my relatives and getting them all into the party, but there was an issue: you have to go outside the venue and enter via a different entrance to get to the ballroom. Everyone on our guest list was trying to access the party at the same time, so there was a big queue, and it was raining. Cue Sarah jumping into action.

'OK everyone, wait in this queue and I'll go and sort it with the security.' Then she went down the front of the line and said to the bouncer, 'I've got Gordon Banks back here stood in the rain. Can I bring them down the front and get straight in?'

'If you have Gordon Banks with you I'll eat my hat.'

'Ta-da,' she said, moments later, 'here he is!'

Everyone stood aside slack-jawed as they all trooped inside. Cue the rest of the evening watching another great big line of blokes all wanting to talk to Gordon and shake his hand.

The following month, November, saw us release another single off *Different Class*. 'Disco 2000' was accompanied by another Pedro Romhanyi video that was the easiest video we ever had to do. It starred our mates Jo and Pat Skinny (named as such 'cos they were, well, thin) as a pair of young things going out on the tiles, meeting and, y'know, getting it on. All of this is observed by six monochrome cut-outs. This meant we didn't have to turn up and hang about all day bored out of our skulls, waiting to get the call to prance about while miming to our song. Oh, how we had changed.

We knew that 'Disco 2000' had a real chance of hitting the top spot in the charts, which had so far eluded us. It was unashamedly going for the pop jugular vein: big chorus, hummable choon and a story everyone could relate to. But who exactly was Deborah? A Sheffield girl from way back when? A mystery to me, I must say, but there have been a few claimants to the character coming out of the woodwork over the years. The track had the added bonus that were it a big hit, someone might want to use it for a mega-bucks ad campaign around all the coming millennium hoo-ha (money grabbing gets), which by this point was only a few years hence.

When Jarvis came up for the riff for 'Disco 2000', we had laughed it off as a straight rip-off of Laura Branigan's eighties hit 'Gloria'. But Jarvis insisted it was 'different'. Once Mark had played it on the guitar through a Marshall stack, it certainly did sound different to 'Gloria'.

Rather than go with the album version, the Alan Tarney remix was chosen to lead the assault on the charts. Alan was a bit of a mystical figure to Jarvis. He'd produced some mega-mega pop records in his career: all the best eighties Cliff Richard stuff, A-ha and even Barbara Dickson. His uber-pop credentials were impeccable and Jarvis was excited to be working with him (I had never heard of him to be honest, but in for a penny as they say). His version of 'Disco . . .' wasn't actually that different from the LP version. Needless to say, the thing that changed the most was my drums. Alan added more of an electronic drum sound, taking away the real drum-playing. That's kind of the way of the remix: change the drums. It's just what we drummers have to put up with.

As we had come to expect nowadays, the single, released on 27 November, was fabulously received by the critics and got loads of immediate airplay.

We were mid-tour in Europe at this point, so couldn't do as much in-person promotion as we'd done for previous releases. This was also the highly competitive Christmas market, and we were fighting some real big hitters for the record-buyer's pound. Even so, when it charted at number seven I, for one, did feel rather disappointed: was this the turning point chart-wise for us? It was our first ever chart placing 'demotion'. All our releases up to now had beaten the previous release's chart placing. I remember us having discussions about holding the release until after Christmas to swerve the crowded market place and probably guarantee a number one in the New Year, as our fans would put it there. But, the consensus was that everyone (Rough Trade and Island) wanted Pulp to be seen as a group that could take on the established order and go toe to toe at Christmas. Island and Rough Trade thought a number seven placing was a great achievement. As I've said, I thought it a little disappointing and would love to have had a number one single. However, we remained optimistic: there's always next time, eh?

33

Pulp Airways

(Boats and Trains)

Release a hit album and you get very, very busy. Everyone wants you. This is nice; this was what we had worked for. We had wanted it. So pretty much straight after our extensive UK tour, it was off to Europe for a couple of months of gigs (during which time 'Disco . . .' was released).

We had only really done French dates on the continent, aside from a couple of shows in Sweden, the Netherlands and Belgium, so I was looking forward to going to new places and seeing how the Germans, Danes and Spanish kids would be getting down to Pulp (we'd be doing plenty of shows in France, too – our seemingly second home).

Before the tour, we did sessions on French radio, two MTV's *Most Wanted* specials (in June and November), BBC Two's *Later . . . with Jools Holland*, all that stuff. We went to Oslo to do a live performance for Norwegian TV, playing a few songs at a kind of nightclub-type place. It didn't go well. First off, Russ, who we have seen did not like flying, refused to go, as the aircraft taking us from Paris was not sufficiently large and thus, to him, safe enough. Never mind, we'll do the TV as a five-piece, Mark filling in on Russ's guitar parts. However, during the show Jarvis had a monumental fit.

We'd really not seen anything like it. Sure, in the early days Jarvis was known for stopping the band mid-gig if something went wrong and thus the song had to be started again (though this had not occurred while I was in the drum seat), and we had all been on the receiving end of a Cocker stare when we'd made a hash of something or other. But this was on a different level.

We first had an inkling that something was wrong as Jarvis started talking to the audience, which was occupied by some very young Norwegian kids, in some most unappealing language: mostly involving getting someone to administer his rear end with a broken bottle. His nibs then moved on to drop kicking the microphone and flouncing off in a major huff. What set him off? Candida's new keyboard set-up, apparently.

After recording the new album it was obvious that we needed to employ some serious tech gear to replicate the electronics on the tracks and try to play the live versions as close to the recorded versions as possible. However, the technological constraints of mid-nineties keyboards were evidently not up to the task. Candida had to load up each song and its sounds from a floppy disk to enable her to play the songs; this led to between-song problems if any of the disks failed to load properly, of which there were many examples on this night. Thus Jarv 'lost it'. The rest of us shuffled off stage, apologising to the Norwegians and finding Jarvis sat backstage under his coat in an obviously foul mood. We sort of laughed it off at the time, but with hindsight, was this a sign that the strain was starting to bite?

We had seen ructions within camp Pulp a little before this incident, too. We had popped over to Paris for a small gig, possibly as part of Rough Trade opening a store there. On the day, the French – as they do – went on strike. All of them, or so it seemed. The streets of Paris filled with marchers, banners held aloft (what the beef was is lost in time to me now), an excited frisson in the Gallic air. We thought about pulling the gig a) in solidarity with the strikers and b) with no public transport running, how were fans going to get into town to see us?

However, Hilda, our lovely French promoter, persuaded us to go ahead – the kids would find a way of getting in and many would be marching anyway, so our show would be good for morale. So, on it went.

All seemed fine until halfway through, when Jarvis started complaining to Justin, who was doing the monitors, that he couldn't hear himself sing. Justin, being a totally amicable bloke who knows his stuff, gamely tried to placate Jarvis, but to no avail. Next thing, I see Jarvis pick up his Marshall Master Lead Combo amplifier and hurl it across the stage (I think he'd had this amp since he was about 16 and it, along with his brown Hopf semi-acoustic guitar, was used in almost every Pulp show since the very start). Jarvis picked the amp up again and hurled it the other way, then proceeded to put his foot through the speakers. A happy bunny he was not. He stomped off stage and the song ground to a halt and we trudged off too. In the dressing room the mood was sombre to say the least, and then things got heated:

'You're fucking up the show!' Russell shouted at Jarvis.

Immediately you could see the red mist descend and Jarvis launched himself across the room at Russell, pinning him to the wall. A couple of blows were exchanged and before the rest of us could pile in to separate them, Jarvis fled to lock himself in the loo. Russell left the room too; all Steve, Candida, Mark and I could do was look at each other incredulous and concerned over how this was going to play out.

Hilda was distraught, thinking she had done something to upset the applecart. Genial Justin was in the corridor, saying he was quitting and he didn't need this shit, and to cap it all, Russ had got his violin off the stage and smashed it into bits by the side of the stage and left. Oh dear, this don't look too good. Oh, and to really top it all off we had 1,000 French kids baying for more songs about 15 feet away. Lots of these kids had walked miles to make the gig with the absence of the Metro. Thoughts of the kids starting a good old 'riot Français' swirled in my mind – I remembered The Stranglers being thrown in a Nice jail many years before as their crowd had gone 'off' one time after they failed to appear for an encore.

The crowd was getting more and more restless and it was very obvious Pulp would not be performing any more that night – or indeed ever. I suggested to Hilda that I go out and address the crowd, the idea being that I could placate them. Yes, good idea, said Hilda. So, there I was, in very unfamiliar territory: centre stage, in front of a potentially hostile crowd, with little grasp of the language, microphone in hand. What could possibly go wrong? I ended up telling 'le punters' a little white lie, that due to a technical hitch we could play no further. Someone at the front suggested I play a drum solo as the encore. Don't think so, Jean-Claude; I have never and would never do a drum solo. Can't stand 'em. I offered that my technical prowess was insufficient for such tasks and proceeded to apologise to all and ended with a spirited '*Vive la révolution!*' Seemed appropriate in Paris during a general strike.

What next? How would we get over this? Well, Russ and Jarvis made up and we coaxed Justin to stay on with the monitors. No dramas.

The remainder of 1995 saw us doing gigs, gigs, and more gigs. All rather triumphant and spectacular. Some highlights being that I managed to walk to Germany one afternoon. Not so fast – it was when we played in Strasbourg, France, and all you have to do is stroll about a mile over the Rhine bridge and there you are. It's great to drop into conversation, though.

Germany was a surprise. We expected to play rather small halls, since we'd never been there before, but small these were not. I can remember playing and watching trays of beer being expertly guided overhead the throngs to thirsty fans below. We had the pleasure of getting acquainted with the famous German efficiency. The record company rep who guided us through meeting radio folk, journalists, competition winners and so on was almost comically well-organised:

'OK, so you meet Radio Hamburg for eight minutes, then you talk viz important music magazine for 12 minutes, meet ze competition winners for sirty minutes exactly, then we go party real fuckin' hard. Ja?'

'Party real hard' became a bit of a saying after that.

We completed the year by whirling round some of our biggest UK venues to date, all strangely beginning with 'B': Blackpool, Bournemouth, Bridlington and Brixton. These shows were not without incident, either.

The authorities in Bridlington (a rather down-at-heel Yorkshire coastal town/resort) had tried to ban our gig after the 'Sorted . . .' kerfuffle but had failed in their quest. So, instead they appeared to encourage the police to come down really heavy-handed on the fans outside, and loads got carted off to the local nick on trifling drug charges. Most were released after the show. It was totally unnecessary. It was almost as if we were like the Sex Pistols or something. Yeah right.

At the same gig, during 'Bar Italia' at the end of the set, I noticed that some bloke right in front of Jarvis was giving him a hard time, heckling and generally being an arsehole. Next thing I know, Steve had thrown his bass to the floor and dived into the audience to have a 'chat' with this chap. He was closely followed by the form of one Colin Lish – our recently hired security chap, ostensibly hired to look after Jarvis but also to make sure venues were safe for us and fans alike – flying over the monitors, his knees tucked into his chest as if doing a 'bomber' into the swimming pool. We all watched agog as Colin 'carefully' took care of the heckler and simultaneously made sure Steve was OK. You really did not want to mess with Colin: a 6ft 4in, 22st die-hard West Ham fan. Let's just say he was good to have on your side in these moments. Meanwhile, we barely kept 'Bar Italia' together but Steve eventually made it back onto the stage and I think we finished off the song. 'I'm not having knobs like him ruin the show.' Fair point, Steve.

The shows kept coming, and at the beginning of 1996 we were finally off to a place I had dreamed of visiting for many years: Japan.

Japan seemed so exotic to me, and an otherworldly place. I fantasised about feeling like a complete alien in an unfamiliar futuristic landscape. Appearing completely different to everyone else around held some kind of odd appeal. I even once wrote to the Japanese Embassy to enquire about working in Japan as an English teacher back in the late eighties. Never got a reply in the end. So, when we had a small Japanese tour lined up, I was beyond excited to be going.

We had five dates organised: Osaka, Nagoya, and three shows in Tokyo over the period of about a week or so. We landed in Osaka and immediately were gobsmacked by everything we saw outside the bus window: elevated motorways going down the middle of rivers, skyscrapers with ferris wheels on the top . . . the heady combination of jet lag and awe made it really appear like a city from the future. It was incredible.

Osaka was especially interesting as it had been one of the main locations of the 1982 sci-fi film *Blade Runner* (one of my favourites), the city's crowded covered alleyways being used as a background for replicant hunting. The sights and smells of these alleys were a real eye (and nose) opener. We soon had the feeling of being an alien beamed down to a strange planet when we stopped into a restaurant where no one spoke English and all the menus were in Japanese (why wouldn't they be?). It was a matter of guesswork to get some food. We survived. Every foray out to find food was a real experience, very hit or miss for a lad from Rotherham who generally found exotic food rather suspicious.

We had heard that the fans in Japan were something else. It was all true. They were waiting for us at the airport in Osaka and were omnipresent, hanging around in the hotel lobby waiting for a member of the band to appear so they could ply us with gifts, usually of the edible nature and all done with extreme politeness and a little giggle (they were almost exclusively girls). It was a bizarre notion to us as to why these kids would wait around all day just for a few seconds of contact, and we'd ask whether they hadn't got better things to be doing . . . obviously not.

The surrealness continued on to the concerts themselves. The venues were usually located on a floor in a skyscraper, and on the other nearby floors would be shops, offices and whatever. They all started and finished really early and it was quite odd to be getting gee'd up to go on stage at 6 p.m. rather than the usual 9 p.m. Everything was over by 8 or so, and you then had to go hunting for late-night adventures. Japanese audiences were very reserved, with polite applause between songs and definitely NO heckling. It was so different from gigs back home. There would be crowds outside the venues, of course, waiting for a chance to meet us (especially Jarvis), and to give us more gifts, get autographs and take photos. We had developed a foolproof strategy when faced with these situations – push Jarvis out first so the crowd would go mental, and we could then slip past unencumbered in a way by shy requests from the kids. We could then watch from afar and laugh as Jarvis was swamped by well-wishers.

We travelled between the stops on our Japanese tour by the world-famous bullet train, which was, again, rather amazing, all the while followed by a devoted mob of Japanese fans, who would, after the daily gift, keep a respectful distance. Unnerving.

Tokyo was just a notch crazier than Osaka and Nagoya. There was more going on, more obsessive fans, more of everything. It was great.

We got taken out by the Japanese record company rep and the tour promoters for a proper Japanese meal, which was all very formal: tatami mats, low tables, hot sake and fugu fish. We'd heard about this Japanese delicacy and some were keen to try it. Not me, thanks; fugu fish, if not sliced correctly, can poison the diner sufficiently to kill. The idea is that you just get enough poison that it numbs the mouth. Yeah, I'll give that a swerve thanks. We all sat cross-legged and the fugu fish was brought out to show us that it was alive and healthy, before the chef expertly (we hoped) filleted and cooked the creature. No quicker did it disappear into the kitchen then it reappeared, ready to eat. No cooking took place of course, just slicing. We noticed that the fins of the poor sod were still flapping as it returned to our table to be devoured.

As the evening progressed, more and more sake was consumed and one of the features of hot sake is that it does go to the head rather swiftly. Next thing we notice Russell being shooed out of the kitchen by some noisy Japanese cook – he had got lost visiting the bathroom and seemed keen to see what was going on in the prep area. Much to everyone's enjoyment, his sake intake now got the better of him and he slumped down on the floor. Maybe it was the fugu!

We had a fellow look after us in Japan, courtesy of the record company, and I have never seen a guy work so hard. His job was basically to ensure that anything we wanted would be catered for (no, stop it). This meant he had to be available for the early risers who fancied sightseeing or shopping, and the late-night owls who wanted to sample the night-time delights of Tokyo, such as karaoke, night clubs and so on. Consequently he was on it from first thing to the wee small hours every day. We must have broken the poor chap.

Another mind-blowing aspect of Japan was the technology. They seemed to have stuff that we could only guess at its purpose. What we did see was our first ever digital camera. And it had a little screen on the back, where you could see the image, rather than a viewfinder.

This was breathtaking, futuristic stuff at the time and we were in awe. We all ended up buying one, even though we had no way of getting the damn pictures off the phone as we didn't really have computers much back then. I lost my digital camera almost immediately in an Oslo taxi the following week. £400 down straight off. Cheesed off.

While in Japan I received some rather special news from back home: Sarah was pregnant. I was going to be a dad. It was rather odd being on the other side of the world getting this news but I was well chuffed – no blanks being fired here!

★　★　★

The rest of 1996 continued pretty much in this vein, a constant stream of concerts all over the shop. We whizzed around Scandinavia in February (pretty chill). Then we hit the heights with our first ever UK arena tour and a triumphant return to Sheffield Arena: all hail the conquering heroes!

We had to get used to playing arenas. It's so very different from playing club dates; the stage sizes were so much bigger and you just aren't used to being so spread out. Still, it's not much to bleat about so I'll stop.

Playing arenas and having mountains of fans wanting a piece of us meant that we'd started booking into hotels under pseudonyms to throw off any unwanted attention. We played Wembley Arena for the first time at the start of March, and as we were on a hectic kind of schedule we hadn't been able to check into our hotel before sound check. Nothing unusual there. We played the gig to the usual rapture and afterwards we piled into our cars – not limos, please; more like plush taxis – and headed to the afterparty at the super posho Mayfair hotel, where we were staying. I was with a couple of chaps who'd worked on our videos and all was well, and I hobnobbed with a few folk I knew from round and about, but did find it rather curious that no other band members seemed to be there. Never mind, have another drink. Anyway, I decided I'd best retire to my room, so I went down to reception to collect my room key.

'I've got a room booked and can I have my key please,' I undoubtedly slurred.

'Certainly sir . . . what name is it?'

'It's Mr Watermelon.'

With just a moment's pause (possibly holding a snigger in), he said, 'Let me look, Mr Watermelon . . . No sorry sir, no one of that name has a room booked.'

'Could you please look again?' I was getting worried now . . .

'No, definitely no one of that name expected, sir.'

I might have started getting irate. 'No, I definitely have a room booked here. You are wrong,' the indignant drunk seethed.

The receptionist paused and looked at me askance: 'Might it be that sir is actually staying at the Mayfair Intercontinental, which is 100 yards up the road, rather than here, which is the Intercontinental Mayfair?'

With this bombshell I abruptly turned on my heels and wobbled out the reception and staggered up the road to the aforementioned Mayfair Intercontinental hotel. Why there was two such similarly named hotels on the same road escapes me – they must get this all the time. On entering the bar was alive with our entire mob, with tales of the star-studded party-goers that I had missed. Where've you been?

Our first headline US tour followed, which was a mixed bag to say the least. We started off on the West Coast, but still in relatively small clubs and it was pretty clear from the outset something was wrong. Jarvis had been on holiday in Hawaii prior to the tour's start (fancy or what? It was a long way from Intake, Sheffield), and was coming down with some ailment. We got through the San Francisco gig but had to cut short the LA show. Jarvis was really struggling, and hats off that he managed to do the LA show at all. The doc said it was some kind of tropical bug he must have picked up in Hawaii and thus it was decided to cancel the following show in Denver, to give him a couple of days' rest and recuperation. This was one of only a couple of gigs that Pulp ever cancelled due to illness (it could actually be the only one). It was a shame, as I loved playing to new crowds and getting the chance to win them over.

Still, this gave us a couple of days in Denver kicking our heels, waiting for JC to get better. So, Steve, Mark and I decided to hire a car and go on an adventure into the Rockies for the day. (Candida would usually hunker down on such days in a fluffy towelling dressing gown, ordering room service and watching black-and-white movies all day. Russ was nowhere to be seen.) Mark suggested we visit the hotel that inspired *The Shining*'s Overlook hotel, which was a couple of hours drive out of Denver, and then hit the Mount Evans Scenic Byway, the highest paved road in North America. Good plan.

We wandered round the 'Overlook' hotel for a while and browsed *The Shining* gift shop, but we were somewhat underwhelmed; didn't look much like the hotel in the film really.★ We shuffled outside (into the pouring rain) to see if it looked any more as it did in the movie – not so much. That is until we noticed a pair of twin girls in white dresses looking at us from a door window – very much like in the film. We gasped at this apparition for a split second until almost simultaneously the rest of the family followed. Just your standard folks staying at the hotel! To say the sight of the girls gave us a start was so very true. Maybe there was something to the Overlook hotel, after all.

We proceeded on to the scenic highway, where we couldn't scenic anything. Thick grey cloud obscured every mountain view we suppos-

---

★ Maybe because the actual exteriors in the movie were filmed at the Timberline Lodge, in Oregon (the Estes Park hotel was just the inspiration for the Overlook in the novel – apparently Stephen King had stayed there one time).

edly came across. The only thing we could experience was feeding the very not-shy chipmunks, or some such, which crowded round every overlook. When the clouds did part, we would slow to a crawl to try and drink in the view. Then, just like in the movies:

Whoop-whoop!

I looked in the rear-view mirror to see the flashing blue and red lights of Colorado's version of the boys in blue (actually, a rather boring beige in real life). I had no idea of any highway infringement, so dutifully pulled over. As I opened the car door to get out the highway patrol man shoved his boot against the door trapping my half exited leg while barking: 'Do not get out the vee-hickle, sir!' (In the UK when pulled over, one gets out to talk to the officer). I sat there thinking, oh shit, this is now serious! What had I done? The trooper drawled:

'Why were you drivin' so slowly?'

'Err, trying to see the view?' This would've been said in a faux posh British accent, which we all know Americans love.

'OK, you seemed to be drivin' a little erratic back there, sir.'

'I do apologise, officer, I was just trying to see the mountains.'

A quick flash of the good ol' UK passport as ID and we were on our way. No rock'n'roll antics here and ending the day being thrown into a local jail on some 'felony'.

We continued up the trail, all the while beginning to feel curiouser and curiouser. When we got out and walked about we instantly felt out of breath. We were feeling the effects of altitude (Denver is already at 1,600 metres and we had been climbing in the car all day and the summit of the trail way is at almost 4,500 metres). I had never experienced this odd feeling of gasping for thin air. We got to the top of the pass besides towering walls of snow that had been cleared off the road and began to descend the other side. Finally the clouds parted, and we got to see some of the absolutely stunning scenery of the majestic Rocky Mountains, all topped off by rounding a corner to come face to face with an enormous moose standing in the middle of the road, eyeing us up, wondering what we were doing in his neck o' the woods. It was days like this that really made me want to use on-tour spare time wisely, rather than hunkering down in a tour-bus berth or hotel room, nursing a hangover. Get out and explore! Must thank Jarvis here for being ill and allowing us the time to do this day trip.

Another place I'd been desperate to see on this trip was Detroit – the famous Motor City and home of Motown Records. I was keen to see the parts of the city that were largely ruined and abandoned with dissolute and dead car factories and block after block of dilapidated houses and buildings, but sadly we didn't get much chance. Nor did we get a chance to see the famous Motown Records building, where so many classic records were made. We did get to experience some extra heavy downtown USA vibes, though, which we weren't expecting.

We had an early evening gig booked in at Detroit's Saint Andrew's Hall. Again, nothing very big at all. The promoter told us that the gig was early because there was a rap night on straight after the gig. 'Wow,' we all said (well, me, Jarvis (now fully recovered) and Steve), 'that sounds amazing, can we stick around after and experience some real homegrown rap in the actual USA?' 'You most certainly cannot!' said the promoter, forcefully. Three British white kids (well, thirty-somethings) in such a hostile environment – he wouldn't allow it. We didn't press the idea, especially once we got onto the street outside the venue. Cars were circling packed with some very heavy-looking dudes who must have been there for the rap event. They looked at us like we were there for the taking. The police had even blocked off the street where Roger and Scotty were loading the bus as lots of bands had been held up and 'liberated' of their gear many times outside the hall. Someone had even been shot there the week before.

The roadies never packed a bus as quickly again. You could feel the threat in the air that night in Detroit. We were rather glad to have taken the promoter's advice and given the rap night a swerve.

This tour of America saw us being booked for our first US festival, though Glastonbury it was not. We were scheduled to play the Riverport Amphitheatre outside St Louis on a sweltering day in late May. It was really starting to hit home just how much work we'd need to do if we were to make any, even the slightest, inroads into America, and especially the Midwest. But the Riverport Amphitheatre sounds pretty grand, I hear you say? You're right, it was. Unfortunately, we were on a stage that was right next to where the festival-goers walked past on their way to the main arena, where the headline bands played. This stage was a small, rather pathetic affair, which reminded us of some pretty dire stages we'd played back in the eighties in Sheffield, such as Dole Busters. So, there we were, playing away to a pitifully small crowd while flocks of young Americans walked past us, totally indifferent to our British squawkings.

What amazed me from my vantage point was how all the American lads really did all look the same:

Baseball cap: tick.
Plaid shirt open over band tee: tick.
Three-quarter-length shorts: tick.
Long white socks hiked up as far as they would go: tick.
'Sneakers': tick.

There was hundreds of them, all in the same identikit style. And not a one of them looked our way. It really did seem a futile exercise in the extreme. Why should we bust our balls doing this if no one was going to take the blindest bit of notice? Plus, it was about 110 degrees that day, so it was no surprise it didn't encourage us to revisit the Midwest anytime soon.

We did, however, play another US festival later in the tour, in Boston with our old mates Lush on the bill. We imagined the sophisticated college-educated Bostonians would be more attuned to our stuff (we had played Boston before, too), but no. The on-site skateboard half-pipe attracted many more punters than us (or indeed Lush). It didn't really look like America was for us.

Anyway, no bother – there were many more places to visit back in euro-land. We even tried to have our first foray into the East – a gig behind the old Iron Curtain in Prague. Lovely! This was our chance to see a beautiful city and to stun the Western music-starved ex-communistas all at the same time (the fall of communism and the Berlin Wall was only five years before at this point, remember). Alas, the Czech border guards were still very much of the old school and although us on the tour bus were allowed entry, the truck with the gear was held up for hours by the over-officious sentries, possibly looking for a juicy bribe that was not forthcoming. By the time they were prepared to let the truck through there would be no time to get to Prague and get set up in time. Turn around everyone; back into Germany. The Czechs would just have to wait.

In June, we found ourselves on the same bill as the reformed Sex Pistols at Denmark's Roskilde Festival. This prompted fierce debate among us Pulpers as to whether the Pistols should be watched or scorned for this most obvious of cash-in concert appearances. I was firmly in the camp of going to see them. I never had the chance to see them back in their heyday, so this seemed as good an opportunity as any.*

After we finished our set, I set off for the arena where the Pistols were playing, thinking I'd watch from afar, studying the events. As I

---

* The Sex Pistols had played at a pub venue in Sheffield in 1976 called The Black Swan, or Mucky Duck as the locals called it. However, I was ten at the time, so even if I had known of this place and/or the Pistols, the chances of going would be precisely zero. They were supported by a new band playing their first ever show: The Clash.

neared I heard the unmistakeable first few bars of 'Holiday In The Sun' being blasted out and I was swept up with excitement to see the band I thought I would never ever get to see. I started to run, at the same time emptying my pockets into the safest zip-up pocket I had, sure that if I was going to get into the middle of the mosh pit I would most likely lose everything not properly secured. I made the moshing's for about four songs when Mr Lydon intoned to the crowd that if anyone throws another thing then they will be off. Needless to say, halfway through the next number Johnny Rotten storms off, never to return. Someone had indeed chucked something at the stage. Deflated, the crowd dispersed to catch the next band. It was only five or six songs, but it was so exhilarating to hear the Sex Pistols at full force – finally.

The next week or so we had possibly the most bizarre event of Pulp's career to date.

We travelled from Roskilde to Turku in Finland for another festival, this time by the shores of a beautiful Finnish fjord. We shared the bill with our buddies Blur so it was nice to see some friendly faces. I suggested to Damon that he greet the vast crowd with the Finnish drinking salutation 'Katpiss' (it's actually '*Kippis*', but the inclusion of that pesky 't' makes it so much more enjoyable, don't ya think?) He looked at me with suspicious eyes – as if I would play such a fiendish trick – but went ahead anyway, to joyous cheers from the hopelessly good-looking young Finlanders.

We also hung out with the incredibly tall Red Hot Chili Peppers fellows, who swanned about backstage in matching burgundy velvet dressing gowns. They took an instant like to our Candida, suggesting she join them in their trailer for some 'fun'. No thanks, deadpanned Doyle.

From Turku we had to get to Iceland, and then over to Norway for more concerting. Some cock-up had occurred at the planning stage, as there were no scheduled flights to get us to each place in time to do our stuff, leaving us with only one alternative: we'd have to hire our own jet. It's all getting a bit Led Zep, you're thinking, and you'd be right. It was all a bit crackers. Priesty hired us a jet from Lithuania or some such, which was crewed by two fearsome-looking Soviet-style stewardesses that wore the most garish eyeshadow seen this side of 1975. Despite this, or maybe because of this, they were professionalism personified.

Anyway, we all sat there on the plane, laughing at the craziness of it all with the Blur lads – they had some time off after Turku so when they heard we had a jet on the go, they jumped at our offer of a seat over to Iceland for a day or two. We sat there for seemingly ages when word got to us that half the gear couldn't go on the plane, as the flight cases made some items too big to get through the smallish hatches into the cargo bay. It was looking increasingly likely that we'd hired a jet to take *us* to Iceland but not our equipment. This would therefore be a colossal waste of money and we would miss the chance to play there. Not happy. Fuck it; we set off anyway, having decided that the plane would go back for the remainder of the gear and stow it somehow and return so the shows could go ahead.

We had a day off in Iceland before the show, so Pulp and Blur went sightseeing on a whirlwind day trip led by our concert promoter, who really did look like some kind of Viking – all long hair and rippling muscles. We did the waterfalls, the blue lagoon and the geysers, and in the afternoon a spot of white water rafting. After all, we had all day, and as the sun didn't set at this time of year it was a long day.

The white water rafting consisted of two rubber boats: one for Blur, and the other for us. There wasn't much in the way of white water-type stuff, but rather a 90-minute-long water fight between the two of us using telescopic water cannons to drown each other, topped off with a challenge to jump 20 metres off a rock into the frigid Icelandic meltwater. It really did dry the mouth, the thought of jumping so far into the cold water. At least we had bright orange cold-water immersion suits on to cushion the blow. So, we all climbed the rock (apart from Webber and our Richard, who put their feet down and said no way!) and we jumped. Jarvis was in front of me and as he neared the top, he turned and said, 'I don't think I can do this.' I was ready to give him the gentlest of nudges to launch him into the ether but thankfully he didn't need it. It was an eerie feeling to step off the tiny ledge and plummet into the green/blue water below. Exhilarating yes, but only the once, thanks.

Pulp Airways deposited us in Norway for our next engagement, a festival where the bands had to access the stage via boat. That's a first. Unfortunately, during the day of the show I developed a searing pain in my side that was agony. Breathing was painful. Laughing excruciating. And don't even ask about sneezing. I really thought I would have to call off the gig it was that bad. What had happened? Had I fallen during our Brennivín (Icelandic firewater)-fuelled après gig bender? Had I got into some altercation with a Viking and come off worst? I had no idea. All I could think of was that 60 minutes of drumming would not be very pleasant. Then it dawned on me: the rafting water fight. I had used my right side with the telescopic water cannon so as to get better purchase and thus force of water ejected towards Damon et al. in the other boat. My ribcage was now exacting its revenge for the battering. Painkillers were sought and the edge just about taken off, enough for me to drum that evening.

The gig was actually quite raucous for the usually reserved Norwegians. I remember being hit full force in the chest mid-song with a pair of expertly thrown spectacles. At least none of the coins thrown our way hit the mark. Perhaps this was payback for Jarv's outburst the previous year in Oslo. Who knows? Word to the wise: do try and look after oneself while white water rafting.

Pulp Airways jetted off into the sunset after this, a bizarre footnote in Pulp's touring career, and we were back into mainland Europe for more. It was strange, and not altogether unwelcome, seeing nighttime again after about a week in the unending polar midsummer sunlight.

Our punishing 1996 concert schedule was, mercifully, drawing to a close, topped off with more Euro fests and an unmissable trip to play to the wonderful people of the Shetland Isles far to the north of Scotland and nestling in the inhospitable North Sea halfway to Norway.

Candida had a lot of relatives in Shetland, who must have been badgering her for ages to get Pulp up to Lerwick, Shetland's capital. Our newfound status as pop stars meant that things like this could happen with seemingly a snap of the fingers – well, not a snap of Candida's fingers. Her arthritis was always pretty bad, but you get what I mean. In fact, we found out ages later that Candida personally funded most of this trip to the outer reaches of the British Isles so that her Shetland clan could finally get to see Pulp live. What a beautiful gesture.

This was another time where we had to hire a plane to get us there, including our equipment, but this time it wasn't a jet, and sadly there were no formidable Lithuanian stewardesses. Never mind. Shetland and its young folk were rather excited to see Pulp play in the only venue large enough on the island, the Clickimin centre, which was of course the hottest ticket in town. No bands ever played Lerwick that were contemporaneously famous down south (the mainland that is), so needless to say the kids were crackers for it.

As usual, though, a trip to an odd destination would not be replete without a spot of sightseeing. Candida arranged for anyone who wanted to go sea fishing off the islands with her Uncle Alan, who had a boat. Russ and I took the bait (so to say) and found ourselves in the early morn bobbing about in the North Sea. Odd that Russ was up for a spot of angling in a small, rickety boat on the unpredictable North Atlantic when he was terrified of travelling on a modern passenger jet bedecked with everything human technology could throw at it, but there you go. We had a grand morning pulling up pollock, ling and cod from the depths, and thankfully didn't bring our breakfasts back up. We had to have a 'wee dram' in the harbour pub once we hit dry land and once the inhabitants found out who we were, they clamoured for us to get them tickets for the show that evening. The gig was, of course, a complete triumph, the Shetlanders going nuts for our antics.

We rounded off an almost solid 12 months of gigging with two big open-air shows of our own in Chelmsford and Warrington with a stellar supporting cast that seemed like a *Who's Who* of these 'Britpop' times: Cast, Supergrass, Stereolab, Elastica, and even goddamn Gary Numan – at Jarvis's behest, I might add. Our set culminated with us getting as many guitarists as possible up on stage for 'Common People'. We even had Chris Thomas guesting at Chelmsford.

To say by now we were knackered would be somewhat of an understatement. Some of us take the rigours of touring better than others. I felt like I could keep going, but others were ready for a rest. We had one last performance to do before we could take a hard-earned break, which bizarrely was a private performance in a Roman-Greco amphitheatre in Barcelona for the beer company Holsten Pils – what a rotten bunch of sell-outs, eh kids? However, it did mean we could fly out loads of mates on Holsten's tab to help us celebrate an amazing year on the road. One that had probably been the pinnacle of our live career.

The Barcelona trip, however, was not our last live performance of 1996. We had been nominated, again, for the Mercury Music Prize and had been asked to perform a song at the ceremony – it's a bit of a giveaway, if you ask me, as to who would be a shoo-in for the win. Would you ask us to play then give the prize to someone else? Exactly.

We went along and played 'Bar Italia' to the suits and our contemporaries in the slum-like surroundings of the Grosvenor Hotel Park Lane.

It was obvious we were in with a really good shout this year, but we were up against Oasis with *What's The Story (Morning Glory)*, plus Manic Street Preachers with *Everything Must Go* and Black Grape's *It's Great When You're Straight . . . Yeah*. Much tougher competition than when we missed out to M–bloody-People in 1994, that's for sure. Thing is, we had become a little paranoid about winning the damn prize. We had noticed that all the previous recipients had suffered career dives immediately after getting the Mercury Prize. We were convinced it was jinxed. It was decided that *if* we won the prize money (a none-too-shabby 25 grand), we should immediately give it to the War Child charity, which had been doing great stuff that year, and *try not to touch the trophy*.

'And the 1996 Mercury Music Prize goes to . . . Pulp and *Different Class*.'

Cue the spraying of the champagne over everyone as if we had just won the Grand Prix. I guess we had. We swaggered onto the stage and Jarvis spoke for us and gave away the 25 grand, and we all avoided touching the Mercury statue. Trouble is, with these affairs the band is supposed to return to their seats holding the gong aloft – we couldn't just leave it there, on the podium. I think Mark crumbled and picked up the prize as we returned to our seats. Thing is, was the prophecy about to come true?

'92: Pulp photo shoot. L-R Jarvis, Me, Candida, Steve Mackey, Russell (standing) GETTY IMAGES

DONALD MILNE

onbury, 1995: from the Candida Doyle collection. Some snaps from that day.

NME awards, 1995: all that was left of the award after a night of debauchery.

Rhythm magazine: me at the kit plus my doppelgänger. From Brixton gig, December 1995. JAMES CUMPSTY

1997, proud dad: Jackson makes a visit to the *This Is Hardcore* writing sessions at the Fortre

group shot, 1998: Mark Webber on the left. MARTYN GOODACRE/GETTY IMAGES

2012, hiking the Andes: L to R Liam Rippon, Steve Mackey, Jarvis Cocker, myself, Matt Butcher and Leo Abrahams.

Live shot from the 2011/2012 gigs. THODORIS MARKOU

Sheffield Arena: taking the applause at the end of the 'last' UK gig (before the 2023 tour), December 2012.

Sheffield FC: SFC under-14s sporting their Pulp kits.

2018: onstage with The Everly Pregnant Brothers using a stripped-down, stand-up kit.

KEVIN WELLS

34

Brit Awards

(The Fear)

I know we've talked about the Mercury Prize already: the nearly winning and the actual winning. But the Brit Awards are another thing altogether. This needs its own chapter, as I'm sure you're gagging to know the inside story of that infamous event.

The Brits is the British Music Industry's (actually the British Phonographic Industry's, to give it fair due) major celebration of all the music produced by British (obvs) acts during the previous 12 months. As we have seen, *Different Class* and Pulp had really hit the big time in 1995 and it would be a big omission if Pulp didn't feature somehow in the awards. And we weren't disappointed. The news came to us that we were nominated in four categories: Best British Group, Best British Video, Best British Single of the Year and, the big one, Best British Album of the Year. This really was the perennial outsiders now comfortably ensconced at the top of the British music scene. Some journey.

We were asked to perform a song at the event, too, which would be broadcast across the nation. 'Sorted . . .' was duly selected (perhaps because 'Common People' was too long for the show format). Once again, the fact we'd been chosen to perform seemed to us like a massive nudge, nudge, wink, wink that we'd be getting our grubby mitts on one of the bronze statuettes.

The ceremony would take place at Earls Court in London and we were required to attend a full rehearsal the day before. These things are always pretty tiresome, but it had to be done. It was here at rehearsal that the enormity of what was taking place kinda hit home: Sony Records were the organisers for this year's shindig and had decided they should use it as a way of getting their megastar, Michael Jackson, a bit of extra publicity – like he needs it, yeah? – by having him perform and receive a totally-made-up-for-him award, Artist of a Generation. Now this really got up our nose for two reasons:

1. Michael Jackson ain't British. Sort of goes against the whole thrust of the Brit Awards, doesn't it?
2. He was poncing his way through his dreary eco-dirge 'Earth Song' and was making it out that only he had the power to save the world from itself and meanwhile protect all the world from destruction with a quick crotch-grab and an industrial-strength wind machine. This sounds like I'm down on MJ. Au contraire: he made some wonderful music in his career – y'know, before all the sordid lawsuits, pay-offs and rumours emerged – and it's just that 'Earth Song' wouldn't get in his Top 20.

We watched Mick go through his performance and were thoroughly sickened by the whole thing. Just didn't seem right or appropriate.

We returned the next day in our best bib and tucker for the show. Russ and I got a cab there, no flash stretch limo. In fact, no red carpet either. No idea how this happened, but we ended up having to queue with the hoi polloi just to get into the building. I bet the Gallaghers got the full flashbulb treatment. I was rather miffed at this. I'm no limelight hugger, but after all we had experienced in the long story of Pulp, a swagger up the red carpet, flashbulbs popping off left, right and centre in full view of the UK TV-watching nation would've been nice. Really nice. But no, jostle with the common people. The indignity!

Never mind, we're here now. And eventually we were called to the stage to do our thing. The best memory of our walk to the stage was seeing a bog-standard (sorry) portaloo, the kind you see at festivals and building sites, sited backstage with a sign affixed:

For the sole use of Mr Michael Jackson

This had us in fits of laughter, imagining Mick was sat in there as we trudged past with his kecks round his ankles, sorting through some pre-show 'nerves'. Should have knocked it over.

We invited our dear friend Martin Wallace to play the acoustic that Jarvis usually played on the song, and we'd around 20–30 ravers to dance about on stage with us. Included in the mob were former Pulp bassist Pete Mansell and Candida's brother, Danny. The song ended with Jarvis being hoisted high into the air on the end of a wire. Quite why and what it was supposed to signify was lost on me: Getting 'high'? It couldn't be 'and then you come down', as he was lowered after we'd finished and the cameras were off somewhere else.

Anyway, once this bit was over it was back to our table to start tucking into the Brit Awards booze. Which we did with gusto. The dishing out of the gongs came and went and we were left empty-handed. Oasis swiped three: Band, Video and Album, while Take That's 'Back For Good' was deemed the best single of '95 – Really?

The wine kind of took the edge off us missing out on an award, so we weren't too disappointed. Music isn't about one group or artist being the 'best' anyway; it's just not like that. But that don't make good telly or sell more records.

On to the grand finale, which was Jacko receiving his faux award and trotting through 'Earth Song' – as I've said, we all found this deeply disturbing, but it was dear little Candida that was the spark to the flame. Jarvis was getting more and more riled up about Jackson and his guff and we noticed that to our right there was the gangway that led directly to the stage and it was unguarded. Opportunity was knocking. Doyle egged Jarv on by saying 'You'll never do anything about it!', and the next thing, Jarvis, accompanied by Peter Mansell, was off across the gangway, stage bound. Manners got the fear just across the bridge and turned back, but Jarvis was not to know this and was off, cavorting around the stage, doing nothing more controversial than lifting his jumper and miming shitting on the Jacko acolytes in the front row. He then had to evade stage security – who were dressed as if from the Old Testament, of course – and make it back to the table. It really wasn't that much of a protest. While he was doing all this we were stood on our chairs shouting, screaming and crying with laughter: 'Go on, son!' What would have happened if MJ was not 30 feet in the air atop a cherry picker machine? No one knows. The whole thing was over in a flash and it was amazing and everything bands should do when faced with utter po-faced pomposity.

Jarvis flopped back in his chair rather wild-eyed and was immediately swamped with folk like Brian Eno slapping his back and saying well done, about time someone did something like that, and all that kind of stuff.

When the ceremony was over it was all back to the dressing rooms backstage and it became somewhat obvious the S.H.I.T. had really hit the fan. We managed to get a bit of 'socialising' done but the main centre of attention was our dressing room and the hoo-ha rapidly erupting around Jarvis. Let's just say that Mr Jackson's people were not best pleased and before long the rozzers were in our dressing room. Comedian Bob Mortimer offered his legal services (he was a solicitor pre-fame, I believe), but I can't imagine how much help he would've been as he seemed somewhat 'refreshed' at this stage of the proceedings. Jackson's folk were out for the blood of an Englishman and all kind of threats were flying around. The main accusation levelled was that Jarvis had pushed some kids off the stage, attacked and injured some. I certainly did not see anything like that happen. The Old Bill decided that Jarvis should accompany them back to Kensington nick for more enquiries and a night in the cells. This was rapidly escalating into a full-blown 'thing'.

Over the next few days a full PR press furore unfolded. Jarvis was all over the front pages (again) and even made international news (no bad thing for a band), especially in the US of A. Trouble is, most of the coverage was toeing the Jackson line – his PR people were somewhat higher powered than our lot. No surprise there, really. Jarv was the villain here, and had caused 'suffering' and 'distress' to the kids taking part in the show. Once the actual evidence was presented, crucially by one Mr David Bowie, who had filmed Jacko's performance – it completely exonerated Jarvis and all charges were dropped, the vid showed that it was Jacko's own stage security that pushed the kids over trying to get to Jarvis. The previously pro-MJ tabloids soon did a reverse ferret once they realised the public was generally on Jarv's side. The *Mirror* even started a 'Free Jarvis' campaign.

The fallout from all this trauma was that Jarvis was pushed even further into the stratosphere of UK fame. Popping out for a quiet pint or just to the shops for a bottle of milk was now impossible without the pap's following his every move and snapping away. Not ideal.

The story fizzled along for a bit and as usual, it was not long until the tabloids found someone else to pick on. Unfortunately for Jarvis, this moment of craziness quickly became a bit of a millstone around his neck. Was this a bit of a turning point?

35

Going Underground

(They Suffocate at Night)

When you get home after a long time on the road you really don't know what to do with yourself. No sound check? No rider to tuck into? No thousands of adoring fans cheering your every move? No adrenaline rush from another crowd wowed by your songs and performance? No aftershow party? Nope, none of that. The bins need taking out, the dog (Our Malcolm) needs walking, and the mundane realities of real life must be addressed. It's a bit of a shock to the system, y'know.

It would seem that during the autumn of '95 and most of '96 we were constantly on the road. Yes, it was probably the most intense series of hard gigging we had ever done, but there was still time for a bit of home life and some R&R.

Sarah and I went on a well-earned holiday to Sri Lanka. In cyclone season. First day, the pizza bar by the beach blew down. Not a good start. It rained every day at 4 o'clock precisely. We booked a trip round the island that would take a couple of days taking in the sights. We expected a coachload of tourists but it ended up just us in a taxi with a driver. Enter one Roger Diaz, who proceeded to run some poor sod over minutes into our adventure and from then on drove with one hand on the horn while playing road chicken with Sri

314

Lankan lorries on precipitous hairpin bends. Relaxing. We bumped into an old acquaintance from Sheffield, as you do, queueing up to glimpse Buddha's tooth (or the outside of the box it might be contained in, in truth), as you do. We ended up in a mountain-top hotel slurping tomato soup and surrounded by the Sri Lankan cricket team, and I just had to pop the eternal question. She would fairly admit that she had been suggesting for days now that a romantic getaway in Sri Lanka would be a *GREAT* time for someone to propose. So, dutifully I did. Guess what? She said yes.

We set a date for April 1996 and duly tied the knot at Aston Hall in good ol' Rotherham. A 'do' was had two days later at the Tapton Masonic Lodge in Sheffield: an odd place, all wood panelling and huge portraits of the Queen with lots of really high-backed chairs to sit on. The police took it upon themselves to cordon off the road in case Elton, Bowie or Bono were going to rock up and cause a kerfuffle with gawpers. None of them bothered to show in the end, mainly because they were not invited. We had best man Ant Genn's dad (on drums) and his organ-playing mate entertain us with the hits of the day played in the inimitable 'club' style. Jarvis modelled a suit festooned with pork pies as Ants ribbed me about my predilection for pastry-encased meat products.

In fact, the rest of Pulp had a right time getting there, as the band had been asked to appear on the David Letterman show in New York, which coincided with the big day. Now this was a BIG deal. If you wanted to make any inroads into your Stateside profile, it could not be turned down. Dave just wouldn't ask again. So, do I pull the wedding to do Letterman or what? I'm sure you will all understand that a bride will dig the heels in about such an adventure and the wedding just could not be moved. Rather than Pulp miss the opportunity of Letterman, Justin Welch from Elastica was asked to deputise for me on the show, where the band played 'Common People'. He did a sterling job of it, too. Sadly, appearing on Letterman didn't really do much for us across the pond in the end. Jarvis, Russell, Mark, Steve and Candida jetted back straightaway and zipped up the M1 just in time to enjoy the party.

The week before Sarah and I were married the final cut from *Different Class* was released as a single: the beautiful love song 'Something Changed' (timing, I think you'll agree). We went on the good ol' *Top of the Pops* the week after it was released and as a surprise for me, everyone had decorated my drum kit in wedding parapher-nalia. Awww! This release was perhaps the record company trying to squeeze every last drop out of *Different Class*. We could've been accused of not giving the single our full push. The video was a very low-key affair: just us sat around playing the song in a kind of warehouse setting. It looked and felt like a band that had got to the end of the line, or at least the end of a particularly gruelling chapter.

'Something Changed' charted at number ten, our fourth Top 10 in a row. I don't think anyone really had any thoughts that it would be storming the highest reaches of the hit parade. Let's face it: the LP had sold, and still was selling, in droves, so why would folk be tempted to buy the fourth single from it? Even record company tricks like producing two different sleeves (a 'boy' sleeve and a 'girl' sleeve) were not enough. Had our chance of a top spot evaporated? Did we care?

In October, two events happened that really changed things. First, our son, Jackson, arrived on the 4th (before you ask, no – nowt to do with Wacko Jacko, but named after my Uncle Jack, a no-nonsense north Norfolk fisherman and lifeboat man. Add in the influence of seeing a Jackson Browne poster prior to his birth to make the name 'Jack' a bit different and there you have it.), and second, during the same week I bought a pub.

Why on earth would anyone who had a career to die for, a new baby and a rosy future buy a Sheffield pub? Well: it needed saving. Back in the eighties, of course, Sheffield folk who weren't beer monsters went to either The Hallamshire on West Street or The Washington on nearby Fitzwilliam Street. The Washy had been run by an old couple called Bill and Barbara for donkeys years who were ready to retire, and as loads of half-decent pubs around Sheffield had been turned into Irish bars or 'theme' bars, we were frightened that one of our last bastions would suffer the same horrific fate. My old mates Mick and Laura Deeley had been running pubs for a while – even The Hallamshire at one point – and were super keen on getting hold of The Washington and saving it. I simply decided to bung a few quid in to help this happen. Mick would run the place day to day. We literally got the keys the week Jackson was born. Talk about piling on the pressure.

Things were great, for a while. My mum and dad would babysit most weekends (they'd been desperate for a grandkid), so we could meet our chums down The Washington while not on Pulp duty. Dad would drop us off at first but then would stay for a diet Tango or two (he never drank alcohol, remember; just didn't like it, he said). He loved meeting the regulars and chatting away.

After a couple of years it was becoming plain that making a pub profitable was very difficult. It felt as if I was personally buying the good people of Sheffield a pint every Saturday night. Mick was great as a gregarious landlord but not so great at keeping the books straight. Worse was to come. Laura, the beautiful Laura who was such a fabulous person, fell ill. Eventually she was diagnosed with kidney cancer. This made looking after a pub very tricky for Mick and things began to slide even further. The cancer eventually became terminal and we lost Laura when she was just 47. Mick had lost his soul mate, and the pub suffered accordingly. This put Sarah and I in a real bind. We couldn't keep funnelling money into a failing business, yet if we abandoned Mick, all the people we hung out with there would shun us as heartless beasts. We tried, we really did, to help Mick keep going, but it was a lost cause and we had to take the risk of selling our half of the pub. Pete, a retired fireman, mate and regular, took my share and my involvement in pubs came to an end. Note to self (and to you reading): don't go into business with a mate. It nearly always ends badly. Especially in a business where you don't really appreciate what's going on. Still, it was great to be a pub owner (at first) for a bit. Info point: The Washington is still going strong and is now owned by Nick and Edie (she's Jarvis's niece) and we still go in from time to time. I really feel that Mick and I did save a piece of Sheffield pub history for the musicians and cool dudes about town. If in Sheffield, give it a try.

Still, the music biz timepiece keeps ticking, and it was time for us to direct our thoughts to the follow-up to *Different Class*. *DC*'s success didn't help us in concocting the next Pulp album. Previously we'd had plenty of time between writing, recording, releasing and touring to have a healthy pot of musical ideas to dip into and develop as necessary, but *Different Class* had taken us around the world and on to a different level of fame and notoriety. Pulp had never been a band where we'd get the guitars out in the tour bus and 'have a jam' and bandy new ideas about. Sound checks were the only place where we really had a chance to try anything out as a band while on tour. Some groups like to do a long sound check, making sure everything is just so. We weren't really like that, and we usually just made sure everything was working correctly and the monitors were set up right so we could hear each other and ourselves. We were always aware that there was a support band who would need a sound check too, and we didn't want to eat into their time (we remembered just how tough it had been rushing gear on stage for a very rudimentary sound check when we were starting out). So, we had managed to develop just one song during sound checks, though it was at least showing promise. This one was about old-age pensioners, maybe. Rock'n'roll.

Studio time was booked and we had Chris Thomas once again fingering the sound board, with a view to getting straight back into making the new album. Trouble is, we had very little to actually record. We had the old people's song and a few other bits but that was it. We did the main bits to the song that would become 'Help The Aged' and some other parts on a song called 'Northern Souls' at the time. However, it was obvious to me that this session was mostly a waste of time. If Jarvis, etc., thought we could conjure up some fantastic music just like that in the (expensive) studio they were very much mistaken. The pot was empty. Never mind, let's release 'Help The Aged' anyway to keep momentum going, and work on songs after that. Remember, Pulp had so very many times suffered from momentum death, so were very wary of letting anything flag. We had gone ahead with an early release for 'Common People' and it had worked, but Island and others in the camp were definitely against trying that this time round. Some even thought 'Help The Aged' wasn't up to much. I disagreed. I thought it was a hoot. A multi-layered tune about old folk getting old and one of Jarvis's favourite charity shops was a great idea. So very Pulp, and it had never been done before. After much 'discussion' it was decided that we should disappear and write. 'Come back when you've got some tunes.' Chris said. Wise words.

Meanwhile, it was time for Pulp to have another crisis. This time it was internal. There was disquiet within the ranks.

Russell had decided to leave. He'd had enough. He jumped. Or was he pushed? There had been some tension at the 'Help The Aged' recording session, which I thought was par for the course. Bands are fragile entities at the best of times so a bit of aggro was easily entertained. However, Russell didn't think the song was strong enough as a single, and could not be dissuaded otherwise. The first I had heard about the impending rift was when I got a call from Steve, asking me to meet him and Jarvis outside a hotel in Sheffield.

I zipped down, curious as to what this was all about, and we had a meeting sat in my car. It transpired that Jarvis had become very weary of Russell and his perceived lack of creativity in the guitar/ violin department. Russ had a very particular style that was firmly rooted in the 'basic' punk technique: certainly not a fancy note-bending 'play as many notes as you can' sort of style. It could easily be said that Russell took this outlook to heart, and never seemed to progress musically beyond it. It looked like Jarvis was going to ask Russell to leave the group. I came down on the side that Russ's style should be tolerated, and that maybe he should be encouraged to experiment further. Get wilder. Neither Steve nor Jarvis seemed to have much faith that he could or perhaps would change. Out of all of us, Jarvis had known Russ the longest, since the early eighties. They'd even shared a flat together once in Crookes, so I acquiesced and thought that Jarvis knew best.

I was disappointed that Pulp was going to fracture again. I always hated it when bands I loved lost a member. Some of the magic would disappear somehow. I could see a backlash from the fans – Russell was very popular with them. I could also see that nothing I could say would have any effect and I'd have to go along with it. But then it sort of didn't happen. I don't think Jarvis ever did put in the call to Russ; he decided to leave anyway.

So that was it. Pulp was a five-piece again. With Russ's departure I really felt something was lost. He wasn't always easy to get along with and could be quite a prickly character, but he was definitely a character, who brought an indiscernible magic to Pulp that disappeared with his departure. He had a unique style, in his guitar playing and his sartorial look – who else would be comfortable going on stage wrapped head-to-foot in tin foil and then a few years later rock Union Jack socks? Russ brought a hard-line edge to Pulp, too, quoting Nietzsche and Arthur Scargill, often in the same sentence. A part of me would perhaps come to miss Russ's hard-line stance in the future. Maybe.

Despite this tremor in the Pulp world it was time to knuckle down and winkle out a new album from the ether. We were in the position now where we could have gone anywhere to settle in and write: USA? Caribbean? Country retreat?

No, we went underground. Literally. We de-camped to a rehearsal complex called the Fortress off Caledonian Road, North London, run by a wild figure called 'Fatty Molloy', who'd done some roadie-ing for The Longpigs. He could usually be found living in a caravan on site and sporting a green beard and bald head. Odd, you could say. Head case, you could also say. He wasn't particularly fat either.

The Fortress basement was a smallish studio room completely covered in dull grey carpet: floors, wall, ceiling. No windows. It would've been difficult to find a more unsuitable room in which to write life-affirming, soaring music, but there we were.

I had played Yamaha drums ever since we got our first advance cheque from Island and just before we went underground, Yamaha had given me one of their brand new electronic drum kits – far removed from the Synare of old and those electronic Simmons kits you used to see Kajagoogoo playing on *Top of the Pops*. It was great: it had hundreds of sounds, some daft, some not, and moreover it was free. It's an odd thing that when you're struggling and having to pour all your disposable income into trying to scrape enough together to buy a half-decent cymbal, as soon as you 'make it' companies are falling over themselves to give you free stuff. Not to worry. I like free stuff as much as anyone. Also the electronic kit had something no acoustic kit could ever have: a volume knob. This is a double-edged sword. My band mates loved the idea that the kit could be turned down so they could hear themselves more clearly, but to me this feature was a pain. One of the best things about the drums is their often-visceral volume – take note: this is the drums coming in! However, as you will have by now gleaned, I'm a person who doesn't like to rock the boat (I know when I'm on to a good thing), so I found myself sat behind this electronic kit for most of the writing sessions in the Fortress (or dungeon – you decide).

We settled into a steady routine. We would gather around midday, wait an hour or so for Jarvis to show and then listen back to the previous days' 'music'. More often than not this would produce gales of laughter at the drivel we'd recorded, but every day there'd be at least one bit we could build on, or maybe even graft on to another bit, perhaps something that sounds like a 'chorus' or another a 'verse'. We would then get with our respective instruments and start working on the stuff we hadn't discarded from the day before. New ideas would come out in a natural way and if Jarvis liked the sound or his interest pricked, he'd press record on the tape to hopefully capture the 'magic' (usually not though).

Steve had got really into music technology and started bringing samplers and such down to the basement to help keep the juices flowing. No one else could get their head around the vagaries of MIDI and interfaces and all that guff. Steve could. He and Jarvis would set up loop samples and we'd play along, adding our own unique style to the sound coming out of the sampler. One such riff we had was a haunting horn part, a bit 'jazz'. Maybe a bit forties? We worked on it forever and the finished song was a graft of probably three or four other parts from other Fortress sessions. It became known as 'This Is Hardcore'. It seemed like such a departure from our previous output. It was slow, it was moody. 'Common People' it was not.

We had had many debates about the direction of the new record. Far more than previous records. Then we just got on with it, seeing where the collective creativity would take us. Now we were bona fide 'rock stars' we were very aware that lots of our new fans were expecting us to serve up 'Different Class II'. It was certainly considered, and a few tentative tracks were attempted as some sort of 'Common People Part II', but they never seemed to reach anywhere near the heady heights of what had in fact become our signature tune. Pulp had never rested artistically on previous music, so why should we start now? We knew instinctively we needed to make a record that was reflective of us *now*. Fame, success, adoration and all that entailed.

Eventually we emerged from the Fortress blinking into the sunlight with perhaps 15 songs of varying quality, ready to put down with Chris Thomas. It would be our sixth studio LP.

36

This is Hardcore

(This is Hardcore)

It didn't feel like groundhog day at all (much). We had recorded *Different Class* at the Townhouse on Goldhawk Road, just up from Shepherd's Bush in that London. So, it seemed the perfect choice of studio to make our follow-up. What could possibly go wrong?

Well, let's see.

It all started pretty much as we expected. Like last time, we beavered away quite diligently, laying down the basics of each track, setting solid foundations. As ever, as drummer, the cursed spotlight fell on me first. It's always tough going first to bat while everyone else kicks their heels waiting for their turn, but that's yer lot.

However, it soon transpired that something was different. In studio sessions of yore, as tracks built up we would start getting more excited about how they were turning out. The extra bits we added were always the cream on the top. But we never seemed to get to that part of the process with this record. Tracks would be put back up on the desk and twiddled with for a week or so, and then swapped out for another track, without, in my opinion, much changing. This seemed to go on for ages. Previously we'd always seemed to know instinctively when a track was finished. Great, can it lads (and lass), it's a wrap! Not this time.

It was decided that everyone needed a change of scenery to get round this block, though I don't remember who suggested it. Was it a case of Chris Thomas wanting to throw off the yoke that the Townhouse may have become? Or maybe our allotted time there was up? Either way, we de-camped to Olympic Sound Studios in Barnes, south-west London.

Olympic was a renowned British recording studio★, famous for producing some of rock and pop music's most iconic albums by artists such as Jimi Hendrix, Led Zeppelin, The Rolling Stones, Queen, David Bowie, Ella Fitzgerald – you name it. Now it was our turn to add to this canon of legends.

We appreciated the change of scenery, that's for sure, but we seemed to be dogged with bad luck. Olympic had put in a brand new desk and it bedevilled us with problems, including stuff we recorded mysteriously disappearing. Though more troubling, the stasis that had set in at Townhouse seemed to have transferred over to Barnes. Again, tracks were worked on, not finished and then replaced by another track, which would also remain unfinished. Frustrating and very, very boring.

Still, there was some moments of light. One day we got a fax (yes, fax – it's a bit like communicating by smoke signals or semaphore, it's that ancient a technology) from James Bond. No, not *the* 'James Bond' (he's a fictional character), but his 'people'. It went something like this:

We would love Pulp to submit a song for consideration as the title track for the forthcoming James Bond movie 'Tomorrow Never Dies'.

Wow. This really was a WOW moment. We were all kids of the sixties and had grown up in the seventies, so we all loved James Bond movies.

★ It's now mostly reverted back to a cinema, its original purpose, as big studios aren't viable nowadays. It still houses a much smaller recording studio.

More to the point, we all loved the classic Bond themes and especially the music of Bond maestro John Barry. So to be asked to contribute a song for consideration was incredible. An opportunity not to be missed. We were all so very excited.

Hold on, what does the rest of the fax say:

Please submit your finished tracks by end of play Friday.

Ah. Today is Wednesday morning. What were the Bond people thinking? Writing, recording and delivering such an important song (for us) in a couple of days was rather a fanciful notion. Never mind that we had got ourselves tied up in knots on our own album. But there was no way we were going to let this one past, no matter what we were confronted with. We decided to finish the day's twiddlings and set Thursday aside to see what we could do. We began dreaming about joining that illustrious group of Bond themers: Shirley Bassey, Tom Jones, Paul McCartney/Wings, Lulu, and even Duran Duran and A-ha.

We assembled at a reasonably early hour (probably about 10 – rock'n'roll is definitely not an early morning bird) and made a start jamming around some suitably Bond/Barry-inspired chords, and after a couple of hours we had a suitable foundation that seemed promising but it needed a middle part. I remembered a bit from the Fortress sessions that could add a dramatic section amidships and surprisingly, it was adopted. We quickly linked the bits together, played through it a few times for familiarisation purposes, and started the afternoon session by recording it. By late afternoon all the parts were recorded, Jarvis did his vocals and when the evening session was over it was all mixed and 'in the can'. Now this what was music recording should be like. All done in a single day: written, recorded and mixed. It was so thrilling and exciting to work this way. It just showed what was possible and threw the work that we were labouring at in the studio into stark relief. In days of yore, bands would record a *whole LP* in a day and it would be ace, but here we were, faffing about for what seemed like an eternity and not getting anywhere.

Still, we sent off 'Tomorrow Never Dies' to the film bods and waited for news. We thought it would slip easily into the Bond canon, with its slinky, tense, Bond-esque chords and car chase-style middle bit. Eventually we got the news: it's a no from Bond. Who got the gig though? Answer: Cheryl Crow? They've decided to go with Cheryl bloody Crow? Pah! There's no justice . . . Anyway, we got a great B-side out of it so all was not lost.

Around this time we had another brush with the film world when we were asked to provide a song for a film in development, *Great Expectations* – a rework of the Dickens novel which would star Gwyneth Paltrow and Ethan Hawke. We set up a TV and video in the Fortress rehearsal dungeon and cued the film up at the part where they wanted the song to go. We diligently worked out a tune to 'fit' the visuals, the song getting frenetic when the action did and cooling down as needed. It was a fun process. The best bit was when we invited the producer and music director along to hear what we had. We dutifully played the piece alongside the film and at the end the film bods were jumping up and down with excitement, saying how absolutely perfect it was, and then they spent the next five minutes animatedly talking over each other as to how the song could be improved. Meanwhile, we just looked at each other and back to this scene, gently smirking at the madness. Once they'd departed we merely shook our heads and asked, 'What the fuck was that all about?' Anyway, 'Like A Friend' ended up appearing in the film (which turned out to be a bit of a duffer in the end) and we got another decent B-side out of it.

Unfortunately, the high-octane shenanigans of finishing a track in a day didn't translate to our daily grind. Technical gremlins returned to haunt us and the new desk at Olympic had developed a habit of throwing a fit every now and again, which didn't help the mood, that's for sure.

One thing I remember from these long old days was that folk stopped hanging around the control room so much, listening to and commenting on the layers as they were being added. The wonder I had felt seeing the magical extra bits added seemed to have gone. Things were much different than before. Perhaps Russell's departure had caused this imbalance? Maybe. Jarvis and possibly Steve were now making the lion's share of the musical decisions, and input from other sources (Mark, Candida and me) was diminished.

This was amplified when we turned up one Monday morning only to find Jarvis already in the control room. This was a brand new venture for all, as Jarvis was never early. More troubling was that on the desk was a completely new track that none of us had heard before. It hadn't come from the Fortress sessions but from an idea Jarvis had developed over the weekend. What was going on? Why had Jarvis decided against presenting the idea to the rest of us to work on collectively rather than taking it straight to Chris Thomas? We were pissed off, to put it mildly.

But no matter how miffed we were, we, or certainly I, felt we had to suck it up. Let's just get on with it. I'm not one to spit my dummy out and cause a fuss. I mean, Jarvis had started the band way back in '78 so it was to all intents *his band* and us lot were supporting actors. Fair enough. The track was based on a sample that bore an uncanny resemblance to the opening riff of Smokey Robinson's 'Tracks Of My Tears'. So, we added our parts and it became 'A Little Soul', a rare Pulp beast in that it is one of the very few tracks that (not counting Jarv's original idea) was solely written in the recording studio.

Eventually the faffing about dissipated and we had 12 finished tracks to make up the LP (plus a few other finished tracks to use as B-sides and 'extras'). One thing that nagged me was that 'Help The Aged' seemed to be the only stand-out, nailed-on, dead-cert single.

This presented a problem. We had up to this point a long, unbroken string of belting bona fide hit singles, and now? Record companies want singles - they treat them as 'adverts' for the album. And we've already learned album sales are where the real profits are. Singles don't generally make anything for the record company. Hit singles = hit album. Simple as that.

At the outset, we had made a conscious decision to avoid making 'Different Class II'. It would probably end up being a watered-down, weaker version anyway. Besides, writing songs is a rather mercurial art. What comes out is what comes out. We had to go off in search of new musical horizons, and *This Is Hardcore* was the result – twelve tracks, warts 'n all.

Originally from an idea labelled as 'Frightened', 'The Fear' sets the scene for the entire album. Jarv had a sort of mental health episode at the beginning of recording *Hardcore*. After years of chasing success and validation, when it arrived it didn't quite live up to the billing. This probably sent him over the edge. I sound like a bit of a crap friend, but I can't say I noticed. Or perhaps he was just really good at keeping things locked in? Mind you, who else could get away with quoting TV magician Paul Daniels?

'Dishes' is a beautiful soft-centred ballad, something we had been pretty good at over the years. It's a great track to play live and has probably the most delightful guitar solo anywhere to be found on a Pulp record.

For 'Party Hard', had we gone all David Bowie? Possibly a bit Scott Walker? Maybe . . . This track took a while to come together, as me and Steve had to sort out the backbeat and rhythm. Jarvis always liked a bit of vocoder (a synthesizer for the voice), and kind of masking his voice with it. The title, of course, derived from the phrase coined a few years back in Germany: 'Party real fucking hard, yes?'

'Help The Aged' was recorded at the very start of the *Hardcore* sessions. It's a rarity for Pulp, since it was written on the road. There's a gap towards the end that is always tricky to replicate live: it's one of those songs where it needs to be all about feel, and choosing the right moment to bring everyone crashing back in. I always got the Jarvis hard stare if I brought it in too quickly or too late. I could never win. Always love this track, though.

'This Is Hardcore' (a title track that actually makes the album, shocker!) is possibly the most grandiose and neurotic piece of music in our entire history. It samples 'Bolero On The Moon Rocks' by Peter Thomas. In rehearsals, we couldn't drop it in and out without going out of time. The answer was to start the song with me playing along to the sample, so that we were locked in from the get-go. That stuck once we recorded it, although the sample kind of comes and goes through the track. It's another song that I don't really do all that much on, as I'm so locked into the sample – which is quite delicate-sounding, thus making it even harder to stay in time. The best approach was just to keep a steady beat. This 'magnum opus' really is up there with the best music Pulp ever made. It took some doing, though, and at first I didn't think it was going anywhere. But it ended up encapsulating the feel of the whole record. Writing and recording it was hardcore, and not necessarily happy hardcore.

'TV Movie' is another sweet ballad, but this time of the break-up variety. After the record came out we heard reports that some buyers had returned it, believing there to be a fault on the CD, as we added radio static noises that come to the fore towards the end of the track.

The 'Tracks Of My Tears' sample in 'A Little Soul' was eventually replaced with a 12-string guitar replicating the feel of the original sample, I believe so that Smokey Robinson wouldn't get in a tizz. Jarvis wrote the song about his dad, who buggered off when him and his sister were kids.

After 'Help The Aged', 'I'm A Man' seemed the best candidate for a single in my mind. It's also one of the few songs on the LP that has an actual chorus. It's one of the worst culprits for being worked on endlessly in the studio to no discernible difference, though. I think it suffered from overwork and fell out of favour as a potential single by those whose opinion mattered.

'Seductive Barry' (this was the working title; it never received a real title) was thought of as a smoochy number à la Barry White, perfect for getting it on (not sure it worked out like that in the end, but hey ho). The delightful Neneh Cherry provided the female vocal part. My main contribution on this track was using that free Yamaha DTX electronic drum kit. It had hundreds of sounds on it. About 80 per cent of them were rubbish but there was some good stuff, one being some drones that seemed to play forever until you hit the pad a second time. There were two slightly different drones, which together made an interesting multi-level sound. Play some swooshing cymbals for effect and there you go. The song seems to outlive its welcome on the record; a more drastic edit could and probably should have been employed.

'Sylvia' is a gargantuan song. The kitchen sink seems to have been thrown at this, and probably not in a good way. It started out as a simple song lamenting a lost girl, but it really goes over the top towards the end. It should have stopped before the last big solo bit. Superfluous. I recall originally playing this with more of a shuffle pattern with prominent snare grace notes (quieter snare hits between the actual correct beat), but in the recording Chris Thomas told me to cut those out. I was really pissed off about it, as I quite liked them. He said they'd put them back in during the mix but never did.

'Glory Days' is the closest we got to 'Common People Part II'. Of course, it's not a patch on 'Common People'. In the end, it was another track I felt didn't really go anywhere. I couldn't get past Bruce Springsteen and his 'Glory Days'.

Probably the last song recorded to make the record was 'The Day After The Revolution'. This is a bit of a lost song, perhaps. I don't think we played it again after we recorded it, and never live as far as

I know. Bit of a shame really, as it's really quite good. It does have an end-of-the-record feel so was placed well.

After such long slog of writing and recording, I think we were just glad that we finally had enough songs in the bag for a record. Blessed relief all round. However, though I probably didn't admit it at the time, I didn't think it was as good as *Different Class*. Yes, it was *different*, but I couldn't see the magic (or hear it) as I had done with *DC*. I knew we had two fantastic tracks on there: 'Help The Aged' and 'This Is Hardcore', but I had this nagging feeling that the rest were a bit patchy to say the least. Music needs to reach in and grab the listener with some unquantifiable 'brilliantness' and maybe I just thought the record didn't have enough of that. The interminable remixing and further remixing rendered some songs rather sludgy and ill-defined in my book. But why? Had Pulp lost confidence after the last five years of ever increasing success? That common purpose that propelled the early Gift and Island singles plus *His 'N' Hers* and *Different Class* appeared to be gone, or at least greatly diminished. We never needed to faff around on those records: we could sense when they were finished. *Hardcore*, though, had been a much more difficult record. We suffered from the loss of Russell, no doubt, and certainly Jarvis (and to a lesser extent Steve) had taken on more of the decision-making process. Had our success changed Jarvis in some way? All those years yearning for fame and success and validation and when you've finally got it, it turns out to be a hollow shell of what you were hoping for – you'd be pissed off too, I expect.

With *This Is Hardcore* it appeared that Pulp had fallen into a music industry trap: second album syndrome. It's that old cliché, where bands have huge success with their debut album and then struggle with the second, usually because they had all the time in the world to hone the first LP and mere months to make the follow-up. Trouble is, this was Pulp's sixth album.

37

Second Album Syndrome

(Seconds)

This Is Hardcore was released on 30 March 1998, five months on from 'Help The Aged', the lead-off single from the record.

So, while we were finishing off the album, it was back to the ol' rigmarole of videos and photoshoots for record covers and such like. Actually, it was a welcome relief from being holed up in the studio for the last millennium (or so it felt like).

The 'Help The Aged' video was shot mostly at Stoke Newington Town Hall. It's a location often used to replicate stern-looking brutalist Eastern European government facilities on film. We had a load of male actors made up to look like old people, with grey wigs on and cardies, etc., and had them interacting with much younger-looking actresses, as if in an odd kind of care home (look hard and you might be able to spot Pat Skinny, the male lead from the 'Disco 2000' video, as an old bloke). The idea was inspired by American artist John Currin, many of whose paintings feature distorted portraits of grotesque young females with equally odd-looking older blokes. The video includes loads of Currin prints in the background.

Jarvis also wanted to use a Stannah stair lift, but when Stannah got wind of the idea for the video, which was that we'd make it appear the lifts were transporting the old dears up to heaven, they passed, saying they didn't want their products to be associated with death (fair enough, I s'pose) Jarvis had to convince them that the video would depict the old folks being transported to *another planet* (it's 'heaven', really). They bought the idea, and gave us the go ahead.

We also had a bit of a problem with the charity Help the Aged. Again, they needed persuading that we weren't taking the piss out of old folk (we were definitely not) and that the song wouldn't denigrate their brand (it wouldn't). Jarvis countered that he in fact found Help the Aged charity shops some of the best on the high street – and he knew them all inside out, being an ardent charity-shop shopper for many, many years.

One thing you'll notice in the 'Help the Aged' cover image (and the video) is the return of Jarvis's trademark glasses. He'd ditched the contacts and returned to his former bespectacled look. Was this a conscious decoupling from the previous few years of Jarvis the Sex Bomb?

The single stalled at number eight in the hit parade and slipped down pretty quickly afterwards. I thought it was a pretty strong single but beyond the 'hardcore' fans, it obviously didn't resonate so much. It certainly didn't get anything like the airplay we thought it would have garnered. Hold on – number eight is pretty good, I hear you say, and generally I would agree, but we felt like we were still cock o' the walk and a this was our much-anticipated return to the lime-light. However, we'd been away for the best part of nearly two years, a very long time in the music world, and others had definitely been reaping the warmth of the spotlight in our absence. Radiohead and The Verve in particular had picked up the 'indie darlings' torch that we had dropped outside the studio as we beavered away on *Hardcore*. We could almost feel that spotlight of relevance moving away from us during this time.

Even though 'Help The Aged' wasn't quite the return to form we had hoped, the UK music presss welcomed *This Is Hardcore* with open arms – the reviews were positive, nay glowing, but with one caveat: this is definitely not *Different Class*; this is dark, brooding, and a lot of new Pulp converts might not like that. Listener beware.

Some folk took against it as soon as they saw the cover, that of a glamorous young lady laying in a 'prone' position, looking rather glassy eyed and without a vest on (she'll catch her death . . .). Apparently this was subjugation of women, leaning towards pornography. Or something. I mean, yes, a lot of the lyrics on *Hardcore* did touch on the subject of pornography – especially the title track – and perhaps how Jarvis had likened his experience of fame to being reduced to a commodity to be traded and demanded of. Heavy shit, man. But I really feel that accusations that we were misogynists or promoting pornography in any way were going a bit far.

The sleeve itself was designed by graphics legend Peter Saville, who had blazed a trail doing sleeves for Manchester's Factory Records, including Joy Division, New Order and even Wham!. The images, of two dazzlingly beautiful Eastern European girls – ice queens who wouldn't (or couldn't) deign themselves to talk to mere 'musicians' (that's probably why I look so pensive, perched on the window sill) – was shot at the prestigious Hilton Hotel Park Lane.

Hardcore was an important release, not just for us but also for Island Records, so it was imperative that we throw a huge launch party for our mates and industry bods. And as the cover images were shot at the Hilton Park Lane, why not rent the top floor? The theme was dress in black and pink and don't come as a scruff.

That night, we crammed onto a tiny stage and played through a selection of tracks from the album:

'The Fear'
'Dishes'
'Party Hard'
'Help The Aged'

'Seductive Barry'
'This Is Hardcore'

Apparently, the bash was 'reasonably' star studded (rumours of David Bowie attending, however, were unfounded). A real mix of TV slebs and the Britpop undercard. We had a busload of Sheffield mates in attendance, too. Mind you, I have almost zero recollection of the party, or the live performance. There must have been oceans of drink to consume and that's my only excuse for these shocking levels of amnesia.

One vague recollection is that we had our own VVIP area in a suite down on the floor below, which we probably used as our dressing room for the performance, and as is the norm after the set we spent more time in there. Late, late on I noticed a couple of lads hanging about and eventually they plucked up the courage to seek out some 'recreational drugs'. They approached big Ray Grange, a London gig promoter (and latterly Amy Winehouse's manager), who was a regular at Pulp shows and is about 6ft 6in tall and built like the proverbial brick outhouse (but is, of course, an absolute top chap). After they had sidled up and made their enquiries Ray straightened himself out to his full height and looked the lads dead in the eye (who were at least a whole head shorter) and bellowed, in his rather RP voice: 'So, you've asked the only black man in the room if he's got any coke. Really?' The lads scuttled away, suitably red-faced. Meanwhile, we guffawed with laughter.

The do went on all night and the mega-expensive suite was eventually used by roadies as a crash pad. Top night all round in the end.

Despite the disappointing single showing, *This Is Hardcore* entered the charts at number one, although it didn't really hang about and over the next few weeks slipped further and further down the charts, eventually spending most of the summer in the forties, fifties and sixties. As I've said before, hit singles really do drive album sales. 'Help The Aged' had done OK, but had largely disappeared from the airwaves by this point. Picking the album's title track as the next single probably wasn't the best move.

As I said before, 'This Is Hardcore' is a towering piece of music – but a single? It's over six minutes long, y'know? Radio 1 (and 2) were clearly going to struggle to fit it into their schedules (never mind commercial radio). 'Common People' it ain't . . .

But, it being easily the strongest material off the record was a decent enough reason (in our books, at least) to release it. So, single it was. Fair play to Island, though; they threw their all behind it and financed our most ambitious video ever.

The '. . . Hardcore' video is an epic of the genre. Should be – it cost over £1 million to make. Just goes to show how far we'd come from filming 'Babies', our first video, in a shopping trolley. The concept for this video was a forties/fifties authentic-looking detective pastiche, the theme being it's a lost movie but with many parts missing. It culminates in a Busby Berkeley-style finale. Phew! Of course, such a venture took ages to film and a load of hanging about (always), but the end product was worth it.

I got a good few appearances in as the barman in the party scene (by the way, I played a great scene as a drunk helping the guy having the heart attack, but the cutting-room floor swallowed it up). Maybe my acting wasn't up to scratch, though it felt great at the time. If you watch me closely in the party fight scene, I look rather as if I'm trying to subdue a laugh as the fight sprawls around me. Truth is, I was . . . the stunt guys were really going for it and I nearly got me head knocked off by a flying bottle! Happy days.* Jarvis did the end scene with the chorus girls separately another time, although he looked like he could have brushed his hair a bit better.

After all the filming was done, I asked what was going to happen

---

* Also featuring in the video is a girl with dark hair and a blue dress. As Lolly, she went on to have a couple of minor hits in the late nineties ('Viva La Radio' and 'Mickey').

with the bright yellow carpet used in the party scene, as I really liked it. 'The skip,' came the answer, and I really wracked my brain as to how I could get it home and installed in my house. I never did in the end. Shame. When we got to view the finished article we all agreed it was absolutely stunning and easily the best video, by a country mile, we'd had ever done.

Nevertheless, 'This Is Hardcore', surprise surprise, didn't garner the airplay required to catapult it into the upper echelons of the charts. Having said that, it did get to number 12, thanks, I'm sure, to our legions of fans getting down the shops to buy it. I thought that 12 was a decent position. Clearly, though it was a sharp divergence from our run of singles with *Different Class*. We had stormed the barricades, fomented the revolution, and been welcomed into the music industry's VIP area. But all we'd found behind the red curtain was Elton John, sat on his own, bored out of his skull.

38

Off We Go Once More

(We Can Dance Again)

With the record out, it was time to hit the road again. I recall reading the *NME* as a young thing and hearing bands moan about getting stuck on the 'rock'n'roll hamster wheel': write, record, tour, write, record, tour, ad infinitum – round and round you go until you can no longer stay on and you fall off. Touring sounded great to me; beats slogging your guts out in a stinking cacophonous factory or teaching slothful ingrates for 30 years. Writing, recording and touring was what I desired (when it was an almost unattainable target) and now we were actively living that rock'n'roll cliché. How did it compare to the myth, I hear you say? Well, to be truthful, mostly great. There was pressure and fall-outs and bits that you wish were better, but we were still playing music, having a laugh, hanging out with mates and doing what we loved. OK, so it wasn't all one big party, but we had our road family who in a way were like extra band mates. Making *Hardcore* had been tough, but once it was done and out there, the pressure was off somewhat. So, after the debauched(ish) night in the Hilton it was time to sally forth and take our new, dark tunes of despair and pornography to the assembled masses. It's gonna be fun again. Honest.

We kicked off by heading out west. No, not Bristol, but across the pond, for several US and Canadian dates. The most prestigious of these was the Tibetan Freedom Festival, held at the Robert F. Kennedy Memorial Stadium in Washington, DC, between 13 and 15 June 1998. Tibet had been part of China since annexation in 1950 and, led by the Dalai Lama, it had been fighting for independence for decades. Chinese repression was getting pretty heavy, and so a group of disparate musicians was brought together to 'sort it all out' in an enormous American football stadium on the other side of the globe. To be honest, I don't really think we had much of an angle regarding the cause, but being on the bill alongside Beastie Boys, R.E.M. and (ahem) Dave Matthews Band was a major opportunity to get out in front of 100,000 Americans and do our funny little dance.

En route to Washington, DC, we encountered a massive rainstorm. Now, Sheffield is known for its rain, but it never rains *that* hard! This was an incredible downpour and seemed to be causing all kinds of problems. We got wind of a situation at the RFK Stadium: the open-air arena had been hit by lightning and a 25-year-old woman in the audience was killed, putting an end to day one of the event. A random, tragic occurrence. No one knew whether the following day's gig would go ahead. This left us at a loss as to what to do.

Someone heard that Radiohead had arranged a last-minute gig at the 9.30 Club in DC that night (MC'd by R.E.M.'s Michael Stipe, no less) as recompense for not being able to play the benefit concert. Why don't we try and muscle in on Radiohead's gig? Ask if we can do a few numbers so our trip wouldn't be a complete waste? The Radiohead boys were amenable as long as we used their gear and didn't alter anything in their set-ups. OK lads, will do.

Later that day we found ourselves ensconced in Radiohead's dressing room, an odd place where the sofas were nailed to the wall at head height so as to make more room down below. The proceedings were enlivened somewhat by our old mucker Rich Hawley (who had joined us as a second guitar and backing vocals for the tour) inadvertently tipping a huge bowl of Bombay mix off the elevated sofa directly onto Thom Yorke's head. I guess you had to be there, but it was hilarious. Thom took it all in his stride.★

The Free Tibet gig did go ahead the next day as planned and we waddled on stage to blank indifference from the gig-goers as we served up our trio of feel-good numbers: 'The Fear', 'Sorted . . .' and 'This Is Hardcore'. I do hope there were no Tibetan refugees in attendance, as they might have run off back home, preferring the jackboot of Chinese oppression to these 'floor fillers'.

After a prestigious show at New York's Hammerstein Ballroom, playing to 2,000-plus East Coast Pulpophiles, it was back home for several European dates. On our return, we boarded our tour bus and set off for Germany, destination Lorelei, a picturesque outcrop over-looking the Rhine, which was due to host a festival with Pulp as a star attraction (alongside David Bowie, no less). As we left London one of our esteemed roadies plonked himself down opposite me and proceeded to reveal a rather large bag of cocaine that needed to be consumed before we hit customs and thus any meddlesome searches that might occur. Well, we all love a challenge, so by Dover the two of us were as wired as could be. I am aware that you may have led a more sheltered life than I, so you might not be aware that one of the side effects of cocaine (along with talking copious amounts of nonsense, usually about yourself) is that one has the ability to drink

---

★ If you think Pulp are renowned for not being very 'rock'n'roll', forget us – Radiohead takes it to a whole other dimension. One time, both bands were playing gigs in Madrid on the same date (different venues, obviously). Since we finished ahead of them, we dashed across town to try and catch the end of their show. We just about managed to hear 'Thank you Madrid, goodnight!', but still we barged backstage to hang out. Radiohead bassist Colin Greenwood engaged us bravely in chitchat but soon noticed we were expecting a rider beer. We were, of course, parched. Colin looked perplexed and nipped off to find something, returning with about four small cans of Spanish beer, sheepishly exclaiming they weren't much of a drinking band and the others probably wouldn't be engaging in post-gig revelry, as they were hard at work on their Open University degree courses, beavering away on their laptops. Wow! Iggy Pop it was not.

prodigious amounts of booze without feeling even a little bit drunk. When I say prodigious, I really do mean it. So, once in Europe, we drank ourselves silly all the way to Germany. And of course when the coke wore off, the hangover kicked in. Big time. I felt awful. Now, by this point I was kind of used to hangovers. After all, during a tour we'd usually get pretty hammered after a gig, the adrenaline of live performance literally forcing you to hit the vodka, so I started most gig days feeling pretty rough. The key was to make it to concert time feeling ready and able enough to do the show. At Lorelei, I decided the only way forward was to seek out a suitable patch of grass and to lay face down on it, enjoying the cool feel of the grass against my skin. Sleep, not surprisingly, was hard to come by, but I thought if I laid still for long enough I'd recover. My rehabilitation was not helped by a constant stream of concerned Germans thinking I was dead. I may have looked it and smelled like it, but I was very much alive. Somehow, I recovered enough to perform and got away with it. The gig was enlivened by Jarvis throwing a bit of a fit (again) about the monitors and at the end tipping them all off the stage. I think he had been enraged because we'd had to borrow a load of David Bowie's amps, as ours had apparently gone to Moscow.

That summer we performed at several more fests as part of the *This Is Hardcore* European Festival Tour and, let's face it, seen one fest, seen 'em all (jaded? Moi?). But these shows could still throw up some unexpected events.

On 21 June we played Hurricane Festival in Scheessel, Germany – a by now rare daytime set, but Jarvis had taken to performing barefoot and the stage was so hot in the sun he could hardly stand. Oh, how we laughed.

Our first visit to Greece was another example of how to have fun on tour. The festival stage was constructed on a beach in Piraeus, the port to the capital Athens. Naturally it was baking hot and as the side of the stage abutted into the sea, japes were afoot. As soon as we finished the last song, while the young Greeks were still a'whooping and a'hollering, Steve and Hawley chucked their guitars off and plunged head-first into the cool waters. Straight into an oil slick. Refreshed, yes. Oily, you bet. The next day we instructed our tour manager Richard Priest to hire us a schooner to take us round the beautiful island of Aegina in the Bay of Piraeus. This is what touring's all about and we loved a boat trip wherever possible. Even better if it involved a spot of fishing. Many a time we'd tour with a small fishing set-up tucked away under the bus. We sailed out into the bay and pushed on to the island, where we enjoyed a splendid lunch, then all back to Athens by the evening. Bliss.

We headlined Glastonbury again in June and it cemented itself in our hearts forever more. The Sunday night crowd showed us as much love as they had in 1995, but this time round we were free of the crippling fear of getting bottled off the stage. Trouble is, without the primordial fear of a bottle of piss taking you out it does sort of remove the memories from the mind.

While we were out touring festivals, to our great surprise the England football team were doing really rather well in the World Cup Championships, and we landed in Porto, Portugal, the day of the quarter-final match between England and Argentina. Priesty had arranged for the hotel to erect a big screen so we could enjoy the match, which we did, until David Beckham was sent off and it went to penalties, which England duly lost. Same old story. Nevertheless, abetted by a very amiable barman, we got stuck into sampling Porto's finest achievement: port, a fortified wine that is lethal in the quantities we were drinking it. Our lovely barman kept upping the ante by pouring an ever more aged port for us to sample, which we did, along with copious amounts of roasted almonds, which Portuguese bars put out to tempt the drinkers. Well, I'm sure you can guess the rest. Later that night the gods of drink were tipping the room from side to side and by the time I found my room, my stomach decided it'd had enough drink and chucked itself up (thankfully down the loo), but it is an unsettling sight indeed to see a stream of jet black vomit pouring out of yourself. Somehow my room got rather trashed with all the 'emotion' of the day. Well, I say trashed; it was probably just a bit messier than usual, but I do recall smashing the bedside lamp (ooh, Mr Rock'n'Roll!). Truth is, once you see how much they charge you for the damage you think twice about smashing anything.★

The European section of the tour ended with a gig in the lovely Stockholm, one of my favourite European cities. The Scandies really seem to have it worked out: everyone is beautiful, everyone is looked after, everyone is intelligent and all seem happy. Sarah flew out with Jackson, who was still only about two years old, to see the gig. Jackson enjoyed having a sit at the drum kit and hitting a few things and I made sure he had a pair of drumsticks to hold as a souvenir. This backfired as gig time approached, as he was really upset, thinking that I wouldn't be able to play without the sticks he had.

On 25 July, we returned home to Blighty to headline a massive show in Finsbury Park, our first gig on home soil in ages. This was a big deal. We were filling a large outdoor space just about on our own name. In that London. Plus it was being filmed for release as a 'Pulp live' video (remember them?). Better get it right, then?

★ As I've already mentioned, Pulp weren't into that rock'n'roll trash the gaff nonsense. The nearest we ever got to trashing a dressing room was at a festival in Sweden. I remember we'd totally smashed the gig – in fact, in my opinion, it was one of the best gigs we ever played. Back at the dressing room Portakabin, high on post-gig adrenaline, we did it in. For fun. Steve looked at the table containing the remains of the rider and asked, 'Who orders this shite?', while holding aloft an unopened bottle of Martini Bianco. No one owned up to it so it went crashing against the side of the 'kabin, smashing into a hundred pieces. We responded by upending the tables, sending drinks/peanuts/Twiglets flying, to gales of laughter. It's hardly driving your Rolls-Royce into a swimming pool but, y'know – gotta get your kicks where you can . . .

Well, such matters were pushed out of my mind (at least initially), as it was Sarah's 30th birthday, and what better way to celebrate than arranging for Pulp security (Colin Lish and Co.) to march the cake – complete with custard and candles, of course – through the heaving crowd to where Sarah and our mates had camped out. Perfect. All the celeb moments pale into insignificance after that really, but as a further birthday treat I managed to persuade Robbie Williams to accompany us to the aftershow club somewhere. The glamour. Suffice to say, we didn't cock any songs up and the video was released to as much success as these things attract. Be forewarned that as a band we were pin-sharp, tight as.

We took the rest of the summer off, before heading to Japan from 18 September for another tour. The same crazy kids were following our every move, burdening us with all manner of trinketry and foul-tasting biscuits (squid flavour? No ta!). We accepted all their gifts (it would be rude not to, and we are all very polite people). However, I fully admit that this time round Japan started to grate on me. I'm no fan of raw food and after the previous visit's highs, this time it was all a bit dull. We were there in the middle of a monsoon, so we couldn't wander about as much and we all felt a bit cooped up inside the hotel.

As we were over on that side of the globe, we dropped down into Australia and New Zealand for a run of shows. We'd been booked to play three shows back-to-back at the Enmore Theatre in Sydney, a bit of a novelty as we almost always did one show per city and moved on. It seemed a good idea: set up the stuff, then sound check, gig, party, hotel, and repeat a further two times minus the set-up/take-down bit.

Never again. It was so dull to be playing to the same four walls three nights running. Torture. We missed the vicarious thrill of looking out into a new venue. It really didn't help that the Enmore Theatre was fully seated, a set-up we abhorred. We survived, but that was the only time we did three consecutive shows in the same place. Ever.

On that trip we played a gig at the furthest geographical point away from Sheffield we'd ever been: Auckland, New Zealand, a full 18,161km (11,285 miles) away from our hometown. We literally had come a long way, baby. I should have been full of it, as I waited to count in 'The Fear', but I remember an odd feeling of dread. Was I tiring of playing these songs for the umpteenth time? Was I sick of seeing the same gyrations in front of me? Was I BORED? I dunno, but I had to shake off these thoughts – I hated making mistakes on stage, and losing concentration was the way to make them. Trouble is, we were so used to playing these tunes by now it was easy to find your mind wandering: Where will we end up after the gig? What's happening tomorrow? That looks like an odd person down the front . . . And before you know it you've dropped a clanger. Maybe no one else notices, but you know it. You just hoped the error wasn't noticeable enough to generate the hard stare from Jarvis, no matter how fleeting.

During our brief stay in New Zealand we managed to fit in another boat trip and hired a small vessel to take us out on to the Tasman Sea for a spot of shark fishing. We didn't catch a shark – mostly red snapper – but my brother Richard (still a crew stalwart) snagged a dogfish, so was King of the Seas for the day. After the run of shows in New Zealand, we had about six weeks before the next stint of gigs, so most everyone decided to spend some of that time exploring the islands and taking in the hot springs and scenery. I couldn't, however, as I had urgent business to take care of back home: the imminent arrival of child number two.

I wasn't looking forward to undergoing the vast and tiring return journey to the UK alone, but luckily my old chum Richard Hawley volunteered to accompany me back home. Now, everyone else saw this as a bit of a double-edged sword. Hawley is usually great company (especially with a beer) but could be, how shall we say, a bit fidgety over a long flight home, especially fag-less. I had visions of me having to control the drunken guitarist for half the time as we traversed the globe. Restful? No. Still, whatever happened would make it all the more interesting. Turned out Richard was a saint all the way home, even when we landed in LA, which due to crossing the International Date Line was the day before we took off. That really did our swedes in. We eventually got back to Sheffield, brains mushed with jet lag, about 36 hours later.

Two weeks later our beautiful daughter (in truth, she looked like a mix of Winston Churchill and American comedian Mike McShane) Jeannie was born. We named her after the person I consider to be Pulp's saviour: our manager, Jeanette Lee of Rough Trade Management.

Once everyone had returned from the other side of the world, it was time to launch into a UK arena tour. Our only UK show since the release of *Hardcore* had been the Finsbury Park date, and it would have been remiss to not to play to our fans at home.

Jarvis decided we needed to shake things up a little, so we employed a lookalike to open the show. Jarvis was a fan of *Stars in their Eyes*, a Saturday-night TV talent show in which members of the public dressed up as one of their heroes and performed one of their classic songs for the audience. The previous year, a young chap named Gareth Dickinson had done a brilliant version of Jarvis. He had the dance moves off just right and had even made the Grand Final. So, he was duly drafted in as part of the UK leg of our *Hardcore* tour.

We'd been opening with 'The Fear' the entire tour and so we decided to employ Gareth to play a visual trick on the audience. We'd start the song and a figure (Gareth) would be seen stage right, pulling the usual Jarvis-style poses and generally larking about, but lit so as you couldn't quite make him out. The figure would start singing the song as per JC, but then from the opposite side of the stage the *real*

Jarvis would emerge (he had been singing offstage all along, of course), and it was always fun to watch the audience's reaction as they realised they'd been cheering on the doppelgänger all along, and that the real Cocker was now in the arena. Jarvis and Gareth would confront each other on stage as if Gareth was some figure of Jarvis's psyche that was there to taunt him. Gareth's job done, he could slope off and put his feet up. To say he was chuffed to be part of a major rock show was certainly an understatement.

At the last show of the year for us, in Bournemouth, we found out that Gareth had really wanted to do Freddie Mercury on *Stars in their Eyes*, but there'd been too many Freddies on the show so the producers had asked him to do someone else – and of course he chose Jarvis. So as a thank you to him, we rehearsed the Queen song 'Crazy Little Thing Called Love' during sound check so he could sing his little Freddie Mercury heart out on stage. It seemed fitting to end our world tour in such a strange way.

39

The Hamster Turns the Wheel

(The Babysitter)

Phew. It felt like a long period of strangeness had finally come to an end. *Hardcore* had been hard work and it was now time to look towards the future. But for the moment there was a window of opportunity to recharge back at home. Hold on a sec; I now had two kids under five, so recharging batteries was a bit tricky to say the least.

Life went on, in a 'walk the dog' and 'look after the kids' sort of way. Jackson was just starting school and Jeannie will have been at nursery. Pulp, however, were never far away, and after what seemed a short break, there was talk of meeting up to start writing again.

We had been somewhat scarred by spending those countless hours, days and weeks in a dank, grey-carpeted, windowless basement writing *Hardcore*, so we agreed a more homely setting for the next album might be nicer. Jarvis suggested we start meeting at his house in Shoreditch, East London, to begin the arduous process once again. We could use the equipment he'd set up in his dank, almost window-less basement studio. What . . . ? Yes, back in the cellar. It was an improvement, certainly, but still a rather damp-smelling cellar, none-theless. Jarvis had set up Candida's Farfisa and a couple of amps, plus a little cocktail drum kit he'd been given. It was pink, sparkly, very, very small and designed to be played standing up. No worries – it was fine to use as a stopgap rather than a big, hairy-chested drum kit that would've been far too loud for sensitive ears, especially in such a small space.

One thing about Jarvis, as we now know, is that he can tend towards the hoarder end of the social spectrum, especially when it comes to music gear. Thus the cellar studio was crammed with all kinds of weird kit, much of it broken or at least in need of repair to make it fully functional. The junk-shop addiction was still going strong. Still, it was nice to be in a home setting after all that had come before, and we would convene during the week to flesh out new ideas.

As always, we'd jam through ideas that Jarvis brought in and we'd record anything interesting and always in a very rudimentary way. The following day we'd play back the previous day's offerings and wonder whether we'd ever produce anything satisfactory again (there's always plenty of muck to dig through when searching for musical diamonds).

One thing we agreed upon was that we needed to get back to road-testing songs before recording them, as we'd done prior to *Hardcore*. This was always a great way of determining how the audience would receive new material. Even more importantly, live playing *changes* songs. Hopefully for the better. The quiet bits could be made quieter and the loud sections louder. There are no set rules. A song, or part, could even be scrapped altogether if the vibe wasn't right. Anything and everything was on the table.

After a couple of months we had a few songs sort of complete, so we booked some tentative live excursions to see how these new songs (most of which only had working titles) stacked up when played to real humans.

Well, I say 'real humans', but can you call the hi-falutin' fine art crowd real humans? Let me explain. Every couple of years the city of Venice, Italy, plays host to the Venice Biennale, a big art show/festival/shindig where all the big-wigs in the fine art world come together to exhibit their wares. The artist Gary Hume, best known for his stylised depictions of ordinary objects, was representing the UK – like it was some kind of Eurovision of the arts or something – and somehow Pulp had been asked to play at his opening (or maybe closing) 'do', and perhaps the thinking went, 'Well, if it's a real "art" crowd they'll be receptive to anything we can throw at them, so we can really go out on a limb if needs be.' So, that's what we did.

We had six new songs to play and that included – hold the front page – one song where I played synthesizer rather than drums. Yep, told you it was far out, maaaan. The piece, working title 'Duck Diving', revolved around Jarvis reading a story about swimming from a book by Philippa Pearce. The band just kind of noodled away with some indiscernible melody and I was tasked with providing synth weirdness courtesy of a vintage Roland SH-09 synthesizer. To be honest, I'm not convinced it was our best moment.

But the strangest concept for the show came courtesy of Jarvis, of course: 'Hey we're playing in Venice, let's get some Venetian blinds and play *behind* them . . . !'

What, covering us up so no one can see us? Well, we are in Venice, y'know. OK, it was rather a lame joke, Jarv said, but the blinds would make us feel more comfortable playing the new material minus the frosty glare of the crowd to unnerve us. We'd also install motors, so that the blinds would slowly rise up as the set went on, fully opening to reveal us by the time we got to play the more familiar material. High concept, see.

Italy had so far eluded Pulp; we'd done most of Western Europe by this point, but never played a full-blown concert in Italy. And as we were playing an 'art event', the actual Pulpsters of Italia would have to wait a bit longer. Never mind.

It transpired that we were also due to play in a Venetian palazzo. That's a palace, to you and me. Down wiv da kidz, eh? Common it was not. We also discovered that the palazzo's conservators were extremely concerned that the noise a 'rock' band would produce could easily damage the delicate 16th-century architecture, maybe even bring the place crashing down (best keep quiet about the Theatre Royal gig from a few years back, then). We assured them that we would play gently, so as to protect their historic palazzo. There was no fear of getting too lairy anyway, as the new stuff was relatively laid back and I would be on the stand-up kit, meaning no chance of loud-monster playing.

It is always rather strange playing to a crowd that haven't paid for tickets. They're usually curious as to what is about to go down, but there's no great feeling of excitement or anticipation. This was ostensibly an art crowd rather than a Pulp crowd. Let's just say they were rather bewildered by the blind thing and definitely subdued. This didn't help us much as we, as players, feed off the energy emitted from a crowd and return it via our playing. We were never going to get that here. Don't get me wrong, everyone was polite and all, but was it really worth it? Well, yes if only for one thing: watching our roadies Roger and Scottie wrestling massive, heavy flight cases off and on to tiny boats (no, they weren't gondolas), as that was the only way of moving all our equipment into the palazzo. We watched, hoping one would fall in. Alas they stayed dry, but some fair old Anglo-Saxon was administered in our direction once they noticed us watching them struggle.

We performed the 'blinds gig' twice more that year: in Edinburgh, as part of the Flux Festival, and at the Liss Ard Festival in Skibbereen, Ireland, both of which were more arts festivals than rock. Always the contrarians.

The Edinburgh gig pulled in a Pulp crowd (in fact it was a fan club show – oh dear, what a way to treat our nearest and dearest), and we could sense the blinds experiment wasn't going down well. Certainly I could tell that the fans were getting rather restless and somewhat pissed off that they couldn't really see what was going off, save for a few silhouettes on the blinds. Perhaps the first few rows might have had a glimpse of Jarv's shoes, but that's about it.

Trekking to a remote site in Ireland wasn't much better. Again, the audience were rather cheesed off that they weren't getting the full Pulp in-your-face experience. I for one was happy that this experiment was brought to a short and swift end. There was no fun in playing like this. I needed to see the crowd and feel the adrenaline coursing to get the excitement going. After all, we had spent years trying to engage with audiences and now it seemed we were putting barriers up. At least we had managed to road-test the new songs and we now had a sense of which of the six newbies to move forward with. However, six new tunes (now four) doth not a new record make. So it was back to writing, to see what would emerge.

Thankfully, writing resumed in more conventional surroundings and we beavered away, teasing tunage from the ether. We were often assigned 'homework' by Jarvis – 'Why doesn't everyone come in tomorrow/next week with one new idea to work on?' This wasn't a particularly new concept, but we used this method several times during these sessions. An idea didn't have to be a chord progression (though it could be); it could be as simple as a word or a phrase, perhaps an emotion – anything, really, to focus the mind into interpreting the notion set before us. We would often then jam around an idea, chord, phrase or word, hoping to tease out a song.

I was still utilising the electronic kit during these sessions and noticed, as part of my homework, that you could trigger little drum loops that had been pre-set into the sound bank, and if you hit the same pad a second time while the first loop was still playing you could get a rather pleasing echo effect as the two loops played together, but a beat out. This idea eventually evolved into the song 'The Night That Minnie Timperley Died'.

Most of the songs that emerged during these sessions had a more bucolic, more organic sound. Certainly more of an acoustic feel compared with the bombast of much of *Hardcore*. There was a real sense of the outdoors rather than gritty urban scenarios or kitchen-sink dramas. This was no doubt down to the surroundings.

We'd held a writing sesh at a rural studio in Monnow Valley, Wales, in an early attempt to get away from it all, the idea being that with patchy mobile coverage folk would have fewer distractions. It sort of worked although the distraction, for me, came from the countryside. Sarah travelled down for a for few days and naturally she brought our dog Malcolm. On one morning walk, Mal and I tried to take a shortcut back to the studio, which involved climbing a barbed wire fence. No bother: I picked up the hound and chucked him over the wire. He was quite young at the time so this was easy for him. I followed, and being unused to such country ways, utilised the top strand of wire to launch myself into the next field. Crump. I ended up in a very painful heap with a searing pain in my left ankle. Oh dear, not good. Mal was jumping around as if this was all jolly good fun. It was not. I hobbled back to the farm, thinking (wrongly, as it turns out) that I had broken my ankle. With most events like this, there's an upside and a downside. The upside was that we'd just about finished the writing sessions (semi-successfully, as I recall), so the injury wouldn't affect the work, thankfully. The downside was we were due to play live on Chris Evans' TV show *TFI Friday* the very next day. Chuff.

I should've known not to use the top strand of a barbed wire fence as a jumping-off point. When I was about 11, I'd split my hand open doing the exact same thing, the barbed wire gouging a cut from the centre of my palm almost to the tip of one of my fingers. Didn't learn my lesson, did I! Anyway, as the showbiz cliché goes, 'the show must go on!', and it did. We played *TFI* (Chris got a face on during the show, as we wouldn't play a bit of 'Disco 2000' as they went to an ad break. I mean, does he think we're performing monkeys or something?). I hobbled on stage using a crutch for support and

354

manfully played away. If I'd sprained my right ankle we'd have had to cancel the show. That's the bass drum leg, and there's no way I would've been able to continue if I'd mashed up that ankle. Us performers kind of live in fear of injuring a limb. Our livelihoods could be at stake, or at the very least we'd have to put our careers on hold. Let's face it, Pulp had benefitted several times in previous years from other musicians' medical misfortunes.

40

Carp or Crap?

(Coy Mistress)

'So, this is where the magic happens, yeah?' I was only being a little sarcastic. Honest. We had set off on a band day trip. Actually it was more of a fact-finding mission, to search for a studio. We had enjoyed the tranquillity of Monnow Valley and thought that recording the new album away from London and its 'distractions' would be a good thing. So we all jumped in Jarv's rather decrepit Toyota Town Ace (sorry Jarv, but I do remember you asking me if I could pinpoint an annoyingly loud squeak coming from the vehicle. I narrowed it down to some very loose wheel nuts, fixed in a trice, but it was scary to think how long he'd been driving around with loose wheels). The Town Ace was a kind of people carrier that looked like something out of *Space: 1999*.*VERY Jarvis and VERY battered (there's a photo of it on the inside cover of the album sleeve). Anyways, we had three or four studios to tour, all of them in the leafy Home Counties, just outside London and beyond the M25 and one of them owned by seventies prog gods Genesis. We wandered around, being shown all kinds of accommodation and barns stuffed with Genesis road gear

---

* A British sci-fi programme which ran for two series from 1977 to 1979 and was set in the far-off future of 1999. It followed the escapades of the inhabitants of Moonbase Alpha, a scientific research base on the Moon.

old and new. The tour's pièce de résistance was the hallowed drum room where Phil Collins honed his signature sound – a room fully lined in stone, as the hard surfaces (along with the tech stuff, such as reverb gates and such like) helped to produce the Phil Collins sound. Now, me being a child of punk, Mr Collins and Genesis were considered 'the enemy' from a formative age. All that prog noodling was for 'others' to enjoy, not snotty-nosed punk wannabes like me. Plus, Phil was all over the airwaves in the late eighties and early nineties with his white boy soul covers that were adored by footballers, mums and middle managers across the nation. Dull, dull, dull. I couldn't stomach the idea of doing a Pulp album with even a smidge of Phil Collins. No way. Thankfully the rest of the band agreed, so that studio was struck off.

We toured others, which were all a much of a muchness: big manor house to stay in, large studio to work at. I think the last one we looked at was at the bottom of the garden of one Roger Taylor from Queen. I say back garden, but as I'm sure you can imagine, this was not some pokey semi-detached house with a shed studio out the back. The grounds were enormous. The studio house was set beside not one, but two fishing lakes (buttons dutifully pressed!) and the 'live room', where the drums and band would set up, was basically Rog's garage just up the lane, connected to the control room via CCTV. The garage, which was of course vast, was home to Mr Taylor's classic Aston Martin and Rolls-Royce and around the edges were many Queen drum kits poking out through protective see-through plastic sheeting. This was certainly ringing my bell – all drummers have to spend their dosh on classic motors and I am no exception. A fan of Italian coupes, I was custodian of a 1972 Lancia Fulvia 1600 at the time, a fine but temperamental beast, make no mistake. Roger's studio, Cosford Mill, seemed a perfect place to get away from it all and record our already rather 'green'-sounding songs in this bucolic landscape for the next Pulp album.

357

We booked the sessions and corralled Chris Thomas to once again man the knobs. After all, he'd done the last two, so it seemed a case of 'If it ain't broke . . .'. We had, as a band, come to the conclusion that we wanted this next record to be done more as a band exercise, rather than relying on computers to fix everything and for it all to be finely polished and 'perfect'. We had road-tested many of the songs by now and we agreed it would be best to capture them as they were played. Great idea. On paper.

Everything started reasonably well (as long as you discount me nearly losing a wheel on the M1 – I staggered on to the destination with one front wheel at an alarming angle. Still, it got me there.). We proceeded to set up, flanked by two beautiful cars and a view out of the windows of swans gliding by on the shimmering lake. We beavered away as we have always done, laying the basics down and then adding the magic stuff on top. The new, old way of doing things meant that we took longer honing each song to try and get a take where everyone was happy with their playing. This wasn't necessarily an easy task, as we'd never put ourselves forward as good technical musicians. We were OK, don't get me wrong. However, Chris was struggling to get the finished article up to the standards he was used to and he started slowly running more and more stuff through the computer, just to 'tidy things up'. I was generally OK with this as it somewhat took the pressure off me, but it soon became obvious that the others were less than happy. This was now getting away from the original blueprint for the record: keep it simple. The finished songs were sounding polished and professional but they definitely lacked a spark. One could even venture that they were lacklustre. Was this down to us and the songs we'd written? Or perhaps by working with Chris again things were running out of our control and we were in danger of getting bogged down in technicalities as per the *Hardcore* sessions (something we knew we never wanted to repeat again)?

Pulp wrapped up the sessions at Cosford Mill and Chris Thomas's run as Pulp's producer was over. Still, I got something out of our time at the Mill: my first attempts at fly-fishing. I even caught one of Roger's trout. We didn't eat it, though – we're not barbarians. The carp fishing in the other lake was pretty good too, so not a wholly wasted time for me. Pulp-wise, however, it really was a case of where do we go from here? Sure, recording in the countryside was great for maintaining focus (aside from the fishing, of course), but it just didn't seem to suit us. We are city kids at heart.

Back to the drawing board. Again. We had songs but no one to tease the best out of them. We're not studio nerds and there was no way we were going to contemplate producing ourselves. That would be a recipe for disaster: welcome to the fall-out zone. So, let's go the other way and get some young tyro in to see what they can do. Worth a shot? You bet.

We set to work with a gent who went by the name Howie B. Who suggested him, I've no idea, but we did a few new songs and the results were again disappointing. It seemed that this LP was going to be just as difficult as *Hardcore* but in a different way; we were stumbling about almost in the dark, trying to find our true direction.

The spotlight of fame, or perhaps infamy, was shifting too. We knew in our heart of hearts that Pulp were slipping into the more comfortable, middle-aged, pipe-and-slippers time in our career. The record company were far less frantic about a new Pulp release and we could sense that the record-buying public were clamouring for other, newer artists. The feeling that Pulp were at the cutting edge of the British music scene was receding. That's the music biz, folks. The spotlight moves fast when you have been in its beam and you'd rather stay in it. But remember: you have no control over it.

Having said that, it didn't really keep us awake at night, as we all had other stuff going on. I started doing a bit of radio presenting. I know? Mental. The truth of the matter is that a radio production

359

company had approached His Jarvis-ness and asked if he wanted to do some stuff on the radio, ostensibly about sport. Now, I don't know if this comes across but Jarv ain't much of a sportsman. Come to think of it, neither am I, but I'd like to think I have a bit of a pedigree: uncle who was a world-famous goalie, school fishing champion, I could go on . . . So the gig was passed to me and I said yes. What's the point of saying no? If you do nothing, nothing happens, but if you do something, something happens (Our Family Motto™).

I was asked to do a one-off late-night live show on BBC Radio 5. I, along with a couple of others, would talk sport with various guests in the studio for a couple of hours, perhaps do a phone interview or two. Easy peasy? Not really; it was a case of being thrown in at the deep end. And just as you think everything's going to be fine the spanner starts getting in the works. One by one the guests we'd lined up started to drop out. Every. Single. One. We had literally 15 minutes before the mics were due to open and we were to start pontificating about the sporting events of the day, swapping 'bants' with our guests, yet we were staring at making it all up on the fly. This was a real mouth-dries-up moment and you could see panic flashing across the producer's face. And everyone else's. The shit looked like it was really ready to hit the fan, so it was a case of pull in the favours, or more realistically, call your uncle. I offered this idea to the folks in charge and they almost dropped to their knees in praise of their saviour. I got Gordon on the line and explained the predicament: everyone's dropped out, can you help me out with a little interview? Of course, he said. He was a true gent.

The show went ahead and it turned out to be almost fun. Talking to Gordon was fantastic. We had various sports folk on the phone (the producer must have rifled through his contacts book at pace, methinks) and apart from a few hairy moments we survived. It was a close-run thing, mind.

Carp or Crap? (Coy Mistress)

I must have impressed someone as I was asked back to do a few more shows before even being commissioned to present a programme solo. I had mentioned to my producer, Richard Berringer, that my dad was good friends with Rotherham scrap metal supremo Ken Booth*, then owner/chairman of Rotherham United (no, sorry, not the seventies reggae superstar). Dad would chauffeur Ken to home matches in his Mercedes, watch the game and then ferry Ken back home. It was a good deal, as Ken only lived up the road from Dad. I had been with Dad and Ken a couple of times to watch RUFC and I could sense the strangeness of the situation: English Third and Fourth Division clubs with no money, dilapidated stadiums and local men made good holding the purse strings. The sight of several elderly, corpulent, male directors and local dignitaries slurping their tomato soup down at half time will stay with me forever.

So, I suggested a behind-the-scenes look at lower division English football to Richard, and he thought it could be an excellent subject. I squared the idea with Ken one day on the way to a match:

'Is there any revenue in it?'

'Err, sorry Chairman, no.'

'Hmmf.'

I took the silence as a tacit yes and was introduced to folk at the club who would actually make it work. We set a date and Richard and I went to the ground and interviewed everyone we could find at the club, from groundsman to kit man to tea ladies to general manager. I even got a grumpy interview from the top man himself, snatched on the 15-minute drive to the ground in Dad's Merc. I don't think the programme went on to win any awards but I thoroughly enjoyed myself and thought that this was something I could do. Store

---

* CF Booth Ltd is a family-owned scrap metal and recycling business based in Rotherham, South Yorkshire. Ken saved Rotherham United from administration in 1987 and was chairman of the club for 17 years.

that idea for the future. The piece was broadcast on BBC Radio 5 under the title *More Soup, Mr Mayor?*.

The other members of the band were also off doing side projects while we decided what to do about Pulp's future. Jarvis had been off making some strange sounds with a fellow who had a thing called a glass harmonica. I'd never heard of this either. It was based on the premise of getting an eerie sound out of a wine glass with your wet finger when rubbed gently across the top. The glass harmonica had about 20 glass bowls, all varying in size, rotating in a cabinet that held water. As the bowls rotated the operator held his fingers to the glass bowls, and lo, an eerie, ethereal sound was produced. This was duly noted as something we could employ in the 'whenever it's coming' next Pulp LP.

Meanwhile, Jarvis was invited to do a spot at the artsy Meltdown Festival in London. Held at the Southbank Centre every year, the festival organisers invite a musical dignitary to select and curate a series of gigs by artists that have piqued their interest or influenced them in some way. This year's dignitary was one Scott Walker – y'know, he of The Walker Brothers fame, including the hit singles 'The Sun Ain't Gonna Shine Anymore', 'Make It Easy On Yourself' and four semi-mythical solo albums that in pre-eBay times were almost impossible to find.* I wasn't asked to participate in the Meltdown appearance but it didn't bother me in the slightest. Let the London dwellers do what they want; I don't get the face on if I'm not asked to participate.

Roll forward a few weeks and our manager, Geoff Travis, is on the phone.

'Hey Nick . . . what do you think about Scott Walker producing the album?'

'Really? THE Scott Walker?' Fair to say I nearly fainted. This was

---

* *Scott* (1967), *Scott 2* (1968), *Scott 3* and *Scott 4* (both released in 1969).

another one of those heart-stopping moments. The chance to record with a genuine icon and someone we pretty much all admired was too good to miss. Was this, finally, the light at the end of the tunnel for Pulp's next record?

'Err, yes. God, yes!'

Geoff explained that at Meltdown he'd had a light-bulb moment and asked Scott's manager if Scott had ever thought about producing a 'pop' album. Miraculously, he had, and so the stars seemed to align and everyone was very excited about what was to come.

Looking back, I'm sure that if I'd said, 'Scott Walker? He's a bit avant-garde, isn't he?' it would've made not a jot of difference. But we were all massive Scott Walker fans and some of my all-time favourite pieces of music are contained on those four solo albums. Some of Scott's later work is, in my mind, unlistenably off the wall and too arty for my rough-neck ears. But still, Scott 'effin Walker!

41

Scott Walker

(Wickerman)

'Hey Nick, put some lead in your ass.'

This was an instruction piped into my headphones from *the* Scott Walker as we started another take of 'Bad Cover Version' at Metropolis Studios in swanky Chiswick, West London. What Scott was trying to get me to do was rather unclear. Was I to play slower? Heavier? Drag behind the click? Absolutely no idea, but I soldiered on regardless and the 'lead' suggestion paid dividends as soon my drums were in the can (studio jargon alert) for that track.

Working with Scott was odd. It was a bit baffling at times (see above), often awe-inspiring, and sometimes surprising. Most evident was the atmosphere in the studio, which was palpably different. Those among our party who were usually most vocal in chipping in with suggestions were less audible this time round. Most everyone deferred to Scott's ideas and suggestions as to which takes were the ones to go with. I was happy to go along with this, not that anyone would've taken my suggestions anyways, so there.

Scott was pretty reserved most of the time in the studio. No regaling of past glories or bursting into song with the legendary voice. He mostly sat there at the studio console under his baseball cap, gently nodding along, exchanging whispers with Pete, his engineer, and sipping his mineral water, which was never without a little paper napkin lid that Scott studiously replaced after each sip. Was he germophobic? Perhaps. Did he see us as unwashed northern English types? Maybe. We will never know. No one asked him about it, of course. Why would we? There were no pub trips after a session or anything like that. We had lunch or dinner together in the studio canteen on a few occasions, but that's about it. It was as if we were all bedazzled by the aura of Scott and it somehow changed us. They say never meet your heroes as they may turn out to be dicks, but Scott was a studious, polite, inscrutable fellow who didn't really say much. I recall at the dinner table wanting to ask Scott about his solo albums *1* and *2*, and if the tracks were arranged in a way that mirrored each other, as I always thought that they were: each album seems to start with an upbeat track, then a guitar-type thing, then maybe a Jacques Brel cover. But I never did ask. Clearly I was tongue-tied by that very British notion of 'if I say what I want to say I may sound like a tit, so don't say it'.

Anyway, we beavered on and the songs were starting to take shape, some more easily than others. The track 'Roadkill', for instance – a quiet, delicate ballad – was recorded with everyone playing live at the same time, which was getting to be quite a rare occurrence for us at this stage in our career. We did what seemed like millions of takes, the vast majority of which sounded just fine to me, but what do I know? Well, what I do know is that, as it's a really quiet song, I was playing the drums with my hands and after said million takes, they were getting rather sore. I can hear the groaning sounds from here, but it really wasn't something I was used to.

During the recording of the album we were presented with a slight diversion to record a track for sixties legend Marianne Faithfull. Jarvis had been asked to contribute a song to her new LP, so as we were all set up and ready to go, it seemed the perfect opportunity to get involved. Jarvis had a song hanging about called 'Sliding Through Life

On Charm', so that was put forward and we worked it up and recorded the instruments in an afternoon. It still remains the only drum recording I've done for someone else since joining Pulp. The track was duly released in 2002 on Marianne's LP *Kissin' Time*, though I don't think I heard the finished version until many years later.

The vibe in the studio was pretty calm. No tiffs or tantrums. There was quite an earnest debate about birdsong of all things. The beautiful track 'Birds In Your Garden' (probably my personal favourite from this record) needed some birdsong adding at the start and no one could seem to agree on the best type. I know: daft. There always seemed to be too much twittering, or the wrong type of twittering, or some such. I always thought we should've had just one bird tweeting away, perhaps being joined by others, but I never suggested it, as by this time I knew that we'd rarely act on anything I said.

Never mind these little gripes, I think the record is deeply underrated. We took our time writing the material and the serendipity of having Scott twiddling the knobs made for a great record. There are some fantastic Pulp moments on that album and we remained true to our underlying credo: make something new and fresh (at least to us). The record certainly has a kind of rural, outdoorsy vibe, a slice of positivity even, and it's certainly a departure from the urban voyeuristic tendencies of *His 'N' Hers* and *Different Class*, and certainly a major swerve from the paranoia and struggle of *This Is Hardcore*. It almost comes across as a concept album, what with the pastoral theme running throughout, illustrated by tracks like 'Weeds', 'Weeds II' (which I don't actually play on), 'The Trees', 'Birds In Your Garden', 'Roadkill', 'Wickerman' and 'Sunrise' (our psychedelic wig-out song and the nearest I ever got to a drum solo. Not that I would countenance such – save us, no one wants to hear a drum solo!).

'Wickerman' took ages to write. It's quite a long song and one of those sort of Frankenstein pieces: it's made up of loads of off-cuts from jam sessions that were good but never evolved into fully formed tracks. The song is essentially a true story. Jarvis often talked about the time he and Russell (perhaps?) went on a boat-based exploration adventure beneath Sheffield, in the Victorian subterranean drainage system of tunnels and archways that all converge in a massive underground manmade cavern called the Megatron. And it really is rather mega. I'm pretty sure the viaduct mentioned in the song is the magnificent 21-arch Conisbrough Viaduct, which can be spotted from the train when travelling between Rotherham and Doncaster (I recall a trip we made to see this rather impressive bit of Victorian engineering). Moreover, Jarvis used to live in a rundown area of inner Sheffield called The Wicker. However, the song itself doesn't do a lot for me. It's too long and unexciting. Sorry, 'Wickerman' fans. However, it is interesting for its inclusion of a sample taken from the 1973 British folk horror movie *The Wicker Man*, one of our favourite films of all time.

The record was finally done and sounding great. A new direction for us? Possibly. Trouble is, it had no title. Jarvis was keeping schtum about what it was to be called. Or more likely was undecided about what it would be. Titles tend to suggest themselves during production, but this time we had nothing. 'The Quiet Revolution' was banded about for a bit but never seemed to gain any traction. For some time it looked like the title would simply be 'Pulp' – no great excitement around that to be honest, but if it has to be, then OK. But 'OK' is not the kind of reaction required. An album title needs to be intriguing, drawing the (potential) listener in to want to explore more. Just titling the thing 'Pulp' seemed like a metaphorical shoulder shrug. Meh. If the band can't be bothered with a more interesting title why should anyone be bothered to listen in? I think Jarvis felt the same too and rejected that idea – knowing him, it was probably due to pressure from the record company wanting a final, definite title so they could proceed with the pressing and manufacture. He also offered 'Love Life', which was certainly better, but then something happened, and we would all remember where we were on that day.

Four American passenger jets were hijacked. Two were flown into the Twin Towers of the World Trade Center in Manhattan, New York; one into the Pentagon, in Washington, DC; and the last, which had also been heading to the capital DC, was brought down in a field in Pennsylvania. We were rehearsing for the album tour and a performance at a gig for John Peel's birthday, of all things, the following day, 12 September. We stopped and watched the TV coverage unfolding in slack-jawed shock, just as everyone else did, all the time looking out across the London skyline at the big jets on their final approach into Heathrow, wondering if one of those was going to come down on the city. The psychological aftermath of the horror was palpable, and it was this that prompted Jarvis to add the 'We' to the title to emphasise the fact that Pulp did indeed 'Love Life'. It was certainly a better fit and conveyed the positivity of the album much more clearly.

We Love Life was released on 22 October 2001 and hit the UK album charts the following week at a rather underwhelming number six. I was deflated. Was our time now spent? Or was this a mere hiccup on the Pulp path? Was it just one of those things, and we shouldn't be too worried about it? Whatever it was, it left me pondering over what the future held.

Once again, we needed a strong single to help with album exposure. We thought that 'Sunrise' was the strongest track on the record, and it had received a rapturous reception when played live prior to recording, so it seemed a bit of a no-brainer to us. But of course Island had other ideas: 'It's too long' or 'The last half is purely instrumental' or 'It's not a "pop" enough song', yadda yadda . . . We had to go with a good old compromise – never satisfactory in my book – and it was decided we'd release a double A-side: 'Sunrise' and 'The Trees'. Now, I liked 'The Trees' as a song, but I'm not sure I saw it as single material. Island thought it had a better chance of radio airplay (that much sought-after commodity) than 'Sunrise'. Trouble is, neither track ended up receiving much airplay. You could easily envisage a scenario where a radio scheduler was deciding what to put on the playlist and having to make a choice; which track to lead with? What if I choose the track that the other stations don't lead with . . . ? I'll look a right plonker. So with seeds of doubt planted, the record is set aside and something else is chosen in its place. Should have stuck to our guns as we had done before, I guess.

Thing is, we could sense the Island bods' enthusiasm for Pulp had cooled. So, with barely an audible whimper, 'Sunrise'/'The Trees' dropped into the hit parade at a heady number 23.

The low-key video didn't help. During filming, one idea was to have me play along to a highly sped-up version of the song and then once the footage was slowed down to the real speed, I would look like I was playing the track in slow motion but at the correct song speed. It didn't work, though, as the speed required to achieve the effect was ridiculous. Keen Pulp observers may know I like to play fast, but this was nuts. Even I couldn't keep up. Idea shelved.

No matter, records still required releasing. It was decided that we needed another single release from the LP. There was some weariness from Island about this. Had they decided to move on from We Love Life and concentrate on other stuff? More than likely. Still, we twisted their arms to get our way as we wanted 'Bad Cover Version' to be the next release from the album. A song that had as much lead inserted as I could manage. It emerged out of a Candida Doyle melody line and a Steve drum loop taken from the Hotlegs (actually 10CC in disguise) 1972 track 'Neanderthal Man' (it was replaced eventually to swerve copyright entanglements). It's got the requisite soaring chorus and a thumping beat; a tale of disappointment and regret, when you realise you should have gone for the real thing rather than a down market replica that doesn't do what it says on the tin. Gosh, it even gently ribs Scott Walker himself in the lyrics as Jarvis chides Scott for an underwhelming 1970 solo LP called 'Til the Band Comes in. Mr Walker agreed the work was sub-par so didn't mind the dis. Mark graced the cover with a picture of him aged about 12, re-constructing the Bowie LP sleeve The Rise and Fall of Ziggy Stardust and the Spiders From Mars.

After the rather lacklustre 'Trees' video, it was great to hear a wonderful idea for the 'Bad Cover Version' clip: get a load of celeb look-a-likes and recreate the Band Aid video for 'Do They Know It's Christmas?'. Perfect; a concept that matched the song completely. So we all gathered at SARM Studios in London (where the original was filmed) and set about our little re-creation. In attendance were the human 'Bad Cover Versions' of: Robbie Williams, Liam Gallagher, Kylie Minogue, David Bowie, George Michael, Bono, Paul McCartney, Craig David, Jennifer Lopez, Sophie Ellis-Bextor, Tom Jones, Björk, Kurt Cobain, Rod Stewart, Meat Loaf, Cher, Jay Kay, Jarvis Cocker and many more.

It was a genuine hoot doing all this (unlike most other video sessions) and having such a laugh with the 'slebs'. I got into the makeup trailer early and had a full beard, moustache and big hairdo applied – a kind of generic kind of 'rock producer' look à la Jeff Lynne of ELO – I had Steve fooled for ages during the shoot, as I had adopted an American drawl for my character. In the video I can be seen at the control desk twiddling knobs and pushing faders alongside Steve and Mark. Candida is resplendent as a production assistant wielding a clipboard, and of course Jarvis is revealed at the end as Brian May, rockin' out with his 'axe'. Top larks all round.

Sadly, even this top-drawer vid failed to push the song up the charts; 'Bad Cover Version' debuted at a deflating number 27. The air seemed to be draining out of Pulp and we could do nothing about it.

Never mind; we could look forward to playing some live dates, which after being cooped up in the studio for ages we – or certainly I – was gagging for. However, it seemed that we were no longer destined for UK arenas and the larger venues. We started playing live shows again in May 2001 while the record was being mastered, sleeves were being printed and all that gubbins, and we kicked off in a most unusual way by playing the Hay Festival of Literature & Arts, in Hay-on-Wye, Wales. Hardly rock'n'roll, but it seemed to fit with the new songs' 'greener' feel. So it was odd, but why not?

The rest of the summer saw the usual jaunt round a dozen Euro festivals. Then, in autumn, we embarked on the *We Love Life* UK Tour, but this time we were playing at venues we hadn't seen since the tour to introduce *Different Class*. We had the very definite sense that we'd summited the peak and were now on the downward slope of the hill we'd been climbing since 1990 or so. Not that we didn't throw ourselves into the live shows with the required gusto: we always did. Even when unwell.

We travelled to Barcelona to play the tenth anniversary of the Razzmatazz club. You can see why they wanted us to play. But I arrived in the city feeling awful. Before you ask, it wasn't a colossal hangover; I was genuinely barely able to function.* Virus? Flu? Man flu, even. Still, we don't let the side down, so I staggered on to play. The sick bucket was strategically placed by the kit just in case of any accidents, and we made it to the end of the gig, at which point we played 'Razzmatazz' for the first time in years, having rehearsed it extensively in the sound check. You couldn't not really, could you? Did we get any thanks from the venue? Nah. Not a jot. Humph.

More interestingly, we did a tour of British forests, from the north

---

* I recall while rehearsing for the *We Love Life* Tour that Mr Hawley and I had been out and rather tied one on. We arrived at rehearsal, hanging like dogs. Now, playing vigorous tunes while hangover is no fun. Ever. Ten minutes into rehearsal and I had chucked up next to the kit. End of rehearsal.

of Scotland to Kent, 'the Garden of England', calling at our 'local' forest Sherwood along the way. It seemed an ideal fit for the album and we played in clearings among the trees to thousands, where idyllic, even magical scenes unfolded. Apart, that is, from my worst onstage cock-up.

There we were, waiting for Candida to start 'Sorted . . .', which she did, impeccably as always, and Jarvis hit the first chord on his acoustic guitar, the signal to start. Which we did. It was all going to plan so far, but for some reason, of which I am at a loss to explain, I simply stopped playing. Just like that. Packed in. It was totally involuntarily. Just stopped. I snapped out of my trance and signalled everyone to keep going and I resumed at the next four-bar phrase. Jarvis mouthed 'Are you OK?' to which I could only shrug and grin inanely. I wanted the ground to swallow me up. We prided ourselves on being right up there as one of, if not *the* best live group in the UK (sod it: the world, yeah?) and I especially hated making mistakes, as it's so easy to dwell on them forever more (hence me writing about it here, decades later). However, no one mentioned it after the gig, to my relief, and we simply got on with it. Why do these errors creep in and mess everything up for us?

We followed the forest shows with a couple of big gigs, double-heading with The Strokes at the Reading and Leeds Festival on 23 and 24 August. We preceded them one night and then they preceded us the next. We blew them off, naturally, and then it was on to the end of the road. No, not the festival of the same name, but literally THE END OF THE ROAD.

Geoff Travis had told us that Jarvis needed a break, to do other 'stuff' outside of Pulp. Nothing was specifically mentioned but we could all sense it. Jarvis certainly never sat us all down and explained his thoughts, about either his need for a 'break' or what he was hoping to do with his time out. As mentioned earlier, he's not the best communicator when it comes to his band mates. Indeed, it would have been a major surprise if he had sat us all down to explain his reasoning. So, with this in mind a sort of homecoming finale gig was organised. Well, it was more of a 'see you later' kind of event rather than a 'goodbye forever' situation. Thing is, we were not to know that at the time, so it was signed off as Pulp's last gig.

Pulp's first 'real' gig (after the City School lunchtime debut) had been at the Rotherham Arts Centre way back in 1980. So, since Jarvis loves a bit of circularity, he chose the Magna Centre in Rotherham – just over the other side of the M1 motorway that separates Sheffield and Rotherham – as the venue for this 'finale' gig and a rather eclectic selection of bands were brought in for the event, titled 'Auto': a mini festival set in an old steelworks that had been converted into a science/industrial museum at the turn of the 21st century. The circle was to be neatly closed by this final return to Rotherham after 22 years of struggle, stubbornness and eventual triumph. And 465 other concerts in between.

We played what we thought would be our final set with our usual verve, élan and bombast, and trooped off and that was that; to all intents and purposes, Pulp had played their last show. There were no tears or wailing from the fans as far as I can recall. We sat backstage afterwards, all seemingly in a rather sombre mood. There was no popping of champers or anything like that. It really felt like an old balloon that had deflated. Gone a bit wrinkly and sad. There was no cheesy group hug to say goodbye, just an 'OK, see yer later'. After all, this was a break; there was no 'split'. No rancorous 'see you in court' type affairs.

The truth was that Pulp had run out of steam. The labour pains of making *Hardcore* and *We Love Life* had taken their toll. We were knackered as a group: tired of each other and tired of just being Pulp. We had been in constant proximity for nigh on 12 years and, as happens with many groups, you just get a bit sick of the sight of each other. Well, in truth I wasn't. I would've been happy for us to stay on the rock'n'roll hamster wheel – write new material, release records, play them live – but I could see that a breather was required. Big time. We would adjust to not being front and centre of the nation's (quirky pop) mindset and would remain content to keep doing what we did best: incendiary live performances and interesting, slightly odd pop music.

Alas, it wasn't to be. Others had already started to map out their futures sans Pulp.

42

What Next?

(Last Day of the Miners' Strike)

The day had to come. What do you do after the band stops working? Kick back next to the drum-shaped swimming pool and smoke fat cigars all day? Don't think so (if you think that was an option, you haven't been paying attention).

So what *do* you do? I had been working at this since I was about 14 and I was now staring into a void. What were my options?

Go solo? Stop it. This is, was, and will always be a non-starter. I'd like to think I contributed to Pulp's writing and success but there's no way I could write my own songs (believe me, I've tried) and try to get them out under my own name.

So how about join another group? This was certainly a possibility. Though I'd hardly had legions of other groups clamouring for my help while in Pulp, so why would they now? I'd probably have to start at the bottom again and see what happened. Did I really want that, after all those struggles with Pulp? Perhaps if the right group came along I could be persuaded. Boy, they'd have to be good though. Ideally, it would be a well-established group. With at least one roadie.

Drugs and ale bender then? Tempting, gotta say. I imagine it's quite common for washed-up rockers to go down that path, so it'd be the perfect excuse. Hold on, though. I'm too boring to do that, plus the kids were still under ten. Becoming a stinking wreck having spent the kids' inheritance on a street corner or down the Dog and Duck is just not me. (Plus, Mrs B would kill me . . .)

Maybe I could become some sort of music Svengali? I could seek out and nurture new talent. Pass on my wisdom gained from years of banding, watching from the side-lines as my protégés scale the heady heights of stardom. Plotting and scheming, I would produce their world-changing music and everyone would be clamouring for it. Hmmm, maybe. I had the contacts and a passable ear for a good band and a tune, or so I thought. However, sitting behind a control desk listening to the same track for hours and hours on end was not my idea of fun. File under 'possible'.

So, if music wasn't going to work, what else was there? I could always go back to running a pub, the go-to end-of-career move for ageing footballers from the sixties/seventies. But, as you know, we'd already tried this – been there, bought the T-shirt, paid the bar tab. I wasn't going back there. No way.

However, I'd really enjoyed my stint at radio presenting. I had some experience, so why not – I could do that? Unfortunately, my producer Richard Berringer had left the biz. Who would be my go-to now? No idea. Case closed? Perhaps.

Maybe I could start a new business. Like what? Sell drums? It used to be the case that old sport stars from way back when would open up sports equipment shops as soon as they aged out. Thing is, I was never much of a tech nerd when it came to drums and all that hog. Does it sound good? Does it look good? That does it for me. Nope. Next.

I suppose I could take over an existing business – I had some experience here through being involved in The Washington when that fell apart. I quite enjoyed toying with the numbers and stuff, so perhaps . . .

Anyway, life goes on I guess. One thing I did do around this time was my last bit of radio reporting. I was asked to comment on and collar various folk at the launch of a posh tailors in London's Soho. There was to be a big party in a nearby underground car park and I was sent along to see what I could find out. Cue the wearing of my wedding suit so that I'd blend in.

Quick story . . .

My wedding suit was made in the less than salubrious Sheffield neighbourhood of Manor Top by a tailor called Ashley Rogers. I nervously went to his shop a few weeks before the big day to be met by a line of cloth reps, enraptured by this old man retelling tales of yore. They were all in hysterics. 'What's this all about?' I thought. Once I could see Mr Rogers, I noticed he was rather fat and seemingly had a weeks' worth of dinner slops down the front of his filthy sweatshirt, a flat cap on his head and a tape measure draped over his shoulders. All became clear.

'What yer after, son?'

'Wedding suit.'

'Yer gettin' married? You daft c★★t! Pick out some material.'

I found a nice black pinstripe and as Ashley measured me up, we literally designed the suit on the back of a fag packet as he wielded the tape with expert hands, all the while a cigarette dangling off his lips as he regaled the remaining reps with all manner of subjects, from fishing to how to hide a Rolls-Royce from a police helicopter and, lastly, all the dark tales about the Cocker family. Jarvis's childhood house was a mere quarter of a mile away, and as I'd told Ashley I was the drummer in Pulp, he began downloading all he knew about the family with a mischievous cackle. All unprintable here, I'm afraid, but hilarious. Once he'd finished with me I was sent on my way: 'F★★k off and come back week on Tuesday for a fittin'.' Two more memorable visits later and I had a beautiful made-to-measure suit, fit to be married in.

Where were we . . .

So, there I was in an underground car park in my Sheffield finery, trying to collar various slebs and get them talking about something, anything. My most successful collar was footballer Mark Bright, a Sheffield Wednesday legend. I also got to interview the proprietor of this posh tailors, who, when I asked him for his opinion about my suit, seemed most impressed, but certainly not when I told him the price. 'For God's sake, keep that quiet round here.'

I like to think of myself as a bit of a doer, not keen to be slobbing about all day, so I started helping out down at Mum's pottery ware-house, Banks Pottery. This was the circle squared, as I felt like I'd gone back to the market stall days of my youth. I started trying to heave the pottery into the 21st century by helping to turn it into a proper business, all professional and that. As is the way of such things, going along a couple of days a week grew and grew, and when Mum and my Aunt Audrey said they wanted to retire, it seemed the done thing to take over the business myself. So I did. The premises were still based in the railway arch at Catcliffe, where we used to rehearse back in the early nineties (it seems as though I have a problem getting away from the gravitational pull of the places from my past).

Taking over an established business was a no-brainer, although I did enrol at Sheffield Hallam University to do an MA course in Business. It seemed a good idea to get some knowledge under the belt so as not to cock up the firm that had been successfully trading for 30-odd years. If my track record of helping steer The Washington was anything to go by (not that I was to blame for its demise) then it would be no bad thing.* Not wishing to bore y'all with all this 'titans of industry' talk – after all, I assume you are still looking for more rollicking tales of rock'n'roll hedonism – I ran the pottery for many years, taking it from a 'walk in and buy what you want

---

* I never did finish the MA in Business Studies. I did a year and thought that was enough. Quitter.

for your café, restaurant or gastro pub' business into an online retailer of the same ilk. It went pretty well. We even became a bit of a specialist in providing custom-decorated messware for several august regiments in the British Army. Odd.

Banks Pottery was eventually killed by the onset of Covid-19 in 2020. Like many small businesses, the bottom fell out overnight and it seemed crazy to continue.

But what about the music, I hear you scream. I was in the position of coming to the sudden end of playing after around 25 years of slog and success. That's a juggernaut that's difficult to jump off. I loved playing and being in a band and all that jazz. So doing something, anything was imperative. I just didn't really have much idea of what at this stage.

I explored the idea of tour management, looking after young'uns on the road, making sure they got from A to B and on to the next stage without mishap, see to it that they were paid their dues and that they didn't kill each other, or indeed themselves, through youthful idiocy. It would be fun.

So, I put a call in to Pulp's management, Rough Trade, and offered my services as genial father figure gently guiding wide-eyed ingénues to fame and fortune. Consequently, RT got back to me about a new (certainly to me) band that I could potentially tour manage. I was sent the itinerary for a series of forthcoming gigs and I started to get rather excited about this change in direction.

A couple of days later, though, RT got back to me and gently let me down, saying they were probably not the right group for me. I was gutted; thwarted before we had even started. I'm keeping you in suspense here about which group it was, aren't I? Well, it transpired that I dodged a bullet, as it was a bunch called The Libertines. Lawks! In the coming months I heard various grisly tales of hardcore debauchery emanating from their quarters and shuddered at the thought of how it could have been: like being thrown to a pack of hungry wolves to be devoured and the bones discarded from a Transit window somewhere on the M4. Phew.

I did, however, get courted by a couple of local groups with a view to drumming for them. Nice to be wanted, yeah? I thought long and hard about this, as I knew I'd be starting right back at the bottom of the ladder again. So, if I was to go for a new group, they had to be good. Let's face it, Pulp would always be a hard act to follow for anyone. I met with a band called The Jim Muir Slideshow: sort of wistful indie pop – not unpleasant, but it didn't do enough to my insides to warrant me joining. Music has to move you, y'know.

Then an old face from the past showed up with an idea: wanna join my band? Paul Infanti (Fannyman, to those in the know) was formerly singer with Treebound Story, alongside me old mucker Rich Hawley. Paul's a great songwriter and suitably eccentric. He'd recently formed a new band, Pollinates, with his old songwriting partner and studio whizz Phil Jones. The music was great; quite heavily electronic but with rocky tendencies, all glued together with Paul's Lou Reedesque drawl and coupled with Victoria's smooth voice – she was a Barnsley lass with only one leg who was also a foundling. I know, you think I'm making this up. I'm not – honest! No one likes to hear and see a band with just a drum machine (not biased), so they asked me to provide some beefy drums. No problem.

We did quite a few gigs, including supporting our Jarvis on one of his early outings as a solo performer. Jarvis went on to pinch Pollinates guitarist Tim McCall for his later tours – we didn't begrudge him, as it was a great opportunity for Tim to get out there. Sadly, Tim died in a tragic accident a few years later, just after his daughter was born. Pollinates continued but it was always tough starting at the bottom and despite some great songs and gigs it just fizzled out; as a seven-piece band, it became increasingly difficult to get everyone together.

What Next? (Last Day of the Miners' Strike)

Still, I did start my own little band with a group of other mates, mostly to play tunes at my 40th birthday bash. Mark (NOT Webber), who had always wanted to play bass without ever having done so before, was allowed to play and it became obvious that it would've been a lot easier to get in a more experienced player. Never mind, we'll call ourselves Big Shambles as a nod to how rubbish we were, and a play on Pete Doherty's new outfit Babyshambles. My dear old friend Dave Kurley was pulled in to sing, and he did a great job. We were a covers band, making a stab at tracks such as ELO's 'Mr. Blue Sky', Rainbow's 'Since You Been Gone', and Blondie's 'Hanging On The Telephone'. In fact, Big Shambles are still going strong, 17 years later and counting. We have improved a little, you will be heartened to know.

Throughout this time, however, I was continually accosted with the same question: when's *Pulp* doing something? All I could do was shrug. Dunno.

43

It's Jarvis on the Phone

(Sink or Swim)

I like a nice soak in the old bath tub. It's good to unwind, cogitate on life, ponder the meaning of the universe an' all that. So there I am, luxuriating in the Matey bubbles, when a phone is thrust through the door:

'It's Jarvis.'

'Would you fancy doing some more music together?' JC drawled.

'Err, YES!'

This was mid-2010 and I did not need asking twice. I had reflected throughout the previous eight years or so about whether Pulp would ever play or indeed record again and I had always harboured a deep-set feeling that we would. At the last gig at Magna, Jarvis had said Pulp were being put on ice for a while, but no one ever said we were splitting up, as bands are wont to do. Pulp just needed dusting down a bit, pump a bit of air into the tyres and we could get back on the road to rocking out again.

Jarvis suggested we all meet up to make sure everyone was on board with new-Pulp. He cheerfully said that we should gather at my house. Certainly.

A date was duly set and we got the choccie biscuits in, as you do for an important pow-wow. The door went and there was Russell.

Now, I had not expected that. Jarvis didn't inform anyone else that he'd asked Russell to be part of new-Pulp. I ushered Russ into the dining room and we had 30 seconds of awkward small talk before the others arrived. Later, Jarvis explained that he wanted Russ back in so we could play the songs that got us up there with accuracy. OK, but a heads-up would have been nice, yeah? The one thing we did make plain was that we weren't going into the studio to make new recordings. This was just a way of playing our songs to our fans. Jarvis had been shaken, as we all had, with Tim McCall's death and thought that any of us could go at any time, so why not get out there and play the tunes? As good an excuse as anything in my mind.

Once the news was released it was obvious that the folk out there were so very excited at the prospect of moshing away to Pulp once again. I was certainly so very excited about performing again. But it wasn't all positive, and we all enjoyed laughing at peoples' negative comments on social media about Pulp playing 'just for the money' – as if professional musicians should do their jobs for free. Buying a ticket for a show was not compulsory last time I looked. Maybe the naysayers would give their 40 hours' a week away for free? 'No thanks, boss, you keep my wages – I don't do this job for the money, y'know.' Thankfully these idiots were almost always shouted down by Pulp loyalists.

We set up Pulp HQ in Axis Studios, downtown Sheffield, where we had recorded some of our earlier stuff, and set about rehearsing the songs we were to play. Russ had spent most of his post-Pulp time as part of Sheffield's antiques mafia, so he used his contacts to fit out the rehearsal space with some really cool seventies retro furniture so that in between playing we could relax and foster the unity bands need. Especially those that have been away from each other for eight years.

We worked steadily, nurturing ourselves back into the swing of things. We knew there were eight songs everyone would want to hear, so it was obvious they'd go on the set-list:

'Common People'
'This Is Hardcore'
'Disco 2000'
'Something Changed'
'Babies'
'Sorted For E's & Wizz'
'Sunrise'
'Do You Remember The First Time?'

We worked on this 'A list' until it was pin sharp. We could then select from this list to keep things fresh for the audience – and us. We also had a 'B list' of more obscure material, which we could call upon if necessary to keep the Pulp obsessives happy. In all, I think we rehearsed around 40 songs for the tour dates. It was all so exciting to be back together and the songs were sounding great. Everyone was pulling in the same direction. Mostly.

It's customary to do a small venue to try out the technology and equipment prior to the first 'real' outing, which was due to take place on 27 May 2011 at Primavera Sound, a totally fab festival in Barcelona. So, we decided to return to Le Bikini club (of burning palm tree fame) in Toulouse, France, on 25 May, to test the waters, so to speak, after the dodgy Catherine wheel 'incident' many years previously. We played our festival set followed by a second section, where we tried some obscurities that had not received a live run-out for ages: 'O.U.', 'Countdown' and 'Mis-Shapes'. We knew loads of Pulp obsessives would be there, so these songs were for them. A thank you if you will. Naturally our set went down a storm – an indicator of what was to come for the next, as it turned out, almost two years.

It's Jarvis on the Phone (Sink or Swim)

Spanish culture is amazing, as is all of Spain, but they do have a very un-British tendency to do everything really, really late. Us Brits are not built for this, so it was a somewhat sobering reality to be told we'd be getting on stage at 2 a.m. We'd have hours and hours to kill before doing the show. Bored bands are usually trouble, but as this was the big 're-entry' we were all extremely nervous about cocking it up. Live bands change from rehearsal; you find the adrenaline surging and your mind can easily wander off the task in hand, especially if bored drummers decide that a cerveza or two might help. No way! We were studiously of the need to keep it straight, so we did. Professional or what! Belle and Sebastian were on before us and had a go at 'Common People' (bit cheeky if you ask me). To be honest, it did sound rather under strength – weedy, we said. We were happy to show the Spanish, and heavily Brit-populated crowd, how it was done. The feeling of seeing the crowd going crazy throughout our set was incredible. The love shown to us was off the scale. We were back. And some.

We could talk about each concert from now to the end of 2012 – each had its own strange idiosyncrasies and eventful moments – but this could get a bit dull, so let's focus on some of the more interesting ones. Most were festivals and they can be similar in nature: hot and dusty or cold and wet, the stench of well-used portaloos gently wafting on the breeze. But for me, there were several major highlights from that run of shows in 2011/12.

First up was the Isle of Wight Festival on 11 June 2011, our first UK gig in almost nine years. Cue rapturous scenes. We stayed in a posho hotel on the mainland, which meant we had to frantically dash across the island to get the last ferry. After a *Starsky and Hutch*-like journey we made it – the last ferry was almost empty apart from us lot, Dave Grohl and Taylor Hawkins (RIP) from Foo Fighters. We shot the breeze as we cruised across the Solent. Bonus: Mrs B was frugging on down to our set next to Joan frickin' Jett (sans Blackhearts, though).

A couple of weeks later we were playing a private party at Central Saint Martins. The building had been sold to developers and the college was moving out, so for sentimental reasons Jarvis wanted to play at the end-of-days party, since he'd been a student there. Let's face it, the place does feature heavily in our meisterwork, after all. We had no idea if the current crop of students gave a toss about Pulp but as we had an important gig the next day, it was seen as worthwhile to help keep the grey cells sharp.

Our real equipment was heading out west, so we had to use rented gear – not something I particularly like doing, as the quality can be a bit hit and miss. Any road, the students went crazy. And I mean *really* crazy. The stage was low and everyone was spilling on to it. It was unlike anything we'd seen since the Swedish scout hut. We heard afterwards that security were discussing pulling the gig midway as they thought it was becoming too dangerous for the punters. It was unbelievable, so different to playing a festival where the nearest audience member is 50 yards away. Bonus: I got to meet a Sex Pistol who'd been in the crowd, Glen Matlock. Two down, two to go. I'd already met my punk hero, Pistol Paul Cook, as he had played with Orange Juice when they supported us on our arena tour in '98.

The following day, we were back at one our favourite places: Glastonbury Festival. This place, as you know, is very dear to us, so to be asked to play again was a privilege. The headliners had already been announced, but we were to do a 'secret' gig on the Park Stage. We were labelled as The Juicers by the festival team, but the secret was out pretty quickly; the Glasto rumour mill had us down to play, among other, incorrect guesses. This was our fourth appearance at this most sacred of music altars and it was still as magical a moment as ever to see and hear everyone losing their shit (often literally) to our songs. Bonus: Beyoncé and Jay-Z were seen strolling around our little VIP campsite of tepees that we'd commandeered during the afternoon. Don't think they stopped for a chat, mind.

The following week we were due to play the Open'er Festival at our only ever date in Poland. It turned out to be the most extreme gig we ever played. Let me explain. We had a beautiful day in Gdańsk before the festival day, and all looked great. However, the Baltic weather systems can be a bit unpredictable. On gig day it started raining. And it never stopped, it just got wilder and wilder. As we were being transported to the stage the rain had reached biblical proportions, only now it was accompanied by a vicious wind. It was grim. As we waited stage-side we could see that the rain was coming in horizontal and the gear was getting a soaking. Now, I know you lot are a knowledgeable crowd and you know that water and electricity don't mix too well. Subsequently, we were concerned about safety. The others were in very real danger of being electrocuted on stage in Poland. A sub-optimal outcome if you ask me – I would have been the only survivor. Strange.

'You're OK,' said Liam, our tour manager, 'there's a 100 millisecond cut-out on the power feed so you'll be alright.' Comforting.

We hit the stage and immediately knew that this would be no ordinary gig. Within seconds even I, right at the back alongside Candida, was absolutely soaked. Every cymbal crash threw up a shower of water that drenched me. We could do nothing but laugh at each other as we dripped from head to toe. Jarvis, Steve and Mark had it hardest, as they were down front in the teeth of this deluge. How Jarvis could put on his usual high-octane performance is anyone's guess, but he did. Cap duly doffed.

After the show the road chaps poured water out of Candida's vintage Farfisa organ, a Pulp mainstay since 1984. We thought it would be the end of the Farf – how could it survive such a drowning? We were all pretty worried, as we had no replacement and we were due to play Hyde Park in London in two days' time to over 75,000 people. Cap doffed once again to sixties Italian electronics, as a good seeing-to with a hairdryer to the circuitry and all was well with the organ. It's still going strong today, I believe.

Although the appearance in Poland was only our sixth gig of the tour, we did it without Russell. As I stated somewhat earlier, Russell had a pathological fear of flying and this had not changed in the interim years. He started off by doing the first two shows in Toulouse and Barcelona by travelling across France and into Spain in a camper van, aided by his driver and all-round Pulp helper Gareth and his own sort of sub-tour manager Ralph Razor. Quite the odd bunch indeed. The rest of us even toyed with the idea of filling Russ's camper with ping-pong balls or some such as a bit of on-the-road japery. We never did it, but had hours of fun thinking of new ways to prank them.

As the rest of us happily travelled to new and exotic gigging locations – a castle in Serbia, surrounded by gigantic earth-moving machinery in Germany, on a beach in Norway, an airport in Slovakia – it was mostly done without Russ. He refused to fly and just couldn't (or wouldn't) logistically get from place to place in time to play, even when he ended up having his own full-size tour bus just to himself and his entourage. Needless to say, this behaviour rankled with the rest of us rather quickly. It was obvious Russ wasn't much of a team player these days, and after the last shows of what had been a quite incredible year we decided not to bother inviting him back for 2012.

To kick off the new year, we started with getting a gong from those nice people at the *NME*, the Teenage Cancer Trust Outstanding Contribution to Music award. Thank you very much. It's always nice to get an award and personally I think we deserved more awards than we actually got over our career, but let's not look back in anger, yeah? Legendary artist Sir Peter Blake presented us with the statue and I managed NOT to break it this time. In fact, I think everyone expressly forbid me to even touch it. Probably for the best. The following night we played at arguably Britain's most prestigious venue, the Royal Albert Hall, in aid of Teenage Cancer Trust.

A couple of nights before we had been invited along to the Royal Albert Hall to see a Paul McCartney show. Who would say no to that? The gig, of course, was dazzling. To see and hear such a talent was awe-inspiring and made all the sweeter by what happened after the show. We were invited to the aftershow party – well, not all of us, as somehow Jarvis hadn't been given the correct accreditation (as you can imagine, security was pretty tight) and couldn't get in, so went home. Meanwhile, the rest of us (actually just Candida, my mate Mike and me) sauntered in to this sumptuously decorated room and started enjoying Paul's hospitality – beer that is – all the while scoffing at the idea of meeting the great man himself. He would be off in the limo, back to his golden palace or something. But no, all of a sudden we spied him at the end of the room, and all heads turned his way. I expected he would do a quick tour round, saying hi (thumbs aloft, of course) and then bugger off. I could see he was coming closer so I seized my moment. I stretched out a hand and introduced myself:

'Hi Paul, I'm Nick from Pulp and we're playing here in a couple of days. Any tips?'

'Yeah, learn some Beatles songs,' he drawled.

'Not sure we've got time for that,' I replied.

'You'll be fine,' said Paul, as his missus ushered him off.

Wow, I thought as I returned to Candida and Mike, *I've just met a Beatle*. I couldn't believe I'd had the chutzpah to do it, nor could Candida or Mike. Gotta grab your chance.

Next moment, Paul appears next to us. 'These yer mates?', as he shook everyone's hand to all-round jaw dropped-ness before moving on. Needless to say we were all totally gobsmacked. The evening continued and I door-stepped Paul's incredible drummer Abe Laboriel Jr. for a chinwag about drums and all that kind of stuff, and of course after five minutes Paul's back with us, slapping us on the shoulder: 'You drummers, eh!'

This was getting a bit crazy now and I couldn't believe the turn of events. We sallied off into the night, slightly the worse for wear, but full in the knowledge that we had a cracking tale to tell tomorrow at rehearsals. Jarvis was duly impressed. He said how he would've loved to have met the great man (which he duly did some years later, I believe).

After a few days away I returned to Sheffield and needed to report back on such momentous happenings. I called a family meeting and solemnly told the kids that while in London I had met Sir Paul McCartney, an actual, real-life Beatle, and this was something they'd want to tell their grandchildren. 'Who?' they both said. Never mind.

While back at home it was becoming increasingly obvious that Dad was coming to the end of his life. He had been declining due to Alzheimer's for a while now and had lived in a care home for the past two years. But it was pretty obvious that he would pass away sooner rather than later. I had to tell the rest of the band that this could easily happen while we were in America and that cancelling shows could be a distinct possibility.

Dad passed away just after his 78th birthday in May 2012. We gave him a grand send-off and it was so heartening to hear so many people say so many kind things about him.

44

Spread the Message

(Babies)

In April 2012, prior to Dad's passing, we flew out to the States for a series of shows, starting with New York's iconic Radio City Music Hall for two nights. Radio City is a truly dazzling art-deco theatre that transports you right smack-bang into the glorious jazz age. To see the word 'Pulp' up in lights on the venue's original twenties frontage was a real highlight. Problem is, Radio City is all seated, and as you're by now aware, we have a bit of an aversion to all-seated venues since they prohibit the audience. It's more a case of tap the fingers and toes rather than get into mosh-pit mode. Never mind; it was an incredible experience to play in that spectacular venue on that vast stage. Twice.

I, or rather Mrs B, had suggested we take my mum, Brenda, out to NYC to give her a week of respite from dealing with Dad and his Alzheimer's. We all stayed at a super posh hotel down in trendy (read as 'expensive') SoHo. One morning we entered the breakfast room and on seeing Brenda, asked if she was joining us for breakfast:

'No,' (adopt Hyacinth Bucket voice), 'I've just had breakfast with Ronnie Wood.'

What? *The* Ronnie Wood? As it happens, yes – the aforementioned Rolling Stone was staying in the same hotel, as he had an exhibition of his art opening round the corner. Brenda had spotted our tour manager Liam chatting with Ronnie, who then invited them all to join him for coffee and a Danish at his table. My mum's a keen amateur (translation: awful) artist and was delighted to brag about how she'd been invited to Ronnie's exhibition opening night. She turned a new version of pale when she saw the artworks and the attached prices. She's from Rotherham, not known for its financial largesse towards anything, let alone impressionistic scrawls of Mick Jagger.

We left Noo Yawk behind and headed out west to play the jewel of the US festival season, Coachella. The annual festival is held in the Colorado Desert near Palm Springs, a couple of hours' drive out of downtown LA, over two weekends on which essentially the same bands play to two different crowds. The crowd is dotted with Hollywood stars (from A-list down) alongside beautiful Californians swanning around with their über-tans, washboard stomachs, macrobiotic skin, bikinis and faux hippy schtick. Unfortunately, weekend one of Coachella was hit by unseasonably cold weather that year. Totally fine by our standards, but the Americans could be seen crying and shivering in the 17-degree nuclear winter. Oh, how we laughed. Any UK festival-goer would never dream of visiting an outdoors music event without at the very least a cagoule to don until the mercury rose north of 22 degrees. Wellies, however, were not required, since Coachella is held at a polo club and the grass is immaculately tended and is more like a green carpet. Glastonbury it is not.

We were shown to our quarters and were delighted to be billeted with the Arctic Monkeys' Portakabins, and so we had a kind of 'Little Sheffield' 5,268 miles from home. We played, we rocked, and we had a laugh with the Monkeys.

The next weekend was the polar opposite: god, it was boiling. Must have been pushing 40 degrees plus. Even the sun-kissed were scrabbling for any shade they could find in the searing desert heat. The thought of playing in that cauldron was sobering. Poor Matt Helders, drummer with the Monkeys, had to play in direct, blistering sun, and it can't have been pleasant. But at least we went on as the sun was setting and a little respite offered. Even so, we left the stage almost as wet as when we departed the rain-sodden Polish stage the year before.

In between the two desert shows, and aside from our own Pulp gigs in LA and San Francisco, we had time to kill. I decided to spend a small fortune (see previous note about being from Rotherham) hiring a 1966 Cadillac Coupe De Ville convertible, red with white leather interior. Nice. And enormous. The family had been booked on a flight home from LA as I waited for my 'new' car to be delivered. I had planned this jaunt for ages and was so excited. I could barely contain my desire to pack them off on to the airport transfer so I could float around LA like a film star. I burbled around Mulholland Drive and up into the canyons, marvelling at the Hollywood homes of the stars and the amazing scenery. I wafted up the Pacific Highway, out towards Malibu and my turn-around spot: Point Dume. There was one parking spot available and it looked tight. You could have got two 'normal' cars in easy, but not this behemoth. Thankfully, as I was sizing up the task in hand a group of very heavy-duty-looking Latino dudes got out of their ride to admire the Cadillac.

'Would you chaps mind awfully helping me reverse into this spot?'

My experience of the USA and its inhabitants was to use your poshest Brit voice and they would do anything for you. They probably think you are a duke or something. The Latino lads couldn't have been more helpful in aiding me berth the red whale so I could go off for a stroll around the headland. Thanks, compadres.

I guess that leads me nicely on to our only ever gig (to date) in Mexico. Stop me if I've said this before, but it was mental. First off, the gig, at Palacio de los Deportes in Mexico City, was our largest ever indoor attendance: 18,000 strong and all going off at once, losing their shit because they were finally getting the opportunity to see Pulp live. They got both barrels, of course.

What I enjoyed most about the gig, and what was an unexpected surprise, was the huge knock-off merch market held outside the venue. I know you're all imagining a couple of stalls with some badly printed T-shirts and posters. No way, José. This was a full-blown market in all senses of the word. Rows and rows of stalls were selling everything Pulp-branded, from T-shirts, mugs, key rings and towels to hats and coasters – anything and everything that you could stamp Pulp on was present. It was quite overwhelming. I wanted to buy so much it was frightening. Mind you, once I had mentioned I was actually in the band they were so pleased to meet me that they attempted to foist all sorts on to me. I managed to limit myself to a couple of mugs. What happened to all the merchandise they didn't sell? It's not like we were regular visitors to Mexico City or anything.

As you know, one thing I always enjoy doing on tour is going for a mystery walk on our days off. Some would stay in bed all day, some would hit the bar. I'd hit the streets with one simple rule: follow whichever road looked most interesting and get a taxi back once knackered.

The Mexico City walk was by far the best. My initial goal was to reach the Zócalo, Mexico City's central square, which houses one of the largest flags and flagpoles in the world. Trouble is, I had not factored in that Mexico City is *vast* and the iPhone suggested it would take five or six hours of walking to get there. Bloody hell. Never mind, I set off anyway.

Immediately outside the hotel was a dual carriageway that was no longer a smog-choked artery of peeping vehicles, but filled with families on bicycles. This was a thing of great beauty and as I wandered along the bike route all sorts of crazy stuff was happening: bands playing, folk doing Zumba classes, dinosaur sculptures made of plastic bottles. I kept walking and as I got further into town the streets were thronged with Mexicans out for their Sunday stroll in their finery, a tent packed to the rafters with people listening intently to a reading of Dickens, the most amazing living statues trying to scrape a living. Eventually, through this madness I reached the Zócalo, to find the square filled with the most incredible customised motor-bikes one is ever likely to see. Native Mexican Indians were performing tribal dances for the tourists and even young Mexican tearaways were fighting each other, presumably over 'turf'. Soak in the vibes and then flag a cab down and back to the hotel. Phew, it was worth it.

We returned to Europe for more festivals and broke new ground by playing Bucharest, Romania – with an added special treat. Jarvis read that Bucharest had a huge population of feral dogs so in salute it was decided we should perform 'Dogs Are Everywhere', a song we'd never played live the entire time I'd been in the band. Cue a 30-minute rehearsal in the dressing room beforehand, and voilà! What a thrill – well, as much as an obscure single from 1984 that sold cock-all copies could be. I'm not sure it went down that well, but it was a real pleasure to do.

My mystery walk for that city took me to the largest building in the world: ex-communist dictator Nicolae Ceausescu's palace. It was shut.

On 13 July, we played our only ever real gig in Italy. How, or why, it got missed over the years is anyone's guess – we had, or seemed to have, loads of Italian fans but they never got to see us in the flesh. So, here we finally were: Rome? Milan? Turin? Naples? Nope, Pordenone. Where, I hear you say? Indeed. Actually, Pordenone is not that far from Venice, as it happens, but as we all said as we arrived at this really quite small town, 'What the . . . ?' Still, playing a small town no one had heard of, yet they/someone/ whomever was paying us shovelfuls of cash to perform, was seen as the way to go. I'll not complain. We played to a small coterie of Italian obsessives and a load of nonplussed locals bedazzled by our larger-than-life stage set.

By now we'd reached mid-2012 and could see the finish line. In the sense of the last few gigs of this run. The future was not, in my memory, put to debate. Rather, it was simply said that Pulp would go back in the cupboard, wrapped in a sheet, drained of vital fluids and quietly left to hibernate again. If it were left to me I would have suggested we had an annual run-out, keep the wheels turning by doing six to ten gigs somewhere across the globe. Let's face it, there's a lot of globe out there that never had a chance to see Pulp play over the years and here would be a chance to remedy that. Plus, it would become a handy regular income, of course. Having said that, I know others had desires to do new stuff and/or take a break from schlepping around the world, getting up close and personal with airport terminals and dusty backstage areas. The horror.

In typical Jarvis circularity, it was decided we'd top off two highly successful and deeply satisfying years of new-Pulp gigs with a grand ta-ra at Sheffield Arena, a kind of homecoming farewell. Before that, though, it was off to the virgin lands of South America, to wow *los hijos* (look it up) with our stuff. I loved breaking new ground and seeing new places, so travelling to South America filled me with excitement: this was a chance to see Chile, Argentina and Brazil (well, a bit of 'em anyhow).

We arrived in Buenos Aires to the kind of reception we hadn't had in ages. Kids were hanging out the outside of the hotel, waiting for a chance to grab an autograph, selfie or a quick word with us. More disconcertingly, though, they would show us their Pulp tattoos. Now, I'm not much of a tat fan, but if that's your thing, knock yourself out. I will say, though, that it was rather freaky to see so many kids permanently etched with images of some poxy indie-disco thumpers from Sheffield, a city some 6,962 miles away. The gig was a quasi-religious experience, as we played a whopping 21-song set. The Argentinians had seen nothing like it.

Getting out and about in Buenos Aires was a real highlight. Our promoter assumed the guise of native guide and took us out on the town. We went to a ping-pong hall, which consisted of dozens of tables all ponging away, but we couldn't get one. So, as her flat was around the corner, we went to play at a promoter's place. Lo and behold, she had a table shoehorned into the front room with just enough room around to move. Cue Argentina v England (away win, 1–2).

The evening culminated in the most Argentinian thing you could envisage: a visit to Teatro del Tango, home of the Argentinian tango. Entrance was through a non-descript door and up some non-descript stairs to a very descript, super ornate yet down-at-heel ballroom full of (mostly) elderly Buenos Aireans tangoing away to gentle accordion music. It was rather quaint, beautiful and bizarre. We were guided through the basic steps by our native guides and away we went. Now, bear in mind we had been on the Cerveza Quilmes for about six hours at this point, so *Strictly* it was not. But we had a go. That's what counts. My favourite moments were when the clientele needed a breather so the accordion soundtrack ended and everyone shuffled to the sides for a slice of orange and a towel down while the DJ (if there was one) soothed the dancers with some ear-splitting Jimi Hendrix. We were, indeed, experienced.

The Buenos Aires mystery walk was a different gravy. Let's go to Uruguay. It could be a new country to tick off the list, as it's 'just' a ferry ride across the River de la Plata (River Plate). The map suggested the ferry terminal was not too far, so I set off. The first obstacle was an eight-lane highway between the terminal and me. I walked and walked but never saw how this torrent could be traversed. Sod it, Uruguay will have to wait. I turned inland, wandering the streets until I happened upon a large group of footie fans going apeshit about, err, football. I watched the fun unfold, eventually asking who the supporters were supporting. Shrugs of shoulders all round (my Spanish is rudimentary to say the least) until I could glean that these were fans of a Colombian team, off to play River Plate FC in some inter-South American competition. They did not hold back, eventually boarding buses to the match packed so full that the roof was as crammed as the insides. Fans were hanging off the outside, too. In an instant the fans were gone and peace restored.

Chile next. How casual that can be said, but it was. We had two shows to do: a festival outside the capital, Santiago, and a smaller intimate club show in the city the next day. The fest was pretty similar to European festivals, of which we were past masters, but the club show was far more interesting, as we were able to trot out a few rarities and lesser-played numbers for the hardcore Pulpers that had mostly forked out their pesos to see us two days running. The sound check was basically a rehearsal of obscurities: long dormant songs like 'She's A Lady', '59 Lyndhurst Grove' and even 'Sheffield: Sex City'. Lucky Santiagans.

The extra-curricular on this section of the tour was a real test. One of our Chilean fans was an actual Andean mountain guide and invited us to go up into the mountains to see a glacial waterfall. This is not something you see every day so I was most keen to go. Jarvis, Liam and Steve went to the mountain equipment shop the day before to kit themselves out, but I decided this was going a bit too far and my Puma trainers, bucket hat and tweed-style jacket would suffice. Why spend extra?

Why did nobody tell me this was going to be one of the hardest physical tests I could possibly endure? We (Steve, Jarvis, Leo Abraham (second guitar), Jean Cook (violin), Liam (tour manager), Gareth Bell (band PA), Matt Butcher (front-of-house sound), me and our Chilean guide) decamped high in the Andes, surrounded by the most breathtaking mountain scenery imaginable. And I really mean breathtaking;

you could physically feel the thin air as you started to walk, your body complaining vociferously at the lack of oxygen. As we started up, the ascent claimed its first casualty: Jean Cook, our buoyant American violinist, fell out due to the harsh atmosphere. Gareth escorted her back to the van. I really felt sorry for Gareth, as he was our unflappable Sheffield/Peak District mountaineer. Guiding Jean down was a noble act, but I bet he was so disappointed not to see the Andes in all their majesty.

We trudged on. And on. We eventually reached the snowline and the first crack in my mountain trekking strategy became apparent: Puma trainers lack traction against a 45-degree snow slope. I overcame this, eventually on hands and knees. Nothing will defeat me in the venture. Luckily the slope never got quite as steep again. We stopped to fill our canteens by a stream of glacial meltwater, where we were caught and overtaken by a group of German octogenarians, who sped up the mountain like spring chickens, leaving us gasping in their wake. The going was getting serious and chitchat dwindled away as everyone concentrated on the simple act of walking and breathing. The group strung out as we neared the goal, and Liam and I started to fall back a little as we had to traverse a section of huge boulders as we neared the glacial waterfall. You could barely do three steps without having to stop to get your breath back; it was torture. I was not going to give in; it would've been like a Channel swimmer nearing a French beach then turning back. At last we could see the others, sat on a huge rock, gazing at a cascade of ice tumbling down a rock face – the frozen waterfall. It was either mesmerising or everyone was so knackered that speech was impossible. I think it was a bit of both. We cracked open the picnic – three peanut energy bars between us all – and after a ten-minute slump we started back down. Strange how the descent was far easier. We got back to the van and stopped at the nearest village for empanadas and Diet Cokes. No one said a word round the table as everyone was so shattered. Back to the hotel and one of the most delicious baths one could ever imagine. Bliss. Early night. It had been knackering, but one of the greatest band days out of all time.

The final destination of our South American getaway was Brazil, one place I had coveted for many years. Trouble is, I wanted to see Rio de Janeiro rather than São Paulo, our actual stopover. This feeling didn't auger well, as the plane seemed to descend for ages over grim, bland and forbidding Soviet-style flat blocks. Everywhere was covered in unintelligible graffiti that appeared to be written in Nordic runes or some such. Our Brazilian guide told us that this was in fact a gang language; members communicated via graffiti and it had developed into a kind of new alphabet so as to evade police intelligence. Far from pretty. São Paulo is a vast urban sprawl, unremitting in its concrete jungle. I'm sorry to say, but it didn't seem to have a lot going for it.

Still, we played to the Pulp-starved Brazilians with as much muster as we could, but by this point we were pining for home and decided to leave a day early to return to dear old Blighty. I didn't tell them back home I was going to be early, so I could see the surprise on their little faces as I drew up outside Banks Towers. They hardly batted an eyelid. 'Dad's back.'

Ho hum.

45

End Game. Bob Lind

(The Only Way is Down)

We could definitely see the finish line now. We knew Pulp weren't doing any more concerts after 2012 and where best to bid farewell? Our glorious hometown of Sheffield, of course. The circle would be joined; first gig City School, Sheffield, way back in 1980, to last show at Sheffield Arena, 8 December 2012. A world traversed, 515 or so gigs played, around 152 songs released (and plenty more not), perhaps 25 current and ex-members later, it was the end game. The last Pulp concert.

Needless to say, the gig sold out in an instant and we wanted to make it special for everyone. We prepared to play as long a set as we could to celebrate all parts of Pulp's career, so we didn't bother with a support band. Why not play some Pulp home movies instead? So we did. It was a full-on Pulp fest, as it should be.

Liam was sent out – or more rightly, he sent someone out – to buy loads and loads of bog roll so we could do a couple of songs with the paper draped over the stage, in remembrance of Pulp's mid-eighties shows, when budgets had been measured in pence. Most of the bog roll was thrown out to the fans in the mosh pit, who reacted like seventies footie fans. Jarvis's sister, Saskia, and her friend Jill were brought on for 'My Lighthouse', as they had done the original backing vocals all those years ago. Mid-era Pulp was illuminated with the gorgeous 'Little Girl (With Blue Eyes)' and *Separations* era by 'Countdown'. For the only time ever, *Different Class* was played in its entirety (not track order, we ain't psychos). Our old chum Richard Hawley was of course invited to twang a guitar on a few, as he often did.

Two and a half hours later, that was it. We gathered on the edge of the stage for one last curtain call and trooped off into the wings. I could finally discard the battered grey trousers and grey shirt I'd worn for every gig since Primavera in 2011.★ We had a big party at a manufacturing firm's warehouse down the road for all our mates and a long guest list. Our Richard was the DJ, spinning some very eclectic choices. The night drew to an end and that was that, as they say.

But hold on, I hear some of you Pulp nerds say. That was not the end, was it though? Was it? There was just one final trip to do. And you would be right.

The bods at Coachella fest had been so dazzled by our brilliance (who wouldn't be?) that they'd asked us to headline the first ever Coachella cruise. Jarvis had said yes, as it seemed a chance not to be missed to see Pulp sail off into the sunset for real.

The ship was due to set sail from Fort Lauderdale, Florida, headed for Nassau in the Bahamas with one boatload, then it would return to Florida, pick up another load and sail to Ocho Rios, Jamaica. Pulp would therefore perform two shows upon the ocean waves.

This was our first experience of a cruise ship, and this one was a

---

★ Yes, before you ask they were laundered by the lovely Catherine after each gig. I had decided to wear the same outfit to avoid having to make a choice for every show – make one choice, and stick with it. Pulp's wardrobe case was a riot of high-fashion designer brands and glittery frocks until you got to my end, where the forlorn George at Asda shirt and Muji trousers lived. Keeping it real, see.

floating palace filled with 'whack' DJs and indie outfits on the scale of Hot Chip and Warpaint. Artists and crew were jumbled together with the punters, who generally seemed to be rich American kids. I've no idea what it cost to bag a ticket, but I'll wager it won't have been cheap. (There might even have been the son of the Mexican president present, but rumour has it he was chucked off at Nassau for being 'naughty'.)

We all had posh suites to lounge around in, but as rubbing shoulders with the rich Americans – pestering and talking a touch too loudly – was no fun, some of the band felt imprisoned in the suites. Not me, though. I could swan about all I liked. For me, cruising was sitting about, watching the sea slide by, while waiting for the next meal or wondering if having a beer at 2 p.m. was too early.

During our ocean jaunt, the itinerary changed; it was decided there weren't enough punters for two cruises, so all acts were pushed on to the one leg. The bands would play one show instead of two and the boat would call at Nassau, then Ocho Rios, then return to Florida. Fine by me.

A trip like this was a once-in-a-lifetime experience, so everyone brought along their kids and partners to join in with the fun. However, one thing that cruise ships can suffer from is passengers coming down with the old norovirus, Delhi belly or Montezuma's revenge, depending on your sensibilities and, unfortunately, my daughter Jeannie succumbed and was now confined to barracks. We docked at Nassau and trekked off to one of the world's most beautiful beaches for a dip. Jeannie came along but could only sit on the beach, puking into a paper cup. We all went to the beach bar for lunch but Jeannie was in no state to contemplate food and so we casually left her on the beach with her paper cup, and a couple of dozen seagulls circling above, looking for scraps. Parents of the year!

It was all aboard and time for the last gig. These huge cruise ships always have a big theatre on board, and the lads set up for the last time. It was disconcerting, feeling the sway of the ship down in the bowels of the ship, and odd to see the huge 'Pulp' neons gently swaying to the rhythm of the seas. By now Sarah had fallen prey to the dreaded lurgy and so missed the very last show, somewhere between Nassau and Miami. We delivered the last ever 'Common People' with its usual thunder, but not without bittersweet thoughts. Would I ever play these songs again? Was that it for my musical adventures? Was worldwide travel with a bunch of like-minded souls now a fading memory?

Forget that for now, we signed up to play bingo with Grimes. Yes. Bingo with Grimes. Note to indie cruise festival organisers: don't get a bored wannabe nu electro Canadian pop star to read out your bingo numbers. Even more importantly, stick with the Brits. Bingo may be played worldwide but surely it's the British that are the masters of calling numbers. There were no 'two fat ladies' and nary a 'Kelly's eye'. Just numbers, delivered in a flat drawl devoid of any Blackpool seaside vibes. However, I did win top prize: a Bluetooth speaker, no less (still use it today – it's brill). Such laughs, waving the winnings in everyone's faces.

After the 'last ever show' we had a mad party in the President's Suite. It had a jacuzzi bath tub on the balcony, which we filled with bubble bath before turning it on. The balcony ended up full of bubbles with just Candida's head poking out topped off with a captain's hat. What larks.

With no second gig to do, my lot decided to bail out in Jamaica and have a couple of days there rather than stay on the boat back to Florida before returning home to the UK. None of us had ever been to Jamaica and we didn't want to miss the chance to experience some cool reggae vibes.

We realised that the night we were heading into town was 'Mad Friday' (as it's known back home), the last Friday before Christmas where all the workers get the afternoon off and have a Christmas party or hit the pub early. Subsequently, the streets resemble a Hogarth painting by 5 o'clock. Turns out, Jamaica was no different. We strolled into town as darkness fell and we were immediately hounded by panhandlers. Thankfully, they weren't too aggressive so were easy enough to swerve. We looked around for a suitable place for a bite, perhaps a homely pizza place (kids, eh?) or some such that would suffice. Nada. Mad Friday was now in full swing and the unlit streets were full of 'celebrants'. Catcalls of 'Hey Papa! Yo man!' came from every dark alleyway as we searched in vain for anything that resembled a restaurant. Barbecues were in full blaze on every corner, but safe to say we didn't fancy going 'al fresco', as we'd already had one horrific stomach bug among us on the trip. We ducked into a Jamaican patty shop, hoping for some pastry treats, but it's never a good sign when the servers are fully encased in clear plastic windows in case of violence. That was it. We hotfooted it to the sanctuary of the hotel and peace returned, away from the hullabaloo of Mad Friday, Jamaican-style.

Before long we were headed home via Virgin Airways to a cold UK Christmas. Richard Branson was on our return flight, and say what you like about him, but I can't imagine any other airline tycoons coming through the cabin for a chitchat with the customers, myself included. Most would probably get a right earful, and rightly so. I declined to fill Rick's ear with particularly anything, as all was plane sailing.

On our return home it was straight into the chaos of Christmas and all that jazz, so I never really got the time to contemplate the future sans Pulp. It was more a case of back to the pottery day job and running the business. I never looked back wistfully at what we had achieved, or contemplated why we were not achieving it again the next year, or indeed perhaps ever again. It just was.

Oh, one more thing . . .

I guess it's about time to wrap up this story (to date). Pulp were popped into the embalming liquid and placed in that cupboard that contains that tin of pilchards from 1985. Y'know, the cupboard that's really hard to reach. Life, however, does go on. Hard to believe, but it does.

Jackson had set his heart on becoming an airline pilot so every couple of weeks we would have a dads'n'lads Sunday out at the aerodrome closest to us. Well, I would drive there, read the paper as he dashed about learning to fly, then take him home while hearing all about pitch, yaw and trim. He had his pilot's licence before he could drive a car and it soon dawned on me that I would be his first solo passenger. Yikes. The day came and all was calm; he really didn't want to crash, almost as much as I didn't want him to crash, so a kind of equilibrium was achieved. We soared into the blue and set the co-ordinates for our house in Sheffield. This was more akin to following the M1 north from 1,500 feet up until you could see the city, then finding our road. I phoned down to Sarah as we were circling above, imploring her to come out and give us a wave, but the nerves of thinking half the family was being held aloft by a bit of aluminium and a mini engine got to her, so she stayed on the sofa. Fair play. Jackson currently flies Airbus A319/20s for EasyJet. No, I don't get freebies.

Meanwhile, Saturdays were dads 'n' lasses days, as Jeannie and I would trek around South Yorkshire while she played football. In all weathers. Eventually I became part of the coaching team – assistant and organiser, really – so that was Tuesday evenings taken care of, too. Jeannie was part of the oldest football club in the world, Sheffield FC, and one year I got Jarvis, Steve, Mark and Candida to chip in a few quid to sponsor the team. The look on Jeannie's team mates' faces as they put the shirts on for the first time and seeing the Pulp logo adorning the front was a scene. Most screwed up their faces, saying: 'Pulp? What's that?' 'Me Dad's crap band,' was the pithy reply. Thanks r kid.

Happens though that having Pulp on the front of a football team kit turned out pretty good. During 2013, Pulp were approached by a 6ft 7in German-Kiwi filmmaker called Florian Habicht, who wanted to make a film on the band, loosely based on our last gig in Sheffield. Jarvis and Steve had seen his stuff and thought his approach was suitably worthy, so the project was given the green light. When I showed Florian the picture of the Sheffield FC under-14s, resplendent in their Pulp-sponsored shirts, he was beside himself with glee. Obviously he could see some great cinematic potential here. From then on, Florian collared us on various occasions to ask questions about Pulp and film us for the doc. When I told the football girls they could be in a film if they wanted too, they were unanimous in saying yes. Of course, you would be.

The documentary, *Pulp: a Film About Life, Death & Supermarkets*, premiered on 9 March 2014 at Sheffield City Hall as part of the Sheffield Doc Fest, and hearing the football girls scream as they appeared on screen was fantastic. Everyone loved it. As did we.

The film brought along some extra benefits. A list was circulated of all the film festivals around the world at which the doc would be screened and if you wanted, you could go along to help promote it – all expenses paid, naturally. Strangely, all the plum destinations had been taken by the time I had got the list: New York? Sydney? Rome? Nah, Jarvis and Steve have bagged them. No bother: Sarah and I could go to Helsinki for a few days on the jolly.

It was brilliant. Watch the movie, answer a few questions after, then get taken out on the town to a Balkan disco by the fabulous Finnish hosts. Even the eye-watering cost of drinks couldn't dampen our enthusiasm. We then went back to Mexico City with the film and on to Guadalajara, again on the jolly. This time the whole family came along to make it a bit of a holiday. Jeannie could not understand why all these kids were queuing up for my autograph (pre-selfie days) after a Q&A session. I guess I was just 'Dad'. I showed them all how mad Mexico City was on a Sunday and it didn't disappoint.

We all moved on to the Guadalajara International Film Festival the following week and I was asked by the genial hosts if there was anything I wanted to do while in their city. Yes, there was.

7 June 1970 saw World Champions England take on World Champions-to-be Brazil in a World Cup group game at the Estadio Jalisco in Guadalajara. Could we visit the stadium please, I asked our Mexican hosts? Of course, they said. They knew why, too. It was here that the greatest save ever made had occurred. By the greatest-ever goalkeeper. Saving a shot by the greatest-ever player. Our Gordon versus Pelé.

Around the ten-minute mark in the match, Jairzinho ripped Terry Conroy a new one on the right and put in the perfect cross, aiming for Pelé's forehead. As the ball arced over, Gordon seemed in the wrong place as Pelé met the ball, powerfully aiming for the corner of the goal. Miraculously, Gordon darted across his net and as Pelé shouted 'Goooaal!', Gordon somehow got his hand to the ball, just as it seemed to have passed him, deflecting it up and over the crossbar.

Not a goal. With typical English sentiment England captain Bobby Moore said, 'You usually catch them, Banksy.'

We eventually walked out on to the pitch around the same time the actual game had been played that day, 44 years before, and it was so hot. How those pasty white English boys managed to play football in those conditions was astounding, let alone facing the ten golden-yellow Brazilian jerseys, one of which inhabited by the one-and-only Pelé.

I had a plan: why don't we recreate the save ourselves on the actual pitch where it happened? Jeannie can be Brazil, I'll be Gordon, Jackson can be the cameraman. Cue rolling of teenage eyes by Jeannie: 'Really? That's sooo lame.' But one twisted arm later, and we were running about the pitch, recreating the legendary scene (I had purposefully worn a blue shirt and pale grey shorts to reflect Gordon's kit from the day). A bit of rudimentary editing later and the addition of David Coleman's commentary, and voila. Barely distinguishable from the real thing. Barely.

The family were packed off after that, as they had school, work and all that palaver to attend to. Meanwhile, I was off to Colombia to continue promoting the film, this time on behalf of the British Council, a government organisation that was there to promote British industry and culture to the Colombians. They asked if I could do something at a university in Bogotá as part of the trip. Like what? was my immediate question. Drums master class? I nearly spat me tea out. Don't think so. I would hardly call myself a master of the craft. OK, I get by, but ask me to illustrate a flammed paradiddle and I'm stumped. What about a talk about Pulp? I parried. Perfect, they said. So, I popped over to Bogotá and had a whale of a time (all the while missing the fam back home, of course). I would always recommend hiring a native guide to show you the sights of the cities' ripped backsides that tourists never get to see. Bogotá was no exception. Who knew they would have bars where the men's loos were just open booths with a urinal proudly on view?

The day prior to the film showing I was due to deliver my talk – nah, let's call it a lecture – on Pulp. I did a bit of prep; well, truth be told I had a playlist of Pulp songs and a rough idea of what the format would be, that's about it.

We settled in a lecture room with a strange corner booth. My ramblings were to be simultaneously translated into Spanish while I spoke to the students. About 30 victims, sorry students, were there, ready for my debut. I started off and there was no stopping me. I rambled on for about two and a half hours, interspersed with the playing of landmark Pulp songs, all the while with my Spanish echo desperately trying to keep up. Most of the audience stayed for the duration and I was surprised they – and I – had such stamina. Result. Next day was the film and the Q&A followed by me spinning a few tunes for the Bogotá Film Festival wrap party. How my bizarre collection of warped tunes went down I don't know, but they were dancing all night, so all right, I'd say.

Back to the humdrum then. Well, yes. But not drum-free, though. I would do the odd gig with the Big Sham and rehearsing was always a laugh. Good excuse to get out the house if you ask me. My expertise, at least, didn't go unnoticed as I was asked to do some drumming for Sheffield local legends The Everly Pregnant Brothers. They were due to play Sheffield's iconic Crucible Theatre and as they were a drum-free band (the horror), they decided they needed to add some 'oomph' to a couple of numbers, so approached me. I don't usually say 'sounds fun', but this did. I knew most of the guys so I knew it would be a blast. Plus it was about as far from Pulp as you could imagine: five lads with ukuleles and a huge singer appropriately called Big Shaun. The repertoire was well-known songs, often repurposed with Sheffield-based lyrics and a LOT of swearing. In a nice way, if that's possible. The set was usually funny, sometimes heart-rending and always very popular. Plus, I got to tick off another Sheffield venue, pretty much completing the set. Along with stand-up double bass-wielding Johnny Wood, we made quite the impression and he and I were asked to join permanently. Why the hell not, it ticked all the boxes. Great bunch of lads, fervent support, great tunes to play: what's not to like? I'm still bashing away with the Evs to this day.

We can now wistfully look back through the lens of time at what has happened. We have weaved our way from a Rotherham start to discovering the Sheffield 'scene'. Finding our rightful berth with some strange failing local musicians and oddballs that could show some potential. And, of course, the flowering of that potential with my little self playing a part. Cue the mentalness of success and how the fallout from that is managed without any kind of 'manual' or 'textbook'. What do you do when it's all over? Indeed, is it ever over? I look back and often it all seems like a mirage. Did it really happen? Was I actually there or was it some other representation of me? Once real life returns it does often feel that it was all experienced by someone else. Surreal. Reminiscing with others who experienced similar events can often throw up viewpoints and memories of which I have zero recollection. Surely I must have been there if that amount of craziness occurred, yet I have very few memories of it? Is the other person delusional or do the events back then warp one's brain so much that all views are correct but variously remembered? In my defence, all I can say is that my recollections inscribed here are what I recall. Pulp obscurists and experts may pick holes in my story and I say let 'em. The others who experienced these events with me may scoff and have an alternative view of what happened. Fair enough. I can only write what my addled brain can recover. At the time of writing, it's now almost ten years since Pulp first sailed off into the Caribbean sunset, clinking piña coladas together in an outdoor hot tub. We look back and all I can think to say is:

'What exactly do you do for an encore?'

Stephen Patrick Mackey

Stephen Patrick Mackey died on 2 March 2023. He was just 56. Steve had become very ill in December 2022 and, despite making incredible progress, he eventually lost his battle.

Steve's impact on the Pulp story is without doubt considerable. He had great drive, such a forward vision and a talent for getting things done where others had tried and failed.

Steve and I were probably closest when we shared the 14th-floor squat in Camberwell, South London. He would be full of schemes to navigate the labyrinth of London survival. When he was not working in the mind-numbing call centre, he was usually found in the bath or often cooking up carrots. Or so my recollection suggests. It might not have always been carrots but definitely something a bit odd.

Steve was probably the first person I knew that used the term 'acid house'. He had been to a club called Shoom and had become obsessed with this new movement, eventually persuading a few of us to follow him down this new path, where we joined in raves such as the one at 'Sunrise'. We were not disappointed, and this new world really influenced Pulp's outlook and therefore music in the late eighties.

Steve and Jarvis were enrolled in film studies at roughly the same time and could call upon fellow students and college equipment to

help Pulp make videos in those early days. They both made a symbi-
otic couple: Jarvis was better at the conceptualisation of how the clips
should look, but Steve was the person who brought it all together:
organising the film crew, locations, equipment performers, all that jazz.

Steve was so brilliant at introducing new music to our circle beyond
'acieeeed'. His enthusiasm was contagious. He was instrumental in
pushing us all to try new stuff with our own creativity, and never
becoming complacent in settling for any old tripe. Once Steve had
experienced what it was like to make records in proper studios he
was a keen student of the entire process. He was never satisfied to
just sit at the back doing the crossword or join in with the endless
games of pool in the upstairs lounge. He introduced samplers to the
Pulp armoury and eventually set up his own studio and set off on a
path to starting his own career as a record producer. The track 'This
Is Hardcore' was probably the culmination of Steve's quest to use
up-to-the-minute technology in the Pulp writing and recording
process. Pulp would never have got there without Steve. Similarly, the
track 'Seductive Barry' was almost wholly a Steve Mackey creation.

Bands, no matter how successful, are greater than the sum of their
parts. Everyone has a part to play, each member of the set-up has
something to give. Steve brought so much to Pulp that it's hard to
quantify.

Steve was a great friend and colleague, and he will be sorely missed.
RIP.

– Nick, March 2023

Acknowledgements

Thanks you lot

Well done. You made it. I admire your perseverance. This is the last bit of the book. It's where we need to acknowledge all those without whom this tale of survival, luck and sheer bloody-mindedness might have turned out oh, so differently.

Let's start with thanking our nearest and dearest who, let's face it, have put up with me for the longest: Sarah, Jackson, Jeannie, our Richard and, of course, Brenda. Dad will always be with us as long as there are memories, and that's going to be a long time. The book started way back in 1929, so I will take this opportunity to thank all the previous Bankses, Fords and all those other ancestors stretching back in time who had the extreme foresight to stick around and procreate so I could arrive and weave this tale. Couldn't have done it without you. Ta.

Now, the meat 'n' taters of this book has been the story of how Pulp went from also-rans to underdogs to chart interlopers. Pretty heady stuff I think you would agree. My part in that trajectory was in tandem with my band mates: Candida Doyle, Steve Mackey, Mark Webber, Russell Senior and one Jarvis Cocker. I cannot thank them enough for:

Acknowledgements

a) Granting me the drum job in the first place, and putting up with my, err, at times 'eccentric' timekeeping.

b) Sticking together during those long months and years of indifference whilst waiting for the fickle finger of fate to point at us.

c) Managing to piece together some amazing, uplifting and soul-searching music over the previous 30-plus years or so. It was sometimes easy; often not.

d) Being a fantastic bunch of people to get to know and laugh away the trials and tribulations of actually being in a band together. God we have had some laughs.

However, let's not forget the multitudes of previous Pulp band members who took their turn, however brief, as a part of this story:

- Tim Allcard (January 1983 to April 1984)
- Peter Boam (August 1982 to September 1983)
- Captain Sleep (November 1986 to December 1986)
- Peter Dalton (November 1978 to July 1982)
- Ian Dalton (November 1978 to January 1979)
- Magnus Doyle (April 1983 to November 1986)
- Antony Genn (January 1988 to August 1988)
- Wayne Furniss (April 1981 to October 1982)
- Steven Havenhand (November 1986 to January 1988)
- David Hinkler (February 1982 to September 1983)
- Simon Hinkler (July 1982 to September 1983)
- David Lockwood (January 1979 to November 1979)
- Peter Mansell (December 1983 to November 1986)
- Glenn Marshall (November 1978 to 1980)
- Michael Paramore (January 1983 to April 1983)
- Jamie Pinchbeck (October 1980 to July 1982)
- Jimmy Sellars (August 1980 to March 1981)

- Mark Swift (March 1979 to July 1980)
- Philip Thompson (December 1979 to September 1980)

You lot helped keep the ship sailing long enough for me to clamber aboard. So I must doff my cap in your direction. Cheers. I thank those who came aboard on a temporary basis to help mould our sound: Saskia Cocker, Richard Hawley, Leo Abrahams, Jean Cook and Pablo Cook (not related).

Getting your band into a position to even try to scale the heady heights of pop stardom is something that cannot be done alone or by sheer will. Other agents are required to help manoeuvre the band through the shark-infested waters of 'the biz'. As you have read, Pulp took ages to get off the ground in this sense and needed others who shared our vision to help facilitate it: Suzanne Catty who was the first music biz insider to say Pulp could go all the way. Scott Piering (RIP) who shaved Pulp into his head and promoted early Pulp records with evangelical zeal. John and Phil and all Savage and Best PR who took a bit of a punt on us and got the press to look in our direction. Rob Mitchell (RIP) and Steve Beckett who set up a whole new record company to help prise us away from Fire Records and thus enabled us to fly to the safety of Island Records and the success we had only dreamed of.

Here's a dilemma: Should Fire Records be thanked in the section? They did put out Pulp records when nobody else wanted to. OK, they were often months and years after they were recorded and almost all of them garnered zero sales, airplay, or interest but they were the only people to invest any money in Pulp for a long time. It is very easy to see that Pulp could have foundered in the mid and late eighties due to lack of interest. Is a band even a band without being able to release music? At least with Fire something was coming out. Just. I am of the belief that the poor relationship that Pulp had with Fire was an essential catalyst in the Pulp story. It gave us something to

416

fight against. I'll leave it to you to decide whether this constitutes a thanks. All at Island Records for putting out our wonky disco songs and angry diatribes, especially Dave Gilmour and Nigel Coxon.

The people who really saved Pulp and showed us the way were Geoff Travis and Jeanette Lee at Rough Trade. I can't thank them enough. Pulp had began to generate some real interest and Island Records were sniffing around but due to our dire legal situation no one would touch us. Not Geoff and Jeanette; they saw the potential and seemed to relish the idea of taking this group of mis-shapes, mistakes, misfits as far as they could go. Without them I doubt Pulp would have got as far as they did. Ably assisted by all at Rough Trade, especially Patsy, Kelly, Pru, and Mog.

I must thank the wider Pulp family in this bit without whom getting Pulp recorded and staged could have been tricky to say the least: Record producers Chris Thomas, Ed Buller, Al Smyth, Scott Walker. Fan co-ordinator Dexy. All those who helped bring Pulp live to a stage near you: Kirky, Mike Timm, Leon, Muttley, John Burton, Simon Dawson, Matt Butcher, Tilde, Justin Grealy, Scotty, Roger Middlecoat, Priesty, Liam, Andy Dimmack, Solj, Matty, Byers, Tom W., Miller, Eric and everyone who ever plugged us in, tightened us up, or moved a flight case. We salute you. I bet I've missed some out here. I can only apologise.

The writing of this book was an impossible task if you just had to solely rely on dredging up the memories of old from the deep dark depths. Rock'n'roll is not so conducive to memory retention in the long term. All that loud music, drum banging and general revelry really doesn't help. What actually did help was the efforts that everyone has put in at Pulp Wiki, an invaluable treasure trove of all things Pulp related; a true velvet goldmine. Thanks a lot. Also, in the quest to rekindle old memories was the excellent book by Mark Sturdy, *Truth and Beauty: The Story of Pulp* (2003) another invaluable reference material to help stimulate the grey matter – I contributed a lot to Mark's book so I hope he doesn't mind re-paying the favour this time round.

Mr Sturdy's book was published by Omnibus who, in a strange quirk of fate, have published my little story and therefore I thank Graham Wrench and all at Electric Canyon Management for putting us together. David Barraclough, Claire Browne, Greg Morton and all at Omnibus. Special shout out to Lucy Beevor who had to massage my ramblings into something readable, ta.

This book was essentially a Covid lockdown project. We all needed something to take our minds off the end of civilisation as we knew it and whether the pubs would re-open. So let's thank all of our mates who helped one another keep the mental demons at bay during those trying times: The Snifters, The Hawleys, Bencey, Anne and Mark, Dean and Sarah, Jim and Jo, Chaz, Pete, Bailes, Big Shaun, Johnny, Klive and all the Everly's fans. Reg, Pete M., Firmo, Gill, Coupe, and L'il Anthony. Let's not forget the Shammers; Al and Jase. A tip of the hat to Sid and Victoria for the advice and encouragement right at the very start and to Joel for his pithy inter-jections along the way.

Scan the QR code here to listen
to a Spotify playlist of the songs and
artists that all did something to me.